Postcolonial Manchester

Manchester University Press

Postcolonial Manchester

Diaspora space and the devolution
of literary culture

*Lynne Pearce, Corinne Fowler
and
Robert Crawshaw*

Manchester University Press

Copyright © Lynne Pearce, Corinne Fowler and Robert Crawshaw 2013

The right of Lynne Pearce, Corinne Fowler and Robert Crawshaw to be identified as the author of this work has been asserted by them in accordance with the Copyright, Designs and Patents Act 1988.

Published by Manchester University Press
Altrincham Street, Manchester M1 7JA, UK
www.manchesteruniversitypress.co.uk

British Library Cataloguing-in-Publication Data is available

ISBN 978 1 5261 2001 4 paperback

First published by Manchester University Press in hardback 2013

This edition first published 2017

The publisher has no responsibility for the persistence or accuracy of URLs for any external or third-party internet websites referred to in this book, and does not guarantee that any content on such websites is, or will remain, accurate or appropriate.

Printed by Lightning Source

This book is dedicated to
PETER KALU
and all those who have worked for
Commonword and Cultureword over the years

Contents

List of figures	*page*	ix
The authors		xiii
Preface		xv
Acknowledgements		xix

Introduction: Manchester and the devolution of British literary culture   1
Corinne Fowler and Lynne Pearce

1   Manchester: the postcolonial city   20
Lynne Pearce

2   Publishing Manchester's black and Asian writers   79
Corinne Fowler

3   Manchester's crime fiction: the mystery of the city's smoking gun   110
Lynne Pearce

4   Collective resistance: Manchester's mixed-genre anthologies and short-story collections   154
Lynne Pearce

5   'Rebels without applause': Manchester's poetry in performance (1960s to the present)   207
Corinne Fowler

Contents

6 Giving voice: the writers' perspective 268
  Robert Crawshaw

Afterword 303
Corinne Fowler and Lynne Pearce
Index 313

List of figures

1.1 A view of Manchester in 1841. Image reproduced courtesy of Manchester Museum of Science and Industry. *page* 21
1.2 Manchester redevelopment, February 1964. Slum clearance makes way for the new Dalton Technical Institute. Photograph by John Cleare, reproduced courtesy of FotoLibra. 26
1.3 Salford, 1962. Photograph by Shirley Baker, reproduced courtesy of the artist. 28
1.4 Hulme Crescents, balcony. Photograph reproduced courtesy of 'exHulme' website. 28
1.5 Salford, 1964. Photograph by Shirley Baker, reproduced courtesy of the artist. 30
1.6 Manchester Royal Exchange, third building, 1847. Image reproduced courtesy of Manchester Libraries, Information and Archives, Manchester City Council. www.images.manchester.gov.uk. 32
1.7 Manchester Royal Exchange, third building, Cross Street, 1900. Image reproduced courtesy of Manchester Libraries, Information and Archives, Manchester City Council. www.images.manchester.gov.uk. 32
1.8 Royal Exchange, bomb damage, Manchester, 1940. Image reproduced courtesy of Manchester Libraries, Information and Archives, Manchester City Council. www.images.manchester.gov.uk 33
1.9 Aftermath of the 1996 (IRA) bomb, Cross Street, looking north towards the Royal Exchange. Image reproduced courtesy of Manchester Libraries, Information and Archives, Manchester City Council. www.images.manchester.gov.uk. 33

List of figures

1.10	Castlefield Quay, 1986. Image reproduced courtesy of Manchester Libraries, Information and Archives, Manchester City Council. www.images.manchester.gov.uk.	35
1.11	Merchant's Warehouse, Castlefield, Castlefield Quay, 1998. Photograph by Aidan O'Rourke, reproduced courtesy of the artist.	35
2.1	Poster advertising 'Young Identity's' showcase. Image reproduced courtesy of Young Identity.	93
4.1	Cover of *Voices* 2 (1972). Image reproduced courtesy of 'the FED'.	157
4.2	Cover of *Voices* 19 (1979). Image reproduced courtesy of 'the FED'.	157
4.3	Cover of *Healing Strategies* (1999). Image reproduced courtesy of Commonword.	170
4.4	Cover of *City Secrets* (2002). Image reproduced courtesy of Commonword.	178
4.5	Cover of the *Hair* anthology (2006). Image reproduced courtesy of Commonword.	181
5.1	Lemn Sissay's 'Rain' poem on Manchester's Oxford Road, 2011. Photograph by Corinne Fowler, reproduced courtesy of the author.	220
5.2	Lemn Sissay's 'Rain' poem on Manchester's Oxford Road, 2011. Photograph by Corinne Fowler, reproduced courtesy of the author.	220
5.3	The opening lines of Lemn Sissay's 'Flags' poem, situated on Tib Street in Central Manchester, 2011. Photograph by Corinne Fowler, reproduced courtesy of the author.	222
5.4	The first plaque on the Manchester Ship Canal Walkway, 2011. Photograph by Corinne Fowler, reproduced courtesy of the author.	222
5.5	One of SuAndi's discs *in situ* on the Manchester Ship Canal Walkway, 2011. Photograph by Corinne Fowler, reproduced courtesy of the author.	223
5.6	The final plaque of SuAndi's Manchester Ship Canal Walkway poem near the Lowry Theatre, Salford, 2011. Photograph by Corinne Fowler, reproduced courtesy of the author.	224
5.7	Another of SuAndi's discs along the Manchester Ship Canal Walkway, 2011. Photograph by Corinne Fowler, reproduced courtesy of the author.	224

List of figures

5.8 Luxury flats near the Lowry Theatre, Salford Quays, 2011. Photograph by Corinne Fowler, reproduced courtesy of the author.   225

5.9 BBC Media City, Salford Quays, 2011. Photograph by Corinne Fowler, reproduced courtesy of the author.   226

5.10 New construction work on Tib Street (2011) with the opening lines of Sissay's landmark poem, 'Flags', laid into the pavement in the foreground. Photograph by Corinne Fowler, reproduced courtesy of the author.   226

5.11 Damaged, repaired and worn tiles of Sissay's 'Flags' poem, 2011. Photograph by Corinne Fowler, reproduced courtesy of the author.   227

5.12 Damaged, repaired and worn tiles of Sissay's 'Flags' poem, 2011. Photograph by Corinne Fowler, reproduced courtesy of the author.   228

5.13 Lemn Sissay. Photograph by Toby Madden, reproduced courtesy of the artist.   231

7.1 View of the 'Writing Manchester' exhibition (Catalogue Hall, Manchester Central Library), 2009. Photograph by Lynne Pearce, reproduced courtesy of the author.   307

The authors

Lynne Pearce is Professor of Literary Theory and Women's Writing at Lancaster University and was Principal Investigator of the AHRC-funded research project, 'Moving Manchester: How the experience of migration has informed writing in Greater Manchester from 1960 to the present' (2006–10). Her previous publications include: *Woman/Image/Text: Readings in Pre-Raphaelite Art & Literature* (1991); *Reading Dialogics* (1994); *Feminism and the Politics of Reading* (1997); *Devolving Identities: Feminist Readings in Home & Belonging* (ed.) (2000); *The Rhetorics of Feminism* (2004); *Romance Writing* (2007). Other publications arising out of the 'Moving Manchester' project include a special issue of *The European Journal of Cultural Studies* (with Ruth Wodak) entitled *Region/Nation/Belonging* (2010); a special issue of *M/C Journal* (with Kath Woodward) entitled 'diasporas' (2011); a special issue of *Crossings: A Journal of Migration and Culture* (with Maggie O'Neill) (2011); a special issue of *Mobilities* entitled 'The Urban Imaginary' (2012); a special issue of *Interventions* entitled 'Cinemas of Displacement and Destitution' (2012). A full list of the articles and chapters she has written in connection with the project is available on the Publications page of the 'Moving Manchester' website at: www.transculturalwriting.com/movingmanchester. [transculturalwriting.com/movingmanchester.]

Corinne Fowler is Director of the Centre for New Writing in the School of English at the University of Leicester where she also lectures in Postcolonial Literature. She was Director of the Arts Council-funded project, 'Grassroutes: Contemporary Leicestershire Writing' (2010–12) and also Research Associate for the AHRC-funded research project, 'Moving Manchester' (2006–10). Her previous publications include: *Travel Writing and Ethics. Theory and Practice* (2013), edited with

The authors

Charles Forsdick and Ludmilla Kostova, and *Chasing Tales. Travel Writing, Journalism and the History of British Ideas about Afghanistan* (2007) together with 'Region/Writing/Home: Relocating British Diasporas', *Moving Worlds,* 9(2) (2009, edited with Graham Mort). She also writes short stories, including 'The Black Devon' (2009) and co-edited a book of short stories with Muli Amaye and Martin de Mello called *Migration Stories* (2009) as part of the 'Moving Manchester' project. A full list of the articles and chapters she has written in connection with the project is available on the Publications page of the 'Moving Manchester' website at: www.transcultural writing.com/movingmanchester.

Robert Crawshaw is Senior Lecturer in French and European Studies at Lancaster University. As co-investigator and initiator of the bid to the AHRC, he brought to the 'Moving Manchester' project an enduring research interest in the interface between literature, mobility and social change reflected in previous publications on the writings of W. G. Sebald and Ismaïl Kadare and in his earlier book *Exploring French Text Analysis: Interpretations of National Identity* (Routledge, 2000). As a former academic adviser to the European Commission, he had been the director of two research projects in intercultural pragmatics: the ESRC-funded 'Pragmatics and Intercultural Communication Project' (2003–6) and the HEFCE-funded 'Interculture Project (1998–2002). In 2010–11, he was a research fellow at the University of Konstanz and is currently Head of the Department of European Languages and Cultures at Lancaster.

Preface

This volume is the final output of the funded research project, 'Moving Manchester: How migration has informed writing in Greater Manchester, 1960 – the present' (2006–10) and the project team would like to thank the Arts and Humanities Research Council for their generous support. Many organizations, groups and individuals have also been crucial to the success of the project (see Acknowledgements) which owes its existence to Manchester's distinctive, polycultural writing scene. Indeed, the reason our funding-bid focused on Manchester was on account of numerous funding bodies and literature development workers sending us in the direction of Commonword, the Manchester-based literature development agency and community publisher which has been operating in the city since the 1970s. Although by no means all the texts discussed in this study are Commonword titles (the organization supports several publishing imprints), our research endorses Lemn Sissay's observation that 'there's not a Manchester black writer who has not, in the past twenty years, been through Cultureword [the branch of Commonword dedicated to black writing]', and arguably very few white writers who have not in some way benefited from the organization's presence in the city. It is in recognition of this achievement that we dedicate *Postcolonial Manchester* to Peter Kalu, current Artistic Director of Commonword, who has worked tirelessly for the organization since the 1980s.

Full details of the 'Moving Manchester' project – its personnel, publications and other outputs (most notably, its electronic catalogue of contemporary Mancunian Writing and its online Writers' Gallery) – may be found on its website at: www.transculturalwriting.com/moving-manchester. In due course, we hope to establish a permanent link between our website / e-catalogue and Manchester Central Library so that our materials will remain available to future generations of researchers and writers. The project's closing conference, 'Glocal Imaginaries: Writing / Migration / Place,' which took place at Lancaster University and the Whitworth Art Gallery, Manchester (9–12 September 2009), has also resulted in six special issues of academic journals that may be of interest to readers of this volume (see 'Publications' section of website for full details). One of the principal objectives of the conference was to situate our research on the diasporic and devolved literatures of a city in the north of England in an international context, and to explore the ways in which art and literature have contributed to a better understanding of the sometimes bewildering intersection of the 'local' and the 'global' in contemporary life. *Postcolonial Manchester*, too, takes as its starting-point a perception of the city or region that stretches beyond its material mapping in both space and time: Manchester, widely invoked as 'Europe's first industrial city' is also, through its trade in cotton, the 'product of Empire' and the hub of a two-centuries-old flow of people and commodities. For this reason, as we outline in the Introduction and Chapter 1, there is good reason to think of Manchester as Britain's pre-eminent 'migrant' city: a dynamic intersection of people and their trades which has never been able to lay claim to anything resembling a fixed, indigenous population.

This indeterminacy is, of course, also replicated in Manchester's fluid – yet politically sensitive – geographical boundaries. On this point it will be noted that the catchment for the 'Moving Manchester' project was purposefully established as 'Greater Manchester' in order that we might include as many authors and texts from the North West as possible. The creation of 'Greater Manchester' in April 1974 (following the implementation of the controversial Local Government Act of 1972) both helps and hinders in this respect, since towns and cities that previously enjoyed independent status – Salford (a city in its own right), Bolton, Bury, Oldham, Rochdale, Stockport, Tameside, Trafford and Wigan – were brought within a regional umbrella that many citizens, even now, refuse to accept. As will be seen in the pages of this book – and likewise the entries on our electronic catalogue – 'Greater Manchester', for us, does indeed include the full gamut of the metropolitan boroughs, towns and cities that now comprize the Greater Manchester Council, though we have also done our best to acknowledge and respect the unique histories and identities of the various locales. As far as what passes for 'Mancunian writing' is concerned, the task is slightly easier inasmuch as many of the contemporary authors with whom we have worked 'self-identify' as 'Mancunian' (including

Preface

recent incomers). In terms of the rationale for the inclusion of texts, meanwhile, we have been broadly inclusive and dealt not only with material written in Manchester, or about Manchester, but also poetry and fiction by writers from Manchester's diasporic communities that is set in their country of origin as well as that written by visitors or temporary residents.

As the 'devolution' in its title suggests, *Postcolonial Manchester* is also a volume that seeks to relocate Manchester and its writing within Britain and its arguably 'London-centric' publishing industry. In this respect, it takes its place alongside, but in contrast to, some excellent recent studies of diasporic and black or Asian literary culture in London: namely, John McLeod's *Postcolonial London* (2004) (whose title inspired our own); *Diaspora City* (2004), introduced by Nick McDowell in association with Arcadia Books; and Sukhdev Sandhu's *London Calling: How Black and Asian Writers Imagined a City* (2003). Nowithstanding the fact that there are, of course, many Mancunian writers who regularly shuttle between here and London, or have made the metropolis their new home (for example, Mike Phillips and Lemn Sissay), we trust that our own focus on the changing literary landscape of a British city or region other than London will contribute towards a more pervasive devolution of what, for centuries, has passed as 'English Literature' in the same way that Scottish, Welsh and Irish literature have now achieved recognition for their distinctive literary cultures.

While the Acknowledgements that follow will, we trust, deliver our heart-felt thanks to all the many organizations and individuals who have supported this project, in my capacity as the 'Moving Manchester' project's principal investigator, I should like to take this opportunity to offer personal thanks to the other members of the 'Moving Manchester' project team, namely: my co-researchers, Robert Crawshaw (who prepared the funding-bid) and Graham Mort (responsible, amongst other things, for the online Writers' Gallery); Corinne Fowler, the project's researcher and AHRC postdoctoral fellow, who conducted the interviews which provided the data for Chapter 6; Rajeev Balasubramanyam and Tariq Mehmood, the project's PhD students (both of whom produced new novels as part of their doctoral submissions); Jo McVicker, the project's administrator and conference organizer; Kate Horsley, who helped design the Writers' Gallery and who, with Corinne Fowler, curated the 'Writing Manchester' exhibition (which ran for six weeks in Manchester Central Library in the autumn of 2009) as well as contributing to all manner of other web-program-

Preface

ming and design; Darien Rozentals, who provided additional administrative support for the conference and curated the conference exhibition held at the Whitworth Gallery, Manchester; and finally, Lee Horsley, who provided invaluable IT and website support during the lifetime of the project. Inasmuch as 'Moving Manchester' was funded before the AHRC committed itself to 'full-economic costing' it should also be noted that many of those listed above gave their time without financial remuneration or buy-out from other duties; neither the project nor, as a consequence, this book would have happened without their goodwill and generosity.

Lynne Pearce (Principal Investigator for
'Moving Manchester', 2006–10)
December 2012

Acknowledgements

As already noted in the Preface, our first thanks are to the Arts and Humanities Research Council who generously funded the 'Moving Manchester' project, in association, of course, with our employers, Lancaster University, who supplied the necessary infrastructure and administrative support. The project team would also like to their Departments (English and Creative Writing and the Department of European Languages and Cultures) for their support of the project team as well as the ex-Dean of the Arts Faculty, Professor David Whitton, who commissioned Robert Crawshaw to write the funding-bid: without his vision and commitment to increasing funded research across the Faculty, this project would never have happened. In addition to the AHRC, the project was also fortunate to receive financial support from Arts Council England (North West) in connection with our closing conference and the 'Writing Manchester' exhibition held at Manchester Central Library in the autumn of 2009, and we would like to take this opportunity to offer special thanks to Avril Heffernan and all other ACE-North West staff for their interest in the project from its earliest days. Finally, in terms of the project's 'prehistory' we are indebted to David Law, whose PhD thesis, '"Guddling for Words": Representations of the North and Northernness in Post-1950 South Pennine Literature' (Lancaster University, 2004), was in many ways a precursor to *Postcolonial Manchester*; it is an outstanding piece of original research and one that is frequently referenced in the chapters that follow.

Moving on to the writers and writing organizations who were the life-blood of the project, our first debt – as detailed in both the Preface and the Introduction – is the literature development organization, Commonword, which has been operating in the city since 1977. Our sincere thanks go not only to Peter Kalu but also Martin de Mello and

Acknowledgements

Cathy Bolton who have granted us their time and support from the very beginning of the project. In addition, we would like to thank literature development worker Steve Dearden, together with members of 'the FED' (formerly the Federation of Worker Writers and Community Publishers) for steering us in the direction of Commonword as well as for their subsequent advice, information and support.

Apart from Commonword, the 'Moving Manchester' project benefited from close working affiliations with Gatehouse, the Black Arts Alliance, Manchester Central Library, Manchester Jewish Museum, the People's History Museum and the Working-Class Museum, Salford, and we would like to extend our thanks to colleagues in all these institutions. Bill Williams, author of *The Making of Manchester Jewry* (1977), was especially encouraging and supportive when we were working on the bid, as was James Procter, whose work was, and continues to be, an inspiration and who has always shown close interest in the project. Thanks, too, to Shirley Chew, who generously dedicated an issue of *Moving Worlds* to the project outputs and shared with us her considerable editorial skills, and to Alan Rice, from the University of Central Manchester, whose ground-breaking research and exhibitions on the North West's share in the 'Black Atlantic' complement our own. Further, although we would ideally like to mention *all* the Manchester-based authors with whom we've worked by name, we shall have to restrict ourselves to the following: the novelist Joe Pemberton, with whom we first made contact when David Law was writing his PhD in the early 2000s and who has generously continued to share his publications, experiences and joyous enthusiasm with us ever since; the author and educationalist Qaisra Shahraz, who has been an invaluable consultant and enthusiastic supporter of the project from its earliest days; the poet Shamshad Khan, who has been a true friend and comrade on our journey and who delighted us with her performances on many occasions; and, finally, poet, novelist and dramatist SuAndi OBE, Director of the Black Arts Alliance and Honorary Creative Writing Fellow at the University of Leicester, who has been a staunch friend and supporter of the project throughout, generously sharing with us her considerable knowledge and challenging us when we needed it most.

The project's management group ('the MAG') met regularly during the lifetime of the project and was invaluable in helping us to refine our research questions and gain access to key archives and individuals. Our MAG members were: SuAndi, Steve Dearden, Avril Heffernan, Peter

Acknowledgements

Kalu, Paul J. King, Qaisra Shahraz and Mei Yuk Wong. Other members of Manchester's writing community who helped steer the project and its research focus, especially in the early days, included our two PhD students, Rajeev Balasubramanyam and Tariq Mehmood, Shamshad Khan, Zahid Hussain, Dominique Tessier, Ra Page, Vijay Medtia, Jane Mathieson, Libby Tempest and Shirley May. We bear a huge debt to all of them and extend our sincere thanks to both the individuals listed here and the groups and organizations they represent. Similarly, the project – and, as a consequence, this book – would not have happened had not we enjoyed the willing participation and support of all those writers and agency-workers who took part in our interviews and agreed to present their work on the Writers' Gallery. Individual names are, in this case, too numerous to mention but we thank you all and trust that your thoughts and contributions will take their place in history as part of the legacy of the project. The Writers' Gallery may be accessed at www.transculturalwriting.com/movingmanchester.

With respect to the production of this book, specifically, the authors would like to extend their thanks to both the commissioning editors and the production team at Manchester University Press. Sincere thanks, also, to Roger Bromley and the anonymous readers of the proposal and the final typescript: your advice has been invaluable. Lynne Pearce would also like to extend thanks to the following individuals (and organizations) for their help with the illustrations to Chapters 1 and 4: Shirley Baker (photographer); Jan Shearsmith (Museum of Science and Industry); Aidan O'Rourke (photographer); Jane Parr (Archives and Local Studies, Manchester City Council); Tee and Tony (exHulme website); Yvonne Seely (FotoLibra); Peter Kalu (Commonword); and Rick Gwilt and Ken Casey (ex-FED). A full list of permissions appears below. Meanwhile, Corinne Fowler extends thanks for the images in her chapters to Toby Madden and members of Young Identity. Still with images, the whole team is immensely grateful to the Manchester-based artist Michael Gutteridge, not only for supplying us with the image for this book's cover but also for the many dozens of beautiful representations of the city that he has allowed us to reproduce free of charge on our website and other publicity material during the life of the project.

Collectively, the authors would once again like extend their heartfelt thanks to Jo McVicker, our project administrator, whose loyalty and commitment well exceeded the call of duty and whose efforts in the months leading up to the conference was truly Herculean. Similarly,

Acknowledgements

and as noted in the Preface, the project, and consequently this book, could not have happened without the amazing web design and IT support of Lee Horsley and her daughter, Kate. More recently we have benefited from the excellent editorial work of Sarah Post, a postgraduate student in the English Department, who provided us with several late entries for the e-catalogue, generally assisted with research in connection with the production of this book and created its index: many thanks for all your efforts, Sarah! In addition, and although he doesn't contribute to this particular 'output' in person, our co-researcher and creative writing colleague, Graham Mort, has been an absolutely crucial pillar to the project overall. Without his expertise and guidance in the field of creative writing (both as a published writer and as an academic), the project would have struggled to negotiate the delicate ground that lies between contemporary writing and research 'about' writing. On many occasions, his judgement and direction was invaluable.

Finally, our individual acknowledgements are as follows.

Lynne Pearce would like to thank Viv Tabner for her unflagging personal support and patience during the long years of the project and the production of this book as well as her practical help and support with the conference and impressive archive of Mancunian music! Also, she would like to acknowledge the good-humoured curiosity shown in both the project and the book from all her friends in the Robin's Nest Tearoom in Taynuilt, Scotland – including Vera Shaw's reminder that, at the risk of alienating some readers, Manchester United should get a mention! As a long-distance supporter of MUFC since she was sixteen, the city and its postcodes (M16 0RA) were seared on Lynne's consciousness several decades before 'Moving Manchester' was born.

Corinne Fowler would like to thank Lynne Pearce for being an inspirational leader and mentor. Thanks, also, to Graham Mort, for his influential and creative approach to the project and to Martin Halliwell, for fostering such a positive working environment in Corinne's subsequent place of work. Corinne would also like to thank her twin, Naomi Fowler, for her sincere interest and wise advice. Thanks also go to Corinne's father, Malcolm Fowler, and to her mother, Yvonne Fowler, for her unfailing encouragement and support. Corinne is grateful to her son, Rafael Lugo-Fowler, for his cheerful greeting upon her return home from work. Finally, heart-felt thanks are due to her partner, Jairo Lugo-Ocando, for his shrewdness and egalitarianism.

Robert Crawshaw would like to thank colleagues and friends in the

Acknowledgements

Institute for Advanced Study at the University of Konstanz, in particular Professor Andreas Langenohl for securing his appointment as a research fellow in the Institute between January and July 2011 and to Nicole Falkenhayner for her insightful advice on the drafts of papers relating to the 'Moving Manchester' project presented at workshops before and during his fellowship.

Permissions

The authors would like to thank the following authors, artists and publishers for their kind permission to reproduce material in our volume as follows: extracts from Lynne Pearce's chapter, 'The Literary Response to Moss Side, Manchester: Fact or (Genre) Fiction?', in Katharine Cockin (ed.) *The Literary North* (2012), Palgrave Macmillan, reproduced with permission of Palgrave Macmillan; the poem, 'Englan no Muddercountry' (1988) reproduced with permission of the author, John Lyons; the poem, 'Black Sister' (1989), reproduced with the permission of the author, Sundar Kanta Walker; substantive extracts from Seán Body's long poem, *Seasons* (2003), reproduced with the permission of the author, Seán Body; substantive extracts from the novel *Lick Shot* (1993), reproduced with the permission of the author, Peter Kalu; the poem 'True Grit' by John Agard, reproduced with permission of Bloodaxe (*Alternative Anthem: Selected Poems with Live DVD* (Bloodaxe Books, 2009).

In addition, we would like to thank the artist, Michael Gutteridge, for his permission to reproduce his painting 'Tram in St. Peter's Square No. 4' (cover image); Manchester Museum of Science and Industry for its permission to reproduce an image of the painting, 'A View of Manchester' 1834' in Chapter 1; FotoLibra, for its permission to reproduce John Cleare's photograph 'Manchester Redevelopment, February 1964' in Chapter 1; the photographer Shirley Baker, for her permission to reproduce the photographs 'Salford, 1962' and Salford, 1964' in Chapter 1; exHulme website, for their permission to reproduce the photograph of 'Salford Crescent, Balcony' in Chapter 1; Manchester Local Image Collection (Manchester City Council (see www.images.manchester.gov.uk)) for its permission to reproduce the following photographs in Chapter 1: 'Manchester Royal Exchange, 1874', 'Manchester Royal Exchange', 1900; 'Manchester Royal Exchange, following Bomb Damage, 1940', 'The Aftermath of the IRA Bomb, 1996', 'Castlefield Quay, by D. Brumhead, 1986'; the photographer Aidan O'Rourke, for his permission to reproduce the photograph, 'Merchant's Warehouse, Castlefield, 1998' in Chapter 1; Young Identity for their permission to reproduce an advertisement for one of their events in Chapter 2; the FED (Federation of Worker Writers and Community Publishers) for its permission to reproduce two cover images of its publications in Chapter 4; Commonword, for its permission to reproduce the following cover images in Chapter 4: *Healing Strategies* (1998), *City Secrets* (2002) and *Hair* (2006); Toby Madden for permission to reproduce his photograph of Lemn Sissay in Chapter 5.

Finally, we would like to thank all the interviewees cited in Chapter 6 (see key at end of chapter) for their permission to reproduce extracts from their interviews with Corinne Fowler.

Introduction:
Manchester and the devolution of British literary culture

Corinne Fowler and Lynne Pearce

As the key components of its title suggest – i.e., postcolonial, diaspora, devolution – this volume arizes out of a recognizable and, in many respects, well-established set of debates concerning the reconfiguration of literary and cultural studies in Britain. The association of 'English literature' with the West's colonial past has been a major, possibly even the predominant, concern of literary scholars around the globe for the best part of thirty years, with our understanding of post/colonialism's reach and complexity becoming ever more nuanced and, arguably, ever more disturbing. 'Diaspora space', a term coined by Avtar Brah in her ground-breaking volume *Cartographies of Diaspora* (1996), represents one such political and theoretical leap forward inasmuch as it compelled scholars, working across the arts and social sciences, to move beyond a binary that posited the world's diasporas as 'others' superimposed upon a pre-existing national or social order and the notionally 'indigenous' inhabitants of the same spaces as implausibly separate from their neighbours. In the introduction to *Cartographies of Diaspora*, Brah presents her thesis thus:

> It is a central argument of this text that 'diaspora space' (as distinct from the concept of diaspora) is inhabited not only by diasporic subjects but equally by those who are constructed and represented as 'indigenous'. As such, the concept of diaspora space foregrounds the entanglement of genealogies of dispersion with those of 'staying put' ... It is a cartography of the politics of intersectionality. (Brah, 1996: 16)

This volume – the culmination of six years' research on the contemporary writing and associated literary cultures to emerge out of Greater

Manchester over the past four decades – presents the North West of England as quintessential 'diaspora space' and, we trust, will contribute positively to a better understanding of the region in social, cultural and aesthetic terms.

In terms of recent academic debates exploring Britain – and, in particular, contemporary British literature – in expressly postcolonial terms, this volume (and, indeed, the 'Moving Manchester' project as a whole) is also indebted to James Procter's work in the early 2000s on postwar black British writing. His book *Dwelling Places* (2003) moved forward popular understanding of diasporic writing in Britain through the simple, yet compelling, observation that it is very different being black 'in London [than] it is in Llandudno' (Procter, 2003: 1); the inference here is that insufficient attention has been paid to the very local and regional specificity of black and Asian 'dwelling places' across the United Kingdom and, by corollary, how this has impacted upon the art and literature produced by the individuals and communities who live there. He writes:

> Black British writing has not been satisfactorily 'placed' in relation to the landscapes and discourses within and alongside which it has been produced, disseminated and consumed. Part of the reason for this prolonged critical neglect of place has to do with the 'placelessness' of those post-national, post-colonial diasporic vocabularies and frameworks currently being used to 'describe' black cultural production. (Procter, 2003: 4)

In other words, there has been too much emphasis (especially from literary scholars) on diasporic identity in terms of the discourses of perceived homelessness, rootlessness and alienation – typically figured in terms of a nostalgia for the lost 'homeland' – and insufficient attention given to the way in which these communities' 'destination homes' (Pearce, 2000: 35–6) have contributed to the development of highly specific local and regional affiliations. In addition, Procter's was one of the first studies of black British writing to spell out the extent to which the profile and status of London as the nation's 'multicultural' heartland has served to marginalize diasporic cultural production in the regions. It is not – as the research conducted by the 'Moving Manchester' project has emphatically proved – that the regions are without their own long-established histories of cultural production, but that these outputs – with the notable exception, in the North West, of popular music and performance poetry – have rarely won metropolitan

Introduction

support and favour. Consequently, both Procter (see Keown et al., 2009) and the 'Moving Manchester' project team, with the support of funded projects, have spent the past decade campaigning for the recognition of a newly devolved canon of English literature which embraces not only ethnic and cultural difference but also *regional* difference. We now proceed to outline this devolved model of English literature, and its associated cultural practices, in more detail.

Devolving literary cultures

> [B]rass bands ... butties in your hands ... headscarves and mushy peas ... fog, smog, sitting on the bog ... gaslight and games in the street (Victoria Wood).[1]

David Law (2004) observes that the comic songs of Victoria Wood offer powerful cultural summaries of northern England. Yet these summaries rarely allude to the significance of immigration to northern life. James Procter observes in his 2006 essay 'The Postcolonial Everyday' that popular filmic representations of northern Britain 'evoke a form of nostalgia for a neighbourly, white working-class community that depends on an image of the north existing at a cultural remove from multiracial Britain' (Procter, 2006: 73). Citing a range of recent films, including *The Full Monty* (1997) and *Billy Elliot* (2000), Procter argues that British cinema represents northern England as 'closeted from and innocent of ... cultural difference' as it is encountered in London (Procter, 2006: 73). It is precisely this imbalance that *Postcolonial Manchester* seeks to redress. Six years' observation of the vibrant literary scene that flourishes in one of Britain's largest conurbations has permitted many distinctive new insights into the way in which increased awareness of Britain's differentiated diaspora space (London is not Llandudno, Llandudno is not Glasgow, Glasgow is not Manchester, Manchester is not Bradford, and so on) has the potential to challenge, invigorate and, above all, *devolve* the nation's literary culture.

In the chapters that follow, we ask how generations of Manchester writers have engaged with the city's distinctive and contrasting settings; we examine the way in which stories, poems and plays set in locales as various as 'the Curry Mile', Moss Side, 'the Gay Village', Salford, Didsbury and Piccadilly Gardens have attempted to reshape, and often to critically appraise, collective visions of Manchester. And in the process we recognize Manchester's twenty-first-century demographic to be profoundly multiracial and multicultural (see discussion following for a gloss on these terms). This study necessarily features an unusually broad demographic of authors and texts emanating from Chinese, Nigerian, Somali, Guyanese, Caribbean, Pakistani, Indian, Bangladeshi, Middle Eastern, Irish, Scottish, Welsh and German diasporic communities and representing a wide range of religious affiliations (Christian, Muslim, Hindi, Sikh, Jewish).

As detailed in Chapters 2 and 4, a suggestive example of Mancunian writers' alternative imaginative cartography of Manchester can be found in the poetry of Seán Body, a founder member of the Manchester Irish Writers' group. Body's long poetry sequence *Seasons* (2003) makes a concerted effort to dispel the imaginative legacy of Friedrich Engels's 1844 work *The Condition of the Working Class in England*. Back in the 1840s, census figures suggested that around a tenth of the city's population was Irish. Most were then living in Ancoats, which Engels notoriously described as the city's 'most disgusting spot' (Engels 1987 [1845]: 54). In *Seasons*, Body vigorously contests Engels's depiction of the Irish. Engels's observations are made to serve as epigraphs to be refuted, albeit implicitly, by the speakers of Body's poem. One such epigraph of Engels reads: '[t]he race that lives in these ruinous cottages ... must really have reached the lowest stage of humanity' (Engels in Body, 2003: 6). Body's poem re-humanizes the city's early Irish immigrants by imaginatively inhabiting their consciousness and narrating the hopes and fears of those who occupy the 'ruinous cottages' to which Engels refers. Meanwhile, the speakers' memories of life back in Ireland are reconsidered in a compassionate light, being likened to 'small pebbles picked up/on a childhood beach' ('Béarla'; Body, 2003: 14). Writers such as Body thus counter tenacious images of monocultural, gritty northern life. Importantly, and led by the literature that we found, this study engages with texts which explore the kinds of immigrant experience that do not figure in comic songs such as Wood's. In this book, therefore, we attend closely to writers' collective exploration of the ways in which the city's refugees and immigrants have, together, integrated Manchester into the world.[2]

Close attention to both diasporic and devolved literary cultures can add to our existing understanding of, in Susheila Nasta's words, 'the extent to which our visions of the national have been built on migrant and diasporic, colonial and postcolonial identities' (McLeod, 2004: inside cover). This book's distinctive contribution thus lies in its attempt to understand the ways in which Manchester's devolved

Introduction

literary cultures challenge and revize our collective sense of Manchester, of diaspora space and, indeed, of Britain itself. Most particularly, we aim to bring significant fresh understandings to some of the unexpected ways in which, as Procter argues, 'the habitual, the mundane and the taken-for-granted are all performing, or capable of performing, important cultural tasks after Empire' (Procter in Fowler, 2008: 87).

Peter Kalu's poem 'Old Radicals' which was published in Kwame Dawes's *Red* anthology in 2010, reflects on a long-standing friendship forged during political protests on Manchester's streets ('our hands on rocks and riot shields' (l. 5)) as well as in its police stations ('5am calls from cells' (l. 7) (Kalu, 2010: 117). As the friends age, however, the speaker's political commitments are increasingly tested by the compulsions of everyday life. He finds himself 'worrying about fresh nappies / as we marched' (ll. 16–17). Similarly, when the 'radicals' meet years later they 'fumbl[e] with the old handshakes' that once symbolized their solidarity against 'apartheid, Special Patrol and the NF' (Kalu, 2010: 117). As a retrospective reflection on several decades of political protest and poetry in Manchester, Kalu's poem reflects on the inevitability of becoming preoccupied with the local and parochial. The challenge, implicit in the poem, is therefore for the political subject – committed to emancipation and equality at a global level – to work out how transnational concerns within the context of the neighbourhood may be brought within the 'practice of everyday life' (de Certeau, 1984), and vice versa.

As Chapter 5 argues in relation to Manchester's long-established history of poetry in performance, Kalu's 'Old Radicals' encapsulates the evolution of certain key social and literary developments in the 'everyday life' of black Britain. On one level, the poem might be read as both a personal and collective coming-of-age poem for British black poets; it explores the social, personal and political implications of what it means to get older in a particular locale. In this sense, 'Old Radicals' charts the perhaps inevitable journey of identification away from the 'Angry Black Poet' – a figure whose popularity with white audiences is parodied in Benjamin Zephaniah's poem (Zephaniah, 1996: 29) of the same name – to the figure of *the neighbour*, a cultural insider who actively shapes its sensibilities. It also marks a parallel transition from the inner-city street to the suburb. As Procter argues, for British black writers, suburbia has gradually become the locus of an 'increasingly differentiated, *devolved* cultural geography of black Britain over the last fifty years' (emphasis in the original) (Procter, 2003: 3,4). Indeed, the figure of the neighbour is one of this book's central metaphors and offers compelling new readings of the kind of devolved texts that were first identified as significant to the field by scholars such as Procter. 'Old Radicals' is just a single example of a text that serves an important literary function by reflecting on the place of British black poets in what Paul Beasley – by emphasizing the link between the regional, the colloquial and the culturally and ethnically diverse – refers to as the 'devolution of British poetry in general' (Beasley in Munden and Wade, 1999: 48), that is, 'a reassertion of the vernacular – the everyday idioms and speech patterns of the poet or the sociolect of the class and cultural group to which the poet belongs'. Beasley identifies poets such as Merle Collins, Ian McMillan and Tom Leonard with the devolution of British poetry in these terms (Beasley in Munden and Wade, 1999: 48), and Kalu's 'Old Radicals' shows a clear affinity with such poets by offering a meditation on the way in which daily, lived experience of Manchester inevitably leads to the devolution of poetry for the city's black and white poets alike.

As well as paying new attention to the local, the regional and 'the everyday', this book also conceptualizes Manchester as an emphatically *global* city in cultural, economic and literary terms. It thus extends the work of John McLeod's 2004 study *Postcolonial London*, which examines how writers of African, Asian, Caribbean and South Pacific heritage have imaginatively transformed Britain's *capital* city. In this book we consider how writers in a non-metropolitan but similarly 'global' city, such as Manchester, have engaged creatively with its 'external geography': a term coined by Doreen Massey in her 2007 study *World City*:

> Ethnic and cultural mixity is only one aspect of being a world city, only one aspect of the city's relationship with the world ... [W]orld cities have lines that run out from them: trade routes, investments, political and cultural influences ... power relations of all sorts that run around the globe ... This is the other geography, the external geography if you like, of a global sense of place ... [The world city] is a command centre, place of orchestration and significant beneficiary of its continuing operation. This city stands, then, as a crucial node in the production of what is an increasingly unequal world. (Massey, 2007: 8)

Following Massey, *Postcolonial Manchester* explores writers' imaginative, and often critical, engagements with the 'external geography' of one of Britain's great northern cities.

Introduction

Such an exploration is strikingly apparent in much of Lemn Sissay's poetry. In 'Island Mentality' (2000a), for example, Britain figures as a 'dot on my world map' that is 'hemmed in by the sea' (1992: 26). As discussed in Chapter 5, his later poem called 'The Gilt of Cain' (2007) – one of his London-based landmark poems – graphically illustrates the capital city's 'external geography', eroding the boundaries between city and coastline, slavery and modern-day commerce. Inscribed upon a sculpture by Michael Vissachi (located near Tower Hill in London) which consists of seventeen sugar canes, representing the slaves, and a slave auctioneer's pulpit, Sissay's poem juxtaposes terminologies associated with the Stock Exchange with descriptions of the suffering slaves. In this way, the poem foregrounds the ongoing relationship between modern finance, capitalism and the exploitation of former colonies around the globe. His poem 'Rage', meanwhile, uses aquatic imagery[3] to reconfigure a Mancunian sense of space:

> Take the sea in handfuls
> and spill it onto this city's streets
> ... It feels so triumphant to let it
> trickle through my fingers into the cracked kerbs
> (Sissay, 2000c: 39)

The poem's speaker thus subverts the salient metaphors of immigration, which is typically described in terms of 'flows', 'floods' and 'waves'. In 'Rage', it is salt water, rather than 'Rivers of Blood',[4] that spills on to Manchester's streets. In this way, the poem draws on an associative link, set up by other poems such as 'Island Mentality', between seawater and an expansive postcolonial consciousness, an awareness of the city's 'external geography' that gradually 'trickle[s]' into the 'cracked kerbs' of everyday life and consciousness.

A further example, Sissay's poem 'Mill Town and Africa' (*Rebel without Applause*, 2000b: 47), begins by expressing solidarity with the political struggles of Ethiopians in the wake of Haile Selassie's deposition in 1974: 'How many fingernails of my own shall I pluck / till she sees that my blood is hers?' (ll. 1 and 2). It also embraces a familiar sense of diasporic identification as a means of countering the material realities of geographical separation:

> Revolutions have passed between us
> emperors dethroned, guns and red flags raised ...
> We scattered on different sides of the debris.
> (Sissay, 2000a: 47)

However, the poem's emphasis on collapsing governments (l. 6), political torture (ll. 1 and 2) and refugees is used as a basis for revealing Manchester's collusion in an 'external geography' in which Africa is personified as female (ll. 10–13) and wilfully exploited:

> I saw her over the Lancashire plain
> fleeing Ethiopia with the remnants of a family.
> She had washed into the hard Manchester rain
> and I into the skating heatwave.
>
> (Sissay, 2000b: 47)

These lines may be seen to enact the kind of spatial reconfiguration described by Massey. The speaker's physical location may be in northern England, yet the way in which the poem reconceptualizes space and place is clearly commensurate with Massey's sense of the global city as a 'crucial node in the production of ... an increasingly unequal world' (Massey, 2007: 8). In 'Mill Town and Africa', it is these inequities of power that operate as a force-field that draws separate locations into a single conceptual and economic space.

With Manchester's devolved location within the United Kingdom, its 'diaspora space' (Brah, 1996) and its 'external geography' (Massey, 2007) to the fore, this book thus attends very closely to the significance of space and place across a wide range of polycultural[5] literary texts. Correspondingly, and perhaps uniquely in this context, it gives sustained consideration to the role of place in defining the perceived relevance and reach of so-called 'provincial' writing. This consideration, which necessarily became a central preoccupation of the 'Moving Manchester' project, is predicated upon the widely acknowledged prejudicial reception of northern writing. As the author Hilary Mantel observes, the regional identity of Manchester's writers continually works against them: '[R]eviewers have trouble focusing on provincial life ... it's all "up there" to them ... Livi Michael [is] a talented ... [Mancunian] writer who writes exclusively about the north, and whom I think has been neglected for it' (Mantel in Fowler, 2008: 81). As the 'Moving Manchester' project has evidenced (see Chapter 6), Manchester writers' regional identity has been particularly detrimental to the profile of the city's black and Asian writers, who have tended to be viewed by commissioning editors and reviewers as anomalies (Fowler, 2008: 81). Our research into the publishing and critical reception of writing from Manchester suggests that the more multiple and complex are writers' perceived identities, the less their work is seen to be of national and international relevance. However, as the following chapters of this book demonstrate, large cities outside London are very far from being strangers to devolved, polycultural expressions of Britishness.

Manchester is frequently depicted as the northern capital of independent publishing on the grounds that its presses have made a strategic decision to specialize proactively in non-commercial publishing formats, such as literary magazines, anthologies and marginalized genres such as the short story. Indeed, this independent sector prides itself on valuing quality and political integrity over more commercial considerations, and many Manchester-based presses argue that they provide genuine alternatives to corporate publishing. Ra Page, the founder of Comma Press, believes that the persistent experience of being overlooked by London's literary establishment has actually been liberating for Manchester's writers, who have consequently embraced a wider range of sources and influences than are found in commercially successful titles (in an interview with Corinne Fowler, 25 October 2007). Further, as Chapter 2 discusses, the emergence of social media, e-books and print-on-demand technologies has the potential to reach new international audiences, thereby bypassing national prejudices about northern writing.

This said, the future of Manchester's distinctive literary and publishing culture is certainly a major concern for all the city's authors and writing organizations at the time of this book going to press (2012) on account of the recession, a point to which we return in the Afterword. In the meantime, the chapters which follow strive hard to pay tribute to the city's proud and distinctive independent writing scene, and, in particular, the literature development organization Commonword, which – for over thirty years – has remained true to its founding principles and played a significant role in the devolution of Britain's literary culture.

'Multiculturalism' – and other contested terms

One of Manchester University Press's reviewers for this volume queried why we hadn't thought of a title that included the more 'obvious' descriptor 'multicultural'. So generic has the use of this term now become that it seemed, to our reviewer, the obvious one to encapsulate our perspective on Manchester and its writing. What the reviewer couldn't know, of course, is that few terms are as disliked, and distrusted, amongst the writers with whom we worked in Manchester as 'multicultural'. By the mid-2000s (when we first began working with groups and individuals in Manchester), 'multiculturalism' was already negatively associated with New Labour's agenda of overtly supporting cultural diversity while at the same time insisting, ever more stridently, on demonstrable loyalty to the nation-state ('England') through mechanisms such as the citizenship exam (commonly thought of as a test of one's 'Englishness').[6] While this is very much an unwritten condition of multicultural freedom, it was striking how many of the authors with whom we worked inferred these caveats and were equally hostile to the concept of the 'multicultural novel'. The latter is widely perceived to be code for 'feel-good' texts (destined primarily for white audiences) in which the alienation and homesickness initially experienced by first- or second-generation British migrants gives way to a 'sense of belonging' (variously achieved). The two texts most often named in this context are Monica Ali's *Brick Lane* (2003) and Zadie Smith's *White Teeth* (2000), and midway through the 'Moving Manchester' project Corinne Fowler wrote an article for the *Journal of Commonwealth Studies* (2008) in which she investigated the parallel publishing histories of *White Teeth* and a novel by the Mancunian novelist Joe Pemberton (*Forever and Ever Amen* (2000)). Fowler revisits this research at the start of Chapter 2, detailing again the ways in which Britain's mainstream publishing houses have a tendency to promote certain kinds of black British texts and certain kinds of authors more than others. Of course, it is important to acknowledge that not all fiction described as 'multicultural' will conform to this 'vanilla' stereotype; in fact, it may apply to very few. The point we are concerned with here, however, is the suspicions the term raises for significant numbers of black writers who know that *their* stories don't fit the bill. With these concerns to the fore, 'multicultural' is clearly not a term we would choose to feature in the title of this book. Further, while the term will be found in the pages that follow – sometimes it presents itself as the most accurate descriptor for the content in hand; and substitute terms, such as 'multiracial', are not without their own problems[7] – as authors we are mindful of its problematic connotations and frequently enclose the term in quotation marks.

With regards to the wider political remit of the 'Moving Manchester' project, the problematic connotations of the term 'multicultural' also point to what we have discovered to be a pervasive misapprehension of what black, Asian and/or diasporic writing in Britain is expected to be *about*. Within months of beginning work on the project's e-catalogue, it became clear that only a small proportion of the texts we were reading were concerned with 'migrant' and/or 'black' experience in terms of identity, alienation, (un)belonging and nostalgia; rather, as is discussed at some length in Chapter 4, the major preoccupation (both in fiction and poetry) is *racism*: in other words, the 'issue' that has concerned Manchester's black and/or migrant writing community more than any other is not 'them' (i.e. the black subject's suffering or alienation) but 'us' (the white 'other' who, individually, collectively or institutionally, is violent and hostile at worst, cold and indifferent at best). This, in turn, raises difficult questions for a project like 'Moving Manchester' which secured government funding on the grounds (sometimes explicit, always implicit) that our research would somehow contribute to an improved sense of 'well-being' for 'marginalized' subjects (typically migrants, asylum-seekers and black or Asian communities) and, though never stated, improve 'social cohesion'[8] in Britain's 'multicultural' towns and cities. Such ideology of course presupposes that the subjects concerned are consumed by a desire to 'belong' and/or be accepted by a separate 'white' community; in fact, what the writers and texts with which we have worked in Manchester evidence is a radical reshaping of 'diaspora space' (Brah, 1996) through the interaction of *all* members of numerous inner-city districts. Understanding, and respecting, what the writers of a twenty-first-century, cosmopolitan city like Manchester are really concerned about – rather than what government policy believes that concern to be – consequently seems to us a matter of huge ethical and political importance. This is a reality-check that a good deal of postcolonial literary criticism, long obsessed with subaltern identity, would also benefit from.

Along with 'multicultural', the authors of this volume have had to negotiate a number of other terms whose contested meaning makes them difficult to deploy (though often equally hard to replace). While it is not possible to attend to all of these here, we would like to note that most of the terms traditionally employed to describe poetry in performance are compromised in some way. For example, the descriptor 'spoken word' has its origins in a particular scene in the US which fails to account for the range of performance scenarios enjoyed in Britain, while 'live literature' – a term espoused by the Arts Council in recent years – is disliked by many poets on account of its 'funder-speak' instrumentality. Arguably even more problematic, however, is the term 'performance poet' itself since the descriptor creates a false distinction between 'poetry for the page' and 'poetry for the stage' (inasmuch as a good deal of 'spoken word' poetry is eventually published, and a good deal of 'page poetry' performed). Consequently, finding an acceptable terminology to describe this particular artistic category has not been easy, and we would ask readers to bear with our sometimes awkward collocations.

Finally, we would advise that our use of the term 'black' is very much context-specific. In some instances, such as the poetry in performance scene just mentioned, 'black' is understood to be a political category that includes performers of African, African-Caribbean and Asian descent who elected to use the single term 'black' to signal their solidarity from the 1970s onwards. On other occasions, we have taken care to identify ethnic groups as precisely as possible, since African, African-Caribbean, Pakistani, Indian and Chinese groups and individuals represent distinctive literary traditions within the city. Further, there are many instances when the conjunction 'black and Asian' is the most acceptable umbrella terminology for the groups or individuals in question and, where possible, we have taken our cue from the writers, publishers and organizations themselves. With regards to the case representation of 'black', we have opted for the lower case except, once again, in those instances when the authors or groups concerned have capitalized (see Procter, 2003: 8–9).

The chapters

The chapters which follow combine close textual analysis of a wide range of texts emanating from Greater Manchester during the past four decades with a consideration of the literary cultures that gave rise to it (i.e. the writing development organizations such as Commonword, the independent publishing houses, the performance poetry scene and the Arts Council). Very little of this discussion takes the form of 'literary criticism' as traditionally understood (i.e. explication and evaluation) but instead it engages with the texts concerned in order to gain a better understanding of the political and cultural issues that have come to define the region and its people since the 1960s. In particular, and picking up on the our opening discussion, it draws upon the literature to demonstrate that Greater Manchester today is a consummately 'diasporic space', not only on account of the fact that it is, and always has been, a 'migrant city' (see Chapter 1) but because all its citizens –

including those sometimes mistakenly represented as its white, 'indigenous' population – live their everyday lives dynamically 'entangled' (Brah, 1996: 16) with one another. Following on from this, many of the chapters explore and pay tribute to the way in which Manchester's writers have been instrumental in 're-presenting' the city to itself in recent times, their intimate portraits of Manchester's fast-changing skyline (both literal and metaphoric) (see Pearce, 2012: 8) and demographic capturing its contemporary identity more astutely than government policy documents and statistics. Between them, the chapters also survey the most popular literary modes and genres to figure in the city's publishing history in recent times: namely, the novel (dealt with principally in Chapter 1); poetry – both print and in performance (Chapters 2 and 5); crime fiction, a sub-genre that has found a suitably noir-ish home in the streets of Manchester (Chapter 3); and the short story and mixed-genre anthologies (Chapter 4). In addition, Chapter 6, which focuses on the interviews that Manchester's authors and agencies kindly granted the 'Moving Manchester' project, provides further insight into why particular modes and genres have been preferred, as well as the challenges the authors have faced in getting their work published. Finally, it should be noted that not all of the texts that feature in our discussions are 'about' Manchester. Along with the early realization that Manchester's writers were typically less concerned with their own 'identities' than with issues that are the responsibility of others (see previous discussion), work on the 'Moving Manchester' e-catalogue quickly established that a large proportion of the texts produced by Mancunian writers, including those belonging to its diasporic communities, were about 'elsewhere' (be this Yorkshire, the Pakistani or Caribbean homeland, London, Ireland, the US or a futuristic, fantasy location). Therefore, while the geographical and analytic focus of this volume remains the Greater Manchester district, it seemed important that variety of fictional locations chosen by its authors were also kept in view. We conclude with a short summary of each of the chapters and their specific contribution to the volume as a whole.

Chapter 1, 'Manchester, the postcolonial city', opens with an overview of the city's social and cultural history in terms of migration, its association (through the cotton industry) with the British Empire and its identity as a profoundly 'diasporic space' (Brah, 1996: 16). This history is evidenced through a combination of recent scholarship, literary texts and the city's architecture which, as numerous commentators have observed (Haslam, 2000; Peck and Ward, 2002), captures the past more vividly than a thousand words. In addition, the chapter seeks to introduce readers to a selection of the authors and texts associated with Manchester's contemporary literary scene as well as its writing and publishing cultures through reference to organizations such as Commonword, Gatehouse and the Black Arts Alliance. The latter part of the chapter then focuses, in some detail, on how Mancunian writers have represented, or re-presented, their city in recent times through the mechanism (both literary and ideological) of 'the view': that is, views of Moss Side; views of the city from the seat of a car; and the 'new views' of the city that have been achieved, paradoxically, by its long-term 'migrant' residents. At every juncture, the chapter seeks to connect the city's present — of which its writers and its writing communities are a part — with its colonial past.

Chapter 2, 'Publishing Manchester's black and Asian writers', explores how the city's writers, principally its black poets, have struggled to achieve recognition within the literary mainstream and yet, partly as a result of exclusion from London-centric, transnational publishing houses, have established a distinctive, internationally renowned reputation for poetry in performance. Both Chapter 2 and Chapter 5 nevertheless also seek to deconstruct what has emerged as a misleading 'page'/'stage' binary as far as black poetry is concerned, and show how a good deal of 'spoken word' poetry found its way into print through the auspices of independent publishers and a tradition of self-publishing.

Chapter 3, 'Manchester's crime fiction: the mystery of the city's smoking gun', draws upon the region's now substantial list of high-profile crime fiction writers to ask the question: 'who, or what, is responsible for the crime of Manchester?' As well as showcasing this most popular sub-genre of the city's fiction writing, the chapter is therefore also, in part, a sociological enquiry into Manchester's unfortunate reputation as one of Britain's 'crime capitals' and uses the fiction, typically astute and nuanced in its analysis, to stretch and complicate more popular explanations (e.g., the link between guns, gangs and the city's black population). Like Chapter 1, the conclusion lays particular responsibility at the doors of the city council's planning department.

Chapter 4, 'Collective resistance', provides a historical overview of Manchester's literary anthologies from the 1970s to the present, paying particular attention to the contexts of their production and the ways in which changing political objectives have gone hand in hand with changing literary objectives and aesthetics. In particular, the chapter observes a transition from writing that was primarily realist, testimonial and militant in nature (i.e., stories and poems that paid tribute to, and supported, political resistance *vis-à-vis* working-class and black oppression) towards experimental, idiosyncratic and more complex political statements. Inasmuch as most of the anthologies considered are Commonword imprints, the chapter also constitutes a brief history of that organization from its origins in 'the FED' (the Federation of Worker Writers and Community Publishers) in the 1970s to the multi-faceted, umbrella organization it has become today. The chapter also pays particular attention to the short story as a literary mode that, according to writer and publisher Ra Page, Manchester has been responsible for rescuing and promoting in recent times (Page, 2002: vii–xii), and ends with a section devoted to the Manchester Irish Writers Group (founded in 1995). This 'case study' looks in detail at how one of the city's many writers' groups has established itself as a distinctive voice within the literary scene, as well as exploring the way in which one of their publications' key preoccupations – temporality – is realized across a selection of poems and stories. Taken as a whole, moreover, the chapter may be seen as an indicative demonstration of Manchester's 'devolved literary culture' at work.

Chapter 5, meanwhile ('Rebels without applause'), constitutes what we believe to be the first in-depth analysis of Manchester's internationally renowned poetry-in-performance scene. Following on from the discussions of how the city's black novelists have struggled to gain a foothold in mainstream publishing but can, in their 'performance poets', claim a powerful, alternative tradition of productivity, this chapter combines close readings of some of the city's best-known performance poets such as Lemn Sissay and SuAndi with analysis of the literary cultures that have both facilitated and challenged their art. Lemn Sissay's career is especially interesting in this respect since it charts a journey from his roots in Manchester and the city's community publishing scene (he was the first Literary Director of Commonword) to the post he holds today as writer-in-residence at London's Southbank Centre (most recently, he was the first British poet commissioned to produce a poem for the 2012 Olympic Games' 'Winning Words' programme, whereby 'landmark poems' are to be permanently sited in the Olympic Park). Very few other black poets from Manchester have enjoyed this degree of success or recognition, however (SuAndi and

John Lyons being notable exceptions), and the chapter ends by speculating on the future of black poetry not only in Manchester but across Britain. As part of its overall argument, the chapter also links Manchester's performance poetry scene (both its black poets and celebrity punk poets like John Cooper Clark from Salford) with Merseybeat poets, Adrian Henri and Roger McGough, and the so-called 'Poetry Revival' of the 1960s. To our knowledge, this connection has never been made before, with most commentators sourcing Britain's black, 'spoken word' poetry scene to transnational contexts. This alternative history of events could, we feel, prove important in challenging the established view that Britain's black poets – and especially its black, northern poets – are not integral to Britain's 'indigenous' literary tradition. The continuity we establish here suggests that they *are*.

Chapter 6, 'Giving voice', affords readers the opportunity to hear many of the authors discussed in the previous chapters 'in their own words'. Focusing on their responses to questions posed in interviews and focus-group discussions, the chapter reflects, amongst other things, on how the writers position themselves in terms of the literary mainstream and (where relevant) their identities as black, migrant and/or diasporic authors.

As noted in the Preface, the discussion and reflection contained in this volume are the culmination of six years of research conducted under the auspices of the 'Moving Manchester' project and, as such, are wholly dependent upon the generosity and support of the writers and organizations with whom we worked. This said, the views and speculations we advance, and the conclusions we draw, are inevitably those of 'outsider' academics working within a set of discourses and debates that are often theoretically and/or textually led. We therefore recognize that not all of the views presented here may not always 'ring true' for the authors on whose texts we draw, but we trust that, taken as a whole, the volume has remained faithful to the 'Moving Manchester' project's first objective which was to support, and promote, contemporary writing in Manchester and pay tribute to its vibrant and radical literary culture.

Notes

1 David Law first drew attention to Victoria Wood's cultural summary of the North in his PhD thesis, '"Guddling for Words"' (2004).

Introduction

2 This idea was first expressed by the Research Institute for Cosmopolitan Cultures in its promotional material for two seminars called 'Creating the Cosmopolitan City: Manchester Migrants Old and New', 22 April and 27 May 2009.
3 Chapter 5 draws on the work of John McLeod in *Postcolonial London* to discuss the wider significance of aquatic imagery to British black writers.
4 John Agard's poem 'Memo to Professor Enoch Powell', in *We Brits* (2006: xx), speaks of 'February shimmer[ing] with rivers of blood / that still flow in the veins of black and white'. Agard's poem refers to the so-called 'rivers of blood' speech made in 1968 by the Conservative MP Enoch Powell, predicting social unrest at the prospect of further immigration from Commonwealth countries: 'As I look ahead I am filled with foreboding; like the Roman, I seem to see the River Tiber foaming with much blood.'
5 John McLeod uses this term, which usefully distances itself from the more loaded terms such as multicultural, in the introduction to *Postcolonial London* (2004).
6 In 2005 the British government (following through legislation first mooted by the Conservative Party in the 1990s) announced that all UK residents born elsewhere would have to take a 'Citizenship Test' in order to be granted permission to settle in the UK permanently. This ruling also applied to long-term foreign nationals with British passports. The test, widely recognized to be challenging (even for long-term residents) lasts 45 minutes and comprizes 24 questions about British laws, customs and social practices. See: www.britishcitizenshiptest.co.uk (accessed 13 April 2012).
7 'Multiracial': as well as being predicated upon a concept (i.e. 'race') that some groups and individuals consider archaic and offensive, this term does not reference religious difference. 'Multicultural', by contrast, is a term that is understood to refer to both ethnic and religious difference.
8 Improved 'social welfare', 'social cohesion' and 'improved national security' are categories that have been invoked by Britain's Higher Education Funding council, HEFCE, as indicators of 'research impact' (i.e. tangible evidence that academic research has been of benefit to the nation or community at large). 'Social cohesion' is an especially troubling concept in this regard since it assumes that all researchers working with groups and individuals deemed to be 'marginal' and/or 'disaffected' recognize them to be 'a problem' and are happy to conspire in their 'integration'. See: www.chugd.ac.uk/docs_Nov09_mtg/3.%20HEFCE%20Indicators.pdf (accessed 13 April 2012).

References

Agard, J. (2006) *We Brits*. Newcastle-upon-Tyne: Bloodaxe.
Ali, M. (2003) *Brick Lane*. London: Doubleday.
Billy Elliot (2000) Dir. S. Daldry. United Pictures UK.

Body, S. (2003) *Seasons*. Mexborough: Glass Head Press.
Brah, A. (1996) *Cartographies of Diaspora*. London: Routledge.
De Certeau, M. (1984) *The Practice of Everyday Life*. Berkeley, Los Angeles and London: University of California Press.
Engels, F. (1987 [1845]) *The Condition of the Working Class in England, 1844*, ed. V. G. Kiernan. Harmondsworth: Penguin.
Fowler, C. (2008) 'A Tale of Two Novels: Developing a Devolved Approach to Black British Writing', *Journal of Commonwealth Literature*, 43 (3), 75–94.
Haslam, D. (2000) *Manchester, England: The Story of the Pop Cult City*. London: Fourth Estate.
Kalu, P. (2010) 'Old Radicals' in Dawes, K. and Sessay, K. (eds), *Red: Contemporary Black British Poetry*, 117.
Keown, M., Murphy, D. and Procter, J. (2009) *Comparing Postcolonial Diasporas*. London: Palgrave Macmillan.
Law, D. (2004) '"Guddling for Words": Representations of the North and Northernness in Post-1950 South Pennine Literature'. Lancaster University. Unpublished PhD thesis.
Massey, D. (2007) *World City*. Cambridge: Polity Press.
McLeod, J. (2004) *Postcolonial London: Rewriting the Metropolis*. London and New York: Routledge.
Munden, P. and Wade, S. (eds) (1999) *Reading the Applause: Reflections on Performance Poetry by Various Artists*. York: Talking Shop, 1999.
Page, R. (2002) 'Introduction' in R. Page (ed.), *Comma*. Manchester: Comma, pp. vii–xiii.
Pearce, L. (ed.) (2000) *Devolving Identities: Feminist Readings in Home and Belonging*. Aldershot: Ashgate.
Pearce, L. (2012a) 'The Urban Imaginary', *Mobilities*, 7 (1), 1–11.
Peck, J. and Ward, K. (eds) (2002) *City of Revolution: Restructuring Manchester*. Manchester and New York: Manchester University Press.
Pemberton, J. (2000) *Forever and Ever Amen*. London: Hodder Headline.
Procter, J. (2003) *Dwelling Places: Postwar Black British Writing*. Manchester and New York: Manchester University Press.
Procter, J. (2006) 'The Postcolonial Everyday', *New Formations: A Journal of Culture / Theory / Politics*, 58, 62–80.
Sissay, L. (2000a) 'Island Mentality' in *Rebel without Applause*. Newcastle-upon-Tyne: Bloodaxe, 35.
Sissay, L. (2000b) 'Mill Town and Africa' in *Rebel without Applause*. Newcastle-upon-Tyne: Bloodaxe, 45.
Sissay, L. (2002c) 'Rage' in *Rebel without Applause*. Newcastle-upon-Tyne: Bloodaxe, 62.
Sissay, L. (2007) 'The Gilt of Cain': www.cityoflondon.gov.uk/NR/rdonlyres/94CC1E18–C97F–4475–B082–C9E92316E5CE/0/MC_cain.pdf.

Smith, Z. (2000) *White Teeth*. Harmondsworth: Penguin.
The Full Monty (1997) Dir. P. Cattaneo. Twentieth-Century Fox.
Zephaniah, B. (1996) 'The Angry Black Poet' in *Propa Propoganda*. Newcastle-upon-Tyne: Bloodaxe.

Internet sources

www.britishcitizenshiptest.co.uk.
www.cityoflondon.gov.uk/NR/rdonlyres/94CC1E18–C97F-4475–B082–C9E92316E5CE/0/MC_cain.pdf.
http://www.chugd.ac.uk/docs_Nov09_mtg/3.%20HEFCE%20Indicators.pdf (accessed 13 April 2012).

1

Manchester: the postcolonial city

Lynne Pearce

Today – the second decade of the twenty-first century – Greater Manchester is home to approximately 2.6 million people.[1] But in what sense 'home'? Despite the postmodern discourses – both academic and popular – which have imbued the concept with provisionality, 'home' still bears powerful connotations of roots, rootedness and heritage (Marangoly George, 1996). 'Home', in this archaic sense, is not where 'you' come from, or even where you were born, but where previous generations of your family come from: your parents, your grandparents and, quite possibly, your great-grandparents. Leaving aside the fact that the extreme mobility of post-Second World War generations has meant that fewer and fewer people in either the Western or developing worlds are able to lay claim to specific geographical roots in this way, Manchester is still an exceptional case. Little more than a hundred and fifty years old, Manchester is frequently invoked as 'the first industrial city of Europe', a spectacular illustration of the way in which enterprise, investment and industry transformed the landscape and demography of northern England in the space of a generation. As Malcolm Bee, writing in 1984, observed:

> Manchester was the capital of cotton, and as the industry grew so did 'Cottonopolis'. The open ground which lay between Manchester and its surrounding towns was shrinking rapidly, and by the middle of the century, these towns were so close together and had so much in common that we can consider each of them to be part of a greater entity – a giant Manchester with a population of a million people. This was Britain's largest urban region by far, excluding London, and it was the largest manufacturing area in the world. (Bee, 1984: 1–2)

The crucial point that follows on from this is that no one living in Manchester today can claim it as home in a definitive, trans-

1.1 A view of Manchester in 1841. © Manchester Museum of Science and Industry

generational sense. Go back a generation or two and your family will almost certainly have come to Manchester from somewhere else, be that near or far. As Dave Haslam sums up:

> As in other cities, Manchester communities can feel transient; it's like we're all somehow strangers, rubbing together, making it up as we go along. Unlike London, which was a thriving metropolis three hundred years ago, Manchester is a hybrid town, born all in a rush one hundred and fifty years ago, when those arriving for work in the fast-growing factories, workshops, warehouses and foundries included large numbers of Catholic Irish, as well as Scots, and Germans and East European Jews. These migrations have been replicated since, with incomers from the Caribbean in the 1950s and from the Asian sub-continent in the 1970s. Then there are the students, appearing every September, many not staying more than three years, but others relocating here permanently. (Haslam, 2000: xi)

This chapter thus seeks to locate Manchester not only as a northern city, and as Europe's premier industrial city, but as a migrant and emphatically postcolonial city whose existence owes as much to the reverse-flows of Empire as to internal migration from the rest of England, as well as Scotland and Ireland. Indeed, even though the British National Party and English Defence League may still be seen to draw distinctions between the so-called indigenous and migrant populations of the north of England, a little history makes it clear that the concept of an indigenous population makes very little sense in the case of Manchester. Put simply, the city (and many of its satellite towns and suburbs) came into being because of a cotton trade that depended upon slave labour to pick the cotton and migrant labour to manufacture it. This dynamic, desperate but above all 'migrant' history is encapsulated in the following paragraph from Gary Messinger's *Manchester in the Victorian Age* (1985):

> Manchester was an extraordinarily open town which took full advantage of its position between a geographic frontier to the north and an economic frontier to the south. It became a kind of Eldorado. From the farms, towns and villages of neighbouring areas, successive waves of English labourers migrated towards it. From across the sea came the poor of Ireland. From the north came Scotsmen fleeing the harsh life of the Highlands and the slums of Edinburgh and Glasgow. And from the Continent, more settlers arrived; some fleeing religious persecutions, others fleeing civil strife, such as the Greeks during the revolution of 1821 and Italians during the wars leading up to national unification in

the 1840s; others, under clandestine conditions, either offering to sell or hoping to steal new industrial techniques; still others, particularly the large numbers of Germans from Hanseatic cities, attracted by the chance of high monetary returns for their business skills. (Messinger, 1985: 8)

To these eloquent portraits by Haslam and Messinger of Manchester's cosmopolitan past should also be added the somewhat belated acknowledgement of the significant numbers of black residents in Britain long before the twentieth century (see Fryer, 1984, and also Chapter 5). Although most social and cultural histories of Manchester and its surrounding 'mill towns' tell a story of 'successive waves' of immigration, recent commentators like Fryer have argued for a more complex demographic evolution which makes clear that the district's ethnic composition was 'always already' mixed.

Further, as we shall see, the region's colonial interests are also writ large on the geography and architecture of the city and have been marked, often in passing, by the city's novelists and poets. As the black Detective Inspector of Peter Kalu's *Yard Dogs* (2002) ironically observes, a long history of enterprise and exploitation links Manchester's present with its past:

> Evenings, I walked the moody streets. Half the city centre buildings were still named after colonial traders – India House, Africa Mill. Its citizenry owed its current prosperity to the black slaves who were the currency of the seventeenth- century's triangular trade. And to the white wage slaves who worked the looms in the nineteenth. Marketing Manchester, Market That. (Kalu, 2002: 37)

The particular link that Kalu makes here, meanwhile, regarding the fact that the Lancashire cotton mills arose as a direct result of the nation's colonial expansion (see also Kalra, 2000), may be read as de facto proof that, as well as its claim to be the world's first industrial city, Manchester may very properly be thought of as Britain's first postcolonial city. For although other British cities can be and have been restyled in these terms (most notably, the metropolis: see John McLeod's *Postcolonial London* (2004) and Sukhdev Sandhu's *London Calling* (2003)), there is a clear argument, following Haslam, that London existed before the era of European colonialism while Manchester was created *because of it*. Further, although the Mancunian authors considered in this volume are, principally, the sons and daughters of the post-1945, postcolonial moment (in particular, second- and third- and fourth- generation members of the city's African, African-Caribbean and Asian diasporic communities whose families migrated to Britain at the end of colonial rule), it can be argued that the white, working-class writers, artists and musicians who have come out of the city and its environs are also, if less obviously, the 'children of Empire'. Inasmuch as it was the rapid contraction of the region's industrial base in the 1950s and 1960s (in particular, the demise of its cotton mills), there is no doubting that the mass-unemployment and economic and social deprivation that Greater Manchester is still struggling to climb out of are a part of the same colonial legacy.

Therefore, while it would be simplistic to attribute all of Manchester's endemic social ills to a handful of ruthless, nineteenth-century cotton barons who got rich from the exploitation of workers both at home and abroad (see Kalra, 2000), it probably would be fair to say that it has been the failure of successive governments (both national and local) to seriously address the complexity of this colonial past on the city that has led to a good many of its social tensions since.

In outlining the city's literary tradition, I shall call upon past research (Pearce, 2007, 2010a and 2010b as well as the 'Moving Manchester' Writers' Gallery: see www.transculturalwriting.com/writersgallery/) to discuss the extent to which the connotations of grime, crime and social deprivation that were attached to the city in the nineteenth century continue to pervade twentieth- and twenty-first-century writing about the city; and I shall also explore the ways in which this perception, and representation, of the city are mediated by the classed and 'raced' positioning of the viewer. My key point here, however, is that no-one can view the city of Manchester with neutral eyes (see Pearce, 2010a): neither the recent migrant nor the long-term resident will be able to see their 'home' outwith the layers of myth (see Taylor, Evans and Fraser, 1996: 19) and defamation laid upon it.

The laying waste of Manchester

The Latin verb *vasto, vastare* (to decimate or 'lay waste') could have been invented with Manchester in mind. Within months of starting work on 'Moving Manchester', the project team was struck by how much of the contemporary writing, music and art associated with the city is preoccupied with its successive waves of demolition and reconstruction Although Manchester's notorious urban redevelopments, especially with respect to its domestic housing stock, are by no means unique in England's industrial North (Taylor, Evans and Fraser, 1996:

60–90), the extent of the personal and community trauma that were its consequence is profound.[2] Indeed, as far as its artists and writers are concerned, there seems to be little doubt that it has been the repeated mistakes of the city's planners and developers that have made Manchester a 'problem city'. Moreover, of particular relevance to the 'Moving Manchester' project is the inference that it has been these enforced internal migrations of large numbers of the city's inhabitants (counted in their hundreds of thousands) that have repeatedly frustrated the efforts of diverse groups, and individuals, to make Manchester 'home' in any meaningful sense (Pearce, 2007).

Friedrich Engels was, of course, one of the first social commentators to draw international attention to the scandal of Manchester's housing and sanitation in the nineteenth century, and it would seem that visitors to the city have turned this reputation into an expectation ever since. Of particular long-term relevance were his observations on the demographic mapping of the city and the way that, although great wealth and great poverty sat cheek by jowl, the location of the workers' housing in a 'girdle' around the city centre (Taylor, Evans and Fraser, 1996: 55) ensured that it developed into a string of ghettos occluded from genteel view:

> Manchester contains at its heart a rather extended commercial district, perhaps half a mile long and about as broad, and consisting wholly of offices and warehouses. Nearly the whole district is abandoned by dwellers, and is lonely and deserted at night: only watchmen and policemen traverse its narrow lanes with lanterns. This district is cut through by several main thoroughfares upon which this vast traffic concentrates, and in which the ground level is lined with brilliant shops ... [but] they suffice to conceal from the eyes of the wealthy men and women of strong stomachs and nerves the misery and grime which form the complement of their wealth. (Engels, 1987 [1845]: 85)

Ever since these somewhat gothic nineteenth-century accounts of Manchester seized the public imagination there has, moreover, been something of a taste for 'alternative' tours of the city (discussed elsewhere in my article on Manchester's 'urban sublime' (Pearce, 2007)). This is most certainly evident in W. G. Sebald's semi-fictionalized account (see note 9) of his first impressions of the city in 1966, for example (see also Pearce, 2012). In the following extract we see the appropriately shocked gaze of the middle-class intellectual whose initial view of the city is from the window of a taxi:

So, with only an occasional traffic light to delay us, we drove swiftly through the not unhandsome suburbs of Gatley, Northenden and Didsbury to Manchester itself. Day was just breaking, and I looked out in amazement at the rows of uniform houses, which seemed the more run-down the closer we got to the city centre. In Moss Side and Hulme there were whole blocks where doors and windows were boarded up, and whole districts where everything had been demolished ... As we drove in among the dark ravines between the brick buildings, most of which were six or eight storeys high and sometimes adorned with glazed ceramic tiles, it turned out that even there, in the heart of the city, not a soul was to be seen. (Sebald, 2002: 151)

While I am not disputing the material accuracy of this impression (see Figure 1.2), Sebald's aestheticization of this 'view of Manchester' betrays the protagonist's failure to recognize it as someone else's (disappearing) home and reflects back on his own privileged migrant status. As I shall explore further in a later section of the chapter, this subject's relationship to a 'destination home' (Pearce, 2000: 32–3) is profoundly class-marked, with consequences not only for himself but also for his relationship to the city's established inhabitants. Meanwhile, Engels's infamous depiction of the city is referenced – and challenged – in Seán Body's poetry cycle *Seasons* (2003), discussed in Chapter 4.

It was in the mid-1950s – also the period when the immigration of Commonwealth citizens, in particular those from the West Indies, was increasing[3] – that the city's authorities faced up to the full extent of

1.2 Manchester redevelopment, February 1964. Slum clearance makes way for the new Dalton Technical Institute. ©FotoLibra.

their housing crisis. Although the notorious 'back-to-back' housing had ceased a century earlier (1844), it was estimated that a third of the city's dwellings were unfit for human habitation (Frangopulo, 1977: 190). In 1963 over eighty thousand homes were deemed 'potentially unfit' and scheduled for demolition, and in 1964 Manchester set up its own Planning Department to put the recommendations into action (Frangopulo, 1977: 1999).

What is most shocking about the accounts of this first 'redevelopment' of the city's housing – both literary and socio-historical – is the speed with which the 'clearances' of people and property took place. Families were exported to alternative housing (other estates or the new mid-rise tower blocks) in their tens of thousands (Haslam, 2000: xxi) and communities torn asunder with particular consequences for the immigrant communities (especially African and Caribbean) who had settled in certain districts of Manchester in large numbers in the 1950s and 1960s. The following pair of illustrations, the first by the celebrated Mancunian photographer Shirley Baker, vividly demonstrate the culture shock involved in moving from the street communities to the new mid-rise 'crescents'.

Contemporary musicians and artists who were children in Manchester during this period and, in particular, those who came from the Hulme and Moss Side districts, remember this migration *within* Manchester as a time of unqualified trauma. Bernard Sumner, a member of Manchester's legendary post-punk band Joy Division, sees this laying-waste of his city as *the* inspiration behind the band's sublime, but uniquely despairing, music:

> Everyone says Joy Division's music is gloomy and heavy ... For me it was because the whole neighbourhood I'd grown up in was completely decimated in the mid-60s. I was born and raised in Lower Broughton in Salford: the River Irwell was about 100 yards away and it stank ...
>
> There was a huge sense of community where we lived. I remember the summer holidays when I was a kid: we could stay up late and play in the street, at twelve o'clock at night there would be old ladies outside the houses, talking to each other. I guess what happened in the 60s was that someone at the council decided that it wasn't very healthy, and something had to go, and unfortunately it was my neighbourhood that went. We were moved over the river into a tower block. At the time I thought it was fantastic: now of course I realise it was an absolute disaster. (Savage, 1994 [no page number])

1.3 Salford, 1962. © Shirley Baker.

1.4 Hulme Crescents, balcony. © 'exHulme' website.

As already indicated, these forced migrations across the city were possibly even more traumatic for the diasporic communities who had come to settle there, and Joe Pemberton (whose work will be discussed in greater detail below) has drawn stark parallels between this relocation and his family's first arrival in Britain. In an interview in *Flux* magazine in April 2000, he refers to his own move from Moss Side to Ashton-under-Lyne in these terms:

> It was like emigration to another country, even though it was only about nine miles up the road. From a multi-cultural area to an area with middle-class pretensions, it was definitely like another world. There were obvious cultural differences, I wouldn't say problems, but at the time it seemed like another world. Emigration is definitely a good word to use. (Pemberton, 2000a)

Pemberton's novel *Forever and Ever Amen* (2000b) also has graphic descriptions of the speed with which this brutal laying-waste of parts of the city (in this case, Moss Side) was effected. Told from a nine-year-old child's point of view, the disorientation entailed is defamiliarized to particular effect:

> Only last week it had been a row of houses. Fairlawn Street next to St. Bees Street next to another road James couldn't remember the name of. Each house had three floors and a million stairs to the top. Only last week the street was full of kids playing catch and cars driving past the women gossiping on the corner. But not any more, all that was gone and all that was left was a pool the size of a school yard and a reflection of a church spire. The church was the only building left, apart from the pub at the end of what used to be St. Bees Street. The pub had a large poster of a man and a woman smiling at the skies like they'd seen a bird. If they'd been looking to the ground they wouldn't be smiling. Who would when all that was left was a big pool the size of a schoolyard. It was like the 'blitts' as Aunty Mary called it, like a bomb had exploded and all the houses disappeared in a puff of smoke and a loud bang. (Pemberton, 2000b: 52)

For the city planners and local authorities, however, the speed and efficiency of this demolition and redevelopment was a source of pride, albeit short-lived. Frangopulo communicates something of this hubris in his 1977 account of the 'evolution' of Greater Manchester:

> By 1974, so thoroughly had the clearance of this city been undertaken that it is evident that the process would be completed by the following year. The extent of this achievement was not only recognised in its early

1.5 Salford, 1964. © Shirley Baker.

stages by the Ministry of Housing and Local Government as 'outstanding' ... but was also acknowledged in a remarkable way by the fact that those responsible were asked by some members of the public to preserve one or two streets 'as a reminder of Coronation Street'. (Frangopulo, 1977: 201)

No irony intended, clearly. For residents who had lived through the Second World War, however, the sudden and absolute way in which their homes and communities were swept away was all too reminiscent of the Blitz (as both the Pemberton extract and Shirley Baker's photograph (Figure 1.5) show). In the small space of ten years, hundreds of thousands of Manchester's residents, the majority of them poor and/or immigrant, were forced to remake their homes in a rapidly moving Manchester.

The colonial cityscape

As numerous artists and critics have observed, Manchester is a city whose fast-changing architectural face (and, indeed, architectural *use*) tells its story more eloquently than a pile of historical documents (Taylor, Evans and Fraser, 1996: 75–9; Haslam, 2000: vii – xxxi; Peck and Ward, 2002)). The following images (Figures 1.6–1.10) sum up why it is important, in certain contexts, to refer to Manchester as an emphatically colonial (as opposed to a notionally *post*-colonial) city on account of the fact that its imperial past has never quite been rubbed out or pasted over.

The first pair of images of the Royal Exchange mark the heyday of this iconic city landmark. Rebuilt and extended many times throughout the nineteenth century, the Exchange was a mart where the city's traders (most notably its mill owners and other industrialists) would meet to buy and sell their goods. Historical documents reveal that the Exchange was a crowded, volatile meeting place that also witnessed political protest from the factory hands on more than one occasion. In 1812, the troops had to be summoned 'when unemployed cotton workers broke in, smashing furniture, lamps and windows' (Manchester Evening News Syndication, 2008: 94–5) and in the mid-nineteenth century the building became the site of protests against the new Corn Laws.

The Exchange, then, may be seen as an iconic symbol of the city's colonial past where much more was exchanged than merchandise: indeed, in this joining of hands between the city's mill hands and the slaves across the water are figured both the human exploitation on which the city's wealth was built and the seeds of protest that would mark the city's literary output in the years to come.[4] Together, the white, working-class musicians and poets who put Manchester on the map in the 1980s and the city's diasporic writers and artists (see Corinne Fowler's discussion in Chapter 5 of how these communities are better understood as a single entity in many respects) may be thought of as the notional avengers of all the (unfair) trade that was executed at the Exchange all those years ago. From the 1930s onwards, however, Britain's cotton industry went into terminal decline as the result of a range of economic and political measures (including India's refusal to purchase English cotton post-1947 (Manchester Evening News Syndication 2007: 78)) and thousands of workers lost their jobs with dire consequence for all concerned.

The Exchange finally closed its doors in 1968 until being taken over by a theatre company in 1973 (later to become the internationally renowned 'Royal Exchange'). In addition, this is a building that has been bombed and rebuilt twice: once in the Blitz (1940) (see Figure 1.8) and, again, in the IRA bombing of 1996 (see Figure 1.9). The latter event features repeatedly in contemporary writing about the city and is, it must be said, a further striking example of how Manchester's architecture bears the mark not only of the city's but of the nation's past.

1.6 Manchester Royal Exchange, third building, 1874. © Manchester City Council.

1.7 Manchester Royal Exchange, third building, Cross Street, 1900. © Manchester City Council.

Manchester: the postcolonial city

1.8 Royal Exchange, bomb damage, Manchester, 1940. © Manchester City Council.

1.9 Aftermath of the 1996 (IRA) bomb, Cross Street, looking north towards the Royal Exchange. © Manchester City Council.

Meanwhile, as Manchester's buildings have risen, fallen and risen again, so have its flocks of citizens moved (or been moved) from one part of the city to another, grouped not only by ethnicity but also by wealth (Peck and Ward, 2002; Kellie, 2010). Indeed, when considering Manchester's identity as a migrant city, it is vital to bear in mind that its incomers – its economic migrants – come from *all* social groups, many of them professional and/or wealthy (see Bill Williams's acclaimed *Making of Manchester Jewry* (1977) as a historical instance of this). And although some housing districts have remained the province of the working class and – more recently – international migrants, we can no longer assume that all nineteenth-century terraces are occupied by these groups or that the suburbs are the exclusive preserve of the white middle class.

A particularly high-profile 'flow' of people since the late 1980s has been the professional classes who have taken up residence in the city's converted warehouses and quays, buildings within striking distance of newly gentrified social spaces – for example, Castlefield and Canal Street (Taylor, Evans and Fraser, 1996: 75–9; Peck and Ward, 2002). My next pair of images shows the Castlefield area before and after its 'makeover' and, once again, it is not difficult to read this more recent change of architectural use in explicitly colonial *and* postcolonial terms. What we see in Figure 1.10 is the canal and area around Castlefield Quay during the mid-1980s when it had fallen into a state of serious dereliction. At this moment in its history it is a typical, if 'grand', example of the demise of the cotton industry: a bold, ostentatious symbol of colonial trade (the warehouses, after all, were where the valuable cotton products were stored) fallen into disuse and ruin with severe, knock-on consequences for the whole district. Figure 1.11, by contrast, shows the nearby Merchant's Warehouse soon after its redevelopment in 1992. This was one of the prize projects of the Manchester Development Corporation (MDC)(1988–96), an organisation that sponsored private–public partnerships to redevelop buildings of this kind.[5] This warehouse was converted into office space at a total cost of £3 million with grant contributions from English Heritage and the European Regional Development Fund as well as MDC and the private sector. Although there are now countless websites and publications celebrating the success of 'Castlefield Estates' and other inner-city regeneration projects (see also Kellie, 2010), there has also been a good deal of criticism of where the money was spent and exactly who were the beneficiaries of the schemes (Peck and Ward, 2002). The generally

Manchester: the postcolonial city

1.10 Castlefield, Castlefield Quay, 1986. © Manchester City Council.

1.11 Merchant's Warehouse, Castlefield, Castlefield Quay, 1998. © Aidan O'Rourke.

'up-market' nature of both the domestic and the commercial architecture erected in districts such as Castlefield means that those individuals, families and communities most affected by the demise of Manchester's industrial past have largely been excluded from a share in the post-industrial prosperity (see Mellor, 2002), notwithstanding the upward mobility of the few. Needless to say, a good deal of the contemporary (i.e. post-1980s) literature coming out of the city reflects upon the symbolic and material meaning of the region's regeneration, and Manchester's fast-changing cityscape forms the backdrop to much of the textual action (see Chapter 5 on 'Crime fiction' in particular).

To conclude this section, then, it can be argued that the internal migrations that have accompanied, and contributed to, the city's regeneration are as important to trace as those of its post-industrial demise, not least because the two flows co-exist and individuals may themselves pass from the one to the other (a theme I shall return to in the final section of this chapter). Manchester is thus a city whose 'ghettos' – socio-economic and ethnic – comprize a map that is continually being redrawn and its buildings 'recycled' (Haslam, 2000: xviii). At the same time, it is important to register that between the first mass-demolition of housing stock in the 1960s and the regeneration that began in late 1980s there was another decade – c. 1977–87 – when the 'resettled' communities of Greater Manchester and, in particular, its large estates like those found in the districts of Hulme and Moss Side appear to have achieved, against all the odds, a fragile sense of community (Haslam, 2000: xx). This was, moreover, the period when community arts projects – and, indeed, Manchester's arts and music scene in general – first came into their own for reasons that I shall explain below (see section entitled 'The Thatcher years'). Before continuing this historical mapping of the city, however, some words are now needed on its early, literary past.

Manchester: the early literary tradition

Time was when any one from the north of England aspiring to be a writer, artist, musician or intellectual would feel compelled to leave the region in order to make their name even if that move (invariably to 'the south' and, in particular, to London) was as traumatic an experience as it was desired.

As David Law (2004) has shown, the North West, including Manchester, spawned a considerable number of publications (some written as autobiographies, the others as fiction) which centred on the story of the grammar-school boy who moved south to 'make good'. Having surveyed a quantity of these 'emigration stories' Law observed that, while most were rather less-than-exciting reads, they nevertheless provided an important insight into what it meant to be a burgeoning writer in North West England in the early part of the twentieth century; and, in particular, into the painful tension that arose between a loyalty to, or nostalgia for, one's 'roots' and desire to turn one's back on such binds and escape:

> The texts I examine reveal shifting and ambiguous positions with regard to the North and northerness. On the one hand there is a surprising level of agreement amongst the authors' texts as to what constitutes northerness, most especially when taken in contrast to the idea of the South. However, it will be seen that the 'North' is used as something of a 'straw man': the life story within is often much more 'anti-Northern' in its sensibilities and predilections, full of hostilities towards the space in which the author spent his childhood. (Law, 2004: 58)

The best-known writers and intellectuals (all male) to belong to this moment of the region's literary legacy include Bill Naughton (born 1910), Richard Hoggart (born 1919), William Woodruff (born 1912), Anthony Burgess (formerly John Wilson, born 1917) and David Storey (born 1933),[6] and their work captures the anguish of the love-hate relationship working-class artists often feel towards a background from which they had personally been ostracized on account of their 'bookish, monkish tendencies' (Law, 2004: 72). Although the action is set not in Manchester but in a Yorkshire mining village, David Storey's *Flight into Camden* (1961) is an outstanding example of the genre in that it explores the central characters' (Margaret's and Michael's) decision to leave home and family from multiple viewpoints (the pain of their 'rejected' parents included) and shows how impossible it was for this generation is to escape a sense of personal and class betrayal (Law, 2004: 137–9). Therefore, although during the postwar period the north of England saw a large number of grammar-school boys make their way south to a better life, the most compelling themes and images in their writings are arguably those which focus on all that they have left behind, often with barely concealed relief.

There are also, of course, a handful of successful white, working-class writers from this early period (1945–70) who elected to stay in the North and make it the subject of their work. The most enduringly successful of these is probably Alan Bennett (born Leeds 1934), but playwrights Shelagh Delaney from Salford (born 1939), and Jim Cartwright from Farnworth (Greater Manchester) (born 1959) are also nationally recognized names whose key works, like Delaney's *A Taste of Honey* (1960 [1959]) and Cartwright's *Road* (1990 [1986]), are regarded as quintessential snapshots of the northern, post-industrial landscape and are often applauded for their 'gritty realism' even if this phrase fails to account fully for the complexity of their aesthetic (especially Cartwright's work which is arguably 'surrealist' rather than 'realist' in form (Law, 2004: 290–1)). It is also interesting to observe the extent to which the film version of *A Taste of Honey* (1962) has become part of the cultural history or collective consciousness of the region: a compelling hyper-real version of what everyone *thinks* they remember about that era, as acknowledged by the musician Morrissey when asked about his childhood home on the BBC Radio 4 programme *Desert Island Discs* (29 November 2009).

As noted above, another writer from the region, this time from the neighbouring town of Bolton, who has written substantially about his life in the region as well as his exodus from it, is Bill Naughton. His two volumes of autobiography, *On the Pig's Back* (1988) and *Saintly Billy* (1989), provide fascinating insights into working-class and, in particular, Irish-migrant life in Bolton in the early twentieth century (Naughton's family migrated there from County Mayo when he was four). As is the case with many of the region's writers born up to and during the Second World War, there is a considerable time-lag between the era in which these autobiographies were written (typically the 1970s and 1980s) and the world they depict. Indeed, when reading Naughton's autobiographies, it is sometimes bewildering to think that the man who wrote the iconic 1960s play, *Alfie* (1963),[7] grew up in a world that appears to have one foot still planted firmly in the nineteenth century: in its coal mines and mills (both described in fascinating detail) as well as in rural Ireland.

In the same decade that the films of *A Taste of Honey*[8] and *Alfie* put working-class life in the north of England on the map, a very different snapshot of the region was provided by the middle-class, immigrant German writer W. G. Sebald. As noted above, Sebald's best-selling *The Emigrants* (2002 [1993]) is an extremely important text not only for the window it offers on to the streets of Manchester when Sebald settled here in the mid-1960s, but also for the view it affords of the middle-class outsider's view of the city (Pearce 2007; 2010a). For although the writerly eloquence of Sebald's prose invites descriptors such as 'evocative', this, as noted above, is an archetypal outsider's view of the city and one that all too easily conspires with the discourse of defamation that has hung over its 'squalid' streets since Engels's oft-cited survey of 1844:

> On those wanderings, when winter light flooded the deserted streets and squares for the few hours of real daylight, I never ceased to be amazed by the completeness with which anthracite-coloured Manchester, the city from which industrialization had spread across the entire world, displayed the clearly chronic process of its impoverishment and degradation for anyone who cared to see. (Sebald, 2002: 156–7)

In his walks through the streets of Manchester in the mid-1960s, Sebald's narrator (and, on this point, it should be noted that *The Emigrants* is itself a work of *fiction*)[9] is arguably a witness to both the colonial and the postcolonial phases of the city's history, taking in both 'immense and time-blackened nineteenth-century buildings' (p. 156) and the slums of Hulme and Moss Side where 'I looked out in amazement on the rows of uniform houses ... blocks where the doors and windowed were boarded up' (p. 151) awaiting demolition. It remains a middle-class flâneur's view of the first phase of Manchester's redevelopment, nonetheless, and is most interesting when placed alongside the work of the writers, musicians and artists discussed above who were themselves involved in the 'slum clearances' and who write about the experience from the perspective of the 'insider'. As I have noted, however (Pearce 2010a: 27–30), the discursive production of a region exists in complex relation to notions of 'authentic' experience making it quite possible for a Mancunian like Morrissey to remember the city of his childhood through Shelagh Delaney's film or, indeed, Sebald's prose, rather than in the raw.

In conclusion, then, it may be seen that, in the decades immediately following the Second World War (the 1940s, 1950s and 1960s), the literature emanating from Manchester (and the north of England generally) was closely linked to the social and historical changes taking place. For the first time, children from working-class backgrounds had some access to good secondary and higher education, and 'intellectual migration' (typically, the removal of the region's grammar-school boys to Oxbridge and London) subsequently gave rise to a significant number of fictional, autobiographical or semi-autobiographical texts which commented upon the demise of the North in the era of post-industrialization as well as their own experiences of alienation and family or class betrayal. Needless to say, publication of these life-stories was, at the time, limited to the tiny, privileged minority who made it into higher education and, as will be shown in Chapters 2 and 4 following, we have to look outside mainstream London publishing houses to discover an alternative 'grassroots' history of writing in the region. By the late 1970s, and especially from the mid-1980s, however, a quite different literary scene had established itself in the region and it is to this new expression of the city's multi-ethnic and postcolonial identity that I shall now turn.

The Thatcher years

The role of the city councils in arts funding

As all those working with the recent past will be aware, it often takes a while before the events and patterns that characterize a particular era become clear. This is certainly the case with Britain in the 1980s: a decade I lived through, mostly as a student, and yet never 'saw' in anything like its true political complexity until recently.

The reason for this blind spot, which I imagine is shared by readers who lived through the moment with me, is arguably Margaret Thatcher. In retrospect it is manifest that both her person and her policies were so brash, and so breathtaking, that she became a blinding focus of opposition.[10] Once those on the Left were mobilized against her via various initiatives (the Falklands, nuclear disarmament, the miners' strike, the women's movement, Clause 28, the Poll Tax), we lost sight of what was also being achieved by way of that opposition. In other words, we failed to appreciate the agency the Left had acquired by having its energies focused in this way. And, in particular, we failed to see that Leftist organizations, including those representing the arts, were the direct, and indirect, beneficiaries of both the recession and the so-called 'enterprise culture' which was seen to be the way of pulling us out of it.

In terms of both the history of its migrant communities and its profile as a regional centre for arts and entertainment, the story of Manchester in the 1980s is indicative of most of the large conurbations in England which were run by metropolitan councils. Together with the high-profile GLC (Greater London Council), these included Merseyside, South Yorkshire, Tyneside, West Midlands and West Yorkshire. The crucial factor which enabled all these regions to become, and remain, strongholds of Left-wing resistance during the 1980s was the fact that a new cycle of local authority elections commenced in 1981: two years *after* the Thatcher government first came to power, and hence *before* either the nation's economic upturn or the Falklands War. Indeed, the polls show that Thatcher's popularity was at an all-time low at this time; a demise which translated into landslide victories for Labour and other Left-wing groups in the council elections. The consequences of this were crucial for the rejuvenation of the arts, in particular, and help to explain, in retrospect, why the decade more typically associated with Yuppies and wine-bars was also the catalyst for so much 'alternative' cultural production. As Robert Hewison sums up:

> These authorities represented alternative centres of political power to Whitehall, and had been the least amenable to attempts to curb public spending. Central government proved the stronger, and all were abolished in 1986, but not before an alternative cultural, as well as political, argument had been developed, most articulately by the GLC. (Hewison, 1995: 237)

What was especially crucial for Manchester, and indeed all the cities which contained large migrant communities, was that this was the moment when these local authorities also began to distribute their funding differently. Instead of allocating specified amounts to each of the generic categories (e.g., theatre, dance, opera, literature) they looked, instead, to support groups centred on political affiliations. Hewison, again:

> By 1986 the arts were seen as the leading edge of the social and economic agenda ... The decline in traditional trades-union power had been one of the reasons why the left-wing group led by Ken Livingstone had been able to take control of the Labour block on the GLC. With the traditional working-class vote in decline, there was a need to establish links with new groups of voters: black British, Asians, middle-class people working in the public sector, and small but articulate pressure groups of gays and lesbians. A cultural policy which addressed the interests of those groups became an alternative form of mobilisation and communication. (Hewison, 1995: 238)

The Arts and Recreation Committee set up by the GLC in 1981, and led by Tony Banks, adopted a significantly 'wider definition of the Arts than the Arts Council's' (Hewison, 1995: 238) and included photography, video, electronic music and community radio within its sponsorship remit. It is also important to note that, under the GLC,

London's budget for ethnic arts rose from £400,000 in 1982–83 to £2 million in 1985–86 (Hewison, 1995: 238) and the Greater Manchester Council [GMC] was involved in a similar redistribution of funding, especially with respect to transport, recreation and local heritage (Taylor, Evans and Fraser, 1996: 75–79).[11]

What emerges from this brief retrospective, then, is the fact that, as a result of the 1981 local authority elections, the early to mid-1980s in Britain constituted a uniquely supportive period for the alternative arts scene despite (or, indirectly, because of) a supremely unsympathetic Conservative government. What Hewison's and subsequent studies have confirmed, moreover, is that, even when the central government finally managed to quash the left-wing councils through its 1985 Local Government Act, their legacy lived on. By then, many of the groups and organizations still with us today had been firmly established (including, in Manchester, Gatehouse, Commonword (initially under the auspices of the Federation of Worker Writers and Community Publishers and Publishers) and the Black Arts Alliance[12] – see Chapters 2 and 4), and the trend for arts activity and funding to be centred on special interest groups rather than the traditional categories of artistic practice (e.g. opera, ballet, literature, visual arts) had become more common. As Hewison concludes *vis-à-vis* the GLC:

> The white working-class benefited less from the GLC's largesse than the newly discovered minorities, but it is clear that the GLC's experiment helped to widen the definition of the arts and what was appropriate for a cultural policy and addressed a new audience in original ways. (Hewison, 1995: 242)

Figured as a key moment in Manchester's postcolonial history, the ascendancy of the Labour-held City Council during this period (i.e. 1981–86) may thus be perceived as the means by which those whose lives were most defined by the nation's rise and fall as a colonial power (i.e. the white, working-class and first- and second-generation migrant communities) were, for the first time, recognized as undervalued minority groups in need of support; further, and notwithstanding the limitations of such support, it is clearly important to pay tribute to the role of the Council from this moment forward in re-profiling Greater Manchester as a vibrant, diverse 'multicultural' city. Indeed, through the auspices of the Central Manchester Development Association (discussed above), the City Council funded the building or refurbishment of a number of new galleries and museums during this period which have been instrumental in retelling the history of the region from the perspective of its subaltern groups. These include the Museum of Science and Industry (MOSI) (which moved to its present site in 1983) and the People's History Museum (formerly the National Museum of Labour History) which moved to Manchester in 1990 and was renamed in 2001.[13]

Grassroots enterprise: the 1980s music scene in Manchester

Yet the redistribution of public funding is only one half of the story of how the articulation of art and society in Britain changed in the 1980s. Although, as Hewison observes, 'the collective nature of this [the GLC's] endeavour was in marked contrast to the privatising, individualistic approach of Thatcherism' (Hewison, 1995: 242), it is clear that, in other respects, both the local authorities and independent ventures became part of an expanding enterprise culture that thrived on purchasing power and competition. In the recent cultural history of Manchester, this other route through the 1980s is nowhere better illustrated than by the music industry.

In his introduction to the *City Life Book of Manchester Short Stories* (1999), the Manchester writer and publisher Ra Page is unequivocal about the signal role of popular music – and its attendant industry – in transforming Manchester during the 1980s. He writes:

> What happened to transform Manchester into a town that stood proudly above the provincial crowd, a place where artists flocked rather than ran from, was quite simply music ... After Manchester's visceral, independent punk scene in the late-seventies, and the diametrically opposed trail blazing of New Order and The Smiths in the mid-eighties, the gathering cultural might of Factory Records with its Situationist super-club, the Haçienda, lit a fuse for an eventual explosion of music from the end of the eighties. 'Madchester', as the music press tagged it, saw a two-pronged revival in dance and guitar music which Manchester bands in particular and British music in general have built on ever since. In the space of ten years Manchester became the place to be. (Page, 1999: xv)

This cultural re-profiling of the city and its environs is clearly crucial for all those of us interested in its literary outputs during the same period, but before we consider the similarities and differences between the music scene and the writing scene we need to account for its wider socio-economic impact on Manchester's status as a specifically migrant city. On this issue, Dave Haslam's compelling portrait of Manchester as a 'pop cult city' is both shrewd and eloquent. Starting from the recognition that Manchester is a city built from the profits of Empire and the immigration of industrial workers in the nineteenth century, Haslam argues that, since the 1960s, contemporary music has become its new, premier social and economic flow:

> Just as the city used to import raw material – cotton – and turn it into something else, so modern Manchester finds itself importing, refashioning and exporting pop music ... Where once the Manchester mill owners and merchants, mill hands and factory operatives created the wealth that financed the Empire, now the city dominates English pop culture, trading in music, the sounds of the city's streets resonating around the globe. (Haslam, 2000: xxviii)

And although it was in the late 1980s, and early 1990s, that Manchester's dance and music industry reached its zenith as a global brand, what makes Haslam's history so riveting is the realization that this cultural renaissance had its roots in a number of authentically 'grassroots', subcultural revolutions that spanned the black and white communities. This is not to deny, of course, that black and white music in the city followed separate trajectories during the 1960s and 1970s (see Haslam (2000: 220–46) on the history of Moss Side and the black, American music that was popular during this period), but the impression given is of multiple, independent catalysts – bonfires being lit all over the city – that, together, captured the spirit of the age: the volatile dizziness, and darkness, and defiance of life in Thatcher's Britain. In this regard, Haslam pays repeated tribute to what he calls 'the do-it-yourself' spirit of the city (Haslam, 2000: 117); not only punk but most of the city's musical and artistic ventures from this period appear to have arizen out of a collective will, or enterprise, and manifestly in spite of the lack of economic or other resources.

The fact that this DIY cultural enterprise crossed ethnic lines is made very clear in Haslam's chapter devoted to Moss Side (2000: 220–46) which details the central role played by the African and West Indian clubs in both sustaining the traditions of the migrant communities in terms of music, dance, food and other recreation and fostering their own subcultural revolutions. At the same time, then, that the members of Joy Division had begun jamming together in the Black Swan, the youth of Moss Side were enjoying their own counter-cultural moment of escape and defiance at the Reno:

> The mix of people was incredible, especially as the clock crept towards 4am: middle-aged Irish women, old domino players always wearing hats,

young black guys off the street, girls with beautiful hair, jazz dancers, people slumped over tables. (Haslam, 2000: 221)

With the benefit of hindsight it is, indeed, possible to see how the period 1978–87 itself flakes into smaller units of social and cultural history. For while 1978–80 may be fashioned as the blind, wilderness, or 'wasteland' years in which artists and politicians struggled to see what was coming next, 1981 is most certainly the year in which the people and politics of England regrouped and moved on as a consequence of both the growing hostility towards Thatcher (as reflected in the results from the local Council elections) and the first significant upturn in the economy for many years. From this moment on, the articulation of art and politics in the UK can be seen to take divergent routes: the first, the self-conscious organization of Leftist groups of all kinds supported by local government funding; the second, typified by Manchester's music industry, constituting the improbable yoking together of the forces of subcultural resistance with capitalism.

Commercial yet 'independent', a typically Thatcherite blend of enterprise and capital, Manchester's indie record labels, led by Factory Records,[14] may therefore be seen to epitomize a strand of arts activity in the city that the literary scene has, arguably, struggled to match. Although some ventures, such as the community publishers Gatehouse, have sought to survive as independent, profit-making ventures after their sources of public funding have been stripped away, it is arguable that regional writing and publishing have never succeeded in doing more than keep their head above water in commercial terms. Indeed, as will be discussed in the next chapter, many established writers' groups and arts organizations operating in the city have long resigned themselves to the fact that they can never compete with international publishing houses on any terms and operate very self-consciously in spite of this.

Yet Manchester's music industry remains, I would suggest, a thought-provoking case study for the arts in general about how, and under what conditions, the provincial can compete with the metropolitan and win. Certainly, for Haslam and others (Reynolds, 2006; Morley, 2007; Robb, 2010; Nice, 2011) convinced of the genius and innovation of Manchester's musicians during the period 1978–81, the cultural industries are capable of creating conditions that will wrench the margin to the centre. Furthermore, if anything has the power to render the provincial 'mainstream', then, it is arguably a region's art and culture. Thus, while it is clearly important to avoid becoming overly utopian in the retelling of this story, it can certainly be argued that Manchester's music scene was the place where black and white cultures spawned very different responses to the 'wilderness years' (1978–81) and yet, finally, came together in a sound, style and mode of entertainment (the 'rave') that expressed a common passion – and revolt (Haslam, 2000: 164).

From the late 1970s, and through to the early 1990s, Manchester's music scene managed to capture, transfix and ultimately reinvent a city whose flux and flow (its people, its buildings) were desperately in need of both continuity and community. Through the lyrics of Manchester's punk, post-punk and (later) acid-house musicians,[15] the streets and districts of Manchester were fixed on a map that was beamed to the world, whilst its dance floors became more celebrated than those in New York. From the mid-1980s onwards, the denomination 'migrant city' meant something very special as far as Manchester was concerned: it was truly a place that the youth of the world wanted to migrate *to*; a margin that had made the centre seem square.

On this point it should also be noted that, although Manchester's authors and publishers have sometimes lamented the fact that the city's writing scene has never achieved the high profile and success of its music scene (e.g. Page, 1999: xv–xvi), its punk bands and performance poets were arguably spawned at the same historical moment, shared the same political consciousness – and frequently performed together. Indeed, as Corinne Fowler argues in Chapter 5, the marginal status of contemporary writing and publication in the city has, in this particular, been exaggerated: while Manchester's fiction writers have, admittedly, struggled to find a foothold in the London-centric mainstream, the city's alternative tradition of poetry in performance is, like its music scene, a well-established, international phenomenon.

Writing postcolonial Manchester: the 1980s to the present

As the result of the re-energized social, cultural and political climate of the early 1980s, Manchester began to develop its own, distinctive, literary scene that shared a good deal of the 'DIY' and 'punk ethic' that Haslam and others have identified in the city's music. This included the establishment not only of writing organizations and community publishers such as Commonword but of more local enterprises such as the Moss Side Arts Group that Lemn Sissay pays tribute to in his preface to his 1988 collection, *Tender Fingers in a Clenched Fist*. It was

Sissay, moreover, who (along with other now internationally renowned Mancunian performers such as John Lyons (born in the Caribbean and now living in Hebden Bridge) and SuAndi) first put the Mancunian 'performance poetry' scene on the map and established Manchester as the largest centre outside London to develop its own, distinctive brand of black performance poetry and help initiate what has arguably been a renaissance for popular oral literature (see Chapter 5).

Having provided something of the social, cultural and political context that rendered Manchester a dynamic centre for the arts in the early 1980s, I now offer a 'first introduction' to some of the writers who have participated in the evolution of its vibrant literary scene. While the chapters that follow will reflect upon the output of these writers in specific generic contexts, my focus, here, is on their literary representation of Manchester as a post-industrial and postcolonial city; this will, I hope, serve to familiarize readers with the diversity of texts to have emanated from the city in the past thirty years at the same time as adding flesh to the chapter's portrait of Manchester as a postcolonial city. For although it is certainly not the case that all the writing to have emanated from Manchester in recent times is interested in writing *about* Manchester per se (see Introduction), those texts which are have provided some remarkably vivid, and often intimate, impressions of the city during an era of accelerated change and modernization. Through the lens of these texts we see the city (its people and its infrastructure) dragged through the trauma of de-industrialization, mass-unemployment and the mixed blessings of regeneration. And we glimpse what these changes meant for particular groups and communities: mothers living on benefits; the young unemployed; the unemployed white working-class; the residents of the mythologized Moss Side estates and the Asian diaspora. Taken together, Manchester's literary output from the early 1980s to the millennium may thus be seen to constitute a moving testament to both the legacy of Empire (inasmuch as the migration of the African, African-Caribbean and Pakistani communities to the North West can be understood as its direct consequence) and the Thatcher government's infamously unsympathetic response to the sudden collapse of Britain's manufacturing base. During these years, Greater Manchester, described by Asa Briggs in 1963 as 'a centre of trade of a whole region, linked to the whole world' (Briggs, [1990] 1963: 103) effectively imploded in economic terms and yet remained, as we shall see, very much a 'world city' (Massey, 2007: see Introduction) in every other respect.

The view from Moss Side

I begin with a short discussion of the work of two writers from Moss Side, Karline Smith and Joe Pemberton. This focus on a single district of the city (albeit its most notorious) was, in part, inspired by James Procter's ground-breaking work on British diasporas in the early 2000s. In *Dwelling Places* (2003), Procter (following Cohen, 1997: 187) proposed that the time had come to counter the universalizing of diasporic experience by shifting attention away from generic discourses of origin (in particular, nostalgia for the lost homeland) and focusing, instead, upon the complexity of re-location. Procter writes:

> Despite the increasingly sophisticated debates over the category 'black' (as an ontological sign of both difference and 'différance') in recent accounts of black British culture, 'Britain', the material site at which these identities are played out, has tended to remain a stable, bland monolith, a singularly undifferentiated setting. The proliferation of difference that has seen black re-energised and rendered multiple has left Britain a homogenous unified flatland, as if it is somehow the same to be black in London as it is in Llandudno. (Procter, 2003: 1)

Following this logic through, it can also be argued that to be a resident of Moss Side, is not the same as being a resident of Whalley Range, or Cheetham Hill, or Ashton-under-Lyne, and movement between the districts (as noted earlier) of a major city is often the (traumatic) measure of this.[16] Further, in the 1960s and 1970s, Moss Side's principal immigrant groups, African (West African, Somali and Guyanan) and Caribbean, were associated with particular streets, clubs and restaurants, and, from the late 1980s onwards, the explosion of drug and gangland culture turned all manner of public space (particular pubs, particular parks, particular cul-de-sacs) into a maze of 'no-go' areas and 'front-lines' (Taylor, Evans and Fraser, 1996: 205–11); Haslam, 2000: 234–7). Understood in this sort of detail, at the level of the street, Moss Side arguably becomes a useful touchstone in our reconceptualization of British 'diaspora space' (Brah, 1996) at the most local level: popularly regarded as a unicultural 'black' ghetto, Moss Side is really anything but.[17]

This carve-up of Moss Side into distinct ethnic areas and, later, gangs, is vividly evoked in Karline Smith's crime thriller *Moss Side Massive* (2000)[18] (discussed in detail in Chapter 4) and, as the following extract testifies, there absolutely nothing 'neutral' or 'monolithic' about this diasporic 'dwelling space':

> The strong aroma of cannabis drifted out to Bedwell Close and Quinney Crescent. This was the Alexandra Park housing estate in the heart of Moss Side. The fact that the Piper Mill headquarters was so close to Grange Close territory was an issue of contention between the two gangs and a surprise attack could not be ruled out. In the pub car park, young boys on mountain bikes roamed in the cold October air, calling out to each other, competing with each other, and surveying their territory with an air of importance. Other boys held pit bull terrier dogs at their sides, with tight grips around their leashes. They were look outs, paid to spot trouble, rival gangs or police. Some were brazen drug couriers, too young to be touched by the law. (Smith, 2000: 10)

Throughout the world, poverty and oppression go hand-in-hand with pressures of space and, in Britain in particular, immigrants have traditionally moved into inner-city areas where the white, working-class population were themselves once squashed into terraces and, later, high-rises. The consequent 'ghettoization' of urban centres like Greater Manchester has, of course, become one of the most visible markers of the nation's neocolonial ethnic diversity, though, as already noted, the perception of areas like Moss Side as 'exclusively black' tend to be grossly exaggerated, and a district's claim to ghetto status (based on the percentage probability of your neighbour being of the same 'minority' ethnic group as yourself) tenuous (Taylor, Evans and Fraser, 1996: 198–205).

By contrast, Smith's novel registers what was, in effect, an extremely complex demographic remapping of Moss Side, decade by decade, with great precision. In the following extract, for example, we see how successive waves of new migrants from Africa and the Caribbean took possession of particular streets, estates and buildings at different times: staking their claims, and shifting the balance of power:

> All this was before the Princess Road became the dual carriage way known as Princess Parkway, to serve those who would rather zoom blinkered through the ghetto. In those days, the Africans owned most of the clubs in Moss Side. Clubs like the Sphinx and Vegas, out on the frontline when it used to be situated on Princess Road, not far from the old police station, before it was knocked down and the brewery erected in its place. Pubs like the Big Apple and the Old Bristol gradually began to see more black faces. The Dandy Lion pub out on Upper Lloyd Street, previously owned and managed by white people, became a frequent haunt of Yardies and eventually got taken over by them ... Nightly gang battles occurred involving gangs from Cheetham Hill and Africans who

drove in from as far as Liverpool. By the mid-seventies things had cooled a bit, but Moss Side's reputation was red hot. Then the African boss of the Sphinx, Musi, got killed over some gambling debts, The Sphinx and the Vegas clubs went underground and were eventually taken over by Yardies, and the two clubs' notoriety for prostitutes, rapes, stabbings, drugs dealing, gambling and extortion increased. Soon after, the Vegas and the Sphinx, along with Curly's café were pulled down. Rubble was all that remained where they once stood. But their legacy lived on amongst the sons of those first immigrants. (Smith, 2000: 214)

As Haslam has also observed (Haslam, 2000: 235–7), Smith's fiction here stays very close to recognized historical events and further illustrates my point about the long-term testimonial significance of these writings. Readers will be interested to learn that the Sphinx and the Vegas are fictional equivalents for the two music clubs, the Nile and the Reno, discussed in the previous section, and it was, indeed, the demolition of these venues when the drug scene took over that coincided with a significant migration of black youth, music and culture into alternative city-centre venues.

From both within and without the black communities of Moss Side, meanwhile, there is widespread consensus that it was the arrival of hard drugs that finally, and fatally, ripped the district apart (Haslam, 2000: 246). This said, there is also 'hard' sociological evidence to suggest that a good deal of the reporting of the district's supposed 'guns 'n' gangs' culture was significantly exaggerated. Taylor, Evans and Fraser (1996) comment on the way that Moss Side was repeatedly, and unhelpfully, linked with South Central Los Angeles during this period, with specific parallels being drawn between the Doddington and Gooch Close gangs of Alexandra Park (Karline Smith's Grange Close and Piper Mill) and Los Angeles's notorious Bloods and the Cripps; as the authors point out, the media had somehow lost sight of the fact that, in 1991, 'Moss Side was home to 13,100 people and South Central Los Angeles, 100,000' (1996: 206). Similarly, of the thirty-four murders committed in Greater Manchester in 1993, only four took place in C Division (the area covering Moss Side and adjacent neighbourhoods) (Taylor, Evans and Fraser, 1996: 207). In other words, by the early 1990s, Moss Side had undeniably become a volatile inner-city area but its reputation was compounded by a mythology from which it is still struggling to escape.

Given the pervasiveness (and longevity) of this mythologization, the alternative views of the district to emanate from its writers must be seen as extremely important. Joe Pemberton's portrait of Moss Side in the

1960s is, as we shall see, the pre-eminent fictional representative of this sort of 'corrective' vision but, as noted earlier, even through the early to mid-1980s, many groups and individuals retained a sense of Moss Side as meaningful community. From the late 1970s onwards, indeed (especially when the deck-level estates of Hulme and Moss Side began to be rented out for student housing), an alternative arts and culture scene sprang up in both these districts. Haslam, reflecting on his interviews with local residents, notes that the mid-1980s are 'now remembered almost fondly in Moss Side' (Haslam, 2000: 230), whilst the short story 'Legoland on Mescalin', by Catriona Smith (1994) (herself a self-confessed middle-class migrant or refugee to the district) testifies to the way in which the heterogeneous population by then living in Hulme had become passionately attached to the type of living it offered (Smith, 1994: 35–44). In this engagingly surreal story, Smith attempts to save Hulme's soul by, literally, giving it a voice: 'All you nice, white, middle class girls, on the run from your backgrounds. Privileged backgrounds ... You come and play housey amongst the proles ... and dress up as urban warriors' (Smith, 1994: 37). Contrived as this is (in Smith's story, it is the building itself that speaks), the text nevertheless captures something of the Left-wing diversity of Moss Side during a period which saw poor whites, poor blacks and poor students living side by side with an equanimity that has caused Dave Haslam to conclude that '1986 and 1987 now seems like a lost golden age in Moss Side' (Haslam, 2000: 232).

As noted above, arguably the most optimistic view of Moss Side to be penned by a Manchester writer is Joe Pemberton's *Forever and Ever Amen* (2000b).[19] Of the fiction writing surveyed for the 'Moving Manchester' project, this novel stands out from other texts from the same period on account both of its, for the most part, positive and celebratory representation of Moss Side in the 1960s and 1970s and of its innovative narrative technique. The latter utilizes a child's imagination and focalization to naturalize a broadly magic-realist narrative method in which the main storyline is regularly interrupted by James's daydreams and fantasies (indicated by an alternative font). It is, indeed, the openness and credulity of James's nine-year old window on to the world that makes this portrait of Manchester, right at the height of the slum clearances, so vivid, and it is only towards the end of the text that the reader fully appreciates the intricacy of the plot and storyline. In the last few pages many secrets are revealed about the history of James's family back in St Kitts, and the fact that, as a nine-year-old, he reports these innocently requires that we, as readers, join up the dots ourselves; it is also why Pemberton's view of Manchester in the 1960s is so strikingly non-stereotypical.

In the novel, James's family (his mother, father, brother and himself) live on Cadogan Street ('Coronation Street with coloured people' (Pemberton, 2000b: 27)), and the multiple representations of this street serve as an useful illustration of Pemberton's method (in terms of both focalization and the text's 'magic-realist' flights of fantasy). Further, it constitutes a uniquely complex view of a part of Manchester that has, too often, been reduced to a cliché. At one level, Cadogan Street is, for James, quite simply 'home'. The exteriors and interiors of the buildings merge with all the things that were most memorable about his childhood, such as local food of various kinds:

> Old terraced houses on cobbled streets, Belle Vue Fair, billy bread with bits of pork in the middle, caterpillars in a jar, Sunday school, mice in the kitchen, cockroaches in the bathroom, ice-cream cornets with chocolate strawberry syrup chopped nuts hundreds and thousands and still have change from a bob for whizzer and chips. (Pemberton, 2000b: 2)

Thus, although, in sociological terms, this hardly counts as a portrait of inner-city Manchester in the 1960s, at an indicative level it does. Knowing, as we do, that James is a second-generation Caribbean child whose parents migrated to Manchester from St Kitts, this 'memory' reveals the extent to which his childhood was indistinguishable from that of any white, working-class schoolboy of the same age, even as other paragraphs (for example, the one which he describes his mother's preparation of West Indian food (Pemberton, 2000b: 6)) illustrate key points of difference. Indeed, considering how strongly the *unheimlich* features in a good deal of Manchester's diasporic writing (see especially Chapter 3), it is important to register the emphasis on the banal and commonplace in this glimpse of James's childhood. At crucial points, indeed, Pemberton uses this everyday perception to undercut James's fantastical visions, of either Manchester or St Kitts:

> This wasn't the time for shimmering streets and terraces of fruit pastilles. Cadogan Street was just a sign with a tarmac road down the middle and houses on both sides. Some had lights on, some didn't. Others had windows boarded up and the one in the corner had a red light. (Pemberton, 2000b: 48)

It is not these quotidian portraits of Cadogan Street that most readers of Pemberton's novel will remember, however, but rather the surreal, 'technicolor' (see dust-jacket description) descriptions of James's fantasies. One of the most spectacular of these involves the whole street coming out of their houses and joining in a dance in true 'West Side Story' fashion:

> James knew the next bit by heart having done it so many times. The street flowed down to a shimmering haze, the houses became a row of fruit pastilles, blah blah blah ...
>
> 'I feel like dancing,' said James. So he sent the violins away and put on a record instead.
>
> 'It's "Madison Time"', said the man on the record. And as if by magic, all the neighbours were out and lined up in rows like school assembly. Only they weren't singing hymns or saying the Lord's Prayer. They were dancing instead. A side-stepping, finger-clicking, hip-on-roller-skates formation as only coloured people on Cadogan Street can. James rushed out to join in. 'Perfect'. (Pemberton, 2000b: 56–7)

By the end of this 'feel-good' musical fantasy, James's vision has swollen to include *everyone* living on the street: whites and well as blacks, the grumpy and miserable as well as the sanguine and benign:

> Everyone was out there. Mr and Mrs Bruce with all their eight children. Even Patricia, though she was meant to be doing her homework. Mrs Green by herself as Mr Green was on night shift. James had never seen Mr Green ever. He wondered if Mrs Green was making him up. Even those white people from the end of the road that didn't speak to nobody but themselves were there. They couldn't do the hips-on-roller-skates bit of course, but they clicked their fingers in the right places. (Pemberton, 2000b: 57)

Focalizing this fantasy through the eyes of a nine-year-old child, Pemberton thus achieves a vision of community integration forever denied the adult consciousness. As a fictional device, it could thus be argued that this particular application of magic realism is of real political significance in that it enables a habitually repressed desire and sentiment to be, at least, *imagined*. Indeed, Pemberton's text as a whole may be seen to exploit James's social and political ignorance on race relations to maximum effect. On the one hand, it intensifies the reader's sympathy for the taunting and bullying he endures (James is unaware that such taunts are racially motivated), while, on the other, it shows us that children make friendships and alliances on grounds quite other than cultural sameness. James's chief inspiration, mentor and mother-substitute throughout the novel is, in fact, an elderly white woman known as 'Aunty Mary' who, despite the occasional racist embarrassment ('How about some scones? You people do like scones, don't you?' (Pemberton, 2000b: 126))), is gratuitously kind and loving. Aunty Mary in fact dies at the beginning of the period of James's life covered by the novel, but her love and spirit support James's fantasies and ensure that Cadogan Street remains very much his home.

This last point relates directly to the key event propelling the novel's plot: that is, James's family's imminent removal to Ashton-under-Lyne. Indeed, the text's intradiegetic action (apparently less than one year of James's life) takes place in the space between when this move is first announced and when it takes place. As already noted above, such moves (even a short distance across, or within, a city) were extremely disorientating for the families concerned, and James looks forward to his own relocation with doubt and trepidation. With this event looming on horizon, the reader becomes quickly aware that *Forever and Ever Amen* is, in fact, not so much an account of one child's experience of growing up in Moss Side in the 1960s as an elegy for a district, and a community, about to be wiped off the map. Fantastical and sentimental as this vision is, its focalization through the nine-year-old James makes it both permissible and credible. Before the demolition of the terraced housing, and before the drugs and guns moved in, Moss Side was a seemingly 'OK' place to live for the black families that took up residence there; indeed, to a very real extent it became a legitimate 'home from home'.[20]

Taken together, then, Pemberton's *Forever and Ever Amem* and Smith's *Moss Side Massive* provide two very different portraits of Moss Side that capture as vividly as Figures 1.3, 1.4 and 1.5 the radical transformation of the district during the period 1960 to 1990. Both authors, moreover (see notes 18 and 20), declare that they were inspired to write partly out of a desire to 'set the record straight' about the area in which they lived, even though this corrective vision means something rather different for Pemberton (who looks back on his childhood in Moss Side with great fondness) than for Smith (who, as a single mother, lived with the fear of her children being drawn into a life of crime). It is the fact that both *Forever and Ever Amen* and *Moss Side Massive* are nevertheless *fictional* texts that should command our attention here, however, since both, in their different ways, remind us of what creative writing can achieve in excess of documentary or sociological studies. As Ben Highmore has observed, inasmuch as urban space is, today, 'experienced as a lived imaginary', then 'belief, art, knowledge and so on will be very much part of that experience' (Highmore, 2005: 17), and it is precisely the rerouting of Manchester's perceived social ills through fictional characters and storylines that provides us with a visceral sense of what it must have meant to live in Moss Side in 1968 or 1988. As such, fictional texts like these can usefully challenge commonsense notions of 'authenticity' and remind us that the Moss Side of Pemberton's childhood was experienced not only in terms of its condemned housing stock and low wages but also through strong family and community connections, music, play and spectacular annual events like the Alexandra Park carnival. And neither, as we have noted elsewhere (Pearce, 2007; Crawshaw and Fowler, 2008; Pearce, 2010b), should the fantastical or highly conventionalized nature of the texts be seen to stand in the way of the texts' testimonial value. The fact that *Forever and Ever Amen* is an exercize in magic realism and *Moss Side Massive* a crime fiction ensures that the district is revealed to us not as a sociological case study but through the mediating consciousnesses of characters and narrators who can communicate the ontology of street life (Smith) and the synthesizing powers of memory[21] (Pemberton) with a complexity sometimes lacking in analytic thought.

Manchester: the rainy city

Rainycitystories.com is the name of a website (begun in 2008) that publishes new writing by Manchester authors.[22] Although by no means all the stories contained in its pages feature rain, the fact that the editors chose this pseudonym for the city says everything about the ongoing predilection for Mancunians to be 'down' on their city in a ways that have become synonymous with its national and international branding. Considering that, in meteorological terms, Manchester is actually no wetter than a lot of other towns and cities in Britain (a typical 858.3mm per year (Taylor, Evans and Fraser, 1996: 23)), this certainly confirms the tenacity of a discourse that settled upon the city, like the proverbial black cloud, many years ago – and stuck. As I have noted elsewhere (Pearce 2010a), the defamation of Manchester that began with Engels and other early social commentators (as quoted earlier) has so dominated social and aesthetic perception of the city and its environs that it would now appear hard for anyone to write about the district without retreading the clichés, especially with regards to its perceived post-industrial ruination. Although some writers have, admittedly, converted this ugly, blasted landscape into an expression of the sublime (see my discussion of Michael Bracewell's 'Blackley,

Crumpsall, Harpurhey' (1999) (Pearce 2007)), the majority do, indeed, employ the imagery of rain – and pervasive 'greyness' – as a backcloth to narratives of depression, alienation and menace. And in this last regard, it may be argued that rain had become a potent *political* trope in a good deal of Mancunian writing.

One, iconic Macunian text that arguably epitomizes just such an appropriation is Lemn Sissay's 'Moods of Rain' (Sissay, 1988) (also dealt with, though with significantly different emphasis, by Corinne Fowler in Chapter 5). Although, ostensibly, a poem about the alienation of an individual on a rainy day in Manchester, it is more radically understood as a poem about racism:

> I'm giving up dodging glassy eyed puddles
> My feet like the kitchen cloth
> Face screwed up no time for scruples
> Head down, walk straight and cough
> And silver speckled my licks are crowned
> Melting black faces drip and shine
> No smile but an unsatisfied frown
> Same goes, I think, for mine
>
> (Sissay, 1998: 16)

As I have observed elsewhere (Pearce, 2010a), the use of the transitive verbs 'slicing' and 'biting' to describe the rain, when placed alongside the cries of 'Get your Manchester Evening News', vividly capture the visceral experience of being a black man on the streets of Manchester in the 1970s and 1980s when racist abuse was a daily and unavoidable occurrence (Procter, 2003: 100–8). The rain in this poem, then, may easily be read as a metaphor for the racist hostility that, through a persistent barrage of angry words, 'sliced' and 'bit' the '[m]elting Black face' of the city's non-white citizens without respite. Read thus, rain becomes much more than a depressing backdrop for a poem 'about alienation': it is rather an agent of angry protest: 'biting' and 'slicing' *back*. As noted in the Introduction, this uncompromising exposure of racism has motivated a good deal of Mancunian writing from the 1970s onwards, and is arguably a more appropriate response to Manchester's post- and neocolonial legacy than the quiescent hymn to 'multiculturalism' that government agencies and publishers would evidently prefer (see the Introduction for further discussion of this).

Meanwhile it is no surprize that Peter Kalu, one of the city's best-known crime writers, should feature rain (with all its noir-ish connotations) in his novels at regular intervals. As in Sissay's poem, however, it is possible to see the perpetually leaden skies as much more than an appropriately moody setting for despairing characters up to desperate deeds. For example, although in *Yard Dogs* (2002) the misery of Manchester's climate is addressed very literally by the text's upmarket, female protagonist ('I hate this city. I'm too big for Manchester. I should be in New York or Paris ... Rain. Rain. Rain. Dingy hotels. Clapped-out clubs' (Kalu 2002: 91)), in *Lick Shot* (1994) the total desperation of Stockborough (a futuristic district of the city) is figured as a dark cloud:

> It was a big place, Stockborough, the biggest and baddest area in the region ... Ordinarily, an air of quiet desperation hung low over the town, so low you could scrape it with your fingers. It hung by the steel grey security grills [sic] of the anti-ram raid posted shop fronts and Fort Knox-walled petrol stations. It hung in the bleak, empty bus stations, in the heaving eucalyptus bushes of every desolate park. It was there in the sudden squeal of tyres, in the sudden clack, clack of a gun, in the scream of fluorescent graffiti, in the slam of glass and in the slam of falling sash-windows. The whole place was treading water, barely hanging together by a 100% proof, Librium-floated, sensi-inspired miracle. (Kalu, 1993: 47)

For while, in this particular extract, the metaphorical 'air of quiet desperation' never converts into 'real' rain as such, it is a trope that clearly draws upon popular knowledge of the city's seemingly inescapable greyness and destitution. With echoes of Dickens's *Hard Times* (1854), this description, for all its notional futurity (although written in 1994, Kalu's story is set in the early twenty-first century), gives the impression that Manchester always has been, and always will be, a damp and desperate place on account of its morphed meteorological and economic 'climate'. In the same way, then, that Sissay's rain may be seen as indicative of racial hostility, so may we see Kalu's as indicative of the district's well-documented post-industrial malaise.

I shall be discussing *Lick Shot* in some detail in my chapter on Manchester's crime fiction (Chapter 3), and so restrict my discussion here to what is most distinctive about its 'view' of the city and its recent past. On this point, it is important to register that, although this is a text ostensibly set in the future, its historical point of reference appears to be the late 1970s and early 1980s when the National Front were at the height of their militancy (Haslam, 2000: 227–8). The action of the novel itself, meanwhile, takes place in the fictional district of

'Stockborough': an ex-suburb of Greater Manchester that has become a site of relocation: 'as war weary residents fled the battle zone the city had become, with crack gangs spilling out of Moss Side, Uzis and Ingrams-a-blazing' (Kalu, 1993:46). To all intents and purposes, however, it would appear that Stockborough in the 2010s is a reincarnation of Moss Side in the 1980s, pointing both to the origins of the dystopia and the uglier continuities of history.

In this last regard, probably the most striking, and frightening, feature of Kalu's futuristic 'Manchester' is that it is a city riven by apartheid. Although Stockborough's population is still only fifty per cent Asian and African-Caribbean (the 1991 demographic of Moss Side), blacks and whites now live very separate lives and occupy the city space in very different ways. This 'view' of the city is first given us by the novel's central character, the black police DI, Ambrose Patterson, on the drive he makes to visit a wealthy Asian businessman known as 'the Rice King':

> At this hour, the traffic was relatively light. The white delivery van people had come and gone, the white reps were somewhere on the motorway in their Ford Twenty's, with their samples, the white secretaries had parked their Rover jeeps and Audi hatchbacks and were taking dictation from their white managers who'd parked their Porsche Saloons and hot hatches in the city's underground car parks.
>
> As in the police force, it was rare to see a black person in any position of power or wealth in the city, despite Stockborough's population being fifty percent Asian and African-Caribbean. The Greater Manchester area was £20 billion in arrears following its failure to secure the Olympic Games yet again. As a result, hundreds of businessmen which had banked on a successful bid, had fallen into receivership. Jobs were at a premium and if you were black you were last in the queue. The black people of Stockborough who succeeded in triumphing over all odds in securing a job, could be found tucked away in factories and mills. Patterson had recently seen one or two in the city centre serving behind counters, but no more. Covert, unwritten 'pass' laws operated throughout Stockborough. Black people weren't allowed in the city until nightfall. They were moved on and out. (Kalu, 1993: 20)

Kalu's portrayal of the unemployment crisis afflicting Stockborough here clearly replicates the one the author himself will have lived through in the 1980s but may also be seen to prophesy our historical present (2012). The inference, then, is clear: Manchester is, and always has been, a city of deep inequality and economic mishandling (as epitomized by

Manchester: the postcolonial city

'its failure to secure the Olympic Games yet again ...' (see Peck and Ward, 2002: 95–115)) which, like the rain, is unlikely to change.

As will be seen in Chapter 3, a good deal of the crime fiction to come out of the city makes the most of Manchester's legendary poor climate to typical noir-ish and/or political effect. And it is also there in Jeff Noon's cyperpunk rendition of the city, as may be seen in this extract from *Vurt* (1993):

> Maybe I'm some kind of romantic fool, especially when the Manchester rain starts to fall in memory, and I'm scribbling this down, chasing the moments. Bridget used to say that the rain around here was special, that something had gone wrong with the city's climate. That you always thought it was just about to start raining, but it always was, anyway. All I know is that looking back I can feel it falling on me, on my skin. The rain means everything to me, all that has been lost. I can see big spots of rain on the gravel. Over the road the black trees of Platt Fields Park are whispering and swaying, receiving the gift of rain gratefully. (Noon, 1993: 19)

By contrast to the texts cited previously, rain is figured here as a welcome constant in a Manchester where all other quotidian points of reference (save for recognisable street names) appear to have been lost. The rain on this occasion serves to reassure the narrator that some continuities between past and future still exist, though, arguably the net result is not dissimilar to Kalu's vision inasmuch as the city itself remains hostile, dangerous and, above all, not to be trusted (even, especially, when it has become a futuristic simulacrum of itself). From whichever direction one approaches it, there appears to be no escape from the discourse that Manchester is a city that is doomed, and writers have made the most of the apocalyptic connotations accruing to both rain and urban sprawl to urge political awareness: for Kalu, this takes the form of a stark warning about where racism begins (a National Front march) and ends (apartheid) while Noon prefers to unsettle his readers with the threat of a creeping, postmodern, capitalist malaise.

In more realist fiction from the post-1980s period, meanwhile, rain features as an equally pervasive, if rather less sinister, signifier of the city's ills. As in the following extract from Livi Michael's *Their Angel Reach* (1994), 'realist' rain is typically presented as an objective correlative for the melancholy of the protagonists' thoughts:

> All over Marley the rain was drumming against the roofs and pavements, there were mothers like Rachel and Julie stuck in their houses, somehow

passing the time by until it stopped. It helped Rachel to know that, but she couldn't help thinking that not everyone's life was the same. (Michael 1994: 129–30)

Once again, however, it may be argued that *how* the rain is deployed in figurative terms matters rather less than the context it is used to evoke, and what ultimately unites all the texts cited here is not rain per se but rather a consensus that Manchester is, and always has been, a 'problem' city in terms of its social, ethnic and economic inequalities. In every case, rain has merely presented itself as a convenient trope to attach this other 'climate' to. For the writers who bore witness to Manchester during the recession of the 1980s, the city's post-industrial decline and neocolonial ghettoization clearly presented itself as a status quo that not even the reimaginings of science fiction could easily escape. This said, and further to the previous discussion of Sissay's poem, it is important to recognize that none of these texts advocates passive quiescence as a political response. Alongside the clear-eyed, depressed, sometimes even despairing, social analysis presented in the work of these Mancunian authors, there is nearly always some sort of challenge or fight-back, either from the actions of feisty and heroic characters or, as I shall now go on to show, through the deployment of empowering focalizing devices.

The view from the driver's seat[23]

As I have discussed elsewhere (Pearce, 2010b), the decision of whether or not to collude in the redemptive endings of certain Mancunian texts is a significant moral and political dilemma. Most of the novels tender that possibility on account of the fact that fiction writing, generally, is invested in plot resolution (especially in the more popular genres) and humanist discourses of individual agency, good overcoming evil, and (on occasion) the upward progress of civilization. One of the great strengths of contemporary Macunian writing is arguably the techniques it has employed to allow these more positive perspectives or reading positions into its texts while refusing to compromise the social and ideological critique at their core. Indeed, as will be shown in the chapters that follow, the city's special relationship with genre fiction, short stories and live literature may be understood as a response to this dilemma since they are all modes of storytelling that depend upon literary and artistic conventions to make large amounts of grief and suffering bearable for their audiences, be this through plot resolution or an interactive dialogue (often humorous) between performer and audience. In addition, as I now proceed to illustrate, the authors in question often focalize parts of their narrative in a way that *empowers* their characters, even if that empowerment is only partial or temporary.

Manchester's roads and transport systems have featured widely in the city's literary output over the years. W. G. Sebald's (2002 [1993]) first view of the inner city in 1966 was, after all, from the back of a taxi, while in Noon's futuristic *Vurt* (1994) the road system often appears to be the *only* tangible set of co-ordinates that have survived into the hyper-reality of the present. Probably the most common and striking use of transport in Manchester writing, however, is the way in which mobility (and, especially *auto*-mobility) is equated with the (temporary) empowerment of otherwise marginalized groups and individuals (children, ethnic 'minorities' and women) (Miller, 2001; Gilroy, 2001; Dant, 2004); further, the way in which the alternative perception of the city facilitated by such transport itself becomes a metaphor for escape, freedom, hope and, at its most utopian, social and political change. While there is not the space here to explore this fictional mechanism in the detail or depth with which I have pursued it elsewhere (Pearce, 2012a), I nevertheless offer some indicative illustrations both here and in Chapter 3.

First, let us return to Kalu's *Lick Shot* (1993). It will be remembered that I have already quoted one extract from Kalu's novel which shows us the Stockborough cityscape from the seat of DI Ambrose Patterson's car. Indeed, from the very beginning of the novel, the extremely high value placed on the car (both as protection or insulation (Sheller, 2004) and status symbol (Gilroy, 2001)) is made clear; for example, DI Patterson may suspect his white sidekick of covert racial prejudice but can still console himself with the knowledge that *his* car (a black Mercedes) is infinitely superior to Moulton's 'wreck' (Kalu, 1993: 17–19). It is towards the end of the novel, however, that a car affords us the most vivid, and arguably most unusual, view of the Manchester cityscape in the context of a wild car chase. In the following extract, Patterson's ex-girlfriend, Cynthia (who has recently become a competitive rally-driver), has taken the wheel, and, glimpsed at ninety miles per hour, Stockborough's bruised and battered streets and buildings are finally blurred into submission:

> Cynthia just shrugged cutely. A squashed Mallieu let out a groan as she unravelled the steering wheel to counter oversteer. The chassis veered up

and they were momentarily on two wheels. They came down on all fours with a thump. The passengers held tight. They were cruising at 90 miles through side streets. Rows of canalside, shored up, back to back and empty, boarded through-terrace houses flashed past. Cynthia checked her wing mirror. The bikes were still on her tail. But they'd dropped back a few seconds. She was doing fine.

As the turbo-charged Audi Ebony sped along the canal route, the smirk on Eddie's face grew to gargantuan proportions. (Kalu, 1993: 153–4)

My point here, then, concerns the way in which a person's mode of transport can radically change his or her relation to, and perception of, a city. Streets that are manifestly unsafe to walk alone are nevertheless safe to drive; especially if you own a powerful, well-armoured car. In the same way that much has been made of the security and freedom cars have afforded women, so too do they offer a similar protection to persecuted ethnic groups (Gilroy, 2001). In the novels of both Kalu and Smith, we certainly see cars play a crucial role in empowering black characters and in changing their relationship to the city streets and highways. This, in turn, advises us of the complexity of perception *vis-à-vis* subject-positioning: no one's relationship to space and place is determined wholly by their 'personal' identity; the means (transport or otherwise) by which that view or experience is mediated is also crucial (Pearce, 2012a).

Of all the texts considered in this chapter so far, Smith's *Moss Side Massive* (2000) presents us with the most varied points of view (both perceptual and ideological) in the telling of her story. This is a text with a wide spectrum of narrators and focalizers, anchored by the black detective, DC Colin Edwards, who is given the role of the text's moral mouthpiece. And *Moss Side Massive* is a text in which the reader is presented with different views of the city on different occasions despite the fact that (in contrast to Kalu's novel) all the protagonists are black and mostly the children, or grandchildren, of African and Caribbean immigrants. As I have argued elsewhere (Pearce 2010b and 2012b), it is also a text in which traditional humanist values (and an associated politics) are very much the order of the day; for example, the protagonists' 'goodness' or 'badness' is not explained in terms of any tensions between ethnicity, religion and culture (or even degrees of poverty and deprivation) but rather their inherent 'character'. Consquently, children from the same family (for example Zukie and Clifton (aka 'Storm')) can be seen to turn out very differently. Thus, despite the fact that this is a text with several long passages attempting to 'explain' how Moss Side has got into the mess it's in ('Blue was a smart kid and had done well in school, but all around him, everywhere he looked, he was bombarded with reminders of the materialistic world that didn't form part of his existence' (Smith, 2000: 9)), the battle between 'good' and 'evil' is essentially fought out on an existential plane. This is especially the case with the story's denouement and ending which has a strong, Shakespearean ring of 'justice' about it.

In terms of the portrait it offers of Manchester, as a multicultural, post-industrial, postcolonial city, the multiple viewpoints offered by these characters and narrators, good and bad, are nevertheless fascinating. For example, a particular point of contrast is made between the views of Zukie (one of the 'good' teenage characters and notional hero of the text), and DC Edwards, the middle-aged, moral 'conscience' of the district. Whereas Edwards appraises the crumbling social infrastructure of the district from either his car or on foot, Zukie sees it from the seat of his mountain-bike: a key, and crucial, means of transport for the youth of the area, especially those who 'make their living' from doing 'runnings' for the drugs gangs. Zukie, a young 'Rasta', has stayed clear of this culture as much as possible, but, via his bike, shares the same, restless, peripatetic view of the urban landscape:

> Zukie rode along Moss Lane East. The squeaking red racing bike seemed to cut through the early morning traffic. The morning was grey and the cold wind blowing in his face, made his grey-green eyes watery and blew his sandy-coloured dreadlocks off his face ...
>
> The drizzle didn't help his mood. Raising his head, Zukie glanced over the dreary grey block of council flats in the distance. Empty, awaiting demolition. Row upon row, block upon block of solid, grimy pigeon-shit concrete which made the area look bleak and cast a feeling of despair over those who lived nearby.
>
> (Smith, 2000: 18)

Bearing in mind that Smith first began writing *Moss Side Massive* in 1984, it would seem that Zukie's description captures the district on the brink of the second wave of mass-demolition. A good deal of the 'new' 1960s and 1970s deck housing had by now been scheduled for clearance (see discussion of the Hulme Crescents earlier), and the community groups and agencies that had started up in the area in the early 1980s (exemplified here by the Black Women's Co-operative) had bitten the dust. In this regard, Zukie's 'witnessing' of his district may be read as a tragic duplication of that of James in Pemberton's *Forever and*

Ever Amen (2000b) twenty years earlier. As a streetwise teenager rather than an innocent child, Zukie is able to see something of the social demise that lies behind the dreariness of his view, though his thoughts stop short of moral or political judgement

However, the fact that Zukie is poised somewhere between childhood and adulthood means that his perception of the world is still sufficiently free of cynicism to entertain possible solutions to the problems that flash before his eyes (Pearce, 2010b). Moreover, his mobility (the comparative speed and freedom provided by his bike) enables Zukie to gain a literal and metaphorical distance on what he sees and, most importantly, to imagine a life 'beyond':

> Zukie glided on the old bicycle, aimlessly cruising out of the Alexandra Park Estate, leaving the blues and shebeens behind him, leaving the early-morning drug-pushers in doorways, like scavenger birds waiting for their prey. (Smith, 2000: 39)

This ability to move 'through' and 'beyond' the region in one's perception of it is in marked contrast with the gloomy and despairing stasis associated with DC Edwards's meditations. As noted above, Edwards is given the role of the text's social and moral analyst and mouthpiece, and what he 'sees' is not a pretty sight:

> Why the fuck were black youths always blasting each other? Things weren't supposed to go down like this. Okay, if you were a villain, fine. Or if you want to make a show of strength or carry out a straightforward robbery. But why did the Moss Side crews always have to come out with their finger on the trigger, blasting. Everywhere you looked kids, no more than fourteen or fifteen, were pulling out guns in wild shootouts in crowded areas, turning the neighbourhood into a war zone and leaving behind a trail of grieving mothers, brothers, fathers, sisters, girlfriends and orphans. He had watched hopelessly as the neighbourhood of his childhood degenerated. (Smith, 2000: 180–1)

With Edwards's analysis of the situation bound up with so much despair, we see even more clearly why Zukie's quasi-innocence and optimism are important for the novel as a whole. On his vulnerable shoulders Smith leaves a good deal resting: not least because his half-brother, Clifton's, story culminates in the sort of tragedy that it is never going to be easy to leave behind. Having turned to drugs crime to accelerate his 'sales' career, Clifton, still the apple of his mother's eye, is quickly caught up in a downward spiral of conflict with the district's rival gang (the Piper Mill Gang) and is framed for a murder he does not commit.

As will be seen in Chapter 3, there are several other crime writers associated with the city who demonstrate the empowerment of car-driving for individuals and groups who may otherwise find themselves vulnerable in the city streets (the female detective of Val McDermid's 'Kate Brannigan' series being an especially interesting example). My main point here, however, has been less concerned with issues of social and political empowerment than with the alternative viewpoint of the city that the car (and, in Zukie's case, the bicycle) literally and figuratively provides. As noted before, most writing to have come out of Manchester in recent years appears to be committed to making visible the city's not inconsiderable social problems. This makes it especially important for readers and critics to attend closely to the mechanics of how an alternative vision is also sutured into the texts. As we have seen, the conventions of particular modes and genres can be especially valuable in this respect, while the fine-tuning of narratological techniques (such as the mobilization of multiple viewpoints discussed here) can prove equally effective. Manchester is a city that has seemingly thwarted the affiliation of large numbers of its citizens, on account of either the fact that its manifestly migrant population has never been made welcome (or allowed to 'settle') or its general economic-social malaise. If we accept this, however reluctantly, as a social 'fact', then literature's capacity for inventing new perspectives (perceptual, psychological and ideological) becomes ever more crucial.

Nice views / new city

Although anxious and ambivalent about his own impending move from Moss Side to Ashton-under-Lyne, James, the nine-year-old narrator of Pemberton's *Forever and Ever Amen* (2000b), expresses genuine excitement when first shown the view from his friend's new flat in Hulme Crescent (see Figure 1.4):

> And there they were, Carl, his sister and James on the balcony of their new apartment overlooking the park with swings and roundabouts and a launderette for mothers to do their washing. (Pemberton, 2000b: 145)

This recognition that change is something that can, and should, be positively embraced in certain circumstances introduces the final set of discussion points that have a bearing on Manchester and its literary legacy.

As readers may have noted, the discourse of 'feel-good' multiculturalism has been kept purposefully in check in the previous sections of this chapter. For although, as we noted in the Preface, this book is, in part, a celebration of the vibrant 'world city' (Massey, 2007) that Manchester has undeniably become, it is clear that we are still many years away from a Britain in which all ethnic groups can stake a claim in its *habitus* as 'different' but 'equal'. This caution has also been informed by the writers with whom we worked on the 'Moving Manchester' project, many of whom remain extremely critical of the political containment and appeasement inherent in the 'multicultural' discourse first promoted by New Labour. This highly circumscribed embrace of 'diversity' has been visited not only upon government policy statements[24] but also upon arts funding and, as will be seen in Chapter 2, the publishing industry. Similarly, the chapter has subscribed to local residents' widespread criticism of Manchester's planning department for getting its social housing policy so badly wrong (not just once, but repeatedly) (Peck and Ward, 2002; Kellie, 2010), as well as the view that the more recent inner-city regeneration projects orchestrated by the Central Manchester Development Corporation from the late 1980s onwards have been partial, and elitist, in their gentrification of what is ultimately a small slice of Greater Manchester (see Figure 1.10) (Mellor, 2002). At every juncture in its history, it would seem, Manchester's governing bodies have failed to listen to, or imagine, what its citizens actually want: a deafness epitomized by their failure to understand that what all too soon became the next generation of 'condemned housing' was nevertheless someone's home (i.e. buildings that, however dysfunctional, might better have been repaired than destroyed). In Manchester's fiction writing, certainly, it is the city's failure to provide durable housing of a kind that would enable families and communities to stay together across generations that is seen as the root of its social problems; a spectacular failure of imagination, then: which, of course, is precisely why the arts have such a crucial role to play in taking Manchester forward.

In this final section of the chapter I therefore turn to a small selection of Manchester's most recent (i.e. post-millennial) writing to see what alternative versions of the contemporary, urban living are being explored. The hope we discover in these texts, I would suggest, pertains directly to a revized sense of home and belonging that is registered (even celebrated) in terms of the habitual, 'the everyday' (Procter, 2006; Fowler, 2008) and the 'taken for granted' precisely because it signals that a semblance of *permanent* residence has been achieved. Not surprisingly, this 'new belonging' (Bromley, 2000) is especially notable in the writings of diasporic communities who now have third- and fourth-generation roots in the district and (to echo the opening lines of this chapter) can stake a claim on Manchester as 'home' in the most archaic sense.

Two texts which illustrate this 'at homeness' with contemporary Manchester are Peter Kalu's *Yard Dogs* (2002) and Zahid Hussain's *The Curry Mile* (2006). Although Kalu's writing remains as critical of British society and culture as it ever was, his central character, DCI Patterson, is very much 'a man of his time': still subject to institutional racism, clearly, but as hooked on post-millennial consumerism as the best of them:

> I wedged my Merc into the Deansgate traffic heave. If money were your God, this was heaven. Bentley dealership to the left, Jaguar dealership to the right. Skywards, hundreds of thousands of square feet of lawyers' offices all pink in the autumn morning sun; ahead, the dome roof of the G-Mex Exhibition Centre, with its awesome cast-iron spans and brickwork. At street level the shop windows displayed Gucci; Moschino; Ralph Lauren ... Ten minutes later I was back in the jam in a new Oswald Boeteng [*sic*]: black cotton, fine double seams, tucked stitching, pattern cut in Japan and stitched in Singapore. Boeteng's were classy, understated, and fit how I liked – loose at the shoulders, an inch of slack at the waist. (Kalu, 2002: 114)

Although it is impossible not to hear the multiple layers of irony in this description (the author's, the narrator's, the character's), Kalu's decision to make his black DCI 'at home' in designer Manchester illustrates well the point made several times in this chapter about the complexity of flows (social, economic and cultural) in the postcolonial city. With recognized social status and, it would seem, considerable wealth, DCI Ambrose can comfortably inhabit spaces and places once the preserve of the white elite, even while he remains an 'outsider' within the force and subject to all manner of discrimination on a daily basis. On this point, it may be noted that Kalu's presentation of his DCI in this text is very different from that in *Lick Shot* (1994) (see preceding discussion) notwithstanding the fact that the latter was set in a future close to our present (early twenty-first century).

Zahid's Hussain's *Curry Mile* (2006) similarly presents the latest generation of Asian Mancunians as being extremely comfortable with contemporary British consumer culture (and, once again, to the point of irony). For example, when we first encounter Sorayah, the central (female) protagonist, at the start of the novel, she is wearing red lipstick and '[rummaging] through her Gucci handbag' (2006: 11). Although the story which follows sees Sorayah gradually being persuaded to re-commit herself to rather more traditional 'family values' by taking over one of her father's famous restaurants, she enjoys an everyday familiarity with all aspects of contemporary culture including the 'white' mainstream. Significantly, perhaps, the text never comments directly on the multiculturalism of this vision and readers are left to make up their own minds over the heroine's preferences and practices. However, there is no mistaking the fact that Sorayah's family is presented as having lived in Manchester long enough to be able to claim it as their home in a meaningful sense.

To conclude this section and, indeed, this chapter, I turn finally to Shamshad Khan's 'Manchester Snow' (2009).[25] This poem, in seven parts, captures superbly the way in which the citizens of a large, multicultural city like Manchester have come to inhabit what Avtar Brah (1996) famously referred to as 'diaspora space'.

Conceived as an intimate dialogue between the speaker and her city (a dialogue so intimate that it may, at first, be mistaken for a love poem), Khan's 'Ode to Manchester' explores the distance between what we desire, and *expect*, of our 'destination homes' (Pearce, 2000) and what we *find*:

> Like all others
> What I thought I came for
>
> And what I end up doing here
> Don't exactly match (Khan, 2009: 43)

As in an interpersonal relationship, our relationship with the place we come to live (for whatever reason) is a dynamic process of 'becoming' that – as Khan's poem dramatizes – engages both you and 'it':

> You dreamed me
> When I was walking the streets of Leeds
>
> I heard your name but other than that
> You hardly existed for me
>
> I can't imagine myself
> Not having met you

Manchester: the postcolonial city

> You have shaped my relationship
> With glitter filled skies
>
> You have made me accept the people
> Who left us
>
> (Khan, 2009: 45)

Throughout the poem, indeed, and especially in the closing section, Khan persists with the nice twist that the city is as subject to *us*, its citizens, as we are to it. Far from being the alien, 'migrant' space that recurs in a good deal of Manchester writing from the 1980s, Khan's city challenges, and is challenged, by all those who settle there: both the city and its people, then, are engaged in an act of becoming, and both must take responsibility for what they produce even if they barely understand how the process comes about:

> VII: Another Loft Conversion
>
> Manchester where do you see yourself in twenty years?
>
> Don't answer straightaway
>
> Let your mind drop into my heart
> Let blood mix with light
>
> Answer after you've decided
> That you'll stay
>
> Khan, 2009: 46)

With a playful echo of *Slumdog Millionaire* (also 2009), Khan's speaker takes peremptory control of the city to which she herself moved as a 'migrant' student and demands commitment (a Manchester that is rather more than its sum total of 'loft conversions') in return for her commitment to it. Further, the dynamics of this long-term relationship (in which the two parties are seen to grow into one another, despite all the irritations ('what I did not notice when we met / is a familiar inconvenience now ...' (Khan, 2009: 45)) is placed in neat contrast with the first attraction:

> Manchester everything I love about you now
> I loved about you then

> Fake gothic promises
> Straight-talking red bricks
> Choose me they said choose me
> And I did
>
> (Khan, 2009: 41)

Whereas twenty years previously, Manchester was the active partner in the affiliation, now it is the speaker who is herself telling the City what to do, putting it in its place, taking ownership – and bearing responsibility. Over time, Khan's text would seem to be saying, the migrant is no longer a migrant and, if sufficient ethnic groups stay long enough ('Romanian, Irish, Iranian, African *Mancunians*' (my italics) (Khan, 2009: 42)), Manchester may eventually earn the right to be designated a meaningfully 'multicultural' rather than a 'migrant' city.

Conclusion

This chapter has sought to introduce readers both to the socio-historical circumstances that have come to define Manchester as a post/colonial city and to the literature that has come out of, and responded to, this past. To this end, it has explored contemporary Mancunian writing for what it has to say about the city and, in particular, how it has both reproduced and challenged some of the more pejorative discourses associated with it. What it has not done, but what the subsequent chapters will redress, is acknowledge all the excellent writing by Manchester authors to emanate from the city without necessarily being *about it*. Indeed, as we noted in the Introduction to this volume, one of our first decisions when setting up the 'Moving Manchester' e-catalogue was to define both 'migrant writing' and 'Manchester writing' as broadly as possible in order to acknowledge the fact that there is no reason whatsoever why second-, third- and fourth-generation Mancunians (of whatever ethnic background, including white) should feel obliged to write about either of these.

This said, most of the writing to have emerged from the city since the early-1980s bears the mark of its migrant and postcolonial past in terms of its production and consumption, if not necessarily its subject matter or theme. As we shall see, the complex politics of British (post)colonialism is seen nowhere more starkly than in its publishing industry which has continued to shun non-metropolitan writing, in particular the work of black and Asian authors, unless it conforms to the problematically restricted model of multiculturalism discussed earlier. The twist here, then, is that, while Manchester arguably has as great a claim as London to the tag 'postcolonial city' the latter has achieved a kudos and a marketability that Manchester has not.

This bias has impacted significantly on the direction of Mancunian writing post-1980, resulting in both an exodus of a good many talented young writers from the city, and an organized resistance in the guise of alternative, community-based writing and publishing practices, 'live literature' and a purposeful investment in popular genres such as crime fiction. All these very material responses to the challenge of becoming a 'Mancunian writer' may therefore be seen to be as consequent upon both the city's, and the nation's, postcolonial past as a more directly thematic engagement with the topic.

Even after six years of research on this great city and its writers, however, the authors of this volume readily acknowledge that our view of both its history and its literature is necessarily partial: not only on account of our status as outsiders and academics but also in recognition of the fact that neither the recent past nor processes of belonging can be 'known' in all their complexity until long after the event. As Shamshad Khan concludes in the poem 'Manchester Snow' discussed in the previous section:

> I get to know myself better
> Every time you answer
> And every time my mind goes blank.
>
> (Khan, 2009: 41)

The lived experience of 'being' and 'belonging' in a city as dynamic as Manchester in the early twenty-first century therefore remains something that we must expect to glimpse rather than fully apprehend.

Notes

1 This figure has been obtained from the Manchester City Council website at www.manchester.gov.uk/downloads/download/4220/corporate_research_and_intelligence_population_publications (accessed 16/08/11) which provides a comprehensive overview of the city's demographic including its ethnic composition and recent migration statistics. Interestingly, although the population of the City of Manchester has increased in recent times (433,000 in 1991 to an estimated 499,000 in 2010), that of Greater Manchester appears to have been steady-state since the 1991 census twenty years ago.

2 The reconstruction of Hulme and Moss Side in the 1960s and 1970s resulted in the displacement of many tens of thousands of people. As Haslam observes: 'The redevelopment in the 1960s of Hulme and Moss Side set new records as the biggest piece of radical urban renewal that had been attempted in Europe; during the transitory years documented by [photographer] Shirley Baker, thirty thousand people were extracted and rehoused' (Haslam, 2000: xxi).
3 During the 1950s significant numbers of African-Caribbean families migrated to the UK, including Manchester (Panayi, 1999: 14) as a consequence of British recruitment campaign to fill vacancies in key sectors (e.g. London Transport). The ship that first brought these families was the *Empire Windrush* (in 1948) and the story of this period in Britain's colonial history has been widely researched and reported on in recent times. See for example the materials written in support of the BBC 'Windrush Season' (first broadcast in 1998): www.bbc.co.uk/history/british/modern/windrush_01.shtml (accessed 16 August 2011).
4 In 2008 an exhibition entitled 'Trade and Empire' was held at the Whitworth Gallery, Manchester, which drew explicit connections between the city's colonial interests (in cotton and the slave trade) and the exploitation and oppression of the mill workers involved in the manufacture of the cotton. The exhibition was curated by Dr Alan Rice, who has written extensively about the involvement of the north west of England in the economies of the 'Black Atlantic'. See: www.revealinghistories.org.uk/legacies-commemorating-the-bicentenary-of-british-abolition/video/trade-and-empire-event-alan-rice-introduction.html.
5 The Central Manchester Development Corporation (CMDC) was an extremely controversial public–private partnership that, during the 1980s and 1990s, came to symbolize Manchester's most recent makeover. It features widely in the literature emanating from the city during this period, creative and otherwise, with many writers sceptical of its objectives and, in particular, its investment in central Manchester rather than the housing districts. Haslam nevertheless observes that the CMDC was 'wary of flaws of past schemes for developing Manchester, and encouraged sensitive use of the existing buildings' (Haslam, 2000: 251).
6 Key autobiographical or quasi-autobiographical texts by these writers include: Burgess, *Little Wilson and Big God* (1987) and *One Man's Chorus: The Uncollected Writings* (2000); Naughton, *On the Pig's Back* (1988) and *Saintly Billy* (1989); Woodruff, *Billy Boy* (1993); Storey, *Flight into Camden* (1964).
7 Even more iconic than Naughton's play *Alfie* (1963) is, of course, the film, starring Michael Caine (dir. Lewis Gilbert, Paramount Pictures, 1966).
8 The film of *A Taste of Honey* (1961) staring Rita Tushingham, was directed by Tony Richardson and distributed by British Lion films.
9 *The Emigrants* (2002 [1993]) is a complex and curious text in terms of its genre. Although the narrator appears to be Sebald himself, the four char-

Manchester: the postcolonial city

acters he encounters and 'researches' are fictional, rendering the whole a sort of pseudo-ethnographic study of Manchester during this period. The text also contains several unlabelled black and white photographs.

10 See Jackie Stacey's article 'Ravishing Maggie' in *New Formations* (2010) for further discussion of Thatcher's iconic status and the impact she had on the lives of all those who grew up in her shadow.

11 Greater Manchester Council (GMC) was operational between 1974 and 1986. The GMC operated from its County Hall headquarters on Portland Street until its abolition following the Conservative government's Local Government Act of 1985. Following its demise, authority was devolved to the ten district councils that had come under its umbrella. Taylor, Evans and Fraser (1996: 77) observe that 'the activities of these county authorities' proved remarkably resilient in the face of the closure as is evidenced by the fact that we can still see their legacy today.

12 The organizations listed here have been the beneficiaries of a wide range of funding over the years including (principally) Arts Council North-West (now ACE) as well as the Greater Manchester Council.

13 Both these museums are the home to important archives chronicling the city's past, a good deal of which is now available online. See Museum of Science and Industry (MOSI) at www.mosi.org.uk/ (which has an outstanding collection of materials on African, Caribbean and Asian history) and the People's History Museum at www.phm.org.uk/.

14 Factory Records is the world-famous, cult record label set up by Tony Wilson and Alan Erasmus in 1978. Many excellent music histories have now been written which include accounts of the Factory scene including Tony Wilson's own *24 Hour Party People: What the Sleeve Notes Never Tell You* (2002) (also a film), Simon Reynolds's *Rip it Up and Start Again* (2006), John Robb's *The North Will Rise Again: Manchester Music City, 1976–1996* (2010), James Nice's *Shadowplayers: The Rise and Fall of Factory Records* (2011) as well as Dave Haslam's *Manchester, England* (2000).

15 For a detailed account of many musical sub-genres of the post-punk era up to an including acid-house see Reynolds (2006).

16 The demographic of Manchester's districts is both specific and evolving. Taylor, Evans and Fraser (1996: 19) note that, according to the 1991 census, Moss Side was 31 per cent black (African-Caribbean) with a further 6 per cent of residents being of Indian or Pakistani background, and Whalley Range was 11 per cent black and 21 per cent Indian or Pakistani; however, by the 1990s, the demographic of Cheetham Hill, Whalley Range and Old Trafford had become increasingly mixed (1996: 202).

17 I have written about Moss Side and its fiction in several articles that preceded the publication of this book and inform the current discussion, most notably: 'Women Writers and the Elusive Urban Sublime' (2007); 'Writing and Region in the Twenty-First Century' (2010a): 'The Literary Response to Moss Side, Manchester: Fact or (Genre) Fiction?' (2012b).

18 Karline Smith's *Moss Side Massive* (2000) is one of the most frequently cited texts to have come out of Moss Side in recent years on account of what continues to be seen as its controversial portrait of Moss Side. It is also invoked frequently, in different contexts, in the chapters that follow (but especially Chapter 4). In our interview with Smith in 2007, the author defends her hard-hitting account on account of her own experience with her son ('I could see where basically if I had gone in there early enough and recognized the signs a lot of things could have been prevented') even if it did bring Moss Side into further disrepute (see also Haslam, 2000, 235–6).
19 Like Karline Smith's *Moss Side Massive*, Pemberton's *Forever and Ever Amen* (2000b) has acquired the status of an iconic text within contemporary Mancunian fiction and has been discussed frequently in publications deriving from the 'Moving Manchester' project (see, especially: Crawshaw and Fowler, 2008; Fowler, 2008). Its incorporation into Manchester City Council's website (www.manchester.gov.uk/info/448/archives_and_local_studies/788/picture_book_moss_side/22: accessed 18/08/11) is seen as demonstrable evidence of its success in positively re-profiling Moss Side (see Crawshaw and Fowler, 2008).
20 In his (2007) interview with us, Pemberton confirmed that the Moss Side he grew up in did not fit the stereotypes that have since become associated with it: 'there was an overwhelming feeling in me saying "Hey, I don't remember Moss Side, where I was born, being like that," and therefore the urge to redress the balance in my own way came and was expressed in the writing ... I remember Moss Side as a place where a normal boy was brought up with his normal family ... being made to go to bed at 9 o'clock in the evening because you'd got to get up for school the next day, having meals around the table, going to church, visiting relatives, having parties.'
21 In their 2008 article on Pemberton's *Forever and Ever Amen* (2000b), Crawshaw and Fowler focus, in particular, on the role of 'post-memory' in James's 'intergrated' fantasies of his own childhood and that of his family back home in St Kitts. I also argue (2010b and 2012b) that the highly conventional nature of Smith's text is at odds with the ostensible 'realism' of its form and reflects upon what this means for its reading and interpretation.
22 See www.rainycitystories.com (accessed 05/04/12).
23 Some of the discussion and textual materials that I draw upon here also feature in my article 'Automobility in Manchester Fiction' (2012a), though with a significantly different intellectual objective inasmuch as the latter is ostensibly about the phenomenology of driving per se.
24 See *Secure Borders, Safe Haven: Integration with Diversity in Modern Britain* (2002). See: www.archive2.official-documents.co.uk/document/cm53/5387/cm5387.pdf (accessed April 2012).
25 Shamshad Khan's poem 'Manchester Snow' was written for the 'Moving Manchester' poetry commission and first published in the special issue of *Moving Worlds* (2009), edited by Corinne Fowler and Graham Mort.

References

A Taste of Honey (1961) Dir. Tony Richardson. British Lion Films.
Alfie (1966) Dir. Lewis Gilbert. Paramount Pictures.
Bee, M. (1984) *Industrial Revolution and Social Reform in the Manchester Region*. Manchester: Neil Richardson.
Body, S. (2003) *Seasons*. Mexborough: Glass Head Press.
Bracewell, M. (1999) 'Blackley, Crumpsall, Harpurhey' in Page, R. (ed.), *The City Life Book of Manchester Short Stories*. Harmondsworth: Penguin, 114–25.
Brah, A. (1996) *Cartographies of Diaspora*. London: Routledge.
Briggs, A. (1990 [1963]) *Victorian Cities*. Harmondsworth: Penguin.
Bromley, R. (2000) *Narratives for a New Belonging: Diasporic Cultural Fictions*. Edinburgh: Edinburgh University Press.
Burgess, A. (1987) *Little Wilson and Big God*. Harmondsworth: Penguin.
Burgess, A. (2000) *One Man's Chorus: The Uncollected Writings*. New York: Carroll and Graf Publishers, Inc.
Cartwright, J. (1990 [1986]) *Road*. London: Methuen Drama.
Cohen, R. (1997) *Global Diasporas: An Introduction*. London and New York: Routledge.
Crawshaw, R. and Fowler, C. (2008) 'Articulation, Imagined Space and Virtual Mobility in Literary Narratives of Migration', *Mobilities*, 3 (3), 455–69.
Dant, T. (2004) 'The Driver-car', *Theory, Culture & Society*, 21 (4/5), 61–79.
Delaney, S. (1960 [1959]) *A Taste of Honey*. London: Methuen.
Engels, F. (1987 [1845]). *The Condition of the Working Class in England, 1844*, ed. V. G. Kiernan. Harmondsworth: Penguin.
Fowler, C. (2008) 'A Tale of Two Novels: Developing a Devolved Approach to Black British Writing', *Journal of Commonwealth Literature*, 43 (3), 75–94.
Frangopulo, N. J. (1977) *Tradition in Action: The Historical Evolution of the Greater Manchester County*. Wakefield: EP Publishing Ltd.
Fryer, P. (1984) *Staying Power: The History of Black People in Britain, since 1504*. London: Pluto.
Gilroy, P. (2001) 'Driving While Black' in Miller, D. (ed.), *Car Cultures*. Oxford: Berg.
Haslam, D. (2000) *Manchester, England: The Story of the Pop Cult City*. London: Fourth Estate.
Hewison, R. (1995) *Culture and Consensus: England, Art and Politics since 1940*. London: Methuen.
Highmore, B. (2005) *Cityscapes: Cultural Readings in the Material and Symbolic City*. London: Palgrave Macmillian.
Hussain, Z. (2006) *The Curry Mile*. Manchester: Suitcase Press.

Kalra, V. S. (2000) *From Textile Mills to Taxi Ranks: Experiences of Migration, Labour and Social Change*. Aldershot: Ashgate.

Kalu, P. (1993) *Lick Shot*. London: X-Press.

Kalu, P. (2002) *Yard Dogs*. London: X-Press.

Kellie, E. (2010) *Rebuilding Manchester*. London: DB Publishing.

Khan, S. (2009) 'Manchester Snow' in Fowler, C. and Mort, G. (eds), 'Region / Writing / Home: Relocating Diasporic Writing in Britain', special issue of *Moving Worlds*, 9 (2), 41–6.

Law, D. (2004) '"Guddling for Words": Representations of the North and Northernness in Post-1950 South Pennine Literature'. Lancaster University. Unpublished PhD thesis.

McLeod, J. (2004) *Postcolonial London: Rewriting the Metropolis*. London and New York: Routledge.

Manchester Evening News Syndication (2008 [2003]) *The Changing Face of Manchester* (Volume 1). Manchester: Manchester Evening News.

Manchester Evening News Syndication (2007) *The Changing Face of Manchester* (Volume 3). Manchester: Manchester Evening News.

Marangoly George, R. (1996) *The Politics of Home*. Cambridge: Cambridge University Press.

Massey, D. (2007) *World City*. Cambridge: Polity Press.

Mellor, R. (2002), 'Hypocritical City: Cycles of Urban Exclusion' in Peck, J. and Ward, K. (eds), *City of Revolution: Restructuring Manchester*. Manchester and New York: Manchester University Press, 214–235.

Messinger, Gary (1985) *Manchester in the Victorian Age: The Half-known City*. Manchester: Manchester University Press.

Michael, L. (1994) *Their Angel Reach*. London: Martin Secker & Warburg.

Miller, D. (2001) *Car Cultures*. Oxford: Berg.

Morley, P. (2007) *Joy Division: Piece by Piece: Writing About Joy Division*. London: Plexus Publishing.

Naughton, W. (1963) *Alfie*. London: Samuel French Limited.

Naughton, W. (1988) *On the Pig's Back*. Oxford: Oxford University Press.

Naughton, W. (1989) *Saintly Billy*. Oxford: Oxford University Press.

Nice, J. (2011) *Shadowplayers: The Rise and Fall of Factory Records*. London: Aurum Press.

Noon, J. (1994) *Vurt*. Manchester: Ringpull.

Page, R. (ed.) (1999) *The City Life Book of Manchester Short Stories*. Harmondsworth: Penguin.

Panayi, P. (1999) *The Impact of Immigration: A Documentary History of the Effects and Experiences of Immigrants in Britain since 1945*. Manchester: Manchester University Press.

Pearce, L. (1994) *Reading Dialogics*. London: Edward Arnold.

Pearce, L. (ed.) (2000) *Devolving Identities: Feminist Readings in Home and Belonging*. Aldershot: Ashgate.

Pearce, L. (2007) 'Women Writers and the Elusive Urban Sublime: The View from Manchester, England', *Contemporary Women's Writing*, 1 (1): 80–97.

Pearce, L. (2010a) 'Writing and Region in the Twenty-First Century: Epistemological Reflections on Regionally-located Art and Literarure in the Wake of the Digital Revolution', *European Journal of Cultural Studies*, 13 (1), 27–42.

Pearce, L. (2010b) 'Beyond Redemption? Mobilizing Affect in Feminist Reading' in Liljestrom, M. and Paasonen, S. (eds), *Working with Affect in Feminist Readings: Disturbing Differences*. London and New York: Routledge, 151–64.

Pearce, L. (2012a) 'Automobility in Manchester Fiction', *Mobilities*, 7 (1), 93–113.

Pearce, L. (2012b). 'The Literary Response to Moss Side, Manchester: Fact or (Genre) Fiction?' in K. Cockin (ed.), *The Literary North*. London: Palgrave, 220–39.

Peck, J. and Ward, K. (eds) (2002) *City of Revolution: Restructuring Manchester*. Manchester and New York: Manchester University Press.

Pemberton, J. (2000a). Interview with *Flux* magazine.

Pemberton, J. (2000b) *Forever and Ever Amen*. London: Hodder Headline.

Pemberton, J. (2007) Interview with Corinne Fowler for the 'Moving Manchester' project. Unpublished transcript.

Procter, J. (2003) *Dwelling Places: Postwar Black British Writing*. Manchester and New York: Manchester University Press.

Procter, J. (2006) 'The Postcolonial Everyday', *New Formations: A Journal of Culture / Theory / Politics*, 58, 62–80.

Reynolds, S. (2006) *Rip It Up and Start Again: Post-punk 1978–1984*. London: Faber.

Robbs, J. (2010) *The North Will Rise Again: Manchester Music City 1976–1996* London: Aurum Press.

Sandhu, S. (2003) *London Calling: How Black and Asian Writers Imagined a City*. London: Harper Perennial.

Savage, J. (1994) Sleeve notes to *Joy Division: Heart and Soul* (career retrospective).

Sebald, W. G. (2002 [1993]) *The Emigrants*. London: Vintage.

Sissay, L. (1988) *Tender Fingers in a Clenched Fist*. London: Bogle L'Ouverture.

Sheller, M. (2004) 'Automotive Emotions: Feeling the Car', *Theory/Culture/Society*, 21 (4/5), 221–42.

Slumdog Millionaire (2009) Dir. Danny Boyle and Loveleen Tandan. Twentieth-Century Fox.

Smith, C. (1994) 'Legoland on Mescalin' in Bolton, C. (ed.), *No Limits*. Manchester: Commonword/Crocus.

Smith, K. (2000) *Moss Side Massive*. London: X-Press.
Stacey, J. (2010) 'Ravishing Maggie: Marcus Harvey and Thatcher Thirty Years On', *New Formations*, 70, 132–51.
Storey, D. (1964) *Flight into Camden*. Harmondsworth: Penguin.
Taylor, I., Evans, K. and Fraser, P. (1996) *A Tale of Two Cities: Global Change, Local Feeling and Everyday Life in the North of England*. London: Routledge.
Williams, W. (1977 [1976]) *The Making of Manchester Jewry*. Manchester: Manchester University Press.
Wilson, T. (2002) *24 Hour Party People: What the Sleeve Notes Never Tell You*. London: Channel 4 Publications.
Woodruff, W. (1993) *Billy Boy: The Story of a Lancashire Weaver's Son*. Edinburgh: Edinburgh University Press.

Internet sources

www.archive2.official-documents.co.uk/document/cm53/5387/cm5387.pdf
www.bbc.co.uk/history/british/modern/windrush_01.shtml
www.manchester.gov.uk/downloads/download/4220/corporate_research_and_intelligence_population_publications
www.manchester.gov.uk/info/448/archives_and_local_studies/788/picture_book_moss_side/22
www.rainystories.com
www.revealinghistories.org.uk/legacies-commemorating-the-bicentenary-of-british-abolition/video/trade-and-empire-event-alan-rice-introduction.html.
www.transculturalwriting.com/movingmanchester.

2

Publishing Manchester's black and Asian writers

Corinne Fowler

[W]hen I was the first black literature development worker in the North of England in 1988 there were only two in the country. One at a place called Centreprise in Hackney, London, and one in Manchester. It is here that I set up Cultureword ... I spent five years in that post. The knock-on effect of its success meant that Liverpool, Bradford, Leeds and Birmingham all went on to produce funds for black literature development workers ... It's one of my proudest achievements in literature and ... there's not a Manchester black writer who has not, in the past twenty years, been through Cultureword! (Lemn Sissay)[1]

The Introduction to this book explored how Manchester's diaspora space has impacted on the city's white writers as well as upon their black and Asian counterparts. Yet when it comes to publishing, it is black and Asian Mancunians who face the most daunting challenges in getting their work accepted by major publishers. Once published, they face a struggle to access wide readerships. In order to explore the obstacles faced by black and Asian writers, this chapter initially takes the example of Joe Pemberton's novel *Forever and Ever Amen* (2000), discussed in an earlier essay published in 2008, before considering how such problems are amplified and complicated for *poets*, whose work is by definition a non-commercial literary form. This chapter considers the prospects for the next generation of British black and British Asian poets in the light of significant changes that are affecting the publishing industry, including the rise of social media, the development of new technologies and, less hearteningly, significantly diminished publishing opportunities for such poets. In order to understand the full implication of these changes, I chart the course of Lemn Sissay's career. A black Mancunian poet, Sissay was honoured with the first commission for the London Olympics 2012.

In 2000, Headline Review published a novel called *Forever and Ever Amen*, set in Manchester's Moss Side district and authored by a black Mancunian called Joe Pemberton. The publication of *Forever and Ever Amen* was an exceptional case of a black, northern working-class author gaining access to, and acceptance by, a major publisher. Its launch in October 2000 exactly coincided with that of another novel by a British black writer, Zadie Smith, which was soon to become an international bestseller: *White Teeth* (2000) (Fowler, 2008: 79). As the novelist Diran Adebayo argues, the publication of *White Teeth* partly reflects the tendency of editors to embrace novels that they perceive to represent celebratory depictions of multiracial Britain, a point Adebayo illustrates by means of an anecdote. Here he recalls his conversation with Margaret Drabble, the novelist, biographer and critic:

> [S]he had very much an idea, as America does – and it's kind of pushed in Zadie's book to some degree – that basically London is this very happy place [with …] lots of happy associations between people of different colours … And I was trying to give Margaret Drabble a sense that other parts of London … it wasn't necessarily like that. But you could see from her world, her sense of what London was … therefore if a Zadie Smith *White Teeth* type of book lands on Margaret Drabble's desk or her publisher's, they would see it as, 'This is the real thing – someone's given voice to all I'm feeling on the streets.' (Adebayo in Sesay, 2011: 124)

Hilary Mantel makes a similar observation: '*White Teeth* accorded with some pictures of a young and vibrant life in the capital, with which reviewers and readers wanted to identify' (Mantel in Fowler, 2008: 81). By contrast, Mantel argues, 'Joe's [Pemberton's] book was … a story about provincial life. I'm a Northerner myself – reviewers have trouble focusing on provincial life … it's all "up there" to them' (Mantel in Fowler, 2008: 81).

Both *White Teeth* and *Forever and Ever Amen* were contracted by transnational publishing houses.[2] Both received highly favourable critical reviews in the national press. Smith's reviewers emphasized the novel's universal appeal in ways that tended to suggest that it was able to transcend its London settings, while the majority of Pemberton's reviewers fell into the established critical tendency to emphasize its northernness in ways that detracted from the wider themes of *Forever and Ever Amen* (such as childhood) or significant stylistic influences (such as magical realism) (Fowler, 2008: 82). Although national reviewers of Pemberton's novel sub-categorized *Forever and Ever Amen* as a northern novel (as opposed to a southern novel, which David Law (2004) argues is invariably viewed simply as 'the novel')[3] they were otherwise loud in their praises. However, it never looked like becoming a bestseller and Pemberton's publisher Hodder was disappointed with the novel's sales figures (Fowler, 2008: 77). The crucial point about Pemberton's novel, though, was not so much that it *ought* to have been a bestseller but that it never *could* have been. As I concluded in my essay, 'A Tale of Two Novels', the destiny of *Forever and Ever Amen* was at least partly related to the perceived social and literary anomaly of black, northern, working-class writing (Fowler, 2008: 87). The 'Moving Manchester' project found that the commercial and critical fate of *Forever and Ever Amen* was broadly representative of the difficulties that regional black novelists have in securing wide audiences for devolved articulations of black Britain outside the publishing capital of London.[4]

Short story writers, playwrights and poets are by definition less likely than novelists to gain national and international readerships. The novel remains the major commercial genre, though – for British black and British Asian writers – with crucial restrictions. In the 1990s, for example, Kadija Sesay points out that mainstream publishers of novels by black writers were 'focused on a particular kind of novel from male writers (urban and gritty) and from women (family and identity)' (Sesay, 2011: 118).

Poets face a different set of obstacles and opportunities. Dania Gioia (2003) argues that, particularly for poetry that is performed, information and communication technologies have the potential to transform the publishing situation for black writers. He argues that the reading public is increasingly inclined towards audiovisual modes of communication, suggesting that 'print has lost its primacy' in this regard. Indeed, he attributes the surge of poetry's popularity to new modes of transmission, noting, in particular, that poets who perform their work increasingly reach their audiences by such means as podcasts and YouTube videos and by using venues that are favoured by the entertainment industry, such as bars and nightclubs (Gioia, 2003: 21, 28). The popularity of poetry in performance is discussed in Chapter 5. As the poet Patience Agbabi notes, however, a published poetry collection remains an important indicator of editorial esteem for poets (Breeze, Agbabi, Tipene, Harrison and Bertram, 1999: 44). Moreover, despite Manchester's thriving performance scene, the city's black poets have yet to gain acceptance by Britain's seven most frequently reviewed poetry publishers: Anvil, Bloodaxe, Carcanet, Faber and Faber, Jonathan Cape, Penguin and Picador (Dawes, 2005: 286).

This problem is not merely restricted to black and Asian poets from the city of Manchester. As Kwame Dawes argues, *all* British black and British Asian poets' chances of publication are adversely affected by their cultural association with performance poetry and by the misleading distinction between 'page' and 'stage' poetry, discussed in Chapter 5 (Dawes, 2005: 282). With the exception of the Manchester-based Carcanet Press, which has published black writers such as Sujata Bhatt, Lorna Goodison and Kei Miller,[5] the seven most frequently reviewed poetry publishing houses only rarely publish titles by black poets and, even then, the trend is to publish writers with established international reputations (Dawes, 2005: 289). In contrast are lesser-reviewed yet respected poetry publishing houses such as Peepal Tree Press, which has published new black poets such as Raman Mundair and Dorothea Smartt (Evaristo in Keane, 2004: 16). Many of Manchester's poets have also been well served by Salt Press, which published Shamshad Khan's *Megalomaniac* in 2007, as well as by the city's own Cheers Ta press, which was established expressly to print the debut collections of poets who perform their work. At the time this volume went to press (2012), Manchester had eleven independent publishers of poetry and fiction, ranging from New Leaf Publishing (formerly Gatehouse Books), which publishes fiction for adult learner readers,[6] to the prestigious poetry publisher Carcanet Press, and Shorelines, an agency committed to publishing the work of working-class migrants and their descendants. However, of these eleven publishing houses, only Carcanet's literary output receives serious, sustained critical attention from established literary reviewers.

Dawes observes that the 'boom time' for the print publication of British black poets has come and gone – with the 1990s representing its heyday – and that situation has appreciably worsened for black poets in recent years; Bloodaxe, which has traditionally published work by poets such as Jean 'Binta' Breeze and Benjamin Zephaniah, now publishes only collections by poets who already have at least one major title with a smaller press, while Canongate (a Scottish publisher based in Edinburgh) has closed an imprint called Payback Press (Dawes, 2005: 288), which was important in establishing the reputation of poets such as Manchester's Lemn Sissay, who was awarded an MBE for his services to poetry in 2009.[7] Payback Press published Sissay's landmark anthology of rap – and reggae-influenced poetry called *The*

Fire People (1998), a volume which included the work of many poets working outside London. The 2004 Decibel report on publishing poetry by British black and Asian writers, entitled *Free Verse*, found that only 8 per cent of Britain's black poets were published by major poetry publishers (Keane, 2004b: 4). Part of the problem, as Margaret Busby, the co-founder of the publishing company Allison and Busby, observes, is that 'there are fewer and fewer independents, as publishing becomes more corporate and conglomerate' (Busby in Sesay, 2011: 119).

Poetry publishing is unique in being an almost wholly non-commercial enterprise concentrated in the independent publishing sector. Owing to this non-commercial remit, much of the current debate about the state of publishing for black poets centres on the vexed issue of quality. Independent publishers have always emphasized the value of quality over commerce, not least because poetry brings tiny revenues and independent poetry publishers across the country rely on Arts Council support or publish fiction titles partly to subsidize their poetry publications (Dawes, 2005: 291). The politics of literary taste thus rears its ugly head since the question 'is it any good?' has retained its powerful – and unaccountable – currency in British poetry publishing. Whereas transnational fiction publishing houses are umbilically connected to celebrity authorship (what sells books is arguably the profile of the author as much as their textual content), notions of 'quality' remain central, if obscure, to publishers of poetry. For Dawes, the problem rests with traditions of 'taste', embraced (or inherited) by leading poetry editors, since such long-established preferences are inevitably predicated upon value-judgements (Dawes, 2005: 286). Bernardine Evaristo, author of *The Emperor's Babe* (Penguin, 2002), *Lara* (Bloodaxe, 2009a), *Blonde Roots* (Penguin, 2009b) and editor (with Daljit Nagra) of the recent anthology *Ten: Poets from Spread the Word* (Bloodaxe 2010), also argues:

> Unlike fiction in this country, which has been so enriched by British writers with origins in so many different cultures, many of whom enjoy great critical and commercial success, the selection criteria for poetry does not have to take into account commercial considerations to the same extent, and so editors' personal taste, which is justified by that most subjective of terms, 'quality', is more of a deciding factor. All the editors of [mainstream] poetry presses in this country are white, and this is generally reflected in their lists. (Evaristo in Keane, 2004a: 14)

For Dawes, the problem is that notions of quality have almost uniformly been used to exclude black poets from the lists of prestigious publishing houses. He believes that contemporary published poetry in the United Kingdom is characterized by 'arch-lyricism' with modernist leanings and 'classical groundings' in Shakespeare, Chaucer, Byron and Ted Hughes (Dawes, 2005: 286, 292). As argued in Chapter 5, Dawes perhaps overlooks the extent to which a significant proportion of British black poets have themselves embraced the modernist legacy. Nonetheless, his point remains that, while poetry publishing in Britain is dominated by a hallowed tradition of independent presses that prize poetic craft (of a demonstrable and highly specified kind) over commercial value, its gatekeepers will continue to hold the reins, and the opportunities for emerging British black and Asian poets to break into elite circles have diminished since the 1990s. When they do, however, the burden to represent black Britons or British Asians frequently exerts pressure on their work. Dave Gunning explores the ironies of such burdens in an essay about Daljit Nagra, whose poetry collection *Look We Have Come to Dover!* was published by Faber and Faber in February 2007: 'While Nagra has been lionized as "the voice of British Asian poetry", his verse actually serves to question the homogenization of diverse individuals and communities implied within such labelling' (Gunning, 2008: 95). Nonetheless, the expectation that such collections are representative is, as Gunning argues, symptomatic of a society 'structured by racialization' (Gunning, 2008: 95).

As noted above, black Mancunian poets have yet to be published by a top poetry publishing house and, as Dawes observed in 2005, what is happening across Britain in the bars, nightclubs and theatres to which Gioia (2003) refers is not currently reflected in the existing range of poetry titles by Britain's most reputable publishing houses. It is often local imprints, such as Crocus Books – one of a range produced by the literature development organization Commonword (see Chapter 4 for discussion of others) – that more accurately reflect this aspect of the literary scene and the evolving trends in work by poets who also perform their poems. This includes writers such as Segun Lee French (*Praise Songs for Aliens*, 2009), Maya Chowdhry (*The Seamstress and the Global Garment*, 2009) and John Siddique's well-received *Poems from a Northern Soul* (2007).

Another important British press in this regard is Flipped Eye Publishing, which emphasizes 'the writer's ability to communicate with a live audience',[8] and which published Martin De Mello's innovative collection *if our love stays above the waist* (2011). Flipped Eye's 'flap' series of poetry pamphlets are embossed by a large 'f', the contours of which mimic those of the curled 'f' of the famous Faber and Faber design. By referencing Faber and Faber, Flipped Eye's 'flap' series capitalizes on the prestige of an established poetry house yet also mocks its exclusionary practices by foregrounding its repeated acts of omission. The single 'f' of the 'flap' series, however, is not quite the mirror image of the double 'f' of Faber and Faber's logo. By bringing the letter's crossbar mid-way down the stem, the Flipped Eye 'flap' series 'f' resembles a pound sign, indicating its status as Faber and Faber's poor relative and foregrounding its own limited budget and resources. Presses that publish work by Manchester-based poets simply cannot compete with the national and global distribution networks of established transnational publishing houses. The single 'f' has another function, however, in asserting its legitimacy as a parallel publishing outlet. It evokes the 'f' word as though to direct it at the group of poetry editors who are often derided as 'the white poetry establishment' and mocked in poems such as Sissay's 'Olympic Invocation' (see Chapter 5).

The politics of literary approbation

Eleven years after the publication of Joe Pemberton's novel *Forever and Ever Amen* (2000), the Manchester-born poet Lemn Sissay[9] became the first commissioned poet for the 2012 Olympics. Sissay is an influential figure in Manchester. He worked at Commonword which, as noted in his statement at the head of this chapter, quickly established itself as the largest writing and publishing organization in the North West. As discussed in Chapter 4, Commonword was established with the support of the Federation of Worker Writers and Community Publishers in the 1970s and Commonword's sister organization, Cultureword, was established in 1986 as a centre for black creative writing. In his role as Cultureword's literature worker and convenor of the 'Tight Fisted Poets' group, Lemn Sissay was central to this endeavour and nurtured new writing talent among many of Manchester's black and Asian writers.[10]

More recently, the Olympic commission has provided a welcome return to the limelight for one of Britain's leading poets, firmly defining Sissay as a poet of national and international, as well as regional, significance. However, this literary accolade is very much an exception to the general rule. As this book argues, most devolved, or regional, articulations of British blackness simply do not register on the radar of major publishers, reviewers and the international readerships that they generally serve.[11]

Significant as it is, Sissay's work is a drop in the ocean of Britain's regional writing.[12] However, justified as is Sissay's success, it seems worth examining how a black, Mancunian poet came to be awarded such an accolade. The key to this question lies in the devolved nature of poetry publishing. Although the major newspaper reviewers and publications such as the *Times Literary Supplement* and *The London Review of Books* are London-based, poetry publishing itself has never centred on the city of London. As Peter Kalu argues, while the publication of novels is concentrated in the hands of publishers in Britain's capital city, the non-commercial nature of poetry publishing means that poets are not quite subject to the same degree of London hegemony as novelists.[13]

Equally significant is the distinctive topography of poetry in performance. Sissay is a poet who is skilled at performing his work, with an established track record of drawing large audiences for his poetry in a wide range of performance venues. After the year 2000, he increasingly harnessed the power of information and communication technologies to transmit his poetry. He was one of the first to engage regularly with audiences through social media sites such as Facebook and Twitter as well as on his blog called 'The Emperor's Watchmaker'.

The following discussion thus attempts to account for Sissay's rise in popularity and status, tracing the route he has taken to his prestigious Winning Words Olympic commission. (Winning Words commissions were awarded also to Carol Ann Duffy, John Burnside, Caroline Bird and Jo Shapcott.) It is not my intention to detract from Sissay's talent as a poet in accounting for his success against the odds. Sissay is an important wordsmith and innovator with a remarkable track record in pioneering British landmark poetry; his rise in status is hard-won and widely welcomed. Nonetheless, it seems important to remove the work of poets from the arena of value-judgement. The wider aim, here, is to understand the politics of literary approbation and to gain insights into the extent to which this approbation relates to the cultural politics of belonging to multiracial Britain. Furthermore, given the generally low profile and status of poetry by black, working-class, northern writers, it seems important to consider the extent to which Manchester's next generation of poets are likely to attain similar levels of international status in Britain's shifting poetry publishing landscape.

At the time of his Olympic commission, Sissay had five published poetry collections: *Tender Fingers in a Clenched Fist* (Bogle L'Ouverture, 1988), *Rebel without Applause* (Payback Press, 2000, originally published by Bloodaxe (2000)), *Morning Breaks in the Elevator* (Payback Press, 1999), *Listener* (Canongate, 2008) and *The Emperor's Watchmaker* (Bloomsbury, 2000), together with an influential edited anthology of work by black poets called *The Fire People* (Payback Press, 1998). Bogle L'Ouverture has long been credited with launching the career of established poets such as Linton Kwesi Johnson, whose *Dread, Beat and Blood* it published in 1975. As Dawes has pointed out, however, Payback Press no longer publishes work by poets associated with the performance scene, while Bloomsbury's publication of Sissay's poetry for children was predicated on a reputation he had earned by means of work published and promoted by the independent poetry publishing sector during the late 1980s and 1990s. As things stand, the traditional publishing route is unlikely to serve Manchester's younger poets as it has the work of Sissay.

Since the year 2000, Sissay's poetry career has really taken off. He frequently embarks on worldwide poetry tours and is a regular contributor to BBC radio, which has also dramatized a number of his plays.[14] In 2011, Sissay announced on his 'The Emperor's Watchmaker' blog that he was the first commissioned poet for the 2012 London Olympics.[15] One of his poems, called 'Spark Catchers', is etched into a wooden structure that houses an electricity transformer in the Olympic Park (now a permanent feature). As Chapter 5 discusses, 'landmark poetry' is integral to Sissay's poetics. In its commitment to hidden working-class histories, 'Spark Catchers' is faithful to Sissay's long-standing ethical commitment as a poet. The poem is inspired by the women who worked in a match factory on the site of the 2012 Olympics. Sissay wanted to write a poem about the Bryant and May match factory, which has since been converted into luxury apartments. The women who worked in the factory were prone to cancer and jaw disease due to the phosphorus that they handled. Sissay investigated the trade union activities of the factory women, who went on strike in 1888, and his poem was partly inspired by an essay by the suffragette Annie Besant called 'White Slavery in London', which was written in support of the strike: '[L]et us strive to touch their [manufacturers'] consciences, i.e. their pockets, and let us at least avoid being "partakers of their sins", by abstaining from using their commodities' ('The First Olympic Poet' in Sissay, 2010). Seizing the opportunity to retell the women's forgotten story for 'posterity', Sissay wrote the following lines:

> The greatest threat to their lives was a spark
> The sulphurous spite-filled spit of Diablo
> So they became spark catchers. Strike.
> (Sissay, 'The Emperor's Watchmaker', 8 March 2011)

In many senses, Sissay's poem counters the celebratory spirit of the Olympic Games by indirectly drawing attention to what anti-Olympics campaigners have implied is a public relations exercize aimed at reducing the visibility of the host country's gangs, riots, anti-strike strictures and underpaid immigrant labour.[16] Sissay's blog suggests that his poem is intended as a permanent reminder to the residents of the Park's many luxury flats that the Olympic Park represents an act of cultural palimpsest: one that promotes a form of amnesia about working-class histories associated with the site. In this way, 'Strike' counters the gentrification of working-class areas on the site of the new Olympic village.

The modern Olympic Games are guided by particular ideals, ideals that have particular resonance for the politics of literary approbation. Schools around the world receive information sheets from the International Olympic Committee about the Olympic creeds, mottos and symbols. The Olympic motto is *Citius, Altius, Fortius*, which means 'Swifter, Higher, Stronger' and embodies the Olympic spirit.[17] This Olympian ideal is arguably also embraced by poets who participate in popular 'poetry slams', an art form (whereby individuals perform their poems in open competition with one another) that arrived in Britain from the United States in the 1980s. The US poetry slams sprang up in venues across the nation, eventually leading to the creation of a high-profile National Slam. Soon afterwards, the slam established itself in Britain and Sweden and this, in turn, gave rise to international events such as the annual 'World Poetry' and 'Women of the World' slams (Somers-Willett, 2009: 4).

There are important parallels, then, between the Olympian ideals and the democratization of poetry, not least because a competitive element has been built into the poetry performance, which embraces the Olympian motto that it is not the winning that matters so much as the taking part (see Chapter 5 for a discussion of earlier manifestations of the Poetry Olympics). Crucially, as Gioia (2003) and Somers-Willett (2009) also each observe, slam poetry is related to a counter-cultural desire to move away from the 'highbrow' poetry readings associated with universities, critics and publication outlets. Both celebrate the fact that these institutions are no longer key arbiters of taste because the poetry slam has developed more democratic approaches to valuing one poem over another[18] (Gioia, 2003: 26; Somers-Willett, 2009: 4, 20). A key feature of evaluating this poetry is by means of Olympic-style scoring. The US-based organization Poetry Slam Inc. (PSI) was set up to administer slams, and PSI-certified slams allow poets three minutes and ten seconds to perform their poems. Scoring is done by volunteers from the audience by scoring from 0 to 10 in the Olympic style (Somers-Willet, 2005: 52). Gary Mex Glazner draws the following comparisons between the Olympics and modern poetry slams in *Poetry Slam: The Competitive Art of Performance Poetry* (2000). He writes:

> Holding poetry competitions is not a new idea. The Greeks gave laurel crowns to the winning poets in the ancient Olympics ... Basho made his living traveling the Japanese countryside judging haiku contests. (Mex Glazner, 2000: 11)

Taken in this context, Sissay's success with the Olympics commission begins to make cultural and poetic sense. Indeed, it seems a fitting tribute to the surge in poetry's popularity since the 1980s, discussed in detail in Chapter 5. His success suggests that early twenty-first-century developments in poetry, such as the burgeoning performance scene, new modes of transmission and landmark poetry, are very much happening off the printed page.

At the same time, British anti-Olympics campaigners and arts organizations are quick to point out that Arts Council funding was diverted from a large number of grassroots arts organizations, including the famous Centreprise[19] – which runs the WordPower Book Fair, dedicated to black diasporic literatures in the United Kingdom – to pay for the 2012 Cultural Olympiad, which ran from 2008 and culminated in a major poetry festival based at the Southbank Centre in London in 2012 called the Poetry Parnassus. This festival had a global focus and employed interpreters and translators in order to ensure that languages other than English were represented. Campaigners from the Big Lottery Refund noted that £425 million, initially destined for community groups, was diverted to the Olympics with catastrophic results since a government announcement suggested that this amount would be 'potentially' repaid to the Big Lottery by the year 2031 (see www.biglotteryrefund.org.uk).

When Sissay was awarded the poetry commission he was already based at the Southbank Centre as a writer in residence. By that time he had become increasingly associated with London rather than Manchester (although not by Mancunians). The official website of the Winning Words commission even refers to him as 'local [i.e., London-based] and renowned poet, Lemn Sissay'.[20] One of Sissay's blog entries in 2012, entitled 'Making Morning Coffee at My Local Deli', simply states, 'I live in Clapton Pond'[21] ('The Emperor's Watchmaker', 3 April 2011), an accurate statement of course, but in literary terms a crucial one.

As Chapter 1 has already outlined, Manchester's literary scene raises compelling questions about the necessary conditions by which the provincial *can* compete with the metropolitan and win. It might well worry the emerging black Mancunian poets, too, that Sissay's profile as a poet of international standing seems subtly predicated on a gradual distance from, and even erasure of, his northern identity. Such erasures – despite Sissay's ongoing loyalty to Manchester – are indicative of the cultural politics of belonging, a politics dominated by what James Procter describes as the collective national 'nostalgia for a neighbourly, white working-class community that depends on an image of the north existing as a cultural remove from multiracial Britain' (Procter, 2006: 73). Further, as Chapters 4 and 5 demonstrate, the politics of cosmopolitan multiculturalism has very evidently been to the detriment of black poets outside London, who are typically overlooked in favour of those who have already gained a foothold in the London literary scene which remains the perceived locus of literary and cultural innovation in the national imagination.

With the depletion of funding for regionally based poetry publishing outlets, this situation seems unlikely to improve in the medium term. In the 2004 Decibel report, commissioned by the Arts Council, researchers found that the majority of black poets surveyed expressed a need for writing mentors (Sesay in Keane, 2004b: 18), a need that cannot be met without a significant increase in current funding levels. The primary recommendations of the Decibel *Free Verse* report was that 'funding is needed to establish development programmes for black and Asian poets whose work is not page ready' (Keane, 2004b: 27). Clearly, any progress that has been made in that respect since 2004 is now (in the recession of 2012) unlikely to be sustained.

In many respects, then, it is possible to read the 2012 Winning Words commission as a form of national poetry slam. Judged by the poet laureate, Carol Ann Duffy, and the bestselling novelist Sebastian Faulks,[22] Winning Words is an influential arbiter of literary taste, not least because it determines whose poetic words have a permanent presence in the Olympic Park. In one sense the outward-facing, globally inflected nature of the Olympic Park is conducive to the strategy of bypassing the partisan politics of literary approbation by seeking international audiences who will be usefully innocent of Britain's national literary bias against regionally based black writers.[23] The senior editor and co-founder of Flipped Eye publishing even observes: 'I actually advise young black poets that if they want to be taken seriously, they should go and get published in the United States and it's sad that I say that because I can only publish three a year' (Parkes in Sesay, 2011: 153). On the other hand, the exceptionality of Sissay's success as a northern, black, working-class poet is indicative of a broader tendency to fetishize a select number of black poets at the expense of a far less visible majority.[24] Like the Booker Prize, the Winning Words commission risks, in Graham Huggan's words, 'rewarding writers that are already established on the international market, thereby, in the words of George Bernard Shaw, throwing "a life belt ... out to a swimmer who has already reached the shore"' (Huggan, 2001: 118), leaving the rest of Manchester's black poets standing on the riverbanks of relative obscurity. Paralleling the discussion of the cultural politics of belonging in Chapter 5, the Winning Words commission acts as yet another literary gatekeeper, embracing a highly selective cultural politics of belonging for British black poets.

Luis Cantarero argues that the Olympic Games have a long association with the ancient Greek oral traditions and, like Homeric poetry, are predicated upon two defining ideals: 'to provide entertainment and to construct a social order' (Cantarero, 2006: 99). I deal first with the issue of entertainment. As Gioia (2003) argues, poets' favoured modes of transmission means that popular poetry of the early twenty-first century is increasingly aligned with the entertainment industry. This is partly because its performance dimension is particularly amenable to multi-media experiences and forums. As Somers-Willett (2009) points out, '[s]lam poetry ... has undeniably and fundamentally changed the relationship between ... popular audiences and poetry ... in tandem with other popular manifestations of the lyric in mass media such as hip-hop and spoken word' (Somers-Willett, 2009: 11). As she also points out, this raises powerful questions about its potential complicity with poetry's commercialization. Bob Holman has observed that the three-minute slam performance is also the length of a pop song (in Somers-Willett, 2009: 6), while poetry in performance has 'penetrated mainstream commercial markets in the United States, finding its way into McDonald's advertisements, Partnership for a Drug-Free America public service advertisements, *MTV News*, and episodes of The Simpsons' (Somers-Wilett, 2009: 6). As Chapter 5 will go on to discuss, this runs counter to the dominant ethics and poetics of black Mancunians such as Peter Kalu, SuAndi and, very much, of Sissay himself.

Nonetheless, as Gioia (2003) and Somers-Willett (2009) have also argued, new information and communication technologies are ideally suited to poets who like to perform their work to large audiences. Sissay has wholeheartedly embraced these new technologies and, as discussed in Chapter 5, the ethical thrust of his work steadfastly resists commodification. The question nevertheless remains as to how regional black and Asian writers are likely to fare in the brave new world of e-books and social media. Many Manchester writers and performers, such as Joe Pemberton, Afrique Like Me and Young Identity, discussed in Chapter 5, are embracing social media just as Sissay has done, adding another crucial dimension in this short history of Manchester's alternative publishing scene to which I now turn.

Technology

The Manchester novelist and social media specialist Zahid Hussain argues that British black and Asian writers should be quick to take advantage of new technology.[25] In the first six months of 2011, there were 12.7 million e-book downloads in the United Kingdom, which was up 101 per cent on the previous year, while e-book sales in Britain increased 600 per cent during the year 2011.[26] While, as Kei Miller argues, the paper-based book will long be fetishized as a 'physical souvenir' of each valued reading experience, he also argues that there is no need to be nostalgic about the 'process of [writing's] re-mediation' and that, just as the advent of the CD did not mean the end of music, the e-book does not mean the end of writing. He argues that black writers, struggling to gain acceptance by the mainstream, should most certainly exploit literature's new mediums. With similar optimism, Hussain argues that 'it's always been about the story: as long as we exist, the story will exist'.[27]

There remains some doubt, however, in the independent publishing

2.1 Poster advertising 'Young Identity's' showcase. © Young Identity.

industry about the longevity of e-books. While they may be enabling in some respects, they also raise serious questions about the status and legacy of the texts concerned. In 2008 the Arts Council commissioned a report, entitled *Read: Write. Digital Possibilities for Literature*, to investigate how 'funded organizations might achieve greater sustainability, self-sufficiency or lower costs by making use of technology' (Harrington and Meade, 2008: 6). Its authors, Mary Harrington and Chris Meade, acknowledge that, while e-books save money on printing costs and partially negate the need for professional gatekeepers, it remains unclear how writers and publishers will actually make money or gain meaningful recognition for their writing. The report concludes that '[n]either Mary [Harrington] nor Chris [Meade] see a clear pathway to economically-sustainable online publishing' (Harrington and Meade, 2008: 64). Moreover, Jeremy Poynting, who established Peepal Tree Press, observes that digital piracy remains an issue for under-resourced publishing houses, since it is common practice for the owners of e-book readers to share titles illegally rather than buying them.[28] Equally problematic for the independent sector is the new generation of young readers who are accustomed to downloading free music and are therefore decreasingly willing to pay for e-books. Nii Parkes, the founder of Flipped Eye Publishing, argues that, while he is comfortable with providing free literary content for people with a low salary, he is reluctant to do so for wealthy readers.[29]

At the time of going to press (2012), the publishing industry – both academic and commercial – readily acknowledges itself to be in an extended transitional period with an end point that is as yet unknown. A survey by Peepal Tree Press found that those who read its books like to build their collections of paper-based books by Caribbean authors since, as Nii Parkes also observes, e-books cannot yet compete at an aesthetic level with physical books.[30] Indeed, the most often-voiced prognosis – across many different fields of publishing – is that the printed book will continue to exist in tandem with its digital counterpart, but the jury is out on the ratio or how, exactly, publishing is going to continue to protect the sales, and elite status, of its authors.

Social media clearly have enormous potential for publishers of writing by black writers and other marginalized groups of authors. As the case of Pemberton's novel *Forever and Ever Amen* indicates, once a manuscript is accepted, it is frequently subject to commercial doubts regarding the perceived breadth of its potential readership. The novelist Diran Adebayo argues that 'a big publisher probably won't take you on unless they feel that [a] white middle class readership, mainly in the South of England ... are likely to buy your book' (Adebayo in Sesay, 2011: 120). Partly because of the novel's provincial setting, and partly because he is a black writer, Pemberton believes that, while the marketing team at Hodder stated that his novel was aimed at a crossover market, their marketing strategies suggested that they believed its chief appeal was likely to be to a regional black audience and the novel was accordingly subject to a modest but relatively narrowly focused marketing campaign (Fowler, 2008: 76). By contrast, as Mantel believes, *White Teeth* (2000) was the product, rather than the focus, of a marketing and publicity campaign that 'started well before the book was in the shops or even sent out to reviewers' (Mantel in Fowler, 2008: 79).

Literary economy is an important concept here, since, while decisions about marketing have a commercial rather than a literary basis, many of the decisions are predicated on assumptions about likely readerships. Adebayo notes that most published novels, for example, fall into obscurity because large publishers make selective judgements about marketing budgets by concentrating on ten or so novels that seem likely to appeal to large readerships (Adebayo in Sesay, 2011: 121). As Jeremy Poynting observes, such decisions are rarely editor-led since it is largely accountants who take responsibility for making judgements about a novel's likely appeal.[31] Nonetheless, at the commissioning stage, the issue remains that editors are overwhelmingly white and middle-class. Indeed, when this book went to press (2012), there was only one black editor working in Britain (Busby in Sessay, 2011: 138). Speaking of her years as a commissioning editor, Busby argues that selecting books for publication has strong class and cultural dimensions. She published black writers partly because she 'was connecting with them ... editors tend to, with the best will in the world, take on things that they connect with – and so if you have a very un-diverse publishing workforce, you're going to get certain books published ... Monica Ali [and ...] Zadie Smith ... are all Oxbridge' (Busby in Sesay, 2011: 123). However, it seems important to qualify such observations, which resonate with Adebayo's words about Smith's *White Teeth* earlier in this chapter. While Ali and Smith are in some ways beneficiaries both of the North–South literary divide and of exceptional literary networks, they cannot be said to be complicit either with this literary divide or with the often problematic commodification of their work. Not only is Smith's novel *White Teeth* resistant in many places to celebratory visions of multiracial London, but Ali, having attained literary success, and perhaps reflecting her own Bolton roots, significantly complicates the North–South literary divide in her London-based novel *In the Kitchen* (2010). This text features a northern-born chef struggling to find his feet in London. The London–Manchester trajectory is, indeed, explored productively by many writers, including Mike Gayle, the crime writer Mike Phillips and Zahid Hussain (Cuban and Fowler, 2012: 295–315). Nonetheless, it remains the case that northern writers are hugely disadvantaged players in the world of publishing and literary recognition, with few managing to attain the status achieved by Ali, Sissay or Smith.

The *Read: write* (Harrington and Meade, 2010) and Decibel *Free Verse* (2004) reports indicate that social media potentially provide an opportunity to test the claims of commercial publishers that the literary output of British black and Asian writers cannot command large audiences. Nonetheless, further problems relate to the way writing is categorized by publishers. The Manchester-based children's author Jacqueline Roy notes that writing for children which is authored by a British black or Asian writer is invariably sub-categorized as 'issue' literature rather than being placed according to its actual genre. Busby argues that 'in certain quarters of publishing, there's a notion of what is authentically "black" … I'm sure there are black writers who've written science fiction and not got taken on' (Busby in Sesay, 2011: 126). Even after a manuscript has been accepted for publication, black children's writers may therefore be seen to encounter promotional problems similar to those experienced by Pemberton since marketing departments will seek to target niche markets of young black readers rather than a broader juvenile readership.[32]

Perhaps fittingly, for a book entitled *Postcolonial Manchester*, the distinctive diasporic consciousness of many writers and independent publishers in northern England promotes global perspectives on the development of e-book technology. Peepal Tree Press has found that readers living in the Caribbean express an overwhelming preference for paper-based books. The Yorkshire-based poet and blogger Simon Murray argues that e-books remain an elite technology that is acquired unevenly in ways that reflect global distributions of wealth.[33] Manchester-based Adam Lowe similarly observes that e-books have an environmental impact; while they save paper, the energy used to power them generates considerable carbon emissions that blight those areas of Africa where the demand for cheap, raw materials potentially perpetuates conflict.[34] Meanwhile, Parkes, Murray, Miller and Lowe all advocate that British black writers should promote alternative routes through information and communication technologies by adopting strategic yet ethical perspectives on e-books' use and potential.

Self-publishing before the e-book

Long before the advent of e-publishing, of course, Mancunian writers were proactively involved in publishing their own work. I end this chapter by considering the case of Blackscribe, which is described by its former members as Britain's first black feminist poetry collective. In keeping with the spirit of this book, I devote a few short pages to the work of this collective and its associates, hoping to draw attention to Britain's vast hidden literatures which – for compelling practical reasons – lie beyond the reach of critics, writers and scholars.

Although SuAndi (a founder member of Blackscribe) established an international reputation as a poet, there are few traces of the pioneering collective's existence today other than limited copies of a poetry anthology, an autobiography by the group's oldest member, Victoria McKenzie, called *Just Lately I Realise*[35] and a handful of leaflets advertising its performances in Birmingham's Vanley Burke archive.[36]

A subsequent women's poetry collective, called Nailah, produced a number of home-made anthologies containing poems about life in Moss Side and dealing with wider struggles against racism and domestic violence.[37] Nailah's many performances for audiences in Moss Side and beyond had a specific political dimension. Inspired by the poetics and politics of Britain's 'Windrush' poets such as Linton Kwesi Johnson, Grace Nicols[38] and John Agard, Nailah's poets sought to convey a devolved sense of struggles and hardships suffered by their local community. Nicols's determination to represent the experience of black women in her poetry (Williams, 2011: 37) was particularly influential in this regard: like her, the Nailah poets found that writing gave them a greater sense of control over a world in which they were under-represented (Williams, 2011: 37). By their own account, their collective expression of their role as 'poet-as-historian' (as discussed in Chapter 5) has a distinctively local orientation and sensibility.[39]

Concurring with the cultural history of Manchester outlined in Chapter 1, the former Blackscribe and Nailah member Elaine Okoro argues that the late 1980s was distinctive era in Manchester when there was a good deal of grassroots community support for ventures like

Blackscribe and Nailah.⁴⁰ Performance spaces were donated free of charge in venues such as Moss Side Community Centre, the Revolutionary Education Development Venues and the Nia Centre, all of which have since closed. Nailah members performed their poems for free, raising money for all kinds of community concerns, from drumming groups for local children to organizations supporting the victims of domestic violence. Members of Blackscribe similarly raised money for concerns such as the Babini, a black children's home of which Lemn Sissay is patron. Blackscribe, meanwhile, regularly performed in Manchester's Green Room, where they received their first standing ovation for their alternative rendition of 'Island in the Sun' by Harry Belafonte Jr, who was widely credited with popularizing the Caribbean calypso. Blackscribe's version of the song featured a black female president. Former members of Blackscribe and Nailah identify 1988 as a watershed moment for the city's poetry in performance; in a concerted collective effort led by the Black Arts Alliance and Blackscribe, the city's black writers managed to persuade Manchester's prestigious Royal Exchange to host a major national event called 'The Revelations of Black'. The headline act was Benjamin Zephaniah, who performed to a packed-out theatre in St Ann's Square.⁴¹

Members of Blackscribe and Nailah were keen to capitalize on their growing popularity by making their poetry available in printed form. Many of these printed poems focus on the hardships of life in Moss Side, an area of Manchester that has traditionally received new immigrants. A prominent example of this is Pauline Omoboye's poem 'Innocent Until Proven Guilty', which achieves its moral force by evoking a local setting. The poem criticizes British policing by providing an eyewitness account of police mistreating a local black resident:

> Although quite innocent
> And still not charged
> The street is a courtroom
> The judge is the Sarge
>
> (Omoboye, 2004: 27)

The rest of the poem operates as a watchdog against institutional racism, highlighting the legitimacy of the speaker's sense of injustice: 'I was a witness / A witness I was'. This credibility is further augmented by means of a repeated refrain: 'I saw' (2004: 27). By mistreating the black Moss-Sider, however, the local police contravene the very legal principle that is enshrined in the poem's title ('Innocent Until Proven Guilty'). In legal terms, the speaker asserts, she is '*only* a witness' (my italics); so long as institutional racism persists, her words will not count for much in a court of law. By contrast, the speaker implies that her poem holds greater weight than her status as legal witness. The poem is clearly imbued here with the ethic of poet-as-historian; in her role as poet she has the power to 'tell you the story so sad and so true' (Omoboye, 2004: 27).[42] This no-nonsense political and aesthetic objective also goes some way to explaining why this group of poets, whose work originated as live performance and whose first concern was to move, and inspire, their audience on the day, were content to self-publish their work rather than to waste time trying to gain the approval of the literary mainstream. The aim here, after all, is manifestly not virtuosity on the page. What the text shares with many other poems in performance is a metrical form designed for both immediate apprehension and 'mnemonic retention' on the part of both poet and audience (Gioia, 2003: 29, 31). And Omoboye has indeed performed 'Innocent Until Proven Guilty' in multiple venues and settings as a rallying point against police misconduct.

Omoboye's poetry also chronicles the lives of first-generation migrants to Manchester. Her mother's exact date of arrival in the city is commemorated in the title of her poem '24th December 1956' (2004). Not only does the poem detail the hardships of her mother's life but it celebrates her achievements in overcoming them by ending on a triumphant note:

> She came
> She saw
> She conquered
>
> (Omoboye, 2004: 29).

A clear celebration of immigrant survival, the poem appropriates and subverts the ultimate colonizer's gloat: *veni vidi vici*. While the experiences of her mother might easily be generalized, the poem's Mancunian setting parochializes the immigrant's triumph: it is Manchester, and not London, that is here transformed into a familiar site of immigrant resistance.

Printed poetry is often valued for its ability to give poets' work longevity and it is therefore not surprising that Blackscribe and Nailah produced anthologies of their work. Nailah's anthologies were assembled page-by-page in Moss Side's[43] living rooms in a communal spirit that Okoro sees as emblematic of the times.[44] As discussed in Chapter 1, Dave Haslam has made similar observations about the city's 'do-it-yourself' spirit (Haslam, 2000: 117), noting that many of Manchester's musical and artistic developments have taken place without the mediation of agents, producers or record companies. Here, however, the question of legacy is a complicating issue. The last remaining copies of the Blackscribe anthologies tell a more sobering story about Manchester's 'do-it-yourself' spirit than Haslam's more celebratory commentary perhaps allows. Copies of the various anthologies are scattered among the houses of the poets who were involved in producing them; the rest lie rotting in cardboard boxes in the basement of the Greenhays Adult Education Centre in Moss Side.[45] Page poetry is often valued for its ability to give poets' work longevity and yet the early poetry of Blackscribe is most likely to exist in the memories of audiences who watched it being performed.

To conclude, then, there are clear advantages of new digital technologies for locally produced and distributed community publications such as these. Had Blackscribe been able to produce poetry anthologies in e-book form in the 1980s and 1990s – laying aside the technical challenges associated with rapidly changing technologies – their work might be more readily accessible today. So, while community and independent publishers cannot compete with the marketing budgets of transnational publishing houses, which ensure that bestsellers such as Simon Armitage and Tim Dee's edited *The Poetry of Birds* (2011) remain by far the most likely titles to be purchased and downloaded,[46] technology *does* allow community writers' groups to edit their own work and make it widely available, even if, as Adam Lowe argues[47] home-grown e-books cannot compete with e-books produced by teams of professional publishers.

Conclusion

With a particular focus on the challenges faced by Manchester's black and Asian poets, this chapter has aimed to provide some insight into the role played by Manchester's independent publishing houses – as well as the city's complementary tradition of 'live literature' and proud history of self-publishing – in creating and sustaining the city's distinctive literary scene. As we have seen, however, the obstacles to success have been – and continue to be – considerable. In theory, while novelists such as Pemberton suffer acutely for their devolved articulations of black British experience, the more regionally dispersed nature of Britain's non-commercial poetry publishers potentially weakens the London-based literary hegemony.[48] In practice, however, not one of Manchester's black and Asian poets has been published by one of Britain's best-reviewed publishing houses.[49]

Today (2012) Manchester has a thriving literary scene with five independent publishers of poetry and a history of committed literary activism spearheaded by figures as Lemn Sissay, SuAndi and Peter Kalu. While small local publishers such as Cheers Ta[50] and Flapjack Press were set up to cater for poetry that is also performed to live audiences, it is arguable that contemporary black poets – both in Manchester and across Britain – suffer from their association with the performance scene. The growing popularity of poetry in performance is acknowledged as an engaging cultural phenomenon, but those who perform their work are rarely recognized as 'poets' per se. As the poet Ruth Harrison argues: 'there are people within the established poetry network who don't approve of performance poetry, [who] don't think it's worthy of being published ... I think that works against a lot of poets who are coming from an oral tradition' (Harrison in Breeze, Agbabi, Tipene, Harrison and Bertram, 1999: 30). To add to poets' woes, the most prestigious poetry publishers are necessarily guarded by a tiny number of gatekeepers. Further, the historical moment that supported investment (both political and commercial) in British black and Asian poets as well as other oppressed and/or marginalized groups such as women and gay people (see Chapter 4 for further discussion) has arguably passed. The situation does not look set to improve; as Dawes (2005) has argued so compellingly, British black poets are decreasingly likely to find major poetry publishers for debut poetry collections (Dawes, 2005).

Nevertheless, as Gioia (2003) and Hussain[51] have both argued, it may be a cause for optimism that the reading public is more and more inclined to pursue multi-media experiences of poetry. As many of Manchester's poets recognize, this is a potential advantage for poets whose work remains closely associated with oral performance. While poetic developments associated with the performance scene are not represented on the pages of poetry collections from Britain's major publishing houses, then, they are represented on computer screens as well as in the nation's bars, theatres and nightclubs. With young audiences increasingly orientated towards audiovisual modes of transmission, it remains possible that black, regional poets can now exercize unprecedented degrees of autonomy to seek audiences for their work without the immediate need for expensive marketing budgets. While this allows them to develop new audiences, the perennial problem – as pointed out by Mary Harrington and Chris Meade (2010) – is that it is not clear how they will make money from their writing.

As this chapter has argued, Sissay's Winning Words commission was an exceptional case of a regional black poet from outside London gaining major recognition for his work. More pessimistically, it perhaps indicates a broader tendency in transnational publishing to fetishize a select band of black poets while simultaneously excluding their counterparts.[52] The chapter has thus asked whether the next generation of black Mancunian poets will be able to follow Sissay's route to critical approval. For reasons already explained above, it seems unlikely that they will be able to follow the traditional publishing route. If this road is now blocked, however, young emerging poets are beginning to explore the potential of e-books and print-on-demand publishing to promote their work to large and diverse national and international audiences. Nonetheless, it seems premature to conclude that social media and new communications technologies are *the* new route to democratizing poetry. There is a world of difference between, on the one hand, online reviews by the reading public or spontaneous audience applause at a poetry slam and, on the other, sustained critical attention[53] by poetry reviewers[54] for *The Guardian*, *The Daily Telegraph* or *The London Review of Books*. Further, so long as white poets continue to dominate the lists of Britain's seven top poetry publishers there remains the risk that poetry publishing embeds a prejudicial distinction between page and stage in its publishing practices. Democratizing poetry should be carefully distinguished from processes that ghettoize it.

At the time of this book's going to press (2012), therefore, the future seemed uncertain for British black poets. The post-2008 'austerity measures' have adversely affected a publishing sector that was already under-resourced. The funding to grassroots writing organizations has also been substantially depleted, partly because additional funding was diverted from these organizations to support the 2012 Cultural Olympiad. In the light of these cuts, it seems decreasingly likely that sufficient funding will be found to implement the recommendations of Decibel's *Free Verse* report that money be allocated to developing mentoring schemes of sufficient quality to allow a new generation of black poets to produce page-ready work.

As noted earlier in the chapter, Lemn Sissay considers his literature development work in Manchester one of his 'proudest achievements' (see epigraph). It is therefore a powerful irony that this work has been badly eroded by the funding cuts of recent times. But surely the most concerning development of all is the proposed closure of Centreprise as this book goes to press. Centreprise was founded nearly forty years ago as the country's foremost hub to serve black artists and writers, and its demise threatens to curtail the hard-won achievements of the writers, agencies and independent publishers across Britain who have struggled so hard to counter the exclusions of Britain's literary and cultural mainstream. We can only hope that enough independent arts and publishing organizations – like Commonword – will survive the present recession to keep recent history fresh and political commitment alive.

Notes

1 Email to Corinne Fowler, 14 August 2007.
2 Pemberton's novel was published by Hodder Headline Review. Smith's was published by Penguin.
3 This observation was first made by David Law (2004: 44) in his thesis '"Guddling for Words"'.
4 See James Procter's seminal study entitled *Dwelling Places. Postwar Black British Writing* (2003: 3–4).
5 Bhatt was born in India, Goodison in Canada and Miller in Jamaica.
6 Many of these books of short fiction are listed in the 'Moving Manchester' e-catalogue at www.transculturalwriting.com/movingmanchester.
7 Blogger Mark Attwood wrote in his blog: 'Lemn Sissay. Friend. Brother. Member of the British Fucking Empire!', www.markattwood.org/family-stuff/lemn-sissay-gets-an-mbe-in-new-year-honours-list/, accessed 2 March 2012.
8 http://uk.flippedeye.net/genres/, accessed 12 March 2012.
9 Sissay is of Ethiopian and Eritrean heritage and grew up in a care home in Manchester. He is patron of the Letterbox Club, a Booktrust initiative to deliver books to young people in care.
10 My interviews with Manchester writers, conducted on behalf of the 'Moving Manchester' project, confirm Sissay's achievements as Cultureword worker.
11 An honourable exception is Bloodaxe's *Out of Bounds* anthology edited by Jackie Kay, Gemma Robinson and James Procter, launched in June 2012.
12 See Corinne Fowler, 'A Tale of Two Novels: Developing a Devolved Approach to Black British Writing' (2008).
13 Written note to the author from Peter Kalu, 1 September 2007.
14 Sissay has a growing reputation as a playwright and one of his plays called

Something Dark was recently published in an anthology of plays called *Hidden Gems: Contemporary Black British Plays*, edited by Deirdre Osborne (2008).

15 'The First Olympic Poet', Friday 10 December 2010 in 'The Emperor's Watchmaker'. http://blog.lemnsissay.com/blog/_archives/2010/12/10/4700875, accessed 2 December, 2011.

16 This is taken from an information leaflet supplied to schoolchildren ahead of the Sydney Olympics in the year 2000. In 2010, meanwhile, an anti-Olympics group called the Olympic Resistance Network wrote: 'It is projected that the number of homeless in Vancouver will triple from 1,000 homeless people since the Olympic bid in 2003 to over 3,200 people by 2010. The hardest hit area has been Vancouver's Downtown Eastside (DTES), the poorest off-reserve postal code in Canada. At present, over 1,200 low income housing units have been lost in the DTES since the Olympic bid in 2003. Meanwhile, real estate speculation and gentrification has led to a projected 1,500 new market housing units, primarily condominiums, being built in the DTES. According to a report by the Geneva-based Centre on Housing Rights and Evictions, the Olympic Games have displaced more than two million people around the world over the last 20 years. This figure does not include the estimated additional 1 million displaced due to the Beijing Games.' http://web.resist.ca/~orn/blog/?page_id=2, accessed 6 September 2011.

17 This guiding principle derives from a quotation by Baron de Coubertin, the founder of the modern Olympic Games, who famously said: 'The most important thing in the Olympic Games is not to win but to take part, just as the most important thing in life is not the triumph but the struggle. The essential thing is not to have conquered but to have fought well', on page 114 of Bryan Forbes's book *International Velvet* (1978).

18 In the poetry slam, a general audience makes a judgement about a poem's worth by means of applause and Olympic-style scoring. As Susan Somers-Willett points out in her book *The Cultural Politics of Slam Poetry* (2009: 9), this puts 'the audience in the dual seats of consumer and evaluator with no critical middleman [sic]'.

19 Centreprise is based in Hackney, London. It was founded in 1970 to promote artistic and literary production by black writers in Britain. The Centreprise website can be found at www.centerprisetrust.org.uk/.

20 See www.london2012.com/games/olympic-park/art-in-the-olympic-park/poetry-in-the-park/winning-words-spark-catchers.php, accessed 12 March 2012.

21 Clapton Pond is in Hackney, East London.

22 The non-literary panel member was the BBC sports presenter John Inverdale.

23 Ra Page, of Comma Press in Manchester, advocates this strategy for short story writers, while poets such as SuAndi and novelists such as Qaisra Shahraz have established strong international followings.

24 See Sarah Brouillette, 'Authorship as Crisis in Salman Rushdie's *Fury*' (2005) and Graham Huggan, *The Postcolonial Exotic: Marketing the Margins* (2001).
25 Panel discussion at the Sixth National Black Writers' Conference, Manchester, Saturday 24 March 2012.
26 Rob Waugh, 'An e-book reader under the Christmas Tree?' The *Mail* online, 16 December 2011.
27 Zahid Hussain, panel discussion at the Sixth National Black Writers' Conference, Manchester, Saturday 24 March 2012.
28 Poynting in discussion at the Sixth National Black Writers' Conference, Manchester, Saturday 24 March 2012.
29 Nii Parkes, 'E-books and social media', panel discussion at the Sixth National Black Writers' Conference, Manchester, Saturday 24 March 2012.
30 Panel discussion at the Sixth National Black Writers' Conference, Manchester, Saturday 24 March 2012.
31 This point was raised by Poynting during a question and answer session after a panel discussion about social media and e-books at the Sixth National Black Writers' Conference, Manchester, Saturday 24 March 2012.
32 Jacqueline Roy, panel discussion at the Sixth National Black Writers' Conference, Manchester, Saturday 24 March 2012.
33 Panel discussion about social media and e-books at the Sixth National Black Writers' Conference, Manchester, Saturday 24 March 2012.
34 Panel discussion at the Sixth National Black Writers' Conference, Saturday 24 March 2012.
35 Date of publication unknown. McKenzie is deceased.
36 Vanley Burke amassed considerable material about black community arts organizations. His collection is housed in the Birmingham Archives and Heritage department of Birmingham City Council.
37 Elaine Okoro in interview with Corinne Fowler for the 'Moving Manchester' project, 22 September 2011.
38 One of Nailah's founder members, Elaine Okoro, was offered a reduced-rate place on an Arvon Foundation Writing Course, where she met (and cooked meals) with black writers outside Manchester for the first time, including Grace Nicols, Caryl Phillips and Ben Okri.
39 Tina Tamsho in interview with Corinne Fowler for the 'Moving Manchester' project, 29 September 2011.
40 Elaine Okoro in interview with Corinne Fowler for the 'Moving Manchester' project, 20 September 2011.
41 SuAndi in interview with Corinne Fowler for the 'Moving Manchester' project, 18 September 2011.
42 Omoboye, *Purple Mother* (2004).
43 Moss Side has traditionally housed immigrants to Manchester and their children. A *Manchester Evening Chronicle* series authored by Barry

Cockcroft in June 1958 called 'A Dream Ends in Squalor' explains how 'maligned' Moss Side's immigrant population was at this time (2 June 1958).
44 Elaine Okoro in interview with Corinne Fowler for the 'Moving Manchester' project, 22 September 2011.
45 I witnessed this while conducting archival research for the 'Moving Manchester' project in 2009.
46 Adam Lowe, panel discussion at the Sixth National Black Writers' Conference, Manchester, Saturday 24 March 2012.
47 Adam Lowe, panel discussion at the Sixth National Black Writers' Conference, Manchester, Saturday 24 March 2012.
48 I am indebted to the expertise of Peter Kalu here for first alerting me to the important differences between novel and poetry publishing for regional writers.
49 A possible exception is Kei Miller, published by Carcanet, who was born in the Caribbean and studied in Manchester before going to live in Scotland.
50 Cheers Ta was established to publish poets who perform their work. It published poetry by the now deceased – and highly popular – poetry slam champion Dike Omeje (*The Mindfield*, 2003) and by Mike Garry (*Mancunian Meander*, 2006). Flapjack Press, based in Salford, is similarly committed to exploring the relationship between the spoken and printed word. Its list includes Ben Mellor, Jackie Hagan and Dominic Berry.
51 Zahid Hussain in discussion at the Sixth National Black Writers' Conference, Manchester, Saturday 24 March 2012.
52 See also Graham Huggan's *The Postcolonial Exotic: Marketing the Margins* (2001) and Timothy Brennan's *At Home in the World* (1997).
53 I am grateful to my colleague Dr Lucy Evans for raising this important question. Dr Evans lectures in the School of English at the University of Leicester.
54 Nii Parkes argues that black reviewers are rarely if ever asked to write pieces unless they are about black writers: 'I don't mind reviewing black writers, but it's as if I'm not qualified to review anything [else] as a black writer' (Parkes in Sesay 2011: 131).

References

Ali, M. (2010) *In the Kitchen*. London: Black Swan.
Armitage, S. and Dee, T. (2011) *The Poetry of Birds*. London: Penguin.
Breeze, 'Binta' J., Agbabi, P., Tipene, G., Harrison, R. and Bertram, V. (1999) 'A Round-table Discussion on Poetry in Performance', *Feminist Review*, 62, 24–54.
Brennan, T. (1997) *At Home in the World. Cosmopolitanism Now*. Cambridge, MA: Harvard University Press.
Brouillette, S. (2005) 'Authorship as Crisis in Salman Rushdie's *Fury*',

Journal of Commonwealth Literature, 40, 137–56.
Cantarero, L. (2006) 'Los Juegos en la Trasmisión Cultural: Los Poemas Homéricos y las Olimpiadas en la Sociedad Oral Griega'. Unpublished paper.
Chowdhry, M. (2009) *The Seamstress and the Global Garment*. Manchester: Crocus.
Cuban, S. and Fowler, C. (2012) 'Carers Cruising Cumbria and Meals on the Mile: Migrants in Fieldwork and Fiction', *Mobilities*, 7:2.
Dawes, K. (2005) 'Black British Poetry: Some Considerations' in Sesay, K. (ed.), *Write Black, Write British: From post-Colonial to Black British*. (London, Hansib).
De Mello, M. (2011) *if our love stays above the waist*. London: Flipped Eye Press.
Evaristo, B. (2002) *The Emperor's Babe*. London: Penguin.
Evaristo, B. (2009a) *Lara*. Newcastle-upon-Tyne: Bloodaxe.
Evaristo, B. (2009b). *Blonde Roots*. London: Penguin.
Evaristo, B. and Nagra, D. (2010) *Ten: Poets from Spread the Word*. Newcastle-upon-Tyne: Bloodaxe.
Forbes, B. (1978) *International Velvet*. London: Macmillan.
Fowler, C. (2008) 'A Tale of Two Novels: Developing a Devolved Approach to Black British Writing', *Journal of Commonwealth Literature*, 43 (3), 75–94.
Lee French, S. (2009) *Praise Songs for Aliens*. Manchester: Commonword/Crocus.
Garry, M. (2006) *Mancunian Meander*. Manchester: Cheers Ta.
Gioia, D. (2003) 'Disappearing Ink: Poetry at the End of Print Culture', *The Hudson Review*, 56:1, 21–49.
Gunning, D. (2008) 'Daljit Nagra, Faber Poet: Burdens of Representation and Anxieties of Influence', *Journal of Commonwealth Literature*, 43 (3), 95–108.
Harrington, M. and Meade, C. (2010) *Read:write: Digital Possibilities for Literature. A Report for Arts Council England*. London: Arts Council.
Haslam, D. (2000) *Manchester, England: The Story of the Pop Cult City*. London: Fourth Estate.
Huggan, G. (2011) *The Postcolonial Exotic: Marketing the Margins*. London: Routledge.
Kay, J., Robinson, G. and Procter, J. (2012) *Out of Bounds. British Black and Asian Poetry*. Newcastle-upon-Tyne: Bloodaxe.
Keane, D. (2004a) *In Full Colour: Cultural Diversity in Publishing*. Manchester: Arts Council.
Keane, D. (2004b) *Free Verse: Publishing Opportunities for Black and Asian Poets*. Manchester: Arts Council.
Kwesi Johnson, L. (1975) *Dread, Beat and Blood*. London: Bogle L'Ouverture.

Law, D. (2004) '"Guddling for Words": Representations of the North and Northernness in Post-1950 South Pennine Literature'. Lancaster University. Unpublished PhD thesis.
McKenzie, V. *Just Lately I Realise*. Manchester. Date of publication unknown.
Mex Glazner, G. (2000) *Poetry Slam: The Competitive Art of Performance Poetry*. San Francisco: Manic D Press.
Omeje, D. (2003) *The Mindfield*. Manchester: Cheers Ta.
Omoboye, P. (2004) *Purple Mother*. Manchester: Crocus Books.
Osborne, D. (ed.) (2008) *Hidden Gems: Contemporary Black British Plays*. London: Oberon.
Pemberton, J. (2000) *Forever and Ever Amen*. London: Hodder Headline.
Procter, J. (2003) *Dwelling Places: Postwar Black British Writing*. Manchester and New York: Manchester University Press.
Procter, J. (2006) 'The Postcolonial Everyday', *New Formations: A Journal of Culture/Theory/Politics*, 58, 62–80.
Sesay, K. (ed.) (2011) *Black British Perspectives. A Series of Conversations on Black Art Forms*. London: Saks Publications.
Siddique, J. (2007) *Poems from a Northern Soul*. Manchester: Commonword.
Sissay, L. (1988) *Tender Fingers in a Clenched Fist*. London: Bogle L'Ouverture.
Sissay, L. (ed.) (1998) *The Fire People: A Collection of Contemporary Black British Poets*. Edinburgh: Payback Press.
Sissay, L. (1999) *Morning Breaks in the Elevator*. Edinburgh: Payback Press.
Sissay, L. (2000) *Rebel without Applause*. Newcastle-upon-Tyne: Bloodaxe.
Sissay, L. (2000) *The Emperor's Watchmaker*. London: Bloomsbury.
Sissay, L. (2008) *Listener*. Edinburgh: Canongate.
Sissay, L. (2010) 'The Emperor's Watchmaker', http//: blog.lemnsissay.com/blog/archives/2010/12/10/4700875.html.
Smith, Z. (2000) *White Teeth*. London: Hamish Hamilton.
Somers-Willett, S. B. A. (2005) 'Slam Poetry and the Cultural Politics of Performing Identity', *The Journal of the Mid-Western Modern Language Association* (Summer), 51–73.
Somers-Willett, S. B. A. (2009) *The Cultural Politics of Slam Poetry: Race, Identity and the Performance of Popular Verse in America*. Ann Arbor, MI: University of Michigan Press.
Waugh, R. (2011) 'An E-book Reader under the Christmas Tree?' *The Mail* online, 16 December.
Williams, N. (2011) *Contemporary Poetry*. Edinburgh: Edinburgh University Press.

Internet sources

http://blog.lemnsissay.com/blog/_archives/2010/12/10/4700875
http://web.resist.ca/~orn/blog/?page_id=2
http://uk.flippedeye.net/genres/
www.centerprisetrust.org.uk/
www.london2012.com/games/olympic-park/art-in-the-olympic-park/poetry-in-the-park/winning-words-spark-catchers.php
www.markattwood.org/family-stuff/lemn-sissay-gets-an-mbe-in-new-year-honours-list/
www.transculturalwriting.com/movingmanchester

3

Manchester's crime fiction: the mystery of the city's smoking gun

Lynne Pearce

Greater Manchester is frequently written and spoken about as one of the UK's top crime hotspots; and many of its districts (Hulme, Moss Side, Wythenshawe, Longsight, Whalley Range) rank high in those league tables used to provide a snapshot of the nation's most socially and economically deprived areas (Taylor, Evans and Fraser, 1996: 275–9;).[1]

It should therefore be no surprise that the fiction genre that has become most associated with Manchester in recent years is crime, although the extent of this output did impress all those of us working on the project. Altogether we have catalogued many scores of authors and titles which may be listed under the 'crime' umbrella, ranging from detective fiction (both private investigators and police procedurals) through to psychological thrillers, urban noir, science fiction and, indeed, a rich seam of 'black-market comedy' (for example, Zahid Hussain's *The Curry Mile* (2006) and Mike Duff's *The Hat Check Boy* (2008)). In this chapter I attempt to capture something of the diversity of Manchester's crime writing in the course of answering a simple but, I trust, provocative question: namely, who, or what, is responsible for the crime of Manchester? Who – as the title of the chapter asks – may we expect to discover brandishing the smoking gun? In advance of this investigation I should, however, like to share some thoughts on another striking feature of these texts (which I have written about elsewhere: Pearce 2007, 2012a, 2012b) and that is their achievement in capturing the urban landscape of the region at a particular moment in its recent history: in other words, the role crime fiction has played in *mapping* the changing economic, social and geographical environment of Greater Manchester.

Mapping

As discussed in Chapter 1, Manchester is a city whose industrial and colonial past is strikingly visible in its architecture and its division into districts, each with its own unique history and profile. Many of the literary descriptions of the city and its environs quoted in that chapter come from the crime fiction texts featured here, but it is, I feel, important to reiterate just how astute and important (in historical and political terms) these novels have been in capturing the changing social and cultural signification of the city's street-map over the past thirty years.

Inasmuch as these authors and texts deal in crime, it is hardly surprising that their descriptions of the city and its environs are acutely sensitive to 'safe' and 'unsafe' areas as far as the threat of robbery and possible violence are concerned. Take, for instance, this extract from Cath Staincliffe's *Dead Wrong* (1998):

> I was only five minutes from the well-appointed Deacon home but already the territory had changed. This was a much poorer area; the terraces along the road had doors opening straight onto the pavements. The place looked tired and drab and hard up. (Staincliffe, 1998: 123)

Of all the authors I work with in this chapter, Staincliffe is the one whose mapping of contemporary Manchester is arguably the most precise. In *Dead Wrong* (1998) alone (the third novel in her successful 'Sal Kilkenny' series), eight districts are name-checked (Belle Vue, Chorlton, Withington, Prestwich, Whitefield, Cheetham Hill, Whalley Range, Hulme) and their socio-economic ranking carefully documented. For example:

> Debbie Gosforth lived on Ivygreen Road, a street of terraced houses near busy Chorlton Green. Chorlton is a cosmopolitan district; the mix of housing means it caters for lots of different people. (Staincliffe, 1998: 130)

> They were big houses [in Prestwich], detached, each one a little different from its neighhour, with Tudor-style facades and leaded windows. Double-garage and gardener territory. (Staincliffe, 1998: 24)

> We drove north skirting Hulme where the infamous crescents had been demolished ready for rebuilding. Thirty years earlier the slum terraces had gone to make way for the shiny new walkways in the sky. Broken concrete, broken dreams. Cracked by poverty. (Staincliffe, 1998: 230)

As can be seen, these descriptions combine visual and aesthetic perception with a finely nuanced taxonomy of socio-economic class. Although, at times, this may be seen to be saying more about the social positioning of Staincliffe's PI than the city itself (Kilkenny, a white, middle-class liberal socialist who lives in Withington, is not without her own class prejudice and capacity for 'othering'), the texts, taken together, constitute a fascinating snapshot of Manchester's human geography from 1994 to the present. 'Mapping' is similarly a feature of Val McDermid's 'Kate Brannigan' series (also 1990s), though the name-checking of districts is not as extensive or precise (or, indeed, as closely linked to the nature of the crimes being investigated) as is the case with Staincliffe's work. Indeed, on this point it is interesting to note that in her award-winning psychological thriller *The Mermaids Singing* (2006), McDermid eschews a materially identifiable Greater Manchester for the fictional *Bradfield*. In her acknowledgements, McDermid refers to Bradfield as 'entirely a creature of my imagination' in what may be seen as an attempt to distance the horrors of serial killing from 'real-life' people and places. That this generic typecasting of 'a northern city' may ultimately prove more damaging to a region's reputation is, however, a concern to which I shall return.

Across the full range of texts researched for this chapter, it is also interesting to observe that certain locales or contexts feature repeatedly.[2] These are:

- Colonial space: the Corn Exchange, the Royal Exchange (see Chapter 1), the dilapidated mansions of Whalley Range, various gentrified warehouses across Greater Manchester (i.e. upmarket domestic housing post-1990)
- Industrial space: nineteenth-century terraced housing across the city and neighbouring towns or districts (i.e. 'Coronation Street'-style representation of 'the North')
- Moss Side and Hulme: the post-1960s new mid-rise 'estates' and their replacements
- Central Manchester Development Corporation (CMDC) inner-city regeneration sites: e.g. Castlefield, Salford Quays
- Canal Street and the Gay Village (post-1990)
- The Haçienda nightclub (home of the Manchester music and dance scene in the 1980s to early 1990s)
- The roads and motorways in, and leading out of, the city (especially Princess Expressway, Stockport Road, the M60 and M62)

- Specific districts or neighbourhoods (such as those cited in Staincliffe's novels, above)
- The Arndale Centre: site of the IRA bombing in 1996.

With reference back to my own mapping of 'postcolonial Manchester' in Chapter 1, we can see that most of these locations have the capacity to be thought of 'crime scenes' in more ways than one. As well as being the favoured locations for the fictional crimes under investigation, these sites are also symbolic, to a greater or lesser extent, of the political, institutional and corporate 'crimes' done to Manchester as the result of its colonial past and/or its neocolonial present; these include both the capitalist exploitation of the city's workforce (past and present) and the City Council's disastrous history of planning and (re)development.

Taken collectively, these locations may thus be seen to be the visible and material expression of the economic and social inequality that is part of Manchester's DNA (from the city's inception, the mill owners, managers and men occupied different districts) and the context ('reason') for its crime and social unrest to this day. While, in some instances, the links between the cityscape and inequality are obvious (i.e. both past ghettoization and present gentrification), others require further explanation: for example, the construction of the Princess Parkway divided the district of Moss Side in two, exacerbating the demise of that already struggling community (see Pearce, 2012a) for a full discussion of this); the Haçienda and other dance and music venues in the city played a crucial role in the integration of the diverse ethnic population of the city as well as becoming sites of drug-related crime (Haslam, 2000: 162–90); the rapid expansion of the Gay Village in the 1980s and 1990s is itself closely linked to the redevelopment and gentrification of areas like Castlefield and the opportunity for sex-related crimes including stalking, blackmail and the porn industry (Taylor, Evans and Fraser, 1996: 180–97); while the IRA bombing may (if controversially) be seen as the consequence of Britain's long-term colonial 'occupation' of Northern Ireland. As will be seen in the discussion which follows, Manchester's crime writers are, by and large, acutely aware how these historical and institutional forces have materially shaped city-space and frequently highlight the link between present crime and the social and cultural violence done to the region in the past.

Perception

It will be remembered that towards the end of Chapter 1 there is a short sub-section in which I explore the cognitive and metaphorical significance of the fact that, in a good deal of Mancunian fiction, the city is perceived through the window of a moving car. Many of the extracts I use to illustrate this discussion come from the pages of the city's crime fiction and, before moving on to the question that is the central preoccupation of this chapter, I would first like to register some of the other ways in which these texts have provided us with a sharp and discerning perspective of Manchester's 'mean streets'.

In her essay on transcultural British crime fiction, Patricia Plummer (2006) observes the way in which Mike Phillips's DI, Sam Dean, assumes the flâneur's mantle in order to 'bear witness' to the political practice of contemporary city life, in particular its racism and social or ethnic inequality:

> The private eye is thus established as the voice of the city. He reports about the misery and injustice of impoverished inner-city areas and the corruption and falseness at work in institutions and political parties. Phillips's detective novels thus assume a function established in realist British fiction since the nineteenth-century, namely that of social criticism. The journalist who records the social changes in the metropolis and appeals strongly to his audience's empathy invariably reminds one of the social reportage of Charles Dickens. (Plummer, 2006: 264)

While Plummer likens Dean's reportage to the realist novelist and the journalist, I would suggest that it is the figure of the flâneur that best captures the way in which the investigator (DI or PI) *looks* at the city: a type of perception that combines movement with a distinctive psychological profile: shrewd, wary, alienated, distrustful – and inclined to both pessimism and cynicism.[3] In other words, the perception of the investigator, like the flâneur (and, indeed, like the criminal), is predicated upon 'otherness': that is, his or her own othering of that which she or he sees. This, inevitably, provides our PIs and DIs with a unique perspective on their crime locations: at once razor-sharp and paranoid. The danger in which they operate (including, most especially, the threat to their lives) also lends their view of the world a particular intensity that may register beauty and wonder as keenly as it registers destitution and horror. Staincliffe's novels, for example, abound with these moments of heightened sensibility (registered, always, as moments in *time* as well as place) such as in this extract from her first novel, *Looking for Trouble* (1994):

> Once outside, a tremor of excitement enlivened me. This was more like it; the beginning of a trail. The night was cool, still. Dew on the car. Orange street lamps lit empty roads. I passed maybe a handful of cars on the way out of town. No queues, no crazy drivers, just the way I like it. (Staincliffe, 1994: 31)

It will be noted that here, once again, the PI's view of the world is 'from the driver's seat' and involves the quality of *moving through* a landscape or cityscape at speed in a way that is massively empowering: the PI in her car (if not on the streets) is temporarily protected, omniscient and predatory.

In his chapter 'Urban Noir: Mobility and Movement in Detective Fiction', Ben Highmore (2005) comments on the way in which:

> The ability to move, often unnoticed, through the city, the knack of reading the streets and interiors of the city, these are the skills that mark the classic detective of urban noir. (Highmore, 2005: 93)

He also observes, however, that this power is typically reserved for white males and observes that female, black and disabled sleuths have to 'make themselves invisible' in order to 'see and not be seen'; hence the importance of cars for PIs like Kilkenny and Brannigan. What is indisputable, however, is that investigators have to learn to see better, and see differently, than the general population in order to succeed at their jobs; and it therefore follows that, across the genre, we may expect to find especially vivid and unorthodox glimpses of the urban landscape – and Manchester is no exception.

Who, or what, is responsible for the crime of Manchester?

I now turn to the substance of this chapter: namely an attempt to answer the question 'who, or what, is responsible for the crime of Manchester?' As my preceding discussion has indicated, there already exists a substantive body of sociological and social policy research that has made an unequivocal link between the poverty and deprivation and the region's high crime rates – but how do Manchester's writers answer the question?

In my survey of crime fiction set in Greater Manchester, I have identified six answers to my question that recur across the texts, all of them demonstrating the way in which literature takes its cue from the sociological explanation yet also moves beyond it by bringing more complex psychological (and, indeed, narratological) factors into play. (Here it is important to remember that in 'detective fiction', though not necessarily psychological thrillers, the compulsion to bring the story of a crime to a satisfactory closure will inevitably impact upon how that crime is posited and understood.) I proceed, then, with my discussion of these 'six motives for crime', many of which, directly or indirectly, bear the mark of the region's colonial past and (post)colonial present.

Social inequality

It is an observational 'fact' that in cities (all cities) wealth and poverty sit cheek-by-jowl and it is clearly important not to make a special case of Greater Manchester in this respect. However, as we saw in Chapter 1, Manchester's rapid expansion into Europe's first great industrial city inevitably meant that its building, especially with regard to its domestic housing stock, was especially chaotic, and ill-thought-through planning and redevelopment have remained an issue ever since. There are certainly *no* Mancunian crime writers that I am aware of who are silent on this feature of the city's past, and their texts draw strong and clear connections between successive waves of urban redevelopment and crime; further, this failure of vision on the part of the planners includes the most recent (i.e. 1990s) 'regeneration' projects as well as the original slum-clearances and the repeated attempts to 'redevelop' districts like Moss Side and Hulme (see Chapter 1 for further discussion of both). As Highmore comments, with respect to the whole of the UK, any 'uneven development' of a region will be detrimental to the community as a whole in time:

> Gentrification is the dynamic of urban uneven development and a number of urban geographers have demonstrated the way that it is structurally reliant on processes of systematic neglect ... Seen as the solution to urban blight, gentrification needs to be seen as a process that is dependent on neglect and lack of investment. Such a process, the gentrification of one area, will, *at some point*, correspond to related disinvestment in another (the cycle is therefore constantly repeatable). As Rosalyn Deutsche puts it, there is a 'concealed relationship between processes such as gentrification and those of abandonment'. The decline of neighbourhoods, rather than being corrected by gentrification, is in fact its precondition. (Highmore, 2005: 104–5)

It could be argued, then, that while the socio-economic mapping of Manchester is by no means unique in the way in which conspicuous wealth and destitution exist in close proximity, the ongoing ghettoization of the city (from the time of the mill-owners to the post-yuppie present) has been instrumental in its unenviable reputation as one of the UK's top 'crime capitals'.[4] Meanwhile, although the starkest, and certainly most publicized, axis of social inequality in the region has an expressly ethnic dimension (see next sub-section) the 'white' crime fiction emanating from the region has plenty to say about social inequality and its consequences.

Both McDermid and Staincliffe began their private investigator series in the early 1990s when Manchester, in common with many of Britain's regional cities (for example, Glasgow, Newcastle, Birmingham), was riding the crest of the inner-city regeneration wave. Their female PIs (Kate Brannigan and Sal Kilkenny) are, however, wary and sceptical about social benefits of this manifestly 'uneven' (Highmore, 2005) redevelopment and expose the new inequalities it has given rise to (some of them linked directly to the crime under investigation).

McDermid's second Brannigan novel, for example (*Kick Back*, 2002 [1993]), shows the way in which the late 1980s and early 1990s property boom facilitated a wave of 'white-collar' crime in which 'ordinary people' (generally those in the low- to middle-income bracket) can become the innocent victims of fraudulent crime. In this somewhat convoluted mystery (which bears the epigraph 'Property is Theft'), the central story follows what happens when an ostensibly 'victimless crime' turns sour: a property developer (Lomax) and a solicitor (Cheetham) rake off interest from temporary mortgages by delaying the registration of Lomax's sales with the Land Registry. This is therefore a tale not only of personal greed but also of the capitalist opportunism that flourished at a particular cultural and historical moment; and what PI Kate Brannigan sees as she trails her criminals through the streets of Manchester in 1993 is a cityscape in which the inequalities of the region's past (symbolized by pockets of run-down nineteenth-century terraced housing) have been replaced by new ones[5] and converted into a fast buck by one of Thatcher's self-made men:

> The houses in [the computer file] RV were all in the seedier areas south and east of Manchester city centre – Gorton, Longsight, Levenshulme. The kind of terraced streets where you can buy run-down property cheap, tart it up and make a modest killing. Or, at least, you could until the bottom began to fall out of the North-West property market a few months ago. (McDermid, 2002 [1993]: 237)

In common with Staincliffe's PI, Brannigan is seen scrutinizing the properties which are at the centre of her crime with great acuity. Through her eyes we see both what they symbolize in terms of Manchester's manifestly unjust social history and their present currency vis-à-vis the contemporary crime scene. Further, what we see are 'real' and recognizable places in Manchester's 'A–Z':

> On the outskirts, he took the M63 towards Stockport. He turned off at the cheaper end of Cheadle, where you don't have to be able to play bridge or golf in order to be allowed to buy a house, and cut across the terraced streets that huddle round Stockport County's training ground. Tailing him through the tight grid of narrow streets was a lot trickier, but luckily I didn't have to do it for long ...
>
> We went through the same routine a couple of more times, in Reddish, then in Levenshulme. All the houses were elderly terraced properties in streets that looked as if they were struggling upwards rather than plunging further downhill. On the third house, it clicked. These were some of the more recent purchases in the RV file. (McDermid, 2002 [1993]: 247)

It is also worth noting, however, that Kate Brannigan sees all this not only as a PI 'casing the joint' but as a comfortably off, middle-class observer whose own house is described as 'one of "thirty professional persons dwellings"' and 'five minutes from every city centre amenity' (Mc Dermid, 2002 [1993]: 24). In this respect, the investigator is both an 'outsider' (see introduction to this chapter) and not: she bears witness to social inequality but from the safe confines of her car and with a desirable 'contemporary' home to return to.

Although very similarly situated to PI Brannigan in terms of social class and cultural outlook, Staincliffe's PI Kilkenny's perception of the world is subtly different from her peer's. Even as Brannigan's 'voice' is Chandleresque in register (the same cryptic summaries, the same self-deprecating jokes), so is her gaze directed by curiosity and her ('hermeneutic') need to solve the crime. By contrast, Kilkenny's apprehension of the world is supersensitive and, above all, empathetic. Although it is clear that Sal, too, sees the streets of Manchester with the eyes of a middle-class flâneuse, she is acutely, often painfully, aware of the smallest details of her locations and their inhabitants, and many passages of the text are dedicated to these moments of perception even when they apparently have very little to do with solving the crime. Take, for instance, this extract from *Missing* (2007b):

> It was another fine day, the central reservation was thick with dandelions and daisies, the trees along the edge of the playing field were lush and leafy, spilling shade across the road. An elderly woman, her back bent over, a Zimmer frame in her hands, made her way, bit by bit along the pavement. I wondered where she was going and whether she was relishing the summer day as I was ...
>
> The traffic lights changed and I moved forward towards the junction where another huge apartment block was being thrown up. BUY NOW! Screamed the hoardings. *Luxury Apartments, only a few remaining.* They are always luxury apartments, aren't they? Never standard or basic or no frills. (Staincliffe, 2007b: 67–8)

In this passage, as in many from across her oeuvre, Staincliffe's PI is Virginia Woolf-like in her apprehension of the scene before her as a unique coincidence of time and space.[6] A few minutes later, the woman will no longer be crossing the road; a few weeks later the dandelions will be no longer in bloom; and a few decades later the 'luxury apartments' advertized on the hoardings may well have gone the way of Manchester's other 'housing experiments'.

Possibly the most provocative of Staincliffe's Sal Kilkenny novels in terms of its focus on social injustice is *Bitter Blue* (also 2007) in which two of the 'victims' (an elderly couple known as Mr and Mrs Smith) die not as the result of a crime but because of social neglect (namely, the public's ability to 'turn a blind eye'):

> I didn't want to accept it. If there was a murder, there was someone to blame, a brutal, mindless, killer. Someone to catch, to punish. Without that ... nothing. Who was responsible, who would bear the guilt? ...
>
> Oh, Lord. I grimaced. My eyes pricked a little. In fashionable West Didsbury, in one of the richest countries on earth. They'd frozen to death. (Staincliffe, 2007a: 207)

Placing this 'mystery' (which is, ultimately, *no mystery*) alongside the others dealt with in the novel (the sad story of the 'psychopath' Lucy Barker, out to get revenge on her a doctor who has spurned her advances; and Minty, the victim of domestic abuse by her lesbian partner) nicely complexifies what counts as 'crime' in the early twenty-first century and prompts us to consider that collective social indifference can give rise to suffering every bit as terrible as that meted out by individuals upon one another (see 'Human Nature' below for further discussion of this).

Indeed, and as I have observed elsewhere (Pearce, 2012b), the notion that social inequality not only *leads* to crime but, in effect, *is* crime is implicit in a great many post-1990s Macunian texts whose action is set amidst the latest wave of inner-city development. Nicholas Blincoe's thriller *Manchester Slingback* (1998) is an especially good example of this. Jake's return to the city after a period in London elicits a peculiarly visceral response (he pukes in a taxi) to the city centre's post-IRA bomb 'makeover' and the narrative is threaded through with observations about what the façade is covering up. Not surprisingly, Jake's distrust is most acute when he visits Canal Street and the Gay Village, the scene of his past life and the sex-crime committed against him. Now, in the late 1990s, the area is almost unrecognizably prosperous:

> What he found there was coffee tables resting on a piazza outside a starkly clean modern bar, disco lights blaring out of the two storeys of glass frontage and skidding across the smooth surface of the canal. The canal itself, that was unbelievable. It had been flushed through and turned into a beauty spot. There was even a cutesy Japanese-style bridge leading to a new waterside café. It was still early but later Jake felt like he was stepping aboard a carousel. (Blincoe, 1998: 141)

Once again, Jake's response to what he sees is profoundly embodied ('As long as he could remain reflective, maybe he could keep on top of the buzzing in his head and his stomach' (Blincoe, 1998: 143)) and clearly predicated upon a suspicion of evil and violence lurking behind the clean and shiny surfaces; as he observes elsewhere: 'What it seemed like, the New Manchester Deal didn't extend as far as the backs of the buildings' (Blincoe, 1998: 137). As we shall see in a later section ('Institutional Crime'), Jake's 'reading' of the New Manchester is closely allied to the nature of the crime committed against him in the past: a crime that was similarly hidden and covered up by the supposedly 'great and the good' of the city.

Before leaving this sub-section, it is important to note (as I have elsewhere: Pearce, 2012b) that social inequality is not always synonymous with *social realism*. Although the texts so far considered may appear to be grounded in a detailed factual knowledge of the city at a given time, these representations are nevertheless the literary evocations of a genre whose narrative objective is to disturb, intrigue and create suspense. Therefore, even the most apparently objective and banal descriptions of the city must be seen to be abiding by the conventions of 'social realism', the literary mode, and *not* 'social reality' per se. As already noted, there is a significant body of crime-related literature emanating from Manchester which is decidedly *non-realist*. This includes Peter Kalu's futuristic Ambrose Patterson series and the cyberpunk fiction of Jeff Noon.

While there is not space to consider the latter in any detail within the remit of this chapter, it is clearly important to register that crime and 'crime as social inequality' are also the thematic preoccupation of both science fiction and cyberpunk to a greater or lesser degree. In terms of their visions of the future, meanwhile, it is worth noting that neither Kalu nor Noon predicts anything very good happening to Manchester. Rather, and as we shall see in the next section, our present ethnically drawn divisions will develop into outright apartheid (Kalu) and crime will become literally intrinsic to the cybernetic operation of everyday life (Noon). In the latter's *Pollen* (1995), for example, Manchester both is and is not recognizable as the city we know today. This is because material reality is now so confused with virtual reality that the streets of the city are only *one* of the places in which a subject 'lives'; and yet, inasmuch drugs, and drug crime, are integral to this future, the reader may not feel that far removed from the world of Karline Smith's *Moss Side Massive* (2000) (discussed below):

> Through the back window I saw a cop car's lights flashing. Its siren was loud, piercing. The Beetle took the corner onto Alexandra Road without slowing. Brid was clinging to the straps, desperate for sleep, her skin full of shadows, The Thing-from-Outer-Space was crying out for a fix ...
>
> Alexandra Park was a dark jungle shimmering the right side windows. We were skirting Bottletown by now and no doubt the park was full of demons: pimps, pros and dealers – real, Vurt or robo. (Noon, 1995: 9–10)

Linked by a century-long tradition of noir conventions, Noon's futuristic vision has much in common with the textual representations of the district's ignoble past (a past which has now, ironically, become a safe haven from the even grimmer present). Even in Noon's late twenty-first century, Alexandra Park (the park and the estate) is still there, and still host to 'criminal' activity, the key variant being that its perpetrators now include 'vurts' and 'robos' as well as humans.[7] What this confirms, I would suggest, is that the links between crime and social inequality are as much part of a literary tradition as they are of the statistics with which I opened this chapter. Social inequality undoubtedly does engender crime in the material world, but it is important to recognize that crime writing (from detective fiction to cyberpunk) has been as instrumental in imagining that nexus as in describing and reporting it.

Racial inequality

Karline Smith's *Moss Side Massive* (2000) is one of the best-known crime fictions to emanate from Manchester in recent times, not least because its purportedly 'negative' representation of Moss Side was a bone of contention for people living and working in the area. In *Manchester, England* (2000), Dave Haslam cites the youth worker Irvine Williams, who was one of Smith's critics:

> For him the book was another knocking exercise, the latest example of over forty years of negativity. He feels that a community has been criminalised, and that this has held back progress. (Haslam, 2000: 240)

The use of the adjective 'criminalised' here is, of course, interesting, implying as it does that Moss Side's 'crime' is the province of fiction rather than a social reality: a myth that writers like Karline Smith are creating rather than a history that they are recording. While this resonates, to a point, with my own emphasis on the literariness of crime fiction (above), the further implication that districts like Moss Side should not be avoided by crime writers because of possible negative connotations arguably overlooks the reading public's ability to distinguish 'fact' from 'fiction' – especially with story-lines as fastmoving (and, on occasion, as overtly fantastical) as Karline Smith's and Peter Kalu's.

In interview (2007), Smith is sanguine about the initial hostility to her first novel from the local, black community and focuses instead on the places where it had a more positive reception (she cites *The Guardian* and *Time Out*).[8] She also presents two, potentially contradictory, motivations for writing *Moss Side Massive*: first, the sharing of personal experience ('I wanted to tell the stories that touched a little bit about my life') and, second, a desire to 'entertain, educate and inform' a readership unfamiliar with Moss Side of the social circumstances that lead to gang culture:

> In the past people have said to me 'Oh, I didn't know that, I didn't know that black people experience this' or 'that was an eye-opener for me. I didn't think these issues affected black people in such a way', talking about issues like poor housing, education. They just didn't realize that there was a domino effect. (Fowler, 2007)

Following on from the previous discussion, what these comments would seem to suggest is that the author is fully aware of the fact that her text derives both from social reality via her own situated experience ('stories that touched a little bit about my life') and from an expressly fictional impulse: the desire to 'entertain and educate'. This clearly reminds us that while *Moss Side Massive* is 'about' crime in Moss Side it is also a crime *fiction* that, in the tradition of Lukács's 'social realism', will necessarily depend on all manner of literary conventions to make its point.[9]

The didacticism of Smith's text is, indeed, felt strongly in those passages where she spells out her unequivocal answer to the question 'who or what is responsible for the crime of Manchester?' For Smith, as the extract quoted above suggests, the gangland crime that has laid siege to Moss Side since the 1980s is the direct consequence of an ever-widening gap between 'haves' and 'have-nots': an economic and social divide which, in cities with a large or diasporic black population like Manchester, is also very markedly racially inflected. In the novel, Smith's narrator also makes clear that the social unrest consequent upon this divide was fuelled by the mushrooming consumerism of the Thatcher era. With reference to one of the novel's central characters she writes:

> Wherever he [Clifton] looked he was bombarded with reminders of the materialistic world that wasn't part of his existence: the top of the range sneakers, the expensive video games, the designer casual wear. Like many young kids his age, he wanted it all. He soon started figuring out that he could sell drugs on the side, while still at school. (Smith, 2000: 9)

The reason, then, that kids like Clifton (aka 'Storm') and Fluxy get into crime is simple: it is their only route to personal wealth and respect. The education system is difficult for children from their backgrounds to succeed in, and the benefits take too long: 'That was how society was set up ... All he could look forward to were minimum wage jobs' (Smith, 2000: 182–3). Drugs, meanwhile (especially from the 1990s onwards) provided both the opportunity and the means for crime. As Haslam observes, 'cocaine and crack replaced marijuana, alchohol and tobacco' and the arrival of heroin 'was to launch Moss Side into a dangerous era, precipitating ferocious gang warfare' (Haslam, 2000: 234). The crucial point to note here is that, for Smith at least, social inequality, compounded by racism, is what started Moss Side's 'criminalization': the drugs and gangs are merely part (albeit a deadly part) of the 'domino effect'.

One of the 'dominoes' which features in all the Mancunian crime fiction whose storylines take in the city's migrant and ethnic communities is the ghettoization of estates like Alexandra Park. As we have already seen, there is an argument to suggest that the city planning which caused the city to evolve into a chequerboard of affluent and deprived areas is, itself, responsible for the 'crime of Manchester'. However, a text like Smith's *Moss Side Massive* quickly reminds us that, no matter how they originally came about, the estates of Hulme and Moss Side are now owned by the drug-traffickers (even as the traffickers, themselves, are forever locked into a life of crime on that particular estate) (Pearce, 2012b).[10]

The territorialization of city-space is, indeed, another feature of crime fiction which combines sociological and aesthetic interest. While Smith's depiction of the carve-up of the Moss Side estate into rival zones is clearly based on historical fact (Haslam recounts how, from the late 1980s, two major gangs known as 'Gooch' and 'Pepperhill' took control of the Alexandra Park estate (Haslam, 2000: 234)), it may be argued that the *concept* of these dark and dangerous corners of city – its proverbial 'mean streets' – also have its roots in a long, literary-noir tradition, as Lee Horsley has observed with respect to the American crime fiction writer Chester Himes (whom Smith cites as one of her chief inspirations) (see note 9):

> In the Harlem cycle, however, naturalism combines with absurdism to produce an invasion of all redemptive possibilities ... Himes provides a powerful picture of the material conditions of Harlem, the poverty and deprivation, but, pushing his prose more to the symbolic than the realistic, he shifts his attention from causes to consequences. (Horsley, 2005: 211)

What Horsley is pointing to here, then, is the way in which the conventions of noir fiction become part of the narratological fabric of the text, determining not only its atmosphere but also its storyline; these are ultimately hyperbolic city spaces which, while originating in the historical reality of Harlem (or Moss Side), reach beyond them to create a terrifyingly claustrophobic vision of the ghetto that is as much psychological as it is material.

In *Moss Side Massive*, Smith's protagonists (at least, the irredeemable ones) are trapped in just such a space: historical *and* hyperbolic, material *and* aesthetic. The extent to which (male) children 'born into' crime are unable, ever, to escape is summed up by the career of Storm who, despite a good deal of conspicuous wealth and local power, is unable to leave his small patch of Moss Side for more than a day. The following extract shows him driving all the way to Coventry in order to enjoy the illusion of freedom, even though he knows that, at the end of the day, he will have to go back since it is the only place in which he is relatively safe (he needs the protection of his gang) and can earn money (albeit by illegal means):

> When he finally looked at the car clock, Storm realised that he had been driving for nearly two hours. The petrol gauge was empty and so was he. Storm caught a glimpse of himself in his rear view mirror. Gaunt, tired, pale and bloodshot. He badly needed a shower. He also needed to eat ...
> It felt so good to simply hit the road, going in no particular direction, with the gas pedal pushed all the way down to the floor and feel himself flying away from all his problems. Oh, if only it were that simple. He turned off the motorway to fill up with petrol and ended up in this sleepy, little town. (Smith, 2000: 147–8)

Inasmuch as the crime depicted in Smith's *Moss Side Massive* and her follow-up, *Full Crew* (2002), is 'black-on-black', the politics of race are both everywhere and nowhere in the pages of the novels. Although, as we have seen, Smith's narrator comments, in passing, on the fact that lack of access to 'good' (i.e. supportive) education is one of the factors that precipitates the young men of gangland Manchester into crime, the racism of British society (institutional or quotidian) is not a discursive feature of her work in which there are very few white characters. The same cannot be said for Peter Kalu's novels. Although, like Smith's, Kalu's (futuristic) Manchester is very visibly ghettoized – to the point of virtual apartheid in some of the novels (see discussion of *Lick Shot* in Chapter 1) – he is committed to making visible the 'white space' in which the zones of black destitution and othering exist, and to hold the white population (both institutions and individuals) responsible for creating the fundamentally unjust society in which crime flourishes. Therefore, although some of the black characters in his texts are themselves involved in criminal activity (the entourage surrounding the black celebrity Desiree Burton in *Yard Dogs* (2002), for example), Kalu always makes clear that racism and racial discrimination are the greater 'crime' and also the local or global context in which Ambrose Patterson's criminal investigations take place. For this reason, I focus on Kalu's work in more detail in the next sub-section of the chapter ('Institutional Crime').

Before proceeding to this section it is, however, worth noting the way in which Manchester's white crime writers like Cath Staincliffe have gradually moved issues of racial as well as social inequality to the centre of their work. Although Staincliffe's novels from the early 1990s are very white (to the extent that even the squatter community in *Looking for Trouble* (1994) includes no identifiably non-white migrants), the most recent (for example, *Bitter Blue* and *Missing* (both 2007)) feature a broad, multicultural mix of characters (both central and minor) and deal with crimes that are racially motivated at both a personal and an institutional level. (I will discuss an instance of the latter – from *Missing* (2007b) – in some detail in the next sub-section.) Especially interesting, however, is the way in which ethnic awareness appears to creep into the Sal Kilkenny series as, for example, in the second novel (*Dead Wrong*, 1998) where it lurks both at the margins of the text and in the protagonists' consciousness *vis-à-vis* the recent wave of riots in Ordsall and Salford:

> 'Heatwave-Crimewave,' screamed the headline. 'Brutal Violence Erupts in Night of Terror'. There'd been riots in Salford. Youths circling the police station, setting fire to the flats and shops. In Cheetham Hill, two teenagers had died in a gun fight, and further south, a young black man had been fished from the Mersey. Police were treating both these cases as part of the on-going drugs war, with rival teenage gangs competing for a share of the lucrative and expanding crack market. (Staincliffe, 1998: 164)

> I had tea and toast while she talked about the crime wave, the Ordsall Riots, the Moss Side shootings. She went through all the acquaintances she'd had who'd ever been mugged or burgled. (Staincliffe, 1998: 230)

As can be seen, neither PI Kilkenny nor the narrator comments directly on these events, although the racism of the press is implied in the ironic treatment of the news headline in the first extract and the seriousness of racial unrest and gangland violence is implicit in the latter. In conclusion, however, it would be fair to say that, until the millennium, Manchester's crime fiction was very clearly divided along race lines, with the series of McDermid and Staincliffe, and the thrillers of Blincoe and Ray Banks, coming from a very different place (and pitched at a very different audience) from the X-Press publications of Smith and Kalu.

Institutional crime

As Horsley observes in *Twentieth-century Crime Fiction* (2005), the X-Press (based in London) has become identified with black crime writing of a particular persuasion:

> The serious objectives of the X-Press writers, however, are not confined to the representation of a particularly controversial form of black masculinity. The 'nerve' that [Victor] Headley claimed to have touched is equally to do with the novels' effort to re-map the British inner-city's terrain, focusing attention on black social decay and institutionalized racism, and developing a critique that has something in common with the socio-economic determinism apparent in Himes's novels. Yardie [West Indian] fiction, it could be argued, implicitly demands a re-assessment of the postcolonial economic and cultural circumstances that made the Yardie underworld possible ... Yardie fiction exposes the economic *need* that underlines the apparent *greed* of the gangland members. (Horsley, 2005: 230)

The crucial point here is that the objective of the X-Press was to sponsor stories that made clear the connections between 'crime on the street' (whether perpetrated by white or black individuals) to the corrupt and racist institutions (government, city councils, the police force) that created the conditions that produced those crimes, whether directly or indirectly. Although, as already observed, Smith's two novels are implicit rather than explicit in making these links and, ideologically, retain a humanist belief in personal responsibility for 'good' and 'evil' (see following sub-section on 'Human Nature'), Kalu's Ambrose Patterson series is totally committed to the project Horsley outlines above; while the DIs and PIs are still involved in fighting crime on the streets, it is indeed 'the postcolonial economic circumstances' (Horsley above) that made the crimes possible – their conditions of possibility – that are under scrutiny.

Kalu's DI Patterson is a sceptical, unorthodox yet warm and likeable character who is totally upfront about the 'chip' he carries on his shoulder. The only black DI in his unit, Patterson presents himself as something of an oddball with no close friends amongst his colleagues and, in the course of the first novel (*Lick Shot*, 1993), it is revealed that the reason he became a police officer was to avenge the death of his father who was killed in police custody (see pp. 144–5 for the back-story). (A vivid vision of his father's treatment comes to Patterson at the climax of the story in chapter 12 with his father's exhortation 'You must lick shot first!' providing the novel with its title (*Lick Shot*,

1993: 167).) Probably the most striking feature of Patterson's life as a police officer, however (certainly for the non-black reader), is the racism and hostility of his work environment and the fact that *none* of his white colleagues can be trusted. In the opening chapter of *Lick Shot* (1993), for example, we are shown how the racism of his particular unit is already having a detrimental effect on his career. Although Patterson was recognized as the district's outstanding new Detective Chief Inspector when first appointed to his post, the 'honeymoon' was soon over:

> That was all over two years ago. Lucky man. Patterson had thought that he was on the fast track to success but instead he and his career had run into the sand. A whole heap of sand!
> Even before he'd been assigned, he'd had a hazy knowledge of the Division's reputation for badness. Slowly, over the months, he'd begun to see more clearly what the badness was. The Division conducted its affairs by means of a Magic White Circle of which he was obviously not a member. The Circle organised key acts of conjuring in the name of effective policing. So crucial defence papers disappeared before you could say abracadabra. (Kalu, 1993: 6)

From page 6 of the first novel onwards, then, the reader is aware that their DI will be fighting the crime of his colleagues as well as the crimes on the streets. The figure of the maverick, morally upright DI pushed to the outskirts of a more or less compromised force is, of course, a staple of crime fiction, but it is the overt racism that Patterson encounters on a day-to-day basis that makes his experiences especially memorable. On this point it is also worth noting that, in Kalu's futuristic Manchester (the novels are typically set in the early twenty-first century), there has been no slackening in the crudeness or the violence of racial hostility, with both Patterson and the narrator frequently invoking the 'n' word to demonstrate the visceral dislike with which black people are still regarded. For example: 'He [Patterson] hadn't yet made up his mind whether the Chief was an out-and-out "nigger hater" but the possibility that this was a set up lingered' (*Lick Shot*, 1993: 14).

It is also significant that Patterson's arch-enemy and nemesis is not a figure from the criminal underworld (a Moriarty (Arthur Conan Doyle) or a Ger Cafferty (Ian Rankin)) but rather another (female) DI: Shirley Decker. From the first pages of the first novel, Decker shows herself to be ruthlessly competitive. It is made clear that, although she is an effective police officer (she has, after all, made it to the rank of DI), all her work is undertaken for personal gain and career advancement. She has no moral interest in fighting crime or seeking justice. Her chief character attribute, meanwhile, is duplicity, with a good deal of the plot demonstrating that we cannot believe a word she says. In *Yard Dogs* (2002), published nine years after *Lick Shot*, she is evidently still up to her tricks and the novel opens with Patterson overhearing her on the phone talking about him:

> I took the stairs to level G and was about to turn into the corridor when I heard my name. I hung back. Decker was on her mobile.
> 'Yes. Too damn black. Good detective actually. Yes. I'll deliver him.'
> I heard her phone flip down. 'Kiss my arse, Anderson,' she intoned. Then her footsteps receding. Decker rooting for me? I thought I'd never live to see it. Don't be naïve, I thought. She had to be scheming. (Kalu, 1993: 8)

Although what she says appears to be complimentary, if racist, in this instance, Patterson is still wary: her person, and personality, wrapped up in the phrase 'she had to be scheming'.

The non-institutional crimes, meanwhile, that Patterson is officially employed to solve are rather more complex in their racial politics. Out on the streets, blacks and Asians as well as whites are engaged in crime of different kinds, although generally the demise of the non-white characters can be traced back to the oppression and/or exploitation of black people by the white, Western world. Typically, however, the most 'evil' characters are white (see discussion following) and most terrifying when seen operating as a pack (for example, in the representation of a latter-day National Front in *Lick Shot* (1993) (see Pearce, 2007 and 2012b for a full discussion of this)). Probably one of Kalu's finest and most memorable novels in this regard is *Professor X* (1995) which sees the wider white community (police, government, financial sector) conspiring to 'take out' a black man who (as the title of novel suggests) bears more than a passing resemblance to 'Malcolm X'.[11]

What is especially interesting about Kalu's series for our interests here is its representation not only of race-related crime but of race-related crime *in Manchester*. Although the series is set in the 'near future', the representation of the city and its environs are geographically familiar, and the novels provide another vivid illustration of the way in which the real and the hyper-real fuse in crime fiction. Since I have written about Kalu's depiction of Manchester at length elsewhere (Pearce 2012b and Chapter 1), I shall not repeat those observations here other than to remind readers of the way in which Kalu's portraits of the city often seem to draw purposefully upon his experience of the recent past (the NF marches and Moss Side uprising ('Riots') (Haslam, 2000: 228) in *Lick Shot* (1993), for instance). He also depicts Manchester as a sharply divided city in terms of both wealth and race, with the description of Stockborough (a futuristic suburb of Manchester) suggesting the ultimate, perhaps inevitable outcome of decades of neocolonialist urban planning: apartheid.

In conclusion, then, it has to be said that Kalu's crime fiction paints an often disturbingly bleak portrait of race relations in Manchester (past, present and future); and, inasmuch as responsibility for the predominant crime with which his work is concerned (i.e., racism) is so widely and completely institutionalized, there is the sense that only a revolution will put things right. This is not a crime that any individual – even Ambrose Patterson (or, in the case of *Little Jack Horner* (2007), PI Delroy Johnson) – can solve.[12]

During the 1980s the Greater Manchester Police force became the centre of a number of corruption scandals, the most high-profile being the 'silencing' of John Stalker after he was involved in a review of the RUC in Northern Ireland. The Chief Constable who was responsible for suspending Stalker was James Anderton, who also became notorious for his views on the Moss Side 'riots' (see Haslam, 2000: 229–30) and his vitriolic hatred of gay people. Known as 'God's Copper' on account of the way in which he used Christianity to justify his views and his actions, Anderton became a figure of contempt and loathing for many artists and activists of the time, and his pseudonym crops us frequently in Manchester writing from the 1980s onwards including, not surprisingly, crime fiction.[13]

Blincoe's *Manchester Slingback* (1998), for example, is a very thinly veiled revenge attack on the Chief Constable's violent homophobia and one that must have edged close to libel (especially since the fictional Chief Constable, Pascal, is shown to be guilty of paedophilia with the children of the care home where the central character, Jake, grew up). The novel's climax takes the form of a showdown between Pascal and Jake at 'Jericho Chapel' in which Jake explicitly references Anderton by calling Pascal 'God's Cop' – before impaling him on a stake improvized from a banner pole (Blincoe, 1998: 251–2):

> Jake was approaching the door now, his feet almost touching the wedge of light that flooded through it. One step he would turn into a black

silhouette in the doorway and a shadow across the floor, measuring the length of the place Pascal stood.

Jake said, 'God's Cop'.

Pascal's arm came up from inside his coat. In his hand some kind of pistol.

Jake kept still between the shelter of the open door and a pillar. Pascal was squinting into the light, but his arm was steady. If Jake moved, he would try to shoot.

Pascal said, 'I knew you were one of them.'

'One of what?'

'Another queer boy, come looking for me.'

'I'm a tourist from London. You're not going to shoot me in church.'

'Wherever the Lord's enemies take the battle.' (Blincoe, 1998: 248)

The name of Chief Constable Anderton also resounds, in even less coded form, in the novels of Kalu and Staincliffe. Kalu's *Yard Dogs* (2002) has a Chief Constable *Anderson* while Staincliffe's *Looking for Trouble* (1994) exposes a corrupt 'DCI Miller' who, like Blincoe's Pascal, has been involved in a paedophile crime ring videoing young boys in care (Staincliffe, 1994: 265). The ending of Staincliffe's novel is, however, arguably truer to life than Blincoe's in as much as Miller 'gets off'. Revenge in this text is limited to DCI Miller having his hand stamped upon (p. 268) and, by the end of the text, we know only that he is the subject of an inquiry. Further, although Sharrocks is exposed by the press, Miller isn't:

> It made the front page in the Evening News for a night: Charity Boss faces Murder Rap – Child Sex Ring Exposed. There was never a peep about Miller's involvement. Funny, that. (Staincliffe, 1994: 270)

Reviewed collectively, this plethora of fictional texts alluding, more or less directly, to the bigotry and hypocrisy of Chief Constable Anderton in particular, and the corruption of Greater Manchester Constabulary in general, renders the city something of a mawkish *cause celèbre* within contemporary British crime fiction. Rather like the 'Moors Murders' whose horror will forever be associated with 'Manchester and crime',[14] so arguably, will this era of institutional corruption and intolerance. And while such questionable policing clearly cannot be held wholly responsible for 'the crime of Manchester' in recent years, crime writers (both white and black) have made vividly clear how lack of trust in, and respect for, a city's police force has a negative impact on a region's relationship to law and order generally.

'Human nature'

For all the documentation there now is that 'explains' crime in terms of capitalism, consumerism, social inequality and poverty or deprivation, there persists a popular counter-claim that crime is not the consequence of the failure of society as much as 'human nature'. Indeed, it is hard to imagine crime *fiction* being so popular were psychology not a key factor in the textual investigations. All the texts I have so far discussed in this chapter deal with the psychological, as well as the material, motives for crime to a greater or lesser extent, though the connection between criminal behaviour and social or political context is variously defined, sometimes within the same author or text. Further, as readers will be aware, criminal activity may derive from a wide range of psychological and moral profiles, with the 'inherently *evil*' at one end of the spectrum and latter-day 'Robin Hoods' at the other. In this section of the chapter I therefore consider a selection of the 'human' factors that are invoked to explain crime in these Mancunian texts including psychopathology, masculinity, greed and human indifference.

The psychopath

At the extreme end of the criminal-profile spectrum is the psychopath:[15] the character that crime fiction readers love to hate, and whose presence is a staple of the serial killer sub-genre. While there is much debate within psychiatry and criminology about whether a person's 'personality' can ever be deemed wholly accountable for their crime(s) without social context also being a factor, there is no question, even within this limited sample of Mancunian texts, that a significant number of fictional criminals are deemed to be suffering from a malignant tendency in excess of their environment. The psychopathic criminal personality is also the one that is most likely to be written and spoken about in terms of 'evil', although the moral judgement implicit in such labelling often, and somewhat paradoxically, brings questions of social responsibility back to the fore ('what was it in X's background that caused him or her to turn to *become* evil in this way?'). On this point, it should also be noted that, in crime fiction texts, psychopaths are typically (though not necessarily) male and violent, hence creating something of a categorical overlap with the next sub-section of this chapter, 'masculinity'.

With respect to this last point, an interesting comparison can be drawn between the two female authors whose work I have been following in this chapter: Val McDermid and Cath Staincliffe.

McDermid's *The Mermaids Singing* (2006) is, in most respects (and notwithstanding the fact that the serial killer operates as a transsexual), a prototypical 'psycho-thriller' in its trailing of a series of brutal murders by an elusive suspect; Staincliffe's *Bitter Blue* (2007a), meanwhile, features a female psychopath whose capacity for violence is not unleashed until the climax of the novel and whose identity is known to us from the first page of what is, in many ways, a classic detective-fiction text. Both authors nevertheless make clear that it is the pathology of their characters rather than the personal or social contexts in which they find themselves that are ultimately responsible for their crimes – as is evidenced in the following extracts:

> Tony sighed. 'I wish to God I'd been brought in sooner on this. Handy Andy's not going to stop here. He's too much in love with his work. Look at these pictures. This bastard's going to carry on capturing and torturing and killing until you catch him. Carol, this guy's a career killer.' (McDermid, 2006: 100)

> She stood on the rug in the middle of the room, pursed her lips, blinked. It was an expression of impatience or irritation. I could see no sign of grief or terror.
> 'He needs help, soon. You're the only one who can help him.'
> 'Stop chattering.' She shook her head fiercely as though my words were insects buzzing in her ears. (Staincliffe, 2007a: 264)

> 'I should have followed my instincts. I didn't trust her but I kept on working for her.'
> 'You didn't know she was a psychopath. She fooled everyone.'
> 'He's dead, Diane.'
> 'She'd have killed eventually. That's what they're saying.' (Staincliffe, 2007a: 279)

As can be seen, both criminals are presented as congenital murderers: McDermid's 'Angelica' (aka Christopher Thorpe) is described by the criminal psychologist Tony Hill as a 'career killer' while PI Kilkenny's best friend, Diane, assures Sal that Lucy Barker (presented in the press as a 'psychopath') would also have 'killed eventually'. Further, in so far as either character can be seen to have a 'motive' for their crimes, we see both Angelica and Lucy conforming to the classic psychopathic trait of feeling 'let down' or betrayed by another (in whom there is a sexual interest). Both these killers stalk individuals around whom they construct sexual fantasies and whom they then seek to punish once they are ignored or rejected.

If, however, we enquire whether there is anything specific to Manchester (and/or the north of England) about these crimes the initial answer is 'probably not'. Psychopathic murder can occur anywhere, even though it is arguable that the most infamous literary psychopaths (for example, Brett Easton Ellis's Patrick Bateman in *American Psycho* (1991)) are associated with social and cultural environments that are themselves 'sick' or 'bad' in some way (typically, the late-capitalist city).

It could, however, be argued that McDermid's and Staincliffe's psychopathic murderers do belong to a disturbing tradition that links violent crime with the north of England via two high-profile serial killers: Ian Brady (the 'Moors Murders') and Peter Sutcliffe (the 'Yorkshire Ripper').[16] The location of 'Angelica's' torture-suite in a remote farmhouse on the 'Bradfield' moors certainly resonates with both, as well, it must be said, with the Gothic literary tradition (most obviously, Emily Brontë's *Wuthering Heights* (1847)). Meanwhile, the 'Moors Murders' are arguably a grim (if silent) point of reference for Mancunian crime fiction in general, and it is worth noting that two of the texts already discussed (Blincoe's *Manchester Slingback* (1998) and Staincliffe's *Looking for Trouble* (1994)) deal with paedophilic sex-rings practising in remote rural locations. The further implication, as the Mancunian singer-songwriter Morrissey has acknowledged in discussion in his famous single 'Over the Moors', is that the *shame* of the 'Moors Murders' has somehow become part of the Mancunian psyche.[17] From that historical moment on, Manchester (and the north of England more generally) was no longer an innocent backwater but a region which hosted crimes of unspeakable perversion and excess; if you told someone that you were from Manchester in the years immediately following the arrest of Ian Brady and Myra Hindley, *this* is what would first spring to mind.

Although several of Staincliffe's novels feature murders that take place outwith the city, often involving a drive across a stretch of moorland or hill country (for example, the description of Kilkenny's drive across the Saddleworth moors in *Missing* (2007b: 160)), her 'psychopath', Lucy Barker, is tucked away in the Manchester suburbs (Levenshulme). While Kilkenny finds Lucy's rented flat disturbing for reasons she cannot quite put her finger on when she visits (Staincliffe, 2007a: 48–9), the bigger point this would seem to be making is that it is not always easy to spot a psychopath: indeed, many of them (like Lucy) hold down responsible jobs and live ostensibly 'ordinary' lives.

The fact that Staincliffe's psychopath is a superficially vulnerable woman is presumably also part of the text's message in this regard; if Lucy Barker (as described below) can end up wielding a hammer and murdering an ex-'boyfriend' then clearly anyone can:

> She looked at me, her face paled and she swayed. She put a hand to her stomach.
> 'Lucy?'
> 'Sorry,' she blurted out. She bent double and began to retch. Nothing came out. After a moment she stopped, straightened, her eyes and nose running.
> 'I'd like to go back.'
> She looked awful. But how convenient, too – a neat sidestep to avoid dealing with my accusations. Like Maddie's sudden tummy aches writ large. (Staincliffe, 2007a: 173)

The manipulation and deviousness that Lucy exhibits here are, according the 'Hare Psychopathy Checklist' typical of the 'type one' psychopath (see note 15), distinguished not only by their lack of empathy for others but also by their charisma and superficial charm, lying and general lack of remorse.

The 'bad seed'

Although not classified as 'psychopaths' per se, several of the fictional characters discussed in this chapter to date do demonstrate 'badness' predicated upon aberrant psychology. In Karline Smith's *Moss Side Massive* (2000), for example, Clifton is compared and contrasted throughout with the text's young Rasta hero (and half-brother), Zukie. Clifton, as noted earlier, turned criminal at an early age in order to claim his stake in contemporary consumer society and, by his early twenties, is caught up in an escalating spiral of drug-related crime. For much of the text, then, Clifton assumes the role of a swaggering gangster who deceives his own mother about the nature of his 'business' and is without pity for anyone who stands in the way of his deals (including his half-brother). The fact that Clifton is ultimately redeemed (Pearce, 2010b: 160–2) by an access of remorse and a desire to save Zukie's life, nevertheless rescues him (and, by implication, the wider Moss Side criminal underworld) from the label of 'psychopath'. Although frequently brutal in their 'turf wars', Clifton and others like him are not totally without empathy or pity.[18] At the same time, Smith's story would seem to imply that crime entails an element of psychological predisposition since Zukie, brought up in similar circumstances to Clifton, does not follow his brother's route.

Peter Kalu's texts, meanwhile, contain a fair number of despicable personalities, most of them white. As already noted, a recurrent feature of Kalu's Ambrose Patterson series is the general untrustworthiness of the DI's white colleagues, which immediately raises a question of whether the selfishness, competitiveness and lack of integrity demonstrated by these characters is understood to depend upon their individual or collective psychological identity. At first glance, it is easy to see this blanket portrayal of white characters as negative stereotyping, and Kalu may, indeed, have been making a political point or exacting revenge on the long history of English literature which has gratuitously portrayed black people in a negative light. Following on from my earlier discussion, I would, however, prefer to read this feature of Kalu's texts as a further comment not on individuals *of any ethnicity* but rather on the systems and institutions that corrupt, and corrupt absolutely. This theory is certainly corroborated by the fact that Kalu's black characters can also exhibit dubious personality traits, especially when motivated by greed (see the discussion following of Dare and Elmershore in *Yard Dogs* (2002)).

One of Kalu's most memorable depictions of aberrant white *group* psychology, meanwhile, occurs in *Lick Shot* (1993). Here the neo-Nazi 'White Tribe' recalls the National Front's reign of terror on the streets of Manchester in the 1970s, as well as the fanaticism of the American Ku Klux Klan (KKK),[19] in its desire to cleanse the streets of the city of immigrants and black people. As discussed in Chapter 1, the fact that this novel is technically set in the future (early twenty-first century) does not prevent it feeling like a return to the 1970s and, in particular, the 'street wars' of that period (Procter, 2003: 69–124). This is a text, then, in which 'evil' is understood largely in terms of ideologically brainwashed *groups* rather than individuals, and on this point it is interesting to see the cover blurb using the adjective 'psychotic' to describe the White Tribe as a whole:

> Down in the dark sewers of Manchester there lies a terrible secret. It's the horrific race-hate weapon that *The White Tribe*, a psychotic group of neo-nazis, plan to unleash on the city's black residents. (Kalu 1993: dust jacket)

As a group, meanwhile, the White Tribe demonstrates truly terrifying collective hatred for Manchester's non-white citizens, as vividly illustrated by Giles Jenkinson's rallying call to his 'troops':

> 'You know, I woke up this morning, a bit groggy as usual on a Monday morning, you know how it is ... and I heard the milk float. I went down and took in the milk. Well, what do you know, an Asian milkman had delivered it! I saw the black bastard disappearing into the milk float as I opened the door!' He paused, his eyebrows suspended in astonishment. The crowd tittered. 'No, I didn't drink the milk friends. I didn't even feed it to my rottweilers! No, that day, I cancelled my milk order from that firm. I wasn't going to drink the milk that had been touched by dark, infected hands.'
>
> The mob applauded with a flurry of Roman salutes.
>
> 'Seig [sic] heil! Seig heil!' ...
>
> 'Brothers in blood, when we march to City square, remember to deliver this message loud and clear to the entire nation.' He enunciated it slowly. 'You can't clean them, so quarantine them! Repatriation. Save the nation!' (Kalu, 1993: 135)

With his overt allusions to Nazism and the KKK (see current website cited in note 19) as well as the National Front, Kalu reminds us of the terrifying thuggery of the mob. *Lick Shot* also features an 'evil' white individual in the figure of Daniel Mallieu, the member of the White Tribe who has been given the job of planting the 'anti-black' bomb in the city's water supply. What is interesting about the portrayal of Mallieu is that he is ultimately revealed to be an effeminate wimp and a coward (caving in to the good cop / bad cop interrogation of (white) DI Moulton and (black) Ambrose Patterson) (Kalu, 1993:159–62)).

Patterson, meanwhile, is revealed to be capable of his own 'blind' propensity to violence as a means of extracting the truth from Mallieu:

> Cynthia looked at Ambrose fuming at the side of the car. He looked distant, so distant ...
>
> Patterson viciously scythed Mallieu's legs from under him. Mallieu flopped silently to his knees and rocked there. Patterson walked around, raised his arm and lashed him with the back of his hand. The head toppled over ...
>
> 'What the fuck are you doing?' Moulton spat.
>
> Patterson looked down at him, furious. 'There are 200,000 lives out there at risk and you ask me what I'm doing?' (Kalu, 1993: 158–9)

What these juxtaposed episodes clearly prompt us to reflect upon is the less-than-straightforward correlation between 'evil behaviour' and 'justified' violence. While Patterson shows that he can be every bit as brutal and unforgiving as the white man he is attempting to screw a confession from (and just as prone to the sudden 'red mist'), his violence is fuelled by a desire for justice, not hatred. Kalu's text is nevertheless brave enough to reveal the fine line that separates these behaviours and to remind us that 'fighting crime' raises complex moral issues.

Masculinity

Many, though by no means all, the male criminals featured in the Manchester crime canon exhibit a capacity for physical violence that has traditionally been associated with both an excess of testosterone and brutal, 'survivalist' acculturation. Readers will also not be surprised to learn that it is the two female authors featured in this chapter who are most inclined to 'explain' Manchester's crimes in terms of violent masculinity and, on occasion, to blur the line between specifically male brutality and 'evil' (a reflex that is arguably similar to Kalu's conflation of 'evil' with racism).

McDermid's *Kick Back* (2002[1993]) is an especially good example of how the threat of physical male violence can rumble through crime fiction texts without necessarily being either the focus or the 'explanation' for the crime per se. As already noted, this particular Brannigan novel is concerned with what is ostensibly a 'victimless crime' (property-market fraud), yet one of the criminals, the builder and property-developer Brian Lomax, presents a physical threat to Brannigan herself throughout the novel and attempts to murder his sister and co-conspirator, Nell, at the end. It is interesting to note, however, that when Brannigan first sets eyes on Lomax (not knowing who he is) she deems him a 'hunk':

> The thought lifted my spirits slightly, but not as much as the hunk I clapped eyes on as I yanked open the street door. He was jumping out of a Transit van that he'd abandoned on the double-yellows, and he was gorgeous. He wore tight jeans and a white T-shirt – on a freezing October day, for God's sake! – stained with plaster and brick dust. He had that solid, muscular build that gives me ideas that nice feminists aren't supposed even to know about, never mind entertain ... He looked slightly dangerous, as if he didn't give a shit. (McDermid, 2002 [1993]: 57)

As the action unwinds we learn that Brannigan's first impressions are correct: her 'hunk' really doesn't 'give a shit' and, within days of this sighting, he has attempted to drive her off the road and into the Manchester Ship Canal (McDermid, 2002[1993]: 85–6). It is not until much later that Brannigan finally discovers that her assassin *is* Lomax, but subsequent encounters cause her to suspect that his 'solid, muscular build' is joined to a ruthless personality. By the end of the novel he is the prime suspect for the murder of his (transvestite) partner-in-crime, Martin Cheetham, and is evidently prepared to kill his sister, Nell, when she threatens to go to the police. While murder is not the *object* of Lomax's crime, then (his motivation is greed), his physical strength and violent temper are integral to his persona and remind us of Kate Millett's observations on the role that 'physical force' plays in the enforcement of patriarchy (that is, it is a constant threat that underlies all other expressions of power) (Millett, 1986 [1969]).

Cath Staincliffe's Sal Kilkenny encounters a number of similarly violent men in the course of her investigations, and much is made of the fact that she carries the scars of these past encounters (both physical and psychological) around with her. One particularly brutal male character, whose propensity for physical violence shades into 'evil', is Rashid Siddiq in *Dead Wrong* (1998). The fact that Siddiq is an Asian character is also of interest here, and may be seen as part of Staincliffe's ongoing project to work against stereotypes at the same time as not being afraid to associate members of 'minority' groups with crime (the lesbian practitioner of domestic violence in *Missing* (2007b) is another example). This said, it is noticeable that Rashid Siddiq's physical violence and psychological 'nastiness' are presented as an index of his *gender* rather than his *ethnicity*:

> 'Get out of the car!' Siddiq screamed at me. I climbed out trying to plot an escape route, uncertain where to run. Siddiq gripped my arm again. It hurt badly. 'No one does this to me,' he hissed. 'You're going to have an accident. Fatal.' (Staincliffe, 1998: 145)

Interestingly, the same latent violence that Kilkenny perceives in Rashid is echoed in numerous other male characters in this particular novel. Closest to Rashid in terms of the threat of physical violence is his partner, Zeb, who engages in several threatening verbal encounters with the PI:

> He struggled to contain his anger, lips pressed tight, jaw working away. Then he lost it. 'You cunt, you fucking —'
> I shut the door quickly. Leant back against the wall for a moment, heart kicking at my stomach. *The knife tip at my throat, needing to swallow, spittle on his lips* ... I concentrated on my breathing. My pulse began to slow. I looked out through the spy-hole. Saw him kicking the gate open, leaving, thank God. (Staincliffe, 1998: 168)

As is indicated by the sentence in italics, the incident causes Kilkenny to have a flashback to a previous physical assault and makes starkly visible the very material threat a female PI faces with regards to male violence. Her undisguised fear and vulnerability are, moreover, in marked contrast to Kate Brannigan's physical revenge on her male assailants (including Lomax, above, whom she slays with a perfectly timed karate kick (McDermid, 2002 [1993]: 264)) and across the series in general. Staincliffe's novels, by contrast, would seem to send out a message that men *are* an ever-present threat because of their greater physical strength and tendency to aggression: not all men, perhaps (her house-mate and eventual lover, Ray, heads the list of 'good guys'), but a great many. *Dead Wrong* (1998), for example, features a male stalker, Gary Crowther, whose latent violence is disturbingly mirrored in the violence of the victim's brother who, while not a criminal himself, is so enraged by his sister's abuse that he ends up attacking and seriously injuring the wrong man (Staincliffe, 1998: 225). Therefore, we must conclude that while masculinity cannot be used to 'explain' Mancunian crime per se, for these feminist crime writers it is a significant contributory factor.

Greed

It will be remembered that in the earlier sub-section of this chapter on 'Racial Inequality' I quoted an extract from Karline Smith's *Moss Side Massive* (2000) in which the narrator attempts to explain why Clifton turned to crime: 'wherever he looked he was bombarded with reminders of the materialistic world' (Smith, 2000: 9). While, for Smith, her characters' consumerist desire is seen to derive, at least in part, from the social deprivation that has led to their lack of prospects, it is also, of course, possible to read it as simple greed: the 'deadly sin' most often associated with crime.

Greed (specifically for material wealth and a yuppie lifestyle) certainly figures high on the list of motives for crime in Mancunian fiction and is the aspect of human nature that most easily cuts across race, gender and class. We see it sinking its claws into black youngsters like Clifton on Moss Side's Alexandra Park estate as well as middle-class white solicitors like John Cheetham (and property-developers like Brian Lomax and his sister Nell) in McDermid's *Kick Back* (2002 [1993]); we see it circulating among a whole group of black celebrities (of both genders) in Peter Kalu's *Yard Dogs* (2002), as well as hardened Asian drug dealers in Staincliffe's *Dead Wrong* (1998); and we see it mixed with sexual exploitation in Blincoe's *Manchester Slingback* (1998) and Staincliffe's *Looking for Trouble* (1994) through (white) male characters who not only engage in paedophilia but profit from it through the sale of videos.

What this reminds us is that the historical context for all these crime fictions is post-Thatcherite Britain. The earliest texts I have considered here date from the early 1990s, and none of them looks back farther than the 1980s, which means that all are dealing with that moment in British culture when, despite some short periods of recession (notably the early 1990s), the trappings of consumer culture (and its associated lifestyle aspirations) had arrived in every corner of Britain, Manchester included. As I noted in the opening section of this chapter, crime fiction has arguably played a vital role in witnessing and recording this dubious 'boom time' in cities like Manchester through close observation of its rebuilding and rebranding. But it is also important to recognize the extent to which the consumerist turn of late capitalism has transformed the nature of crime itself, manufacturing both a new set of motives and a new *context* for the crimes. Blincoe's novels are especially indicative in the last regard inasmuch as Manchester's latest 'makeover' is seen to have hollowed out the city's organic community[20] in much the same way that its new buildings give the impression of being merely a façade (see earlier quotations).

In *Twentieth-century Crime Fiction* (2005), Horsley notes the impact of consumerism on the genre in general:

> The protagonists of contemporary crime novels rather than being lured into a dangerous demi-monde, find themselves endangered by a seductive commodity culture and a society of spectacle, in which complicity and assimilation are major sources of anxiety. These shifts are particularly evident in literary noir, which is one of the most inherently critical forms of crime writing and is also one of the variants most likely to slip its generic moorings, slipping over into mainstream fiction. (Horsley, 2005: 161)

Something of this 'anxiety' is marked at the end of Kalu's *Yard Dogs* (2002) in a conversation between DI Patterson and PI Delroy in which they reflect upon the vanity, egotism and greed that led Desiree Burton's entourage to commit murder:

> How come everybody wants money and fame? How about knowledge, spirituality, integrity? Don't those count any more? [Patterson]
> Softest pillow's the one stuffed with fifty-pound notes. That's how come. [Delroy] (Kalu, 2002: 247–8)

This leads Patterson to an uncharacteristically melancholy closing comment: having spent a lifetime fighting racism and working for a better life for black people in Manchester and elsewhere, there is the worry that 'human nature', in the form of consumerist greed, has taken possession of the whole world and, in the process, made a mockery of true freedom:

> Then I was nudging my car through the late night traffic, thinking Strawberry Fields was a hallucination, a nether world of scheming and double-dealing behind saccharine fonts.
> It took a murder to cut through to the real. (Kalu, 2002: 252)

Yet it must also be acknowledged that Manchester's DIs and PIs (including, especially, DI Patterson) are arguably as invested in a 'yuppie' lifestyle as the criminals they seek to foil. As I observed in Chapter 1, DI Patterson is a top-of-the-range dresser, and all the novels pay close attention to the clothes (and brands) he is wearing. The fact that his early morning shopping spree in Deansgate (Kalu, 2002: 114: quoted in Chapter 1) occurs in the same text that ends with the anti-materialist meditation cited above makes its own point: globalized material(ist) culture and its associated value-system are everywhere. Patterson does not disguise the fact that he dresses expensively precisely in order to counter racial prejudice with a visible demonstration of wealth and class.

Not surprisingly, the two female PIs featured in this chapter, Kate Brannigan and Sal Kilkenny, have rather less flashy tastes and consumer desires than DI Patterson, but this is not to say that they are free from them entirely. Brannigan, as we have already seen, has a 'yuppie' house close enough to the city centre to satisfy all her consumer needs (McDermid, 2002 [1993]) while Kilkenny, who lives in (part of) a substantial Victorian villa with a large garden in Withington, has a taste for gourmet food and holidays in the sun (even if she cannot afford them). Therefore, while it would be wrong to suggest that these 'good-living', socialist-feminist PIs are greedy, it is arguable that they share many of the same desires and aspirations as the criminals they are in pursuit of: the difference hinges on the fact that that they don't *need* to commit crimes to enjoy them.

Human indifference
I end this section with a brief discussion of one final aspect of 'human nature' that has quietly taken its place alongside more obvious crime in Cath Staincliffe's work, and that is complicity with, or indifference to,

the individual suffering that results from various expressions of social injustice.

Vis-à-vis this preoccupation, I have already cited Staincliffe's sad tale of Mr and Mrs Smith in *Bitter Blue* (2007a): the dysfunctional elderly couple who freeze to death in their own home. On discovering how and why they died, Sal Kilkenny rages at 'the system' that enabled this to happen and also reflects upon our 'human' responsibility to our neighbours. Is not the middle-class's refusal to get involved in cases like the Smiths' comparable to armed robbery? Both result in the suffering and death of innocent people, after all. In the following conversation with her social worker friend Rachel, we see Kilkenny struggling with the implications of this 'criminal-less crime' including her own sense of guilt:

> 'The place was filthy. There was no heat, no gas or electricity, the water was off too. They were using a bucket for a toilet. How can that happen?'
> 'If we'd only ... Sal, I don't know. Some people don't want intervention.'
> 'They died like animals, Rachel, worse, there was no dignity.' ...
> 'You don't know, Sal. They may have chosen not to accept any help. People do.'
> 'What I saw – that wasn't a choice. It stinks,' I said. ...
> 'I'm sorry,' I sighed, 'I'm all over the place today. I feel so cross, and it's so sad and then I start to feel guilty.' (Staincliffe, 2007a: 216–17)

The fine line between 'neglect' and 'crime' is, moreover, emphasized by the fact that when Kilkenny first sees the bodies she believes them to have been bludgeoned to death; in actual fact, the marks on Mr Smith's face have been caused by rats (Staincliffe, 2007a: 193).

Staincliffe's second title from 2007, *Missing*, also features what is arguably a crime without a criminal: the suicide of an Iranian asylum seeker called Berfan. In a text which deals with three categories of 'missing person', Berfan's story is the 'mystery which is no mystery': he 'disappears' from the streets of Manchester and later escapes from the psychiatric ward of Wythenshawe Hospital in order to kill himself for the simple reason that he has been refused asylum. As with the case of the Smiths, Kilkenny is seen struggling with the implications of such tragedy when placed alongside her more normal caseload. At the same time she is tracking down Berfan, she is also attempting to reunite an abandoned child with his lost mother and discover what has happened to Janet Florin, a young mother (who, it turns out, has been murdered by her best friend's husband with whom she had been having an affair).

Like the Smiths', Berfan's death is especially distressing: not least because, like theirs, it could have been avoided. The climax of this storyline follows a phone call Berfan makes to his brother (Ramin) from somewhere on the motorway. He has recently gone missing again, this time from the psychiatric ward at Wythenshawe Hospital and, as we discover subsequently, the phone call was to say goodbye. Kilkenny correctly guesses that he is calling from a service station and makes for the nearest: Knutsford Services. She and Ramin apprehend him just as he is about to throw himself under an articulated lorry, but he subsequently escapes again and heads for the petrol pumps where he douses himself with petrol and sets himself alight. He is determined to commit suicide, and – before their eyes – he succeeds:

> Berfan stopped at the edge of the forecourt. He put his hand in his pocket, withdrew it and flicked with his thumb. The spark from the lighter caught the vapour and a sheet of flame ignited over Berfan's upper body. Berfan twisted and staggered, a pillar of fire. Ramin flew to him, knocking him over and smothering the flames in an embrace. (Staincliffe, 2007b: 281)

So shocking and 'sensational' is this horrific event that readers may be as surprised as I was to learn that it closely resembles a real-life suicide by an asylum seeker. Attached to the IRR News Website (Independent Race and Refugee News Network)[21] is a list of asylum-seeker suicides in the UK which includes Babak Ahadi (aged thirty-three) who set fire to himself in Bristol. Of course we cannot know if Staincliffe had this or another 'real-life' suicide in mind when she wrote about Berfan's tragic fate, but the IRR list is a sharp reminder that there is a very material context to this storyline. Not only is Berfan's death 'no mystery' in the world of crime fiction; it is the frequent, if unspoken, fate of rejected asylum seekers in Britain today.

As with the Smiths' deaths, meanwhile, Kilkenny's reflection on Berfan's suicide focuses on the ambiguous nature of 'crime', and the way in which the inaction of the public, either through complicity or indifference, can facilitate events every bit as bloody as armed robbery or murder. In this case, the UK's government's 'hard line' on asylum seekers is arguably the 'cause' of Berfan's death, with everyone who has failed to challenge the existing regulatory practices notionally complicit. Once again, PI Kilkenny mediates this dilemma for the

Manchester's crime fiction

reader: by reflecting upon her own shame and guilt, she causes each one of us to reflect upon what it means to ignore stories like Berfan's:

> Sitting down at my desk, I thought about the sequence of events, tried to explain to myself what had happened ... Berfan had been imprisoned and tortured in Iran. He'd fled to the UK with Ramin. The brothers had applied for asylum and Berfan's request had been denied. He became mentally ill and was sectioned. He ran away from hospital. He was suicidal. He ran in front of a truck. Then he set himself on fire. No mystery.
> Would it have made any difference if his application has been granted? ... Was it inevitable that his mental health would deteriorate so dramatically? Should I have acted differently? ...
> I lay my head on my arms and closed my eyes and stayed there until my limbs grew stiff and my hands got numb. (Staincliffe, 2007b: 293)

Sal Kilkenny's physiological response to the crimes she solves and the atrocities she witnesses is very much a feature of Staincliffe's writing and, I would argue, distinguishes her female PI from many of her sisters, McDermid's Kate Brannigan included. Although not without the guts and determination we now routinely expect of our women PIs and DIs, Kilkenny's visceral response to her environment makes her an extremely empathetic figure and, as illustrated here, something of a moral and political conduit for the reader.

Conclusion

When placed in the context of the crime fiction genre as a whole, it would be difficult to argue that these Macunian texts come up with any significantly different *motives* for crime from those set in London, Chicago, Detroit or Los Angeles.[22] With respect to the motives that fall under the umbrella of 'human nature', especially, we (as readers) are positioned to accept the banal, yet profoundly nihilist, conclusion that 'human nature' (read 'human badness') is the same everywhere. However, as Horsley (2005) and other commentators have shown, crime fiction, in all its variants, has typically exposed the tension between this human(ist) rationale and one grounded is sociological critiques of a kind that render criminality culturally and historically specific. Similarly, if we return to the question of 'who or what is responsible for the crime of Manchester?', all the texts considered here are committed, albeit to a greater or lesser extent, to the view that the crimes perpetrated by individuals must be understood in the context of the crimes done to a district like Greater Manchester as the result of anonymous, institutional forces.

On this last point it also important to acknowledge that my fictional sample does not come close to referencing all the crime writing to have emerged from Manchester in recent times.[23] Key names are missing, most notably Ray Banks, whose novel *Saturday's Child* (2006) headed the Amazon 'Manchester Crime Top Ten' list in 2008 ahead of Smith, McDermid and Staincliffe. Banks was initially passed over by the 'Moving Manchester' project on account of the fact that as a white, mainstream author his work was less likely to address the concerns of migration and diaspora with which we were centrally concerned. Our subsequent review of his work (see e-catalogue) reveals, however, that although primarily concerned with white gangland culture, his fiction is similarly concerned with the economic and social demise of the city and, in particular, with how brutal environments 'breed' brutal characters.[24] Banks's more mainstream fiction can, moreover, be usefully invoked to help specify the dedicated politics and social conscience of the authors dealt with in this chapter who all very recognizably subscribe to a Left-of-Labour critique of contemporary Britain.[25]

The question remains, however, of whether the critique of contemporary society and its institutions found in the city's crime fiction is, ultimately, specific to Manchester. Common sense would tell us that the social and economic factors informing crime in Greater Manchester are, like 'human nature', very much the same the world over and (as noted throughout the chapter) its crime fiction writers may well have based their analysis of such problems on their reading of Raymond Chandler or Chester Himes rather than their familiarity with the city per se. Similarly, there is also the argument (following Taylor, Evans and Fraser, 1996: 206–7) that Manchester may purposely have been chosen as a location by some of the writers on account of its generic reputation as a 'crime capital' rather for any more specific qualities. However, inasmuch as all the writers dealt with here are long-term residents of the city there is, I would suggest, little chance of Manchester having been chosen as a location simply on account of its 'bad-city' reputation. Instead, this chapter has, I trust, provided numerous instances of the specificity of Manchester's social and historical domain being taken into account in the analysis of the crimes committed, be this the institutional racism and homophobia of the Greater Manchester Police in the 1970s and 1980s, the rise of gangland culture in the 1990s or the repeated mistakes of the planning department in attending the city's housing and inner-city redevelopment.

By way of conclusion, I would, indeed, propose that what distinguishes Mancunian crime fiction from other national and international variants is its focus on the city's architectural mapping. Although, on occasion, the roads, buildings, alleyways and cemeteries featured in these texts take on the character of a generic, noirish façade (this could be Leeds, Liverpool or Birmingham as well as Manchester), more often the streets and districts are name-checked with great precision and (as discussed at the beginning of the chapter) carefully graded in terms of their socio-economic class. Similarly, the city's urban redevelopment (whether domestic housing or the gentrification of districts like Canal Street and Castlefield) is noted with a forensic attention to detail comparable to that afforded the investigations themselves, and storylines concerning property development (McDermid, 2002 [1993]), squatting (Staincliffe, 1994), homelessness (Staincliffe, 2007b) and ghettoization (Kalu, 1993, and Smith, 2000) abound.

In other words, if the finger *is* to be pointed anywhere in response to the question 'who or what is responsible for Manchester's crime?' it is surely towards the planners and developers who have created an environment that has shattered communities and exacerbated social and ethnic divisions. Moreover, inasmuch as the practice of residualization (see note 5) has effectively replaced white, working-class slums with black ghettos, the legacy of colonialism continues to be writ tragically, and ironically, large. What Manchester's crime fiction therefore appears to be saying with one voice is that *this*, then, is the 'crime' and that an improvement in the GMC (Greater Manchester Police) crime statistics with which I opened the chapter is unlikely until both houses and communities start to be repaired rather than demolished.

Notes

1 Detailed records of criminal behaviour (including anti-social behaviour (ASB)) are now available on the police website for England and Wales. Localities (including specific streets) can be searched using a googlemap or postcode facility. See: www.police.uk/crime/ (accessed 22 August 2011). A search of the Manchester districts listed here confirms that high levels of crime (including ASB) are still being recorded on a month to month basis, although readers may find it instructive to compare Moss Side and Hulme with more 'upmarket' areas such as Didsbury and Middleton which also register comparatively high levels of crime of all varieties (though less ASB).

Needless to say, these police 'official statistics' may themselves be subject to interpretation.

2 See Chapter 1 for further discussion of the symbolic resonance of these buildings, districts and urban developments; also Pearce (2012a) on the city's road-system.

3 Flânerie has been widely discussed across the field of literary and cultural theory over the past twenty years. See, in particular, Wilson (1991); Parsons (2000) and Highmore (2005) and also Rajeev Balasubramanyam's unpublished PhD thesis (2009).

4 A casual web search will bring up countless articles and reports that identify Manchester as one of the UK's 'crime capitals'. See for example, Ian Wylie's article in the *Manchester Evening News* (2005) at www.menmedia.co.uk/manchestereveningnews/news/s/177/177533_why_we_are_the_capital_of_crime.html (accessed 22 August 2011) or John Steel's 'Britain's murder capital revealed in survey' (*Daily Telegraph*, 2006) at www.telegraph.co.uk/news/uknews/1519123/Britains-murder-capital-revealed-in-survey.html (accessed 22 August 2011). With respect to the juxtaposition of wealth and poverty it should, however, be noted that the location of Manchester's poorest areas in a 'girdle' (see Chapter 1) around the city centre means that expensive shops and low-grade housing are less contiguous than is the case in London (as was demonstrated by the August 2011 'riots').

5 The technical term used to describe this recycling of low-grade housing in inner-city areas is *residualization*: 'By residualization is meant the process whereby public housing in Britain, which was once housing for the bulk of the white working class, becomes housing for the unemployed, minorities, single parents (mostly women) and others on benefit' (Wilson, 1991:148).

6 In common with those of many other modernist writers, Virginia Woolf's plots are structured around moments of sudden illumination ('epiphanies') in which the subject is granted a profound, new insight into the nature of Being. This ('synchronic') moment-in-time is contrasted with ongoing, chronological time, and its spatial dimension also chimes with Bakhtin's work on the chronotope (Pearce, 2004: 67–72).

7 It is also worth noting that in both Jeff Noon's *Vurt* (1993) and *Pollen* (1995) new social hierarchies are formed after the interbreeding of the different species, mimicking the class and 'race' politics of the present. I am grateful to Sarah Post for this observation.

8 Karline Smith was interviewed by Corinne Fowler for the 'Moving Manchester' project on 6 November 2007. In it, she discusses her literary influences (Thomas H. Cook, John Grisham and Chester Himes) and the mixed reception of *Moss Side Massive*, including the (for her frustrating) comparison with Victor Headley (published, like Smith, by X-Press). See also note 18 to Chapter 1.

9 'Social realism': a mode of fiction writing championed by the Marxist critic Georg Lukács that, notwithstanding the terminology, stood in complex

relation to both 'reality' and 'realism'. Lukács expected the socialist realist text both to truthfully describe and analyse the workings of capitalism *and* to create heroic (i.e. idealized or 'typical') characters who would resist and lead the revolution against it. Lukács's most famous work is *The Historical Novel* published in 1937.

10 See also Lyndsey Hanley's excellent study *Estates* (2007) and the chapter on Courttia Newland in Kadija Sesay's *Write Black, Write British* (2005).
11 Malcolm X was an African-American Muslim minister and public rights activist active in the US and across the world in the 1960s. See the official Malcolm X website at: www.malcolmx.com/ (accessed 22 August 2011).
12 The PI, Delroy Johnson, features as a minor character (and friend of Ambrose Patterson) in the earlier novels and one could interpret Kalu's move to PI-centred crime fiction from the police procedural as a political statement on Kalu's part regarding the ever-increasing ineffectiveness of the police force to deal with the crime and injustice suffered by those on the margins of society.
13 See Taylor, Evans and Fraser (1996: 342): 'James Anderton, a police officer of extremely fundamentalist views and notably homophobic sentiment, was appointed Chief Constable of greater Manchester in 1976. Within two years, the Greater Manchester Police (GMP) were conducting regular raids on clubs in central Manchester thought to be used by homosexual people. One of these raids, on Napoleon's, led to an outcry, especially among sections of the local student community. A period of very low key policing followed ... a further raid on Napoleon's, in November 1984 gave rise to further protest from "the gay community". Anderton resigned from office in June 1991.'
14 See http://en.wikipedia.org/wiki/Moors_murders (accessed 22 August 2011): 'The "Moors Murders" were carried out by Ian Brady and Myra Hindley between July 1963 and October 1965 in and around the area of Greater Manchester. The victims were five children aged between 10 and 17 ... at least four of whom were sexually assaulted. The murders are so named because two of their victims were discovered in graves dug on Saddleworth Moor and a third grave was discovered in 1987, over 20 years after Brady and Hindley's trial in 1966. The body of a fourth victim, Keith Bennett, is also suspected to be buried there. Despite repeated searches of the area, it remains undiscovered. Myra Hindley died in 2002; Ian Brady remains (2012) in a high security psychiatric hospital.'
15 Following the 'pop psychologist' Robert D. Hare's 'psychopathy checklist', the psychopath is typically defined as a person possessing some or all of the following characteristics: glib and superficial charm, grandiosity (i.e., sense of one's own importance), need for stimulation, pathological lying, conning and manipulation, lack of remorse, callousness, poor behavioural controls, impulsivity, irresponsibility, failure to accept responsibility for one's own actions. These traits may or may not result in criminal behaviour, but the inability to empathize with one's victims or show remorse for cruel or

brutal behaviour is cited frequently in the assessment and conviction of murderers. See http://en.wikipedia.org/wiki/Hare_Psychopathy_Checklist (accessed 23 August 2011). Robert Hare's book *Without Conscience: The Disturbing World of the Psychopaths Among Us* was first published in 1999.

16 See note 14 for background on the 'Moors murders'. Peter Sutcliffe, 'The Yorkshire Ripper', was responsible for the murder of thirteen women between 1975 and his conviction in 1981. Most of the murders took place in West Yorkshire (Leeds, Huddersfield, Bradford) but two bodies were discovered in Manchester (the allotments close to Southern Cemetery and the grounds of Manchester Royal Infirmary). See http://en.wikipedia.org/wiki/Peter_Sutcliffe (accessed 23 August 2011).

17 Morrissey made this point when interviewed by Kirsty Young for *Desert Island Discs* on 29 November 2009. See: www.bbc.co.uk/programmes/b00p068y (accessed 23 August 2011).

18 It should also be noted that in *Full Crew* (2002), Smith's second 'Moss Side' novel, the character Easy severs all bonds and relationships and is depicted as out-and-out 'bad', especially in comparison with the other characters who continue to demonstrate 'human' values such as compassion and loyalty notwithstanding the criminality in which they are engaged. I am grateful to Sarah Post for this further point.

19 For a history of the Ku Klux Klan who have been operating in the USA since the 1860s see http://en.wikipedia.org/wiki/Ku_Klux_Klan (accessed 23 August 2011). The KKK official site may be viewed at http://kukluxklan.bz/ (accessed 23 August 2011).

20 'Organic community': a concept associated with the cultural theorist Raymond Williams, whose work is centrally concerned with the erosion of local communities (comprized of people of all walks of life and social class) in Western, post-industrial society. See, especially, *Culture and Society* (1958) and *The Country and the City* (1973).

21 The Independent Race and Refugee News Network can be found at: www.irr.org.uk/IRR (accessed 23 August 2011).

22 See Horsley (2005) for discussion of the symbolic resonance of certain American cities in the history of crime fiction: 'Much less comprehensible than Holmes's London, this is an intractable, uncontainable, ultimately unknowable terrain, to be grasped only in a fragmentary way' (2005: 72).

23 This 'recommended' list was compiled by Andy Hansford of Manchester. See: www.amazon.co.uk/Manchester-crime-random-10/lm/R3X4NIMJ 5MU8H/ref (accessed 20/08/08). The authors featured (in list order) are: Ray Banks; Karline Smith; Val McDermid; Cath Staincliffe; Paul Southern; Frank Lean; Nicholas Blincoe; Philip Caverney; Peter Kalu; Chris Simms.

24 See the 'Moving Manchester' e-catalogue for full details (including synopses) of Ray Banks's *Saturday's Child* (2006) and *Beast of Burden* (2009).

25 It is also worth noting that most of the writers dealt with in this chapter

have been affiliated to Commonword at some point in their careers. See Chapters 2 and 4 for further discussion of how influential this organization has been in developing the work of new writers in the city.

References

Arana, V. R. (2005) 'Courttia Newland's Psychological Realism and Consequentialist Ethics', in K. Sesay (ed.), *Write Black, Write British, From Post Colonial to Black British Literature* (Hereford: Hansib).
Balasubramanyan, R. (2009) 'The Evolution of the Compound in Black British Male-Authored Literature: From Arrival to Siege to the Black Flâneur.' Lancaster University, unpublished Phd dissertation.
Banks, R. (2006) *Saturday's Child*. Edinburgh: Polygon.
Banks, R. (2009) *Beast of Burden*. Edinburgh: Polygon.
Blincoe, N. (1998) *Manchester Slingback*. London and Basingstoke: Picador.
Bronte, E. (1995 [1847]) *Wuthering Heights*. Harmondsworth: Penguin.
Duff, M. (2008) *The Hat Check Boy*. Manchester: Commonword/Crocus.
Easton Ellis, B. (1991) *American Psycho*. New York: Picador.
Hanley, L. (2007) *Estates*. London: Granta Paperbacks.
Hare, R. (1999) *Without Conscience: The Disturbing World of the Psychopaths among Us*. Guildford Press.
Haslam, D. (2000) *Manchester, England: The Story of a Pop Cult City*. London: Fourth Estate.
Highmore, B. (2005) *Cityscapes: Cultural Readings in the Material and Symbolic City*. London: Palgrave Macmillian.
Horsley, L. (2005) *Twentieth-century Crime Fiction*. Oxford: Oxford University Press.
Hussain, Z. (2006) *The Curry Mile*. Manchester: Suitcase Press.
Kalu, P. (1993) *Lick Shot*. London: X-Press.
Kalu, P. (1995) *Professor X*. London: X-Press.
Kalu, P. (2002) *Yard Dogs*. London: X-Press.
Kalu, P. (2007) *Little Jack Horner*. Manchester: Shorelines/Suitcase.
Lukács, G. (1989 [1937]) *The Historical Novel*. Trans. H. Mitchell and S. Mitchell. London: Merlin Press.
McDermid, V. (2002 [1993]) *Kick Back*. London: Harper.
McDermid, V. (2006) *The Mermaids Singing*. London: HarperCollins.
Millett, K. (1986 [1969]) *Sexual Politics*. London: Virago.
Noon, J. (1993) *Vurt*. Manchester: Ringpull.
Noon, J. (1995) *Pollen*. Manchester: Ringpull.
Parsons, D. (2000) *Streetwalking the Metropolis: Women, the City and Modernity*. Oxford: Oxford University Press.
Pearce, L. (2004) *Reading Dialogics*. London: Edward Arnold.

Pearce, L. (2007) 'Women Writers and the Elusive Urban Sublime: the View from Manchester, England', *Contemporary Women's Writing*, 1(1), 80–97.

Pearce, L. (2010a) 'Writing and Region in the 21st Century: Epistemological Reflections on Regionally-located Art and Literarure in the Wake of the Digital Revolution', *European Journal of Cultural Studies*, 13 (1), 27–42.

Pearce, L. (2010b), 'Beyond Redemption? Mobilizing Affect in Feminist Reading' in Liljestrom, M. and Paasonen, S. (eds), *Working with Affect in Feminist Readings: Disturbing Differences*. London and New York: Routledge, 151–64.

Pearce, L. (2012a) 'Automobility in Manchester Fiction', *Mobilities*, 7(1), 93–113.

Pearce, L. (2012b). 'The Literary Response to Moss Side, Manchester: Fact or (Genre) Fiction?' in Cockin, K. (ed.), *The Literary North*. London: Palgrave, 220–39.

Pemberton, J. (2000) *Forever and Ever Amen*. London: Hodder Headline.

Plummer, P. (2006) 'Transcultural British Crime Fiction. Mike Phillips's Sam Dean in Matzke, C. and Mühleisen, S. (eds), *Postcolonial Postmortems: Crime Fiction from a Transcultural Perspective*. Amsterdam and New York: Rodophi, 255–87.

Procter, J. (2003) *Dwelling Places: Postwar Black British Writing*. Manchester and New York: Manchester University Press.

Smith, K. (2000) *Moss Side Massive*. London: X-Press.

Smith, K. (2002) *Full Crew*. London: X-Press.

Smith, K. (2007) Interview with Corinne Fowler for the 'Moving Manchester' project. Unpublished transcript.

Staincliffe, C. (1994) *Looking for Trouble: A Sal Kilkenny Mystery*. Manchester: Crocus.

Staincliffe, C. (1998) *Dead Wrong*. London: Hodder.

Staincliffe, C. (2007a) *Bitter Blue*. London: Allison and Busby Limited.

Staincliffe, C. (2007b) *Missing*. London: Allison and Busby Limited.

Taylor, I., Evans, K. and Fraser, P. (1996) *A Tale of Two Cities: Global Change, Local Feeling and Everyday Life in the North of England*. London: Routledge.

Williams, R. (1958) *Culture and Society, 1780–1850*. New York: Columbia University Press.

Williams, R. (1985 [1973]) *The Country and the City*. London: The Hogarth Press.

Wilson, E. (1991) *The Sphinx in the City: Urban Life, the Control of Disorder, and Women*. Berkeley, Los Angeles and Oxford: University of California Press.

Internet sources

www.amazon.co.uk/Manchester-crime-random-10/lm/R3X4NIMJ5MU8H/ref
www.bbc.co.uk/programmes/b00p068y
www.irr.org.uk/IRR
http://kukluxklan.bz/
www.malcolmx.com/
www.menmedia.co.uk/manchestereveningnews/news/s/177/177533_whywe_are_the_capital_of_crime.html
www.police.uk/crime/
www.telegraph.co.uk/news/uknews/1519123/Britains-murder-capital-revealed-in-survey.html
http://en.wikipedia.org/wiki/Hare_Psychopathy_Checklist
http://en.wikipedia.org/wiki/Ku_Klux_Klan
http:/en.wikipedia.org/wiki/Moors murders
http://en.wikipedia.org/wiki/Peter_Sutcliffe

4

Collective resistance
Manchester's mixed-genre anthologies and short-story collections

Lynne Pearce

Along with the crime fiction featured in Chapter 3, the anthology (that is, a multi-authored collection of poetry or prose fiction or – very often – a mixture of both) is the most popular literary genre to emanate from Manchester in recent years.[1] Inasmuch as short stories and poems constitute a more manageable undertaking for non-professional writers than the novel, this is hardly surprising, and the anthology format has, of course, long been a staple of community publishing. However, more radical aesthetic and political claims can be, and have been, made for such anthologies – and, in particular, the short-story collection – which this chapter seeks to endorse with reference to Manchester's literary scene.[2]

The discussion which follows aims to provide an overview of some of the most indicative and distinctive anthologies to have emanated from Manchester in the past four decades followed, in the final section, by a case-study focus on the writings of the Manchester Irish Writers' Group. Combining discussion of the anthologies' thematic preoccupations with their publishing history, I attempt to show how these collectively-authored texts are symptomatic of the social and political function of writing in postcolonial Manchester: through their cross-cultural authorship and interrogation of concepts such as 'migrant', 'exile' and 'home', unrepresentative stereotypes of the city and its people are repeatedly called to account and new voices heard.

Following on from the discussion in Chapter 2 of how Manchester's community publishing and 'live literature' scene has responded to the exclusion of mainstream publishing with regards to poetry, the first part of this chapter pays tribute to the role of both the writing development organization Commonword (and, in particular, its black writing wing, Cultureword, founded in the 1986 by Lemn Sissay) and Comma Press (conceived and managed by Ra Page) in commissioning and promoting mixed-genre anthologies and short-story collections from the 1970s to the present; in so doing, it also charts a journey from the Commonword Writers' Workshop early involvement with working-class writing (as promoted by the Federation of Worker Writers and Community Publishers (hereafter FWWCP) magazine, *The Voice* (1972–84)), through the shift, in the 1980s, to the sponsorship of a wide range of interest groups (e.g. black writing, women's writing, gay and lesbian writing) to the multicultural, cosmopolitan and more esoteric collections of recent times (for example, *The City Life Book of Manchester Short Stories* (Penguin, 1999) and Ra Page's *Comma* anthology (2002)). What it does not include is any close discussion of the single-authored poetry collections to come out of city during this period since poetry is dealt with by Corinne Fowler in Chapter 2.

The final part of the chapter presents the Manchester Irish Writers' Group (founded in 1995) as a case study of a writers' collective operating in the city, and samples their poems and short stories to reflect upon all that is unique in the Irish migration story. Discussion is structured around the theme of temporality with a particular focus on the dislocation of time and space occasioned by the migrant's repeated 'journeys home' in the context of Ireland's tantalizing proximity to the north-west of England.

The evolution of Manchester's mixed-genre anthologies and short story collections

The 1970s

Notwithstanding my opening remarks, not all Manchester's short-story and mixed-genre anthologies are most usefully evaluated in terms of their technical innovation. Since the early 1970s, the city's commitment to adult literacy, writing development and community arts programmes (spearheaded by the Commonword Writers' Workshop (in association with the FWWCP now 'the Fed') and, later, the Gatehouse Project has produced many scores of collections whose claim to literary experiment is small but whose social-historical and political legacy is immense.[3] This is not to suggest that the stories, poems and essays contained in these publications are without artistic merit (many are innovative, eloquent and technically accomplished) but it is clear that the motivation behind the writing of many of the texts that comprize Commonword's flagship 'Write On' series[4] and *The Voice* (the publication of the FWWCP/Fed) was political before it was aesthetic[5] and, as I shall go on to discuss, collective before it was personal.

In this section, then, I begin with a brief overview of the grassroots of Manchester's earliest, extant anthologized writings, before tracing their evolution into the increasingly confident and cutting-edge publications that we associate with the city today. This includes discussion of the parallel history of women's writing in the city which tells its own unique story of social, political and artistic enterprise.

As noted above, and in Chapter 2, the FWWCP/Fed is the national organization that did most to promote working-class literature development and community publishing during the 1970s and early 1980s. In the editorial to *Voices* 19 (Spring 1979) (which was effectively a relaunch of the quarterly magazine) (see Figure 4.2), Michael Rowe identifies the roots of the organization in the TUC (Trades Union Congress) Resolution 42 of 1960 and reaffirms *Voices*' commitment to publishing 'Working Class poems and prose with a Socialist appeal', even though, by this time, some of its early sponsors (such as the TUC's 'Unity of Arts' society) had been disbanded.[6] Looking back through the thirty issues of *Voices* (1972–84) (now available online through the Fed website at www.mancvoices.co.uk),[7] the pre-eminence of Manchester (both as the publishing base and as the home of most of the contributors) is striking, even though this was officially a 'national' magazine. In the very first editorial, Ben Ainley (Ainley, 1972: 1) pays special tribute to the Manchester and District Labour Movement for 'getting the publication underway':

> I can make no great claims for these pieces, except that they are, it seems to me, varied, interesting, freshly written, and in most cases the work of men and women taking up a pen late in life; with some qualms, though with real curiosity as to how it will turn out. We offer this collection to the Labour movement at large, but especially to Manchester and district.

With respect to the particular concerns of *Postcolonial Manchester*, meanwhile, it is possible to point to the relaunch of *Voices* in 1978/79 as the moment when ethnic diversity and racism become central to both the magazine's and the contributors' agenda. The Autumn 1978 edition carries an advertizement for the 'Anti-Nazi League'[8] and a protest song by Jim Ward ('Who are the English?': 38–9) which lambasts the racism and xenophobia of Enoch Powell and his followers. It should be noted,

4.1 Cover of *Voices* 2 (1972).
© The FED.

4.2 Cover of *Voices* 19 (1979).
© The FED.

however, that the Autumn 1978 issue contains only two poems by self-identified black contributors, W. Lloyd Thomas (21–2), and Val McKenzie (54), and the representation of 'black voices' (and, indeed, 'women's voices') versus the magazine's historical focus on the male 'working class' was to prove increasingly divisive in the years ahead.

McKenzie's poem, written when the author was only fourteen, is a brave and impassioned statement on the impossible double-bind of being an 'English/Asian Woman' who wants *both* to 'belong' to the country into which she has been born ('I have been brought up in a Western country / I have gone to school with the other girls' (McKenzie, 1978: 54)) at the same time to stay faithful to her Asian culture except for the pressure to succumb to an arranged marriage:

> But I'm a woman, and Asian woman and proud of it,
> but I want to live my life fully, work, and marry whom I please
> I do not wish to marry a man my parents pay to take me.
> but I am not rebelling against my culture
> and so my difficulty is no longer oppression
> because the only alternative to oppression is Westernisation
> and it is not what I seek.
>
> (McKenzie, 1978: 54)

The repeated 'but' at the beginning of three of McKenzie's sentences encapsulates what has arguably become *the* contradiction for British

Asian women over the past thirty years and the syntactic awkwardness ('but, but, but ...') performs the intractability of the problem more emphatically than any number of sophisticated analyzes. It should also be noted that Val McKenzie's complaint is presented not as personal but collective (the poem is entitled 'One Voice, Many Voices') and, in contrast to a good deal of later writing produced under 'the personal is political' remit, is not fuelled by the quest for individual identity or personhood per se:

> So I'm a voice speaking and wishing to be heard
> Speaking not just for myself but for many other women
> So it is no longer just I, but we, and it's we who are fighting.
> (McKenzie, 1978: 54)

Given the evident urgency of McKenzie's appeal, not to mention its implicit socialism, the rift that subsequently emerged between the members of the FWWCP who believed that *Voices* should continue to be defined by class and those who wished to open it up to other interest groups is surely regrettable. By the end of the magazine's life in 1984, this polarization had come to a very frank, and vocal, head, with the Manchester writer Ailsa Cox (editor of issue 30) proclaiming that 'there is no one working class, any more than one writer's experience will be identical to another's ... There are teenagers and pensioners, women and men, black, white, Asian, Chinese, gay and heterosexual worker writers' (Cox, 1984) at the same time that the Liverpool branch of the FWWCP ('Scotland Road '83') was arguing (in the 'discussion' section of the same issue), equally passionately, for keeping the organization free from the 'dilution' of 'separatist groups'. The Liverpool group proposed that women, gay and black or Asian writers were best served by their own groups and publications ('there are lots of other magazines catering for these separatist groups and the Federation was not designed for them' (*Voices* 30)) and took constitutional issue with the Commonword collective for becoming, de facto, an 'umbrella organization' with multiple 'sub-groups'. What history tells us (see Chapter 2) is that Commonword ultimately won the argument by seceding from the FWWCP and pursuing its own agenda, but the ferocity of the exchanges recorded in these final issues of *Voices* is a salutary reminder of the 'lived' politics at stake in these early anthologies. McKenzie's poem gives voice to one, terrible 'personal and political' dilemma; its publication in an ostensibly working-class literary magazine to another.

The 1980s

Following this schism with FWWCP, Commonword did, indeed, evolve into an umbrella organization with a number of sub-groups, many of which survive to this day. From the early 1980s these included a black writers' group and a women writers' group, both of which have produced numerous anthologies of new writing emanating from Manchester.[9] One of the most important of these early anthologies was *Black and Priceless* (1988). As with most subsequent Crocus anthologies,[10] the stories and poems that comprize the collection are the prize winners of a new writing competition[11] and, although most of the authors are from the North West, a few are London-based (thus challenging the perception of Commonword as an entirely regional organization). The collection also includes a preface by Benjamin Zephaniah (one of Britain's best-known black writers at that time), who looks ahead to a future when publications like *Black and Priceless* will stand as a testament to Britain's black history:

> These words come from a generation who have no real voice in society. They are their own historians; the historians of the future shall have to relate to them if they are to obtain an insight into Black British life in the 1980s (*Black and Priceless*, 1988: ix)

As one of Zephaniah's 'historians of the future', it is hard for me not be moved by his words and, indeed, by the anthology itself which takes us back to the decade when (as outlined in Chapter 1) a new wave of racism, fuelled by unemployment and Thatcherite ideology, made being 'black' and 'British' very difficult indeed. The violence and misery of this historical moment are felt in virtually all of the contributions (see, especially, poems by Karryn Ewers, Peter Kalu and Lemn Sissay) and are well summed up in the frustrated appeal of this extract from John Lyons's 'Englan no Muddercountry':[12]

> Englan no muddercountry.
> Ol West Indian 'istry book
> was tellin lies:
> is white man mamaguy.
>
> Englan
> no 'Land of Hope and Glory',
> ask de so-called black minority,
> dey go tell yuh a different story.

> ...
>
> Man, dis is National Front country
> wid aerosol can graffiti:
> 'Gas the Blacks',
> say di writin on di wall.
>
> Here any Black man can carry
> di collective identity:
> wog, nigger, alien disgrace,
> slum-maker, wife stealer,
> contaminator of di English race,
> job-tief, sociological case;
>
> an yuh tellin mi
> Englan is muddercountry,
> cheups!!
>
> (Lyons, 1988: 69–70)

In addition, the collection addresses international political concerns (e.g. apartheid in South Africa, the Australian government's treatment of Aborigines), thus figuring the 'glocal' and profoundly interrelated nature of racism in a (post)colonial world. On this point, it cannot be stressed enough that (in common with most of the other early Commonword anthologies that I go on to describe) these authors are far less concerned with the traumas of displacement, and the quest for 'belonging', that postcolonial scholars have typically ascribed to first- and second-generation migrants than with the racism of the *white* 'other'. This means that (as in the preceding example) the texts are less introspective and abject than many white readers have been given to suppose since *we*, not *they*, are 'the problem'. In the terms laid down by Gwendolyn Mae Henderson in her seminal essay, 'Speaking in Other Tongues', these are texts that 'enter into familial dialogue with black addressees' and 'contestorial dialogue' with white addressees (Henderson, 1989: 20). Finally, it is important to note that the collection includes many poems and stories that may be considered pilot-texts for the authors concerned and their future careers: Peter Kalu's early detective story 'The Adventures of Maud Mellington', for example, and Qaisra Shahraz's short fiction.

Although *Black and Priceless* itself included more female contributors than male, the late 1980s was also the time when the women writers' group at Commonword started to publish prolifically. Two early anthologies from this period are *Holding Out* (1988) and *Talkers through Dream Doors: Poetry and Short Stories by Black Women* hereafter *Talkers* (1989) which, together, give some indication of the diversity of the women involved in Manchester's writing scene at this time. Both anthologies are edited and produced collectively (to the extent that neither has named editors) and are written out of the 'common experiences' of womanhood as it had come to be understood, and politicized, during the feminist consciousness-raising movement of the late 1970s and early 1980s. The specific violence and oppression of racism for black women is, nevertheless, a feature of both collections even though in *Holding Out* the only black or Asian writers are SuAndi and Qaisra Shahraz.

The support and challenge of living, and living up to, a newly acquired feminist consciousness is referred to directly in Kanta Walker's 'Black Sisters' (*Talkers*) which is also important for its frank acknowledgement of the fact that black women and white women remained differently positioned during this moment in history and also that, *in both camps*, the pressure to 'do one's duty' was immense:

> Black sister
> I haven't seen for a full year
> Rushes up to me
> Like a long lost friend
> Gives me a firm hug
> And a peck on the cheek.
> (Very English –
> Not much of the East in such gestures!)
>
> I return her affection
> Guilt ridden, ashamed
> Why didn't I give her the greetings first?
> She must think of me
> Horribly cold!
>
> ...
>
> 'Life is hard', she starts
> 'Under this racist regime.
> Thatcherite bastards want us out, out.
> See what is happening to Viraj Mendis!
> Yes, they want us out!'
> With vehemence she pronounces.

> ...
>
> 'I would, I would try,
> I would come, of course,
> Of course, it is only for a day',
> I limply say.
>
> She pecks my cheek again, hugs perfunctorily
> And departs looking for another sister
> Who regards
> Love and solidarity among Black sisters
> Another game to be played
> In front of well meaning, white audiences!
>
> (Walker, 1989: 57–8)

Many other entries in these two anthologies nevertheless find solace and support in giving voice to the common experiences of womanhood such as childbirth, unwanted pregnancy, unsatisfactory or abusive sexual relations and what we would now (post-Judith Butler (1990)) think of as the 'performance of femininity'. Indeed, it is in this last particular that the commonality-within-difference of black/white 'sisterhood' becomes especially interesting with Qaisra Shahraz's 'A Pair of Jeans', SuAndi's 'Maidenhood, Motherhood, Womanhood', Ailsa Cox's 'Be a Good Girl' (all from *Holding Out*) and Carlene Montoute's 'Simmy' and Sally Neaser's 'Being a Woman' (both from *Talkers*) all dealing with the requirements involved in 'growing up a woman' and, in particular, the collusion of mothers in a domesticated, obedient version of the female self. Although coming from different cultures, it is striking how many of the young, female narrators of these stories were brought up to be 'quiet', 'docile' and 'good' and how 'appropriate' behaviour was seen as the guarantee of femininity.

In Ailsa's Cox's story, the title phrase 'Be a good girl' is associated with the ridiculous propriety of not being allowed to go to the toilet when visiting elderly relatives ('Be a good girl. Just behave yourself until we get home ... Haven't I told you, you can't go round to people's houses asking to use the toilet' (Cox, 1988: 142)) but echoes, menacingly, through everything that is said to poor Marietta ('And are you a good girl for the teachers, Marietta?' (Cox, 1988: 143)). Reiterated thus, we see how 'being a good girl' is commensurate with covert cruelty and oppression: all that matters to the mother and her female relatives is the keeping up of appearances. In Montoute's 'Simmy',

Collective resistance

meanwhile, we see a young Caribbean girl undergoing another form of physical torture for the sake of appearances: this time, the hot waxing and chemical straightening of her hair. In this instance, the collusion of Simmy's mother is more complex in that she genuinely has her daughter's own interests at heart inasmuch as the latter has been bullied relentlessly at school on account of her 'bad hair'. However, yielding to orthodoxies of Western femininity is still a betrayal of sorts, especially since it will commit poor Simmy to not insignificant pain on a regular basis:

> Simone's heart felt good.
> Her hair problems were finally over . . .
> But this little girl didn't realise that her hair problems had only just begun. (Montoute, 1989: 74)

Crossing cultures yet again, we see similar regulatory practices at work in Qaisra Shahraz's 'A Pair of Jeans'. Shahraz's story has been reprinted twelve times since its first publication in 1988, and is now used throughout the world as a text to help young people think through the lived reality of cultural difference (see 'Moving Manchester' Writers' Gallery for full details). The further twist to Shahraz's story, when placed alongside Cox's, however, is the extent to which its protagonist has internalized the shame of appearing in front of her future in-laws dressed in her jeans. While Cox's story ends with an act of defiance from the young protagonist (when she gets home, she urinates through her knickers), Miriam takes revenge only on the jeans that have shown her up:

> She drew out the repugnant looking article and threw it on the floor, as if it burned her to hold it. She stared at it as if mesmerized by it. Then with her foot she gave it a vicious kick. Her mouth resumed its cynical twist. Her friends would never believe her if she told them.
>
> The shabby looking and much worn pair of jeans lay nonchalantly near the end of the bed, blissfully unaware of the havoc it had created in the life of its wearer. (Shahraz, 1988: 54)

The strength and complexity of Shahraz's story is that it presents us with a female character who genuinely *does* want to be a modest Muslim woman, a 'good girl', even as she enjoys the Western aspects of her life like college and going walking with her friends.[13]

In SuAndi's story, meanwhile, as in Sally Neaser's poem, the impossible pressures of adolescent femininity (being a 'good girl' at home;

being a popular girl at school; having a boyfriend) snap under the strain of an unplanned pregnancy. In such circumstances, girls are forced to grow up quickly (hence the title of SuAndi's story, 'Maidenhood, Motherhood, Womanhood'). In both texts, racial difference is the context rather than the focus of the story, but the extra challenge it lends to young lives trying to do 'the right thing' is heartfelt. Even before she falls pregnant, SuAndi's protagonist has to contend with the fact that, to her boyfriend's brother, she is effectively an 'un-woman': 'although he didn't really like Niggers, he never objected to someone screwing one' (SuAndi, 1988: 100). Surrounded by such bigotry, being a 'good girl' is clearly pushed to the point of impossibility.

Given the profoundly racist context that young black, Asian and mixed-race people had to grow up in during the 1970s and 1980s, it is hardly surprising that a good deal of the poetry contained in the anthologies from the period tackles it head-on. As noted above, a feature of much of this literature is the way in which it calls the white 'other' to account and focuses on him or her as 'the problem'. As a consequence, remarkably few of these texts feature a confessional 'I' and are directed, instead, to the culpable '*you*'. For example, this poem by Sua Huab entitled 'You':

> You live
> In a white-walled city
> And have
> White-washed opinions
> And feel nothing.
>
> You have
> Clear cut conceptions
> Of the situation
> And you feel nothing.
> ...
> But
> ...
> Although you feel
> Nothing
> We feel
> Despite your indifference

Collective resistance

> We feel
> We feel
> We feel.
> (Huab, 1989: 20–1)

With admirable economy and technical finesse (note the poem's skilful use of alliteration, repetition and prepositions to nail home its point), Huab calls the white population of Britain to account for their indifference. In Nayaba Aghedo's 'Invasion', meanwhile, the accusation extends back into the West's postcolonial past and swaps linguistic control for visceral anger:

> For ten thousand years
> We survived
> We built our cities
> We built our pride
> And then you came
> Like a thief in the night
> And stole all you could
> That was ours by right
> You came with your guns
>   Your bible
>   Your beads
> You raped our lands
> And neglected our needs
>
> [...]
>
> But listen now fat Whiteman
> Wipe the blood from your eyes
> AFRIKA is angry
> And now she will arise
> (Aghedo, 1989: 34–5)

Bearing in mind the popular characterization of women's writing from this period as the collective expression of common oppression (as exemplified above), it is important to recognize that *this too* is 'women's writing'. Without any express mention of women or women's suffering (save the gendering of the African land as female), this text's emotion is focused entirely on the 'fat Whiteman' responsible for Africa's ten thousand years of exploitation: at which juncture we should note that this is also the voice of postcolonial Manchester in the

1980s. Looking back to that time through the prism of these texts, we see that Manchester was an ideologically as well as materially contested city upon which many centuries' worth of grievance was deposited, lending new meaning entirely to Avtar Brah's 'diaspora space' (Brah, 1996: 16).

The 1990s

As we move from the 1980s into the 1990s, it is worth pausing to review the evolution of the poetry and prose presented in the Crocus anthologies during this period. As will be evident from the thematic focus to my discussion, it would be fair to say that the majority of the short stories considered thus far have been typically conservative in form. Realist in convention, focused on a single narrator or protagonist and with a plot that stays close to the storyline, most of these narratives are committed to making (or sharing) their point as simply and accessibly as possible. As we shall now see, this is in significant contrast to a good deal of the new fiction that emerges out of Manchester in the 1990s and early 2000s whose formal experimentation is consistent with what is arguably a conceptual and aesthetic turning point in diasporic writing in Britain during this period (see Procter, 2003).[14] With respect to the poetry included in the anthologies, however, the transition is less marked, owing to the fact that, by the late 1980s, Manchester had already established itself as the UK's leading city outside London for radical, performance-based poetry (see Chapters 2 and 5). Therefore, although by no means all the poetry considered thus far belongs to the same tradition as Linton Kwesi Johnson, Lemn Sissay, SuAndi or John Lyons, the ambitious, outspoken nature of these high-profile performers clearly inspired confidence and fostered innovation. On this point, and following on from Corinne Fowler's discussion in Chapter 2, it is clear that Lemn Sissay's anthology, *The Fire People: A Collection of Contemporary Black British Poets* (1998), marked a sea-change in the profile of black poetry in Britain, and the collection includes the work of several Manchester-based poets including Shamshad Khan, John Siddique, SuAndi and Marie Guise Williams. Sissay advertized the collection as 'the new generation of poets who are knocking on the doors of publishing houses ... the new poets, the raw, the fresh Black and British poets – The Fire People' (1998: 8), and the Manchester presence is certainly a testimony to the city's vibrant poetry scene at this transitional time.

Moving from poetry to fiction, the 1990s may be seen as the decade

Collective resistance

in which the city's short-story writing began to catch up with inter/national reputation for poetry – and, of course, music (see Chapter 1). This is not to say that the willingness to experiment was wholesale or immediate: the 1994 Crocus anthology *No Limits: Urban Short Stories* (Bolton et al., 1994) features stories that are still predominantly realist in form but which, as expressions of the contemporary, Mancunian, imagination, are more stylistically adventurous than those featured (for example) in the *Holding Out* (1988) collection discussed above. Instead of reproducing carefully reconstructed autobiographical experiences that, even when fictionalized, are very evidently committed to 'telling the truth' or 'bearing witness', the stories in *No Limits* typically concentrate on a single bizarre, quirky or disturbing incident from everyday life as indicative of the anthology's thematic focus (i.e. contemporary urban living). There is also significantly more interiority and psychological complexity to the stories, with both first- and third-person narrators giving voice to 'mixed emotions' rather than clearly determined passions or beliefs. This 'psychological turn' is evident, for example, in Julie Farrand's 'The Dragon on the Wall' which (as I have observed elsewhere: Pearce, 2007) creates an aesthetic and 'beautiful' portrait of the back streets of Manchester via the consciousness of the story's alienated narrator:

> The weather has been very warm just recently. It makes everyone very lazy and even the dust doesn't move about like it usually does. I sit out on the steps by the back door when it's nice, and get a bit of sun. It really catches it in the yard in the afternoons. I had some pansies in a tub by the gate, but the cats dug them up and pissed in the pots. There aren't many trees or flowers around here. Only the rubbish blooms in the spring, and you catch a waft of it when the breeze is blowing. Some days I feel as though I've been fossilised in a layer of dirt. (Farrand, 1994: 9–10)

Yet this is arguably a middle-class, outsider's view of the city: a positioning reproduced in several of the stories and contextualized via the biographical notes where we learn that several of the authors have come to Manchester to work or study and never left. In this regard it is, indeed, very much a collection arising from the experience of migration even though all the contributors, with the exception of Qaisra Shahraz, are white and (with the exception of Fokkina McDonnell who was Dutch) have moved to Manchester from elsewhere in the UK.

Yet it is here, too, in the stories of white, middle-class migrants, that we can, and should, look for 'postcolonial Manchester'. Read closely, a good many of the stories in the *No Limits* collection reveal something about the city as a 'diaspora space' (Brah, 1996): even if it's no more than a sense of uncertainty of fear about where one lives (as in the Farrand story cited above) or, oppositely, an enthusiasm to immerse oneself in the city's trendily deprived, multicultural cauldron (as in Catriona Smith's 'Legoland on Mescalin' (Bolton et al., 1994: 35–44). The latter, which must be considered one of the anthology's more experimental stories on account of its dramatic form (the story is effectively a dramatic monologue between the narrator and the 'wall' of her student flat in Hulme Crescent), is especially interesting in this respect inasmuch as, while the district's poverty is vividly described, its ethnic mix remains embedded, incidental. We know only that the narrator's immediate neighbour, Tina, is black on account of her dreadlocks even though Hulme itself (see Chapter 1) is synonymous with the mass relocation of Manchester's black population. While this may, indeed, be read positively in political terms (i.e. the multiculturalism of the district is a 'given'), we may also find the silence disquieting: middle-class liberalism, politeness and reserve – not knowing quite *what* to say. In this respect, Noel Hannan's futuristic story that opens the collection is an interesting variant inasmuch as it features a central protagonist, Luisa, of unspecified race who is seen to feel very *unsafe* about living in the 'war zone' her city has become:

> Downtown is in uproar, a usual Saturday night.
> Animosity develops through fistfights into knifefights, knifefights into gun battles, and gun battles into turf war, all fuelled by long-standing hatreds and alcohol and drug consumption.
> My city is a war zone.
> (my city) (Hannan, 1994: 6)

Here, both the surrealist representation of the futuristic city that Manchester has become, and the willingness to dramatize rather than evade the ethnic and other conflicts that are indicative of contemporary urban living, look forward to the next generation of Mancunian short stories as well as the crime sci-fi of Peter Kalu and the cyberpunk fiction of writers like Jeff Noon (see Chapter 3).

The boldness that distinguishes Hannan's story also finds its way into the next generation of the city's female-authored anthologies. While a sense of collective, cross-cultural 'sisterhood' still inspires the production of these volumes (up to and including the time of writing),[15] the woman-centred suffering and injustice that preoccupied the early

Collective resistance

anthologies has, by the late 1990s, been replaced by poetry and stories that are more nuanced in both their emotional range and their politics. One especially stylish collection from this period is *Healing Strategies for Women at War: Seven Black Women Poets* from 1999. Another Crocus/Commonword publication, this anthology nevertheless looks, and reads, very differently from *Talkers through Dream Doors* published ten years previously (see Figure 4.3). With an introduction by the Manchester writer and University lecturer Jacqueline Roy, its contribution to postcolonial literature and criticism (as well as to black British writing) is made explicit, and the reader invited to reflect upon the issues and debates that the poems enter into (such as an interrogation of Britishness) rather than the simple fact that they were written by black women.

Another departure for this volume (not strictly an anthology) is the fact that the seven poets represented (namely, Maya Chowdhry, Marie Guise Williams, SuAndi, Shamshad Khan, Trudy Blake, Tang Lin and Seni Seneviratne) are each represented by a substantive number of poems: an approach deemed necessary by the editors who note that, here, 'each poet is given enough space to do justice to her own poetic voice' (Chowdhry et al., 1999: xiv). This decision distinguishes the collection markedly from the earlier anthologies we have looked at, forcing the reader to come to terms with the thematic and formal preoccupations of each individual poet rather than leaping from one eye-catching title to another. Moreover, the multiethnic spread of authors whose diasporic roots are in Sri Lanka, India, Pakistan, China and the Caribbean causes us to think carefully about the diversity implicit in 'black British' subjecthood and the way in which different cultural traditions impact upon the function and aesthetics of writing.

Two poems which illustrate this last point well are Shamshad Khan's 'Silver Threads' and Tang Lin's 'naked frame' since both draw upon the aesthetic conventions and cultural traditions associated with their 'parent' culture (Pakistan and China) to capture the experience of romantic love. In each case, the poet (re)presents deep feeling through imagery, tropes and verse forms that will be unfamiliar to most Western readers. In Khan's case, the 'code' is both sensual and visceral:

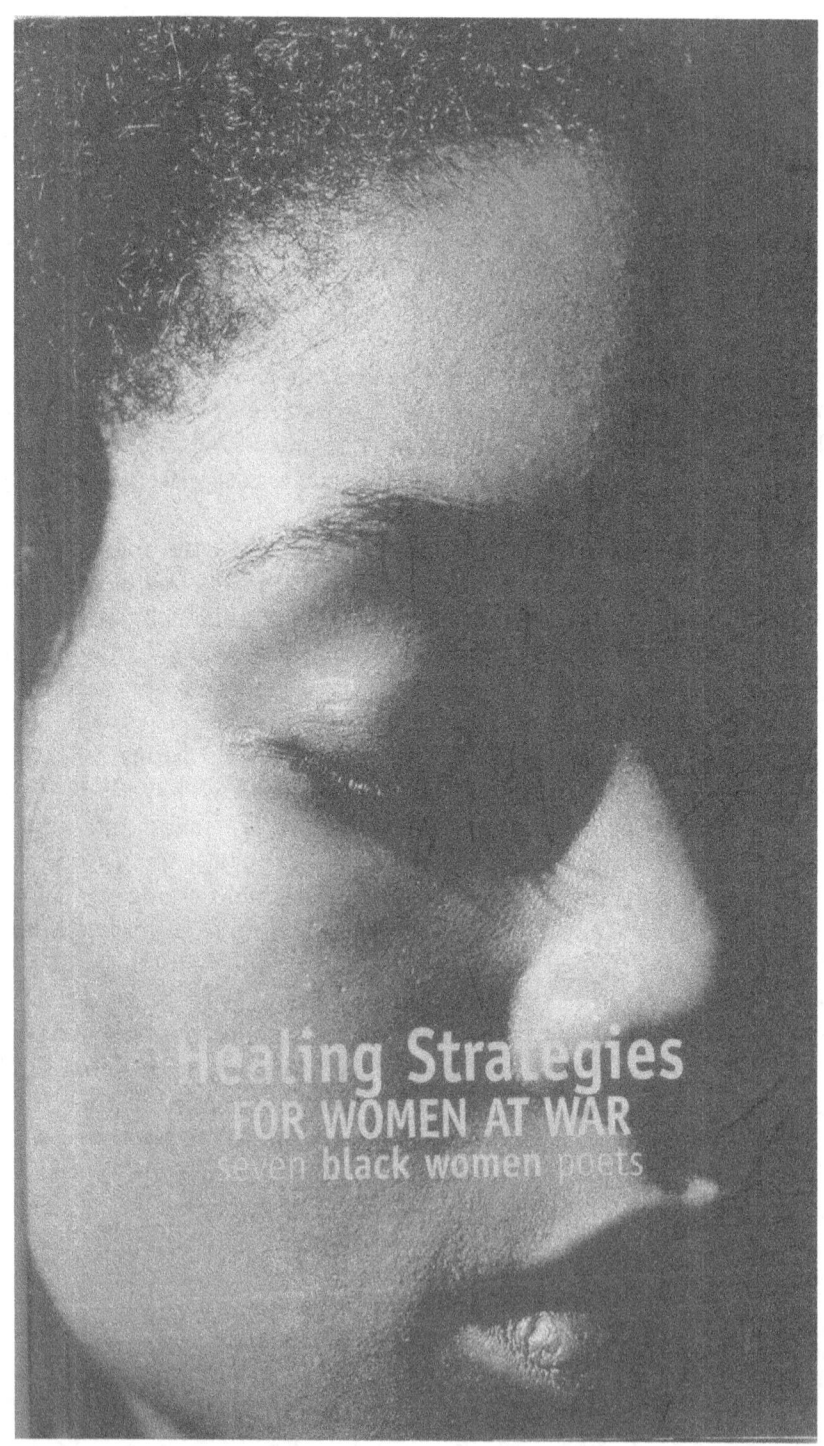

4.3 Cover of *Healing Strategies* (1999). © Commonword.

Collective resistance

> Together we built a palace
> mahal
> domes and minarets
> tiny blue tiles and mirrors.
>
> Wandered
> hand in hand
> warm feet
> on cool floors.
>
> Ran up stairs to call
> from towers piercing skies.
>
> Rushed through gardens
> pomegranates and white flowers
> ruby sweet pungent scent.
>
> (Khan, 1999: 63)

For Lin, however, the sensual is rapidly *dis*-embodied; rendered intellectual, spiritual:

> you touch me
>   you kiss me
>   you make love to me
>
> water
>   floods
>   the earth
>
> i hear the song of love
>   in the wind
>
> the grass
>   drinks the rain
> i hear the song of love
>   in the wind
>
> the wind
>   is singing
>
> the song of love
>   is in the wind
>
> (Lin, 1999: 100)

In both cases, however, literary form and cultural convention fuse to create a version of the love song (indeed of love itself) that is unfamiliar to the Western reader and which renders the English language fresh and 'other' to itself: another instance of how the writing that has emanated from Manchester in the past thirty years is manifestly 'postcolonial'. When taken as whole, moreover, this collection of seven poets at the top of their game arguably takes both women's writing and black British writing to a new level of technical accomplishment.

The millennium and after

The 'new look' of this Crocus collection, published in 1999, spills over into the millennium with a raft of anthologies that sought to gain wider recognition for the Manchester literary scene. A key mover in this enterprise has been the writer and publisher Ra Page, who set up Comma Press with the express purpose of selling Manchester writing to a wide, international audience. Previous to this, his *City Life Book of Manchester Short Stories* (1999), published by Penguin, laid down a manifesto for the type of new writing and new audiences he was trying to capture. Drawing a direct connection with the success and international renown of the city's popular music industry (see Chapter 1), Page insists that a similar innovation, dynamism and edge are to be found in its contemporary writing, another expression of the region's hard-wired *musicality*:

> [Because] the natural voice of the city, its language, perspective and character are, I believe, intrinsically wrapped up in its musical lyricism: 'the ready-made poetry of Mancunian conversation' ... the song-infused speech that laced the early plays of Shelagh Delaney with obscure ballads and nursery rhymes ... the rich rhythms of Jeff Noon or in the career trajectory of Factory-signed-rapper turned best-selling novelist Nicholas Blincoe. (Page, 1999: xv–xvi)

The links that Page draws between Manchester's writing scene and its music scene are, in the first instance, very literal. Three of the anthology's authors are also big names in the music business: Nicholas Blincoe (ex-rapper); Dave Haslam (Haçienda DJ and author of *Manchester, England* (2000)); and Mark E. Smith, lead-singer and songwriter with the long-standing cult rock band The Fall.

Compiling the *City Life Book of Manchester Short Stories* when he did, at the end of the 1990s, Page was certainly able to capitalize on Manchester's recent celebrity status as one of the world's coolest cities and to target the young, educated, upwardly mobile readership associated with *City Life*, the fortnightly city entertainment guide and the book's sponsors. This is a somewhat different demographic to that associated with the Commonword anthologies, not least because the contributors (with two exceptions, Jackie Kay and Karline Smith) are white and all, without exception, published writers of some standing. Other well-known names in the collection include: the crime fiction writers Cath Staincliffe and Val McDermid (see Chapter 3); the best-selling author of *Once in a House on Fire* (1998), Andrea Ashworth; the founding editor of Carcanet Press, Michael Schmidt; the sci-fi author Jeff Noon; prize-winning novelists such as Michael Bracewell and Livi Michael; and two icons of twentieth-century northern literature, Shelagh Delaney (*A Taste of Honey*, 1958) and Bill Naughton (*Alfie*, 1963).

In the Foreword, meanwhile, the *City Life* editor, Chris Sharratt, makes a special pitch for the short story genre and *City Life*'s role in its regeneration. He writes: 'The anthology began as a germ of an idea that could only grow into something much bigger: a desire to reflect the city's contemporary literary scene and promote that most undervalued of literary forms, the short story' (Page, 1999: xix). Packaging aside, the extent to which this collection really does break new ground *vis-à-vis* the short story form remains debatable; with one or two exceptions (discussed below), most of the stories abide by the genre's tried and tested conventions. This said, taken as a whole, the collection does have a touch of *zeitgeist* about it and contains some memorable depictions of millennial Manchester.

Two of the most resonant of these cityscapes are, for me, Livi Michael's 'Robinson Street' (1999) (discussed in Chapter 1) and Michael Bracewell's 'Blackley, Crumpsall, Harpurhey' (1999). Indeed, the latter featured as the centrepiece of my article on the 'urban sublime' (Pearce, 2007) which explored the aestheticization of Manchester and its environs with specific reference to class and gender. While undertaking this research for a journal on contemporary women's writing, I nevertheless confessed to being both moved and amazed by the beauty and sublimity of Bracewell's portrait of the urban landscape: 'Here, at last, was a view of the city that rendered daily features of urban life – the houses, the streets, the bins, the detritus – sublime rather than abject and, by implication, expressed love for, and affiliation towards, the carefully labelled districts concerned' (Pearce, 2007: 86). In contrast to the other Mancunian authors under consideration who, for a range of very good reasons (i.e. poverty, racism, social exclusion, the threat of sexual violence), were unable to discover beauty in their home town or, indeed, to *love* it, here was a writer who managed to render even a patch of derelict land exquisite:

> Tall grey bins have been left upturned at crazy angles, and some stacked waste timber, swollen with damp, is catching the pink light of the afternoon sun. A mongrel dog, its coat the colour of cigarette ash ... is trotting towards the main road – where shattered glass glints around the edges of a telephone box, and the low sweep of vivid turf makes a child's drawing of the new estate. (Bracewell, 1999: 114–15)

Aestheticizing the cityscape at the expense of its 'material reality' as Bracewell arguably does here is arguably one of the ways in which Manchester has had its colonial past airbrushed out; nevertheless, as I discuss in the 2007 article, aesthetic perception clearly plays a crucial role in our affiliation to a place, and the stereotyping of Manchester as 'rainy', 'grey' and 'cold' is a discourse that may have unhelpfully stood in the way of many incomers' relationship to their 'destination home' (Pearce, 2000: 32 and Chapter 1 above).

The high-octane aestheticism of Bracewell's vision of the city was certainly spotted by the sci-fi or cyberpunk author Jeff Noon, whose own contribution to the *City Life* anthology is a tongue-in-cheek parody of 'Blackley, Crumpsall, Harpurhey' entitled 'Cobralingus Remix'. Presumably drawing upon both authors' long-standing investment in the Manchester music scene, this 'remix' leaps off the page as the most experimental piece in the *City Life* collection. Not only does Noon's text disrespect Bracewell's purple prose but, more profoundly, it disrespects *the short-story form itself*, through the mutilation of what has traditionally been seen to be its most important ingredient: that is, *the story* (Narayan, 1985).[16] Hacked into short gobbits, a selection of Bracewell's descriptive passages (including the one cited above), are 'purified' into text reminiscent of an imagist poem (see below) before being 'randomized' and 'enhanced' into a (song) 'sample' entitled 'Manchester Streets' that, presumably, would sit well on top of the electronic dance-rhythms of a band like New Order:[17]

PURIFY
Clouds
White remnants held in a stillness
Where Sunday lays sorrow on the heart,
Swollen with a damp pink light.
A mongrel dog.
Cigarette ash
Descending.

(Noon, 1999: 128)

SAMPLE

Dusk, the near future. Saturday night at the Rust Club, where Mongrel Gothic performs songs from their latest release, *Bouquets of Drone* ...

Outside the club, lank children play, dreams of petrol in their eyes. While, in the nearby churchyard, a lonely kid makes a drawing of Manchester, all crazy angels and swollen clouds. Sodden flowers, wired to a cross.

His sister's grave. (Noon, 1999: 129–30)

What Noon produces here (and one has to admire the ingenuity!) is a version of the Bracewell original that calls into question whether stories really *need* all the connective tissue that is traditionally built into them in order to function as stories. 'Blackley, Crumpsall, Harpurhey' is, at this stage of Noon's reprocessing, no more than a collection of disaggregated 'stage directions' and yet, with the help of a proactive imagination, the reader can easily find *a* story in the lines and take it whichever way he or she chooses.

The second part of Noon's remix is, effectively, a masterclass in how this is done: having 'enhanced' the 'purified' sample into a new set of narrative possibilities in which the 'mongrel dog' has morphed into a Gothic rock band, and the 'crazy *angles*' of Bracewell's 'grey bins' into the 'crazy *angels*' of a bereaved child, a whole new set of narrative possibilities emerge. By the end of Noon's processing, this has included relocating the cityscape and its characters to a futuristic Saturn ('[a]t dusk, on the lakes of aroma, the people of Saturn gather relic songs from the mist' (Noon, 1999: 133)) and, ultimately a distillation of the whole into a *sonnet* (entitled 'Outlet'). The latter would appear to give voice to the 'essence' of Bracewell's story without the encumbrance of character, location or storyline: a tongue-in-cheek performance, perhaps, of Edgar Allan Poe's view that, to succeed, a short story (like a poem) has to be built upon 'unity of effect or impression' (Poe in Rau (2005): 316).

> Along the crescent of the tongue allow
> These words . . .
> Allow the ghost, the skin, the sky inspire;
> And soft in sorrow's cloud, allow the sun.
> Allow that wings be fixed to every brow;
> And every child of dust, a tongue endow.
>
> (Noon, 1999: 135)

Needless to say, all this is at the expense of a textual location called 'Manchester': but what Noon's ransacking of Bracewell's lyrical adjectives has perhaps shown us is that there may not have been very much 'Manchester' in the original text.

As noted above, it was in part the success of the *City Life Book of Manchester Short Stories* that inspired Ra Page to set up his own press, Comma, devoted both to the genre and to writing from the north of England. In the introduction to the first anthology (entitled, simply, *Comma* (2002)), Page offers a short overview of the genre and the (generally unsatisfactory) attempts to define it before setting forth his own critical opinion: namely, that the short story (at its sharpest, most radical and therefore most interesting) is (like poetry) *about gaps*:

> In short stories, the gaps are less uniform. Ostensibly they're the before and after; the back-story we're never told which, if the author's timing is right, we don't need to be told; and the outcome, the ever after, the next episode in the protagonist's evidently episodic existence. Or rather they're the *lack* of an existence either side. (Page, 2002: ix)

This vision of the short story being defined by its gaps was precisely what caused Page to call his press 'Comma' ('These blank canvases, these hesitations are the spots of time, that appear within the spots of time. Hence "Comma"' (Page, 2002: x)), and this first anthology (whose contributors are writers and journalists living in, or associated with, Manchester) is certainly a credit to the artistry of the form in this respect. What Page doesn't mention in his introduction, and what is unquestionably another feature of the anthology, is the way that it 'challenges our perceptions and understandings of the world' (see 'Moving Manchester' e-catalogue)[18] through its mixture of realist, surrealist and fantastical contributions. In contrast to the anthologies considered thus far which have remained predominantly realist in form,[19] *Comma* purposefully moves between 'other lives and other worlds' (e-catalogue) in ways that intrigue and unsettle the reader in a manner similar to the juxtaposition of the Bracewell story and Noon 'remix' discussed above.

Collective resistance

In terms of its postcolonial footprint and general politics, *Comma* is rather harder to pin down. With the exception of Tariq Mehmood (whose story 'The Peacock's Dance' takes the form of a powerful allegory set in Pakistan) all the contributors are white and, without exception, professional writers and/or journalists. There is only one story (Anthony Wilson's tense and unresolved micro-thriller about a Muslim waiting to be interviewed by Al Jazeera: is he about to blow himself up in front of the cameras?) which is ostensibly 'about' issues of race and ethnicity, and fewer that are recognizably located on the streets of Manchester than in the *City Life* collection. Michael Bracewell ('Nocturne'), Shelagh Delaney ('Abduction'), Wayne Clews ('Going to the Dogs') and Clare Pollard ('Kirsten vs the City') are the notable exceptions to this, and the latter's chilling account of a young girl's fear ('paranoia'?) of being stalked and murdered in her own city – her 'home' – is certainly one of the strongest and most memorable stories in the collection.

With Page's re-profiling of the Mancunian anthology in mind, I now complete my survey of its evolution by returning to Commonword/ Crocus and investigating how its publications adapted to the creative and commercial challenges of the 2000s. The good news is that, up to and including the time of writing (2012), the Commonword organization continues to survive every political and economic uncertainty thrown in its way (which, most recently, has included a change of national government and uncertainty about the future of Arts Council funding). This survival, moreover, reflected in the tremendous variety of publications it continues to bring out (see www.commonword.org), clearly owes a good deal to its diversification into an 'umbrella organization' in the late 1970s (i.e. the very move that was looked upon so unfavourably by some factions within the FWWCP). Now, thirty years on, it is arguable that it is precisely this diversification into different communities of writers (black writers, Asian writers, women writers, black and gay writers etc.) that has ensured both its survival and its publishing success, even if its modus operandi and informing ideology (niche publications with dedicated authorships or readerships) is the polar opposite of the Comma initiative. Indeed, Commonword's strongly independent response to the post-millennial publishing environment and the pressures of a multicultural orthodoxy has led to a further raft of highly distinctive publications.

While it is clearly impossible to do justice to the full backlist of titles published by Commonword/Crocus since 2000 (see Commonword

4.4 Cover of *City Secrets* (2002). © Commonword.

website), the following sample will, I hope, offer some indication of how the press has moved forward in the past ten years. The first anthology I should like to mention in this context is *City Secrets*, edited by Cathy Bolton and P. P. Hartnett and published in 2002. Bolton, the co-author of one of the early anthologies considered here (*No Limits: Urban Short Stories*, 1994), has been a pivotal figure in the Manchester literary scene (especially with regards to women's writing and gay and lesbian writing) for many years. In both appearance and content, *City Secrets* is nevertheless a world away from the earlier publication. Although the words 'gay, 'lesbian' or 'queer' do not feature in its title (itself an interesting decision which marks this out as a 2000s rather than an 1980s anthology), the blurb on the back cover of the volume nevertheless makes clear that this is a collection of stories by 'lesbian, gay, bisexual and transgender writers' whose point of cultural reference is the (then) hip TV series *Sex in the City* and *Queer as Folk*. As well as signalling that LGBT writing is now as cool as it is political, the collection also attempts to break new ground *vis-à-vis* the 'non-politically correct' nature of many of the storylines. In the introduction, figured as a dialogue between the two editors, the reader is advized that these are not tales for those in search of a happy, comfortable gay romance:

> P-P H: Many of them explore less than wholesome lifestyles and not-so loving relationships. I think it's a sign of maturity that we can own up to being as obsessive, vindictive, manipulative and downright perverse as straight people.
>
> CB: Mm. There's been one fuck of a lot of blinkered thinking and self-censorship in the past. Here people are just doing their own thing, rather than playing to a formula or working a really obvious commercial angle for a market that is long dead. (Bolton and Hartnett, 2002: 8)

Bolton's running together of form and aesthetic ('playing to a formula'), political conservatism ('blinkered thinking and self-censorship') and 'the market' is especially interesting here, and invites us to look back over some of the earlier anthologies (her own included) from this freshly liberated perspective. In much the same way that Queer Theory exposed the way in which all orthodoxies (within the field of race as well as gender and sexuality) depend upon the existence of the deviant 'other' to sustain their illusion of normativity (Pearce, 1998: 17–18, n.2), so does Bolton, here, hint at the way in which gay writing has responded to this positioning with its *own* orthodoxy and censorship (i.e. a covert desire for approval).

The stories that constitute *City Secrets* certainly make a good job of throwing all aspects of orthodoxy to the wind, favouring writing styles that are, in many instances, as nonconformist as the sex. P. P. Harnett's own story, 'CCTV Eyes', Keith Munro's 'Gutted' and Sean Burn's 'Edgecity' certainly stand out in this respect and, taken together, the anthology arguably exceeds the stylistic experimentation found in the other anthologies considered thus far including *City Limits* and *Comma*. This is significant inasmuch as it suggests that the revitalization of the short-story form that Page was consciously promoting in his collections can also be found in avant-garde, niche publishing. On this point it is, of course, important to acknowledge that there is significant trade and overlap between Comma and Commonword/Crocus from this moment forth: Hartnett was himself a contributor to the *City Life* anthology and, in appearance and pitch, this whole wave of anthologies would appear to belong to the same, 'out' and stylish cosmopolitan moment.[20] It should, however, be noted that *City Secrets* (like the *City Life* and *Comma* anthologies) is a predominantly 'white' anthology, with only two stories (Helen Smith's 'That's Adolescence' and R. Stockdale's 'After the Queen's Head') dealing with a multiethnic cast of characters. However, this is arguably not a problem if we think of *City Life* as just one of the 'niche' publications emanating from Commonword/Cultureword and the Crocus imprint at this time, many of which would have represented the work of black and Asian writers.

Many of the things that have been said about the style, politics and political context of *City Secrets* could also be said about the Crocus anthology *Bitch Lit* from 2006. Edited by Maya Chowdhry and Mary Sharratt, *Bitch Lit* is another example of smart, hard-edged contemporary writing to which the term 'cosmopolitan' could easily be applied without the reader thinking too carefully about what that might actually mean. In this case, the presence of Chowdhry herself, as both contributor and editor, diversifies the ethnic profile of the collection, though it is interesting to observe that in Chowdhry's own story, 'Acting Real', the ethnicity of the characters (while visible in their names) is not overtly significant within a highly complex tale of S&M sex, fake identity, power, exploitation and revenge. In common with the remit of *City Secrets*, discussed above, *Bitch Lit* is evidently committed to moving beyond a laudable but safe consciousness-raising agenda and to commissioning stories in which female characters follow their desires rather than their consciousnesses. In the Introduction, Chowdhry and Sharratt present their radical agenda thus:

> Is Bitch Lit a new genre?
>
> Maya Chowdhry: It's not a term you'll find in the dictionary – yet! Of course, women were creating stories about strong female characters before we came up with the idea of Bitch Lit, just in the same way that there were lots of books written about simpering women before someone in a marketing department coined the term Chick Lit.
>
> ...
>
> MC: All these stories, in one way or another, are about women and power. They are the opposite of cautionary tales. They goad us and dare us to strip off our niceness, to be real, leave our safe haven and go out into the dark woods knowing that the most dangerously sublime thing to be encountered in that forest is ourselves unleashed. (Chowdhry and Sharratt, 2006: 6–8)

Read alongside some of the early anthologies reviewed here, this mission statement is, indeed, a striking reminder of the ideological and

4.5 Cover of the *Hair* anthology (2006). © Commonword.

literary distance Manchester's women writers have travelled since the 1970s. Instead of coming together to challenge patriarchal oppression through consciousness-raising and political marches, Chowdhry and Sharratt are proposing that women writers initiate a new genre of 'revenge fantasy' that will unleash their 'inner demons' and (one presumes) make whatever stands in their way take note. On this point, it is important to observe that, whilst the spectre of patriarchy still lurks in several of the stories, by no means are 'men' the only target of these writers. A number of stories (Rosie Lugosi's 'My Dear', Michelle Green's 'Forklift Trucks', Chowdhry's 'Acting Real' and Jo Stanley's 'Die, You Bastard') feature lesbian characters and storylines and, true to Chowdhry's clarion-call, the *majority* feature narrators who are rather less than 'nice'. While it would clearly be wrong to describe any publication coming out of Commonword (which still holds its women's group meetings on a regular basis and is faithful to its roots in every regard) as *post*-feminist, it is evident that power, and politics, mean something rather different to this group of writers. However, the empowerment that comes with writing itself is a recognizable thread binding past and present, and the fact that in *Bitch Lit* the authors are prepared to 'pack a punch' in more senses than one suggests that this is a raison d'être by no means exhausted.

Finally, to end this compressed but, I trust, indicative overview of Manchester's anthologies, I turn to the 2006 Commonword/Suitcase[21] volume *Hair: A Journey into the Afro & Asian Experience*. Edited by Peter Kalu and Shirley May, *Hair* includes no fewer than 118 poems, fiction extracts and, as it says on the cover, 'styling tips'. Although, at first sight, this might appear to be a rather idiosyncratic themed anthology, closer inspection reveals it to go to the heart not only of black experience (personal and political) but also to the Commonword/Cultureword mission of providing writers operating outside the mainstream to have their voices heard in defiance of market forces and publishing trends.[22] This is not to imply that *Hair* is a less contemporary or innovative publication than the City Life and Comma anthologies discussed above (indeed, the eye-catching cover signals the opposite), but, as with all Commonword/Crocus/Suitcase publications from the past thirty years, a concern with the market or audience is secondary to a commitment to the writing itself: writing that may, or may not, be about things in which the wider (white) public are interested. In the editorial, Kalu and May explain that the anthology began life as an open call for writing on the subject of 'hair':

> The contributors' backgrounds are wide ranging: from office workers and landladies to teachers and plumbers, from teenagers to poets in their eighties. The only criterion has been that the poems must move and engage, tell something new, or reveal something old in a new light. (Kalu and May, 2006: 14)

It is this editorial policy that makes Commonword titles, even today, very different publications from the City Life and Comma anthologies discussed above where the contributors were hand-picked with a particular product or audience in mind.

Now into its fourth decade, Commonword is nevertheless an organization that attracts submissions from well-known and established writers as well as non-professionals. Notwithstanding the egalitarian note struck in the preceding extract, the *Hair* anthology includes poems and stories from several high-profile black writers (e.g. Kanta Walker, Shamshad Khan, John Lyons, Jackie Kay, and SuAndi), and it is the juxtaposition of these established figures with a plethora of new voices that gives anthologies like *Hair* their freshness and integrity. In the opening section ('At Mama's Feet'), for example, writers of all ages and backgrounds reflect upon the horrors of the 'hot comb' traditionally used to tame and straighten Afro-hair: a covert, routine, domestic torture which all too many black women of a certain age seem to have shared:

> Watch the comb
> Heat up on top of the stove
> Til the devil-thing turns red
> Just like the priest promised:
> Red-hot torture
> For all my sins.
>
> ...
>
> Play statue
> While it sizzles in my still-wet hair,
> Pray it doesn't burn my ear.
> (It's embarrassing to go to school
> With comb-marks on your neck).
> (Martin, 2006: 20–1)

In itself, such 'giving testament to' black experience is indistinguishable from the many poems and stories in Commonword's earliest anthologies (and, indeed, Carlene Montoute's story 'Simmy', featured in

Talkers through Dream Doors (Montoute, 1989) and discussed above, tells a very similar story to this). Context is all, however, and the *Hair* anthology sets up a very different dynamic between authors, readers and texts from that created by the early anthologies that were defined, and distinguished, primarily by the authors' ethnicity, gender or sexual orientation. The focus on a cultural commodity such as hair, or, in the case of *Bitch Lit*, female empowerment and revenge, enables both authors and editors to approach historical and ongoing political concerns 'slant'. This is no way diminishes the political purpose of the project but does, arguably, inspire more innovative writing through processes of defamiliarization and (in the case of the short story) an unusual topical focus. Therefore, despite Ra Page's call (in the introduction to the *Comma* anthology) for writers and editors to renounce the 'indifference' of 'themed' anthologies (Page, 2002: viii), Commonword's *City Secrets*, *Bitch Lit* and *Hair* prove that the 'formula' still has a good deal to commend it.

Manchester Irish writers' group

In the final section of this chapter, I turn to the writings of the Manchester Irish Writers' group,[23] founded in 1995, and the anthologies and collections published by the group's imprint, Scribhneoiri Press.[24] My focus is the highly distinctive temporalities featured in the poems and stories which speak both to the powerful collective consciousness of the Irish diaspora and also to the somewhat unusual experience of having one's natal and destination 'homes' so close together.

For while all Manchester's diasporas will necessarily experience time and space in unique, and often disconcerting, ways, the history of the Manchester Irish has arguably been defined by the fact that Ireland (both the north and the Republic) has always been no more than a short step 'across the water' to and from north-west England; and this, in turn, has given rise to migrant experience marked by repetition and reprize. Needless to say, travel backwards and forwards from one's place of origin (Rouse's (1991) 'circuits of migration')[25] is now increasingly common across all the world's diasporas, but for the Irish relocated in Britain, and the North West in particular, it has become not only a possibility but an expectation. Apart from the family and cultural pressures that arize from this, the extreme proximity of one's past life has given rise to a complex, and often confused, sense of diasporic identity for migrants who sometimes return home with the frequency of commuters. As Breda Gray has observed: 'It may also be the case that the act of emigration is more immanent when the country of immigration is geographically proximate to the country of origin' (Gray, 2000: 76). The inference here is that, for members of the Irish-English diaspora, migration is experienced as a process of perpetual leave-taking and endlessly deferred arrival; moreover, in terms of a locational or national identity, it means always to remain *filiated* to the country left behind rather than *affiliated* to the new one (in contradistinction to what Edward Said has deemed the 'natural' trajectory).[26] Further, this would seem to be as true for those migrants who never, or rarely, return home despite the promixity as for those who make the journey regularly (i.e. the abiding contingency of one's old home is the crucial factor).

On this last point, there is striking evidence that the early twentieth-century north-west Irish diaspora into which the Bolton writer Bill Naughton was born still identified with the people and places left behind, even though the families concerned might never expect to see Ireland again. In *Saintly Billy* (1988), Naughton depicts his mother chatting to extended-family members about people and places in Ireland as though it were only a street or two away, and on one memorable occasion, during the Miners' Strike of 1921, she is suddenly transfixed by a breeze which reminds her of home:

> 'I came down Thomas Rostron Street there,' she said, 'an' do you know I couldn't believe it, the breeze that was there! I stood in the street a minute – the people must have thought me mad – I stood for a full minute, feelin' the way it was blowin' across one's face, and within the eyes, so it seemed. It was just like I was comin' down the little hill back at home.' (Naughton, 1988: 66)

Naughton observes 'I had never realized before how much she missed Ireland' (Naughton, 1988: 66), though we could equally read the incident as evidence that she has never properly left it.

In a poem written shortly after she had first been introduced to the work of the Manchester Irish Writers' Group, Eileen Holroyd recognizes this same preoccupation with migration as both 'endless' and 'endlessly repeated':

> The little histories interest me
> not differences but repeated
> patterns of migration leaving
> reasons to imagine
> (Hinchcliffe and Hughes, 2001: 13)

In significant contrast to the writings of other diasporic communities featured on the 'Moving Manchester' e-catalogue, then, these Irish writers (second- as well as first-generation migrants) show little inclination to leave either their homeland or the iconic moment of departure behind. Indeed, there is a very real sense, when reading the four volumes of short stories and poems that were published by the Scribhneoiri Press between 1995 and 2005, of hearing the same story over and over again. This is not meant as a criticism, nor does it overlook the fact that the same writers feature across the four volumes. Rather it would seem to confirm the view expressed by many critics of Irish literature that this is a canon that is hard pressed to escape key moments in its country's past (or the mythologies that have followed them), and for which the themes of migration and exile are *the* defining topoi; as George O'Brien has observed: 'It seems only a slight exaggeration to say that without exile there would be no contemporary Irish fiction' (O'Brien, 2000: 35). What this observation perhaps fails to acknowledge, however, is the nuanced variety of grief and longing that the experience of exile has given rise to or its associated temporal expression. The latter includes such variants as: the legacy of the mythic past; the representation of childhood; the juxtaposition of rural and urban chronotopes;[27] the dislocation of time and space associated with 'the journey home'; and, finally, the invocation of a parallel life that 'might have been' as a special type of national mourning. Owing to restrictions of space, I have had to limit myself to the first and last of these in the discussion that follows and trust that readers will discover the texts' preoccupation with the temporalities of childhood and rural life (both indicative of Bakhtin's 'idyllic chronotope' (see note 27)) without too much difficulty themselves.

The Mythic Past

In the same way that no Irish writer can ostensibly escape writing about 'exile', neither can most escape writing about the Great Famine (O'Brien, 2000: 53). Moreover, although the famine of the 1840s and 1850s is over a hundred and fifty years distant, there is widespread evidence that it remains as much a tangible 'memory' for the present generations as for their ancestors. Here, the concept of 'post-memory' is especially helpful in explaining how individuals can remember, or feel that they remember, events and situations they never lived through themselves.[28] Seán Body, one of the founder members of the Manchester Irish Writers' group, has noted something to this effect in a personal reflection posted in the 'Moving Manchester' Writers' Gallery:

> My poems are frequently driven by memory, not necessarily my own, but a folk memory, composed largely of images, word associations, the oral history and stories that, in childhood, establish who we are. When I was growing up in rural West Limerick, the Great Famine, though it had been a hundred years before, had become part of consciousness, seared into the very geography, the half-obliterated paths; those defeated, hopeless people setting out on tortuous journeys, ending in death or exile, the people with their backs to the land … It was time to leave, a mass emigration that continued for the next hundred years, which I was forced to join at one of its peaks. (Seán Body, 'Moving Manchester' Writers' Gallery)

There is certainly plenty of evidence in the poetry produced by the Manchester Irish Writers' Group of a 'sense' of the Famine that goes beyond the history book and which has all the rawness of personal mourning. Body's own poem 'Blight' (2001) links the plight of his ancestors with his own, presented through the 'burden' of the descendant-witness:

> You could tell our history
> in stone: this a shawled head
> back to the land
>
> expects no one;
> The weight of its grief
> binding like roots.
> A bruised sun lies low,
> hardly revealed
> by the small wing of shadow.
>
> I almost listen
> for the dry-throated cormorant –
> and I'm back
> walking a winter strand
> everywhere the eye turns
> is tormented.[29]
>   (Body: 'Moving Manchester' Writers' Gallery)

Within this particular mythic space 'all time' is, to invoke T. S. Eliot, 'eternally present' (1959 [1944]), and there appears to be little prospect of the 'collective unconscious' moving on to the next stages of mourning. Similarly visceral and immediate in its recollection of the Famine is Mary McGonagle Johnson's poem 'Famine Imagined':

> Children crawl over rocks
> Like old men they search.
> Wizened arms starved of flesh
> Pull dregs of dulse from rocks
> To stuff lips where flies feast.
> ...
> At home the sodden turf still smoulders.
> The old man lies, now stiff and cold,
> His scrawny hand still clutching
> A tiny seed potato saved in hope.
> It has just begun a tiny bud.
>
> (McGonagle Johnson, 2001: 28)

Although this is a third-person portrait which does not show collective memory at work in quite the same way as Body's poem, the incongruous assemblage of images (including what appears to be a purposeful repetition of certain words or tropes – e.g. wizened, 'scrawny' flesh) – creates the impression that this famine has been imagined via sources other than books or paintings. What McGonagle Johnson presents us with is effectively a list of traumatic details of the sort that live long in a people's memory. Most arresting, however, is the 'present-ness' of the picture she paints which, like the old man clutching the budding seed potato, is both 'dead' and 'alive', 'then' and 'now'. What both these poems attest to, then, is the responsibility subsequent generations have felt to bear witness to the sufferings of their ancestors: to keep the memory fresh by defamiliarizing acts of the imagination.

A similar desire to cut through the mythology at the same time as honouring the past to which it refers is found in the texts which deal with the nineteenth-century migrant experience. As observed in Chapter 1, the living conditions of the working classes (and, in particular, the Irish) in Manchester in the mid-nineteenth century presented a ghoulish spectacle to the middle classes sent to report on them. According to these contemporary accounts, the most shocking aspects of the living conditions appear to have been overcrowding, starvation and lack of sanitation; though the more disturbing feature of the

Collective resistance

reports for readers today is their prejudice. As noted in Chapter 1, the migrant Irish population (estimated, even in 1835, to account for about one-fifth of Manchester's total population) (Hylton, 2003: 121), were consistently represented as the lowest, and most bestial, tier in the city's social infrastructure, and it is shocking to see how unsympathetic social reformers like Engels were in their reports. The 'poor Irish' were all too frequently cast as not only a symptom but the *cause*, of all Manchester's socio-economic ills (Hylton, 2003: 121). And this, of course, was the impression even *before* the Great Famine which caused both temporary, and permanent, Irish migration to soar to new heights. Biased or not, the first-hand accounts of Engels and other commentators remain luridly compelling for the reader coming upon them for the first time, and it has taken considerable scholarly effort to prove that the experiences of the many thousand migrants were not necessarily the same[30] and that the notion of 'Irish ghettos' existing in all Britain's major towns and cities has been significantly exaggerated (Davis, 2000: 24–6).

Needless to say, poets and fiction writers have faced similar challenges when engaging with the mythology surrounding the nineteenth-century migrant experience and have been necessarily guilty of a certain 'impressionism' in their attempts to capture that 'moment' (in truth, *many* moments) in their people's past. Seán Body, for example, in his long poem *Seasons* (2003a), appears to have drawn upon generic historical sources in conjuring up a picture of the streets of Manchester in the mid-nineteenth century, albeit with the intentions of accessing the material suffering that lies beneath the rhetoric. Following an epigraph from Engels ('The cottages are old, dirty, and of the smallest sort, the streets uneven, fallen into ruts and in part without drains or pavement, masses of refuse, offal and sickening filth lie among standing pools in all directions'), the poem opens with the following 'analysis':

> Hunger drove them here
> where only the spirit starved.
> Of all places, one
> they would not have chosen.
>
> Among outcasts, they
> were outcast; carriers
> of disease, poverty,
> their unforgiven history.

> And unforgiving. Fed
> cotton mills, dissension,
> a plethora of wars; kept intact
> a dream of Ireland.
>
> (Body, 2003a: 7)

Nonetheless it is arguable that, in his failure to specify which group, or generation, of migrants is referred to here, Body may be seen to be corroborating the generic stereotype of Ireland's suffering. From this purposefully ahistorical perspective, Ireland is 'always-already' suffering, and successive waves of migrant sons and daughters are a testament to a problem that the country has failed to solve. Indeed, the fact that this time is archetypal also renders it disconcertingly continuous with the present, and, as in 'Blight', we see Body's speaker slipping into his ancestral past with ease:

> Today, their memory's
> an entertainment, a guided walk,
> a footnote in the history
> of old Manchester – Yet
>
> so bleak this morning
> they might still be here, gaunt
> against the grudged light,
> recognisable
>
> (Body, 2003: 7)

However, while a historian might regard Body's apparent flattening-out of history as perpetuating the mythologies and stereotypes associated with Irish migration to Britain, it can also be argued that his decision to present the migrant past as a continuity is politically, and in terms of temporality, valid. Ireland's diaspora is, after all, defined by its never-endingness. As Timothy O'Grady has observed:

> The past in Ireland, drip-fed on pain, has this kind of intense coherence. The histories of larger, more powerful and expanding countries are neither as painful nor as repetitious. (O'Grady, 2006: 259)

The journey home

Alongside this investment in, and interrogation of, Ireland's mythic past, the writings of the Manchester Irish Writers' Group are widely preoccupied with the staging of the 'journey home'. And while these stories and poems may well incorporate instances of other temporalities (e.g. myth, childhood, rural idyll), their defining characteristic is the spatio-temporal dislocation consequent upon a sudden invasion of the present into the past. For this reason, most of the Irish 'journey home' stories represented in these anthologies include an element of trauma and/or the 'uncanny', and the extent to which an uncomfortable situation is redeemed is, as we shall see, variable. A significant difference also emerges between the stories and experiences of migrants who travel backwards and forwards frequently (most evident in the work of the post-1980s generation) and those for whom journeys home have been delayed for a complex range of reasons.

Two stories by Alrene Hughes, 'Incidental Snow' (2002) and 'A Missed Heartbeat' (2003), are exemplary of this sub-genre of migrant writing in a number of respects. First, and, perhaps most interestingly, they detail the anxious and complicated feelings involved in making the decision to return home, especially when long years have elapsed. The narrator of 'A Missed Heartbeat' explains the convoluted process to herself thus:

> The truth was there were reasons why I wanted to go back. Many reasons, but they were all tangled up in my mind like the scraps of wool my mother used to keep for mending. I had once spent a rainy afternoon untangling them, working patiently, following each colour to its end. Now I had to trace back the threads of my life undoing the knots time had tied. I'd lived in England longer than I'd lived in Ireland. Was it only the place name on my birth certificate that gave me any claim to Irishness? (Hughes, 2003: 45)

'Return' for this protagonist would seem to be linked to a desire to reconnect with her 'roots', though the metaphor she uses, the muddled skeins of wool, exposes the uncertainty of her intentions. What she appears to want most is clarification of the choices she made to get to where she is now, including the one that rendered her 'English'. That she *is* 'no longer Irish' is made painfully clear to her by her Uncle John whose first words are 'You've an English accent' (Hughes, 2003: 47); and even though she tries to deny it – because in England her accent is seen as 'not English' – she is eventually forced to concede: 'But, my voice didn't match his' (Hughes, 2003:45). Game over.

Rather than pursue the full complexity of the narrator's decision to return, however, this story invokes the 'Troubles' as an explanation for both the protagonist's long absence and her feelings of guilt. In the same paragraph that she invokes the metaphor of the 'tangled wool' she admits that there may be 'some truth' in the fact that she was only coming back now, 'when it was safe to do so' (Hughes, 2003: 45). This 'theory' subsequently underpins the story's denouement in which the narrator's escalating sense of alienation and guilt is absolved by Aunt Kate who tells her niece she had every reason to leave ('Look, if I'd been your age, I'd have done the same, but my roots were too deep' (Hughes, 2003: 51)). The further implication here is that the narrator has given her own children a 'better chance' by leaving, but that now (post ceasefire) a new generation of Irish children can begin to enjoy what they themselves enjoyed ('the trouble [pun?] was only a missed heartbeat' (Hughes, 2003: 52)).

I would suggest, however, that this neat and somewhat sentimental resolution to the story sidesteps the deeper complexity of the narrator's reasons both for 'going home' and for 'staying away'. Indeed, the doubts she raises about her motives via the metaphor of the tangled wool are echoed by Uncle John, who is overheard to remark: 'Twenty five years, she never sets foot in the country, twenty four hours notice and she's back. Seems to me there must be some reason' (Hughes, 2003: 46). What Uncle John's words would seem to point to is the rather unpalatable truth that 'long lost relatives' (Hughes, 2003: 46) *don't* return to their homelands to *give* but to *take*, even when that 'taking' is focused on symbolic rather than material capital. People 'go home' to 'discover their roots', to 'reconnect with themselves' or to revisit the places of their childhood, often with little corresponding interest in those who have continued to live there. Indeed, the story of the migrant's return home is frequently (perhaps typically?) a deeply introverted, solipsistic affair in which the protagonist's sense of alienation is experienced as what is, in many ways, an irrational 'rejection' inasmuch as he or she was the one who left (notwithstanding some admittedly 'good reasons').

What could be seen to emerge from this particular body of literature, then, is the proposition that the migrant's journey home (when made after a long period of absence) will necessarily involve psychological agendas that escape rationalization. Moreover, when it is a belated journey home to a country as proximate as Ireland is to the UK, the question marks proliferate. Why now? Why so long? What was it that kept him or her away? It is perhaps for this reason that Hughes is one of the few writers to dwell upon this moment in the 'returning home' process at any length, with others preferring to focus on the dislocation of arrival. Her story 'Incidental Snow' also interrogates the narrator's final decision to make the trip 'across the water', although in this instance the complexities are disguised, initially at least, as epiphany:

> I couldn't say with any certainty when the idea first occurred to me. Maybe it had always been there beneath the surface of every day like one of those seeds in the desert waiting years for rain. But the fact was, it bloomed suddenly on the morning of my fiftieth birthday. The sleep cleared, I opened my eyes and the idea was there fully formed. I would go home. (Hughes, 2002: 29)

What makes this story arguably more honest than 'A Missed Heartbeat' from the protagonist's point of view is that it openly confronts the vague, and somewhat fatuous, 'fantasy of return'. As the result of a chance meeting with a young Irish woman and a baby newly arrived at Stranraer, the narrator is freshly reminded that emigration is, in many cases, a purposeful *choice* ('Haven't the Irish always found paths away from their home more often than they've found them back?' (Hughes, 2002: 31)) and is finally able to embrace her own 'in-between', diasporic identity. In this instance, then, the 'visit home' is ultimately rejected and considered no longer necessary as the narrator is seized by an image of 'the path to my house [in Manchester]' where her husband and sons wait for her (Hughes, 2002: 31).

Another text which is extremely 'honest' about the reasons for not returning to Ireland – albeit only a couple of hours' journey away – is Mary McGonagle Johnson's 'Cleaning the Slate' (2002) in which the protagonist, Jim, has fled to Manchester after the death of his wife and children in a car crash for which he feels himself responsible. Although a daughter survived, he has been too scared to go back and confront the extent of his loss and his shame. Meeting a group of young Manchester United fans from his home town in a Manchester pub, he is eventually persuaded to make the journey home. What is especially interesting here is the extent to which a sense of national or cultural identification combines with his longing to see his daughter in his final decision to make the journey home: 'community' and 'family' come together in a uniquely Irish way ('[s]o proud they were of qualifying and so proud to be Irish in this country, that the pride was rising in him too' (McGonagle Johnson, 2002: 34)).

For the migrants who do 'make it home', the dislocation of time and space consequent upon visiting 'old haunts' is often immense. Hughes draws out the nightmarish nature of the experience in her story 'A

Missed Heartbeat', in which the small, but significant, changes to virtually every landmark in her old town convince her that 'it had been a mistake to come back' (Hughes, 2003: 49):

> Halfway along the High Street, I looked for the café, the haunt of my teenage years ... The café was boarded up and the plywood daubed with para-military slogans ... The town was crowding in on me, places I knew yet didn't know, recognised but hadn't seen before, like a distorted dream, a warped déjà vu. It had been a mistake to come back. (Hughes, 2003: 48–9)

Construed in terms of temporality, it will be seen that what has most disoriented the narrator is the sudden realization that the spaces and places of her memory, held perfectly intact for twenty-five years, have been subject to a change and degradation that makes inescapably material her own absence and 'neglect'. The nature of 'mythic' time, both frozen and continuous, is blasted asunder by her 'present tense' intrusion and this, in turn, rocks her fragile sense of identity.

Not all the stories and poems in the Manchester Irish Writers' collections represent 'returning home' as a traumatic experience, though I would suggest that those that focus on the 'warm embrace' of home, family and the past serve mostly to make visible the *absence* of these things in the stories where the journeys are less happy. In this regard, Catherine Breen's 'Coming Home' (2003) takes on iconic status: climaxing in the dramatic discovery of her 'real' father, the protagonist moves a step closer to discovering her 'true self' and is positively reconnected with the spaces and places of childhood. In contrast to Hughes's protagonist, for whom a walk in her old neighbourhood is profoundly alienating, this narrator feels immediately 'at home'. The family revelation which follows is, essentially, part of the same fantasy: in much the same way that she is pleased to discover who her 'true father' really is so does she embrace Ireland as her 'true home': 'It was enough. I knew her words were true. I felt a calm I had not known before, a sense of being at ease with myself, as if my life had been a journey to this moment' (Breen, 2003: 63).

The parallel life

These stories of a return to Ireland from England by middle-aged women after long absence are, of course, only one small sub-section of texts on the theme of travels 'home and away'. Although none of the writers belonging to the Manchester Irish Writers' group has produced texts which are dynamically involved in 'circuits of migration' (Rouse, 1991) of the kind evidenced in Breda Gray's ethnographic study of the contemporary Irish diaspora (2000),[31] many of the texts are preoccupied with fantasies of 'the life that might have been' had they stayed. This fascinating game of 'what if' is, of course, a 'circuit of migration' all of its own, and sees the authors and their protagonists travelling between their Anglo-present and Irish parallel-universe on a frequent basis (a spatio-temporal projection that may be compared with Qaisra Shahraz's novels about the Pakistan she has never lived in since a young child).[32]

Such fantastical journeying, not simply to a dimly remembered homeland of childhood (or, indeed, of one's parents) but to a parallel life that might have been just 'across the water', is especially resonant in the work of the Manchester Irish for the good reason that it *is* a permanent geographical possibility even if the political reasons for staying away (once the Famine, more recently the Troubles) are equally material. Further, what we see in the work of the Manchester Irish Writers' Group, and arguably postwar Irish literature more generally, is a romantic fantasy of what the country itself might have been at different moments in its history had not oppression and tragedy intervened. In this respect, literature becomes a crucial space in which to imagine an alternative, parallel life for the country and its people.

For the emigrant writer, meanwhile, this vision of what Ireland 'might have been' inevitably combines with more personal fantasies of the life he or she might have had if he or she had 'never left' or 'returned home'. It is certainly the sentiment that sets the scene for Marion Riley's 'The Ashes of Betrayal' (2004: 5–8), with the narrator reflecting repeatedly: 'If only I'd stayed in Ireland'. Indeed, the ghosts of untold, alternative lives haunt the pages of the Scribhneoiri anthologies, contributing an intense, and disquieting, impression of successive waves of Ireland's young people disappearing into thin air. Something of the profound melancholy of this is captured by Mary Willner in her story 'DeValera's Wild Geese' (Willner, 2002: 48–51) which 'follows' a bus from Ballina to Dun Laoghaire as it picks up young men en route to Holyhead. Although many of the men are planning on return ('I'll stick it out 'til I've made enough money to buy the tractor' (Willner, 2002: 50)), the elegiac narrator makes it clear that very few will ever return, and that the Christmas dance will have to go on without them. For these young men, Ireland will soon be not so much a memory as a life that might have been but now never will:

> Dun Laoghaire. Seagulls wheeling and diving and crying out, crying out for the Wild Geese. DeValera's Wild Geese. The lonely sound of the ship's siren, like a dirge, sounding out as they watch the lights of Dublin disappear on the horizon. The sea taking them far away.
>
> They would miss the girls and the dancing; the waterfall tumbling down the mountain, past purple heather and yellow gorse, making music from the stones as it hurries to the sea; the sun rising behind the river, turning it to dazzling silver. (Willner, 2002: 50)

For those left behind, meanwhile (the mothers, lovers and extended families), emigration to England is figured as a cruel inevitability that sees Ireland 'frozen in time' in a rather less utopian way: '*Only the stones are static. Standing from dawn to dusk impervious to the situation. Why do they not weep? Silent witnesses of the dying population*' (Willner, 2002: 51 (italics in the original)). On both sides of the Irish Sea, then, the process of migration may be seen to have created a hyperreal version of Ireland as it might have been had its ghostly sons and daughters stayed at home. For all its manifest social and economic transformation in recent times, moreover, there is little sign of the Irish diaspora giving up on its parallel universe just yet; possibly out of respect for the many thousands of lives spent waiting for loved ones to return from just 'across the water'. So near (in time, in space), and yet so far.

Conclusion

Looking back across the varied and dynamic list of titles represented in this chapter, and the forty years of Mancunian history that they bear witness to, it is evident that there is a hitherto neglected strand in contemporary British literary studies still to be written. As with the performance-poetry scene investigated in Chapter 5, Manchester has arguably led the way in inventing and sustaining an alternative canon of writing and performance that, by virtue of its independence from the mainstream, has been able to stay true to the artistic and political vision of its authors and eschew the pressure to write (for example) a particular type of novel for a particular type of audience.

In particular, the anti-individualist, anti-capitalist nature of the writings and performances considered in this and the following chapter of *Postcolonial Manchester* cause us to reflect upon just how far writing, publishing and the creative industries have drifted towards a corporate and profit-led agenda since the 1970s and 1980s. During this former era, the spirit of collectivity was widespread: across the academic world, political organizations, the trades union movement and the music industry, individuals regularly, and repeatedly, put their political commitment and artistic integrity before professional achievement or financial gain.[33]

The fact that this spirit and ethos have survived in the Manchester literary scene for the best part of forty years on account of organizations like Commonword, and groups like Manchester Irish Writers, should therefore make literary critics and social historians take note, since our conversations with independent publishers and literature development workers[34] have made it clear that similar, alternative literary cultures are to be found across the Midlands and the north of England which, taken together, seriously challenge the curricular version of the contemporary English literature canon. In this age of 'international bestseller' authorship it would, admittedly, be difficult to get teachers and/or academics to teach one of the anthologies featured here (many of them purposefully bereft of even an editor's name) but they are texts that may well speak more immediately, and more meaningfully, to young people than more 'feel-good' titles; further, they may encourage the students concerned to co-author a project of their own.[35]

Before anthologies such as those reported upon in this chapter can be taken seriously enough to feature on school and university syllabuses, however, we need more academics to attend to their artistic and political significance. Following the efforts of Ra Page (2002), Ailsa Cox (2005) and the recent 'Save our Short Stories' campaign (see note 22), we need books and articles that will demonstrate how technically innovative and culturally relevant short fiction is; and we need postcolonial scholars who recognize that Britain's black, Asian and diasporic writing is not (and, arguably, has never been) characterized by stories about alienated individuals who (after long suffering) overcome their marginalization to achieve a sense of belonging in contemporary, 'multicultural' Britain. In other words, we need a new generation of academics, commentators and (ideally) publishers who will be brave enough to reveal, and pay tribute to, writing that is experimental on account of its collective, oral and/or performed authorship rather than (or in addition to) its avant-garde literary devices, and which, *vis-à-vis* the teaching of black British or postcolonial studies, attends to what is demonstrably a long tradition of black and working-class *protest* literature. As we have seen in this and the other chapters, successive generations of young, black writers have got together to publish and perform not because they feel alienated and marginalized but because they are angry about the racism they are forced to endure. These, too, are the voices of 'multicultural Britain' and they deserve to be heard.

In terms of their witnessing of Greater Manchester's own colonial past and postcolonial present, meanwhile, the literary anthologies presented here must been seen as social-historical documents of the utmost importance; in years to come they will serve as a testament not only to the discrimination and oppression that successive generations of diasporic groups within the city have endured but, even more importantly, how the hitherto disregarded anthology form enabled them to fight back, collectively, through their writing.

Notes

1 See: 'Moving Manchester' e-catalogue at www.transculturalwriting.com. Please note that, since many of the anthologies are multi-authored and/or edited it may be easier to call them up using a 'title' search.
2 See, in particular, Ailsa Cox's *Writing Short Stories* (2005) in which she observes: 'One of the great strengths of the short-story form is this very ability to break generic boundaries. The distinctions between experimental and mainstream, or between literary and mass-market, crumble in a technically-adventurous piece such as Stephen King's "That Feeling, You Can Only Say What it is in French" (2002)' (Cox, 2005: 7).
3 See Roger Bromley's *Lost Narratives: Popular Fictions, Politics and Recent History* (1988) and Ian Heywood's *Working-class Fiction: From Chartism to 'Trainspotting'* (1997) for further discussion of the complexity that accrues to 'value' when considering working-class literature and writers with restricted literacy.
4 There is scarce availability of the earliest editions of 'Write On' (published in the early to mid-1980s); see also Chapter 2 for Corinne Fowler's discussion of some of the work produced by groups like Blackscribe during this period.
5 In the editorial of *Voices* 29, Ailsa Cox tackles the issue of the artistic value of working-class writing head-on: 'Literary merit? Don't let it scare you. When I look at the more tasteful magazines – those which represent the flower of "our" culture – I feel proud to be a part of VOICES. Not only because we care about what we have to say, but for the sake of technical proficiency. Look at "Decline of the Hull Fishing Industry ..." in VOICES 26 or "Last Liner" (27). Yet many of the best pieces in VOICES draw their power from a waning source. Poems, in particular, are often farewells to a world their author knows is dying. They describe an industry in decline, or they may dwell on an ageing workmate or relative. Fewer and fewer of us

belong to that world of traditional manual industry. That doesn't mean we don't need to be told what it is (or was) like. But if working class writers are to have a future outside of absorption into the "mainstream", we must have more to show of ourselves.'

6   The earliest edition of *Voices* (see Figure 4.1) acknowledges that the Manchester district of the TUC's 'Unity of Arts' organization was a key player in the early days of the magazine. See 'Moving Manchester' e-catalogue, 'Voices: Verse and Prose', for further details of an early edition.

7   *Voices* has been archived on the (new) FED website at: www.mancvoices.co.uk/ (accessed September 2011). This is an excellent resource for anyone interested in the history of working-class and/or diasporic writing in the UK in general and in Manchester in particular. On this point, it should be made clear that, although *Voices* operated out of Manchester (and in association with the early 'Commonword' writing groups), it published contributions from groups and individuals from across the UK (writers from London and Scotland being especially well represented).

8   Anti-Nazi League: the Anti-Nazi League was active in the UK between 1977 and 1981 after which it was reformed as 'Unite Against Fascism' (see: http://uaf.org.uk/: accessed September 2011). The following site provides interesting information about the history of the organization and the associated 'Rock against Racism' initiatives of the period: www.dkrenton.co.uk/anl/anl.html (accessed September 2011).

9   For more information about the history of Commonword and Cultureword and their various writing groups see: www.cultureword.org.uk. Both the 'Monday night group' and the 'Women Writers Group' (now 'Womanswrite') have been in existence since the late 1970s. It is worth noting also that, until the appointment of Peter Kalu as artistic director of Cultureword in 2007, the organization and its various groups eschewed managerial hierarchy and ran the organization through a team of 'workers' and a Management Committee. This is also reflected in the format of the Commonword/Crows publications, which, in most cases, are without named editors. However, for reference purposes I have listed these volumes according to the names of the authors of the Preface or Introduction; where no lead names are obvious, the volume is referenced under its title.

10 Crocus is one of the publishing imprints of Commonword (others include 'Suitcase' and 'Satchel').

11 This was the 1987 'Peterloo Black and Asian' poetry competition. See 'Moving Manchester' e-catalogue for further details.

12 John Lyons is one of Manchester's earliest and most important performance poets. See Chapter 5 for a full discussion of his work and also the 'Moving Manchester' Writers' Gallery at www.transculturalwriting.com.

13 This focus on the complexity which surrounds the contemporary Asian woman's relationship to clothing as a signifier of modesty, sexuality and religious faith is also at the core of Shahraz's best-selling novel *The Holy Woman* (2007 [2001]).

14 In his chapter on 'The Street' in *Dwelling Places* (2003), Procter traces this trajectory from 'realist' to more experimental forms of black British writing, noting, in particular, the focus on orality and realism in 1970s and 1980s black 'protest' writing. He also cites Linton Kwesi Johnson who has observed that: 'from the very beginning I saw myself giving voice to, and documenting, the experiences of my generation' (Procter, 2003: 103). In other words, the primary objective of the black writer at this time was to bear witness and provide testimony.

15 See, for example, the new 'Womanswrite' anthology, *Life, Death ... The Whole Damn Thing* (Bolton et al., 2011).

16 In the introduction to *Under the Banyan Tree and Other Stories* (1985), R. K. Narayan cites a lecturer he once heard who cryptically observed that 'A short story must be short and have a story' (Rau, 2005: 319).

17 New Order was the band that evolved out of iconic post-punk Manchester band Joy Division (see Chapter 1) following the death of Ian Curtis. See the New Order website at: www.neworderonline.com (accessed September 2011).

18 This entry was written by Sarah Post who contributed some late entries for the catalogue in the summer of 2011. The 'Moving Manchester' team would like to acknowledge her incisive synopses both here and elsewhere.

19 There are, of course, exceptions: the Commonword women writers' group publication *Herzone: Fantasy Short Stories by Women* (Brown, Broughton and Williams, 1991) being a particularly notable example.

20 On this point it is also worth acknowledging that the discourse of 'cosmopolitanism' also entered academic discourse around this time. The year 2008 saw the instigation of RICC (Research Institute for Cosmopolitan Cultures) at Manchester University and 2009 the publication of Berthold Schoene's study *The Cosmopolitan Novel*.

21 'Suitcase' is a new imprint from Commonword dedicated to the publication of radical black writing. See: www.suitcasebooks.info/ (accessed September 2011).

22 See: http://savetheshortstory.org/our-manifesto/ (accessed September 2011)

23 Manchester Irish Writers' Group was founded by Alrene Hughes and Seán Body in 1995 and continues to meet at the Irish World Heritage Centre building in Cheetham Hill every Tuesday night. See: www.iwhc.com/oldsite/education.htm (accessed 06/09/11).

24 Scribhneoiri is the imprint of the Manchester Irish Writers' group. Discussion here focuses on the four early anthologies: *Rodden*, ed. S. Body 2003 [1997]; *The Retting Dam*, ed. Hinchcliffe and Hughes (2001); *A Stone of the Heart*, ed. Hinchcliffe and Hughes (2002); *Drawing Breath*, ed. Alrene Hughes (2004).

25 'Circuits of migration': in this much cited article on Mexican migration and the 'social space of postmodernism', Roger Rouse (1991) was one of the first commentators to note the fact that migration is no longer necessarily a 'one-way journey' and that diasporic subjects the world over (including

Collective resistance 201

those in low-paid jobs) are more able to return 'home' on a regular basis.
26 Filiation/affiliation: Rosemary Marangoly George (1996) provides a useful gloss on these concepts (from Edward Said): 'Said calls "filiation" the ties that an individual has with places and people that are based on his / her natal culture; that is, ties of biology and geography. "Affiliations" are what come to replace "filiations", are links that are forged with institutions, associations and communities and other social creations. The movement is always from filiations to affiliations' (Marangoly George, 1996: 16).
27 A term coined by the Russian theorist Mikhail Bakhtin to describe the conflation of time and space observable in certain events and situations: 'the intrinsic interconnectedness of temporal and spatial relations that are expressed in literature' (Bakhtin, 1981: 84). Particular literary chronotopes that Bakhtin discusses in *The Dialogic Imagination* (1981) include the 'idyllic chronotope' in which a dominant 'unity of place in the life of generations weakens and renders less distinct all temporal boundaries' (Bakhtin, 1981: 225). See Pearce 1994 (67–72) for a full discussion.
28 Post-memory: the invention of this term is usually attributed to Marianne Hirsch who, in her essay on the Nazi holocaust in Mieke Bal et al.'s *Acts of Memory* (Hirsch, 1999), used it to describe the way in which those who did not experience the atrocity first-hand nevertheless appear to participate in its memory as vividly as those who were there.
29 This poem is available only on the 'Moving Manchester' Writers' Gallery site and not included in Body's published collections, *Seasons* (2003) and *Witness* (1998).
30 A useful distinction exists, for example, between 'emigrants of hope' (e.g. small farmers with some capital) and 'emigrants of despair' (Davis, 2000: 19). Similarly, all destinations were not the same (even with respect to Manchester and Liverpool).
31 In contrast to the female migrants of the 1980s and 1990s who are the subject of Gray's study, the members of the Irish Writers' Group are mostly of the generation who moved to Manchester in the 1950s and 1960s and thus travelled back and forth less frequently.
32 See Qaisra Shahraz's 'reflection' on her page in the 'Moving Manchester' Writers' Gallery in which she observes: 'The rural world I have created in *Typhoon* is far removed from that of Manchester, my home city. It has captured my imagination since I was seven and still continues to fascinate me. A friend from my school days, marvelled as to how I could have created such a world ("It is so real!" she exclaimed) having lived most of my life in England. It was from my childhood memories on writing about Pakistan.'
33 Academics in the UK, for example, organized themselves into groups such as the Marxist-Feminist Literature Collective and LTP (Literature, Teaching, Politics) which published radical, co-authored books, articles and pamphlets.
34 In the process of setting up the 'Moving Manchester' project, we consulted

with long-serving literature development workers in the north of England such as Steve Dearden, who generously provided us with information about a wide range of community writing organizations and publishers in the region and pointed to Sheffield, Leeds and Newcastle-upon-Tyne as other cities with lively, multicultural literary scenes. More recently, Corinne Fowler's work with the black and Asian writing communities of the East Midlands has confirmed that Manchester, although a leading-player, is not the only British city to have created an 'alternative canon' of contemporary British literature.

35 In the course of the 'Moving Manchester' project, Graham Mort and Muli Amaye ran a workshop at Manchester College which encouraged people to do just this, and in the course of the two days they produced their own collectively authored poem on the subject of 'Moving Manchester'.

References

Aghedo, N. (1989) 'Invasion', in Walker, K., Craven, J., Aghedo, N., Shahraz, Q. and Ansar, L. (eds), *Talkers through Dream Doors*. Manchester: Commonword/Crocus, 34–5.

Ainley, B. (1972) 'Editorial', *Voices* 1 (1) [no page numbers].

Bakhtin, M. (1981) *The Dialogic Imagination: Four Essays*. Ed. M. Holquist. Trans. C. Emerson and M. Holquist. Austin, TX: University of Texas Press.

Bilenberg, A. (2000) *The Irish Diaspora*. London: Longman.

Bloom, V. and Walker, F. *Black and Priceless* (1988). Manchester: Commonword/Crocus.

Body, S. (1998 [1995]) *Witness*. Salford: Tarantula Publications.

Body, S. (2001) 'Blight' in 'Moving Manchester' Writers' Gallery at: www.transculturalwriting.com/movingmanchester.

Body, S. (2003) *Seasons*. Mexborough: Glass Head Press.

Body, S. (ed.) (2003 [1997]) *At the End of the Rodden*. Manchester: Scribhneoiri.

Body, S. (2007) Entry in 'Moving Manchester' Writers' Gallery at: www.transculturalwriting.com/movingmanchester.

Bolton, C. et al. (1994) *No Limits: Urban Short Stories*. Manchester: Commonword/Crocus.

Bolton, C. et al. (2011) *Life, Death ... The Whole Damn Thing*. Manchester: Commonword/Crocus.

Bolton, C. and Hartnett, P. P. (eds) (2002) *City Secrets*. Manchester: Commonword/Crocus.

Bracewell, M. (1999) 'Blackley, Crumpsall, Harpurhey' in Page, R. (ed.), *The City Life Book of Manchester Short Stories*. Harmondsworth: Penguin, 114–25.

Bracewell, M. (2002) 'Nocturne' in Page, R. (ed.), *Comma*. Manchester: Comma Books, 71–80.
Brah, A. (1996) *Cartographies of Diaspora*. London: Routledge.
Breen, C. (2003) 'Coming Home' in Body, S. (ed.), *At the End of the Rodden*. Manchester: Scribhneoiri, 56–65.
Bromley, R. (1988) *Lost Narratives: Popular Fictions, Politics and Recent History*. London: Routledge.
Bromley, R. (2000) *Narratives for a New Belonging: Diasporic Cultural Fictions*. Edinburgh: Edinburgh University Press.
Brown, N., Broughton, J. and Williams, D. (1991) *Herzone: Fantasy Short Stories by Women*. Manchester: Commonword/Crocus.
Burn, S. (2002) 'Edgecity' in Bolton, C. and Hartnett P. P. (eds), *City Secrets* (Manchester: Commonword/Crocus), 35–43.
Butler, J. (1990) *Gender Trouble*. London and New York: Routledge.
Cox, A. (1983) 'Editorial', *Voices* 29 (1) [no page numbers].
Cox, A. (1984) 'Editorial', *Voices* 30 (1), [no page numbers].
Cox, A. (1988) 'Be a Good Girl' in *Holding Out*. Manchester: Commonword/Crocus.
Cox, A. (2005) *Writing Short Stories: A Routledge Writer's Guide*. London and New York: Routledge.
Chowdhry, M. (2006) 'Acting Real' in Chowdhry, M. and Sharratt, M., *Bitch Lit*. Manchester: Commonword/Crocus, 163–80.
Chowdhry, M. and Sharratt, M. (2006) *Bitch Lit*. Manchester: Commonword/Crocus.
Clews, W. (2002) 'Going to the Dogs' *in* Page, R. (ed.), *Comma*. Manchester: Comma Books, 123–6.
Davis, G. (2000) 'The Irish in Britain, 1815–39' in Bilenberg, A. (ed.), *The Irish Diaspora*. London: Longman, 19–36.
Delaney, S. (1960 [1959]) *A Taste of Honey*. London: Metheun.
Delaney, S. (2002) 'Abduction' in Page, R. (ed.), *Comma*. Manchester: Comma Books, 99–106.
Eliot, T. S. (1959 [1944]) *Four Quartets*. London: Faber & Faber.
Farrand, J. (1994), 'The Dragon on the Wall' in Bolton, C. et al., *No Limits: Urban Short Stories*. Manchester: Commonword/Crocus, 9–21.
Gray, B. (2000) *Women and the Irish Diaspora*. London and New York: Routledge.
Green, M. (2006) 'Forklift Trucks' in Chowdhry, M. and Sharratt, M., *Bitch Lit*. Manchester: Commonword/Crocus, 103–14.
Hannan, N. (1994) in Bolton, C. et al., *No Limits: Urban Short Stories*. Manchester: Commonword/Crocus, 1–8.
Hartnett, P. P. (2002) 'CCTV Eyes' in Bolton, C. and Hartnett, P. P., *City Secrets*. Manchester: Commonword/Crocus, 99–121.
Healing Strategies for Women at War: Seven Black Women Poets (1999).

Manchester: Commonword/Crocus.
Henderson, G. M. (1989) 'Speaking in Tongues: Dialogics, Dialetics and the Black Woman Writer's Literary Tradition', in Wall, C. A. (ed.), *Changing Our Own Words: Essays, Theory and Criticism by Black Women*. New Brunswick, NJ, and London: Rutgers University Press.
Heywood, I. (1997) *Working-class Fiction: From Chartism to 'Trainspotting'*. Tavistock: Northcote House Publishers Ltd.
Hinchcliffe, S. and Hughes, A. (eds) (2001) *The Retting Dam*. Manchester: Scribhneoiri.
Hinchcliffe, S. and Hughes, A. (eds) (2002) *A Stone of the Heart*. Manchester: Scribhneoiri.
Hirsch, M. (1999) 'Projected Memory: Holocaust Photographs in Personal and Public Fantasy' in Bal, M., Crewe, J. and Spitzer, L. (eds), *Acts of Memory: Cultural Recall in the Present*. Hanover, NH, and London: Dartmouth College, 3–23.
Holding Out: Short Stories by Women [no named editor or lead author] (1988). Manchester: Commonword/Crocus.
Holroyd, E. (2001) 'Collection' in Hinchcliffe, S. and Hughes, A. (eds), *The Retting Dam*. Manchester: Scribhneoiri, 44.
Huab, S. (1989) 'You' in Walker, K., Craven, J., Aghedo, N., Shahraz, Q. and Ansar, L. (eds), *Talkers through Dream Doors*. Manchester: Commonword/Crocus, 20–1.
Hughes, A. (2002) 'Incidental Snow' in Hinchcliffe, S. and Hughes, A. (ed.), *A Stone of the Heart*. Manchester: Scribhneoiri, 29–31.
Hughes, A. (2003 [1997]) 'A Missed Heartbeat' in Body, S. (ed.), *At the End of the Rodden*. Manchester: Scribhneoiri.
Hughes, A. (ed.) (2004) *Drawing Breath*. Manchester: Scribhneoiri.
Hylton, S. (2003) *A History of Manchester*. Chichester: Phillimore and Co. Ltd.
Kalu, P. and May, S. (eds) (2006). *Hair: A Journey into the Afro & Asian Experience*. Manchester: Commonword/Crocus.
Khan, S. (1999) 'Silver Threads' in Chowdhry, M., Guise Williams, M., Khan, S. and Lin, T. (eds), *Healing Strategies for Women at War: Seven Black Women Poets*. Manchester: Commonword/Crocus, 63–5.
Lin, T. (1999) 'naked frame' in Chowdhry, M., Guise Williams, M., Khan, S. and Lin, T. (eds), *Healing Strategies for Women at War: Seven Black Women Poets* (Manchester: Commonword/Crocus), 95–105.
Lloyd Thomas, W. (1978) 'Richman, Poorman, Beggarman', *Voices* 18 (2), 21–2.
Lugosi, R. (2006) 'My Dear' in Chowdhry, M. and Sharratt, M., *Bitch Lit*. Manchester: Commonword/Crocus, 17–24.
Lyons, J. (1988) 'Englan no Muddercountry' in Bloom, V. and Walker, F., *Black and Priceless*. Manchester: Commonword/Crocus, 69–70.

Marangoly George, R. (1996) *The Politics of Home*. Cambridge: Cambridge University Press.
Martin, C. (2006) 'The Hot Comb' in Kalu, P. and May, S. (eds), *Hair: An Anthology*. Manchester: Commonword/Crocus, 20–1.
McGonagle Johnson, M. (2001) 'Famine Imagined' in Hinchcliffe, S. and Hughes, A. (eds) *The Retting Dam*. Manchester: Scribhneoiri, 28.
McGonagle Johnson, M. (2002) 'Cleaning the Slate' in Hinchcliffe, S. and Hughes, A. (ed.) *A Stone of the Heart*. Manchester: Scribhneoiri, 32–5.
Michael, L. (1999) 'Robinson Street' in Page, R. (ed.) (1999) *The City Life Book of Manchester Short Stories*. Harmondsworth: Penguin, 23–30.
McKenzie, V. (1978) 'One Voice, Many Voices', *Voices*, 18 (2), 54.
Mehmood, T. (2002) 'The Peacock's Dance' in Page, R. (ed.) (2002) *Comma*. Manchester: Comma Books, 57–68.
Montoute, C. (1989) 'Simmy' in *Talkers through Dream Doors*. Manchester: Commonword/Crocus, 69–74.
Munro, K. (2002) 'Gutted' in Bolton, C. and Hartnett, P.P. (eds), *City Secrets*. Manchester: Commonword/Crocus, 191–211.
Narayan, R. K. (1985) *Under the Banyan Tree and Other Stories*. New York: Viking.
Naughton, W. (1963) *Alfie*. London: Samuel French Limited.
Naughton, W. (1988) *Saintly Billy*. Oxford: Oxford University Press.
Noon, J. (1999) 'Cobralingus Remix' in Page, R. (ed.), *The City Life Book of Manchester Short Stories*. Harmondsworth: Penguin, 126–35.
O'Brien, G. (2000) 'The Aesthetics of Exile' in Harte, L. and Parker, M. (eds), *Contemporary Irish Fiction: Themes, Tropes, Theories*. Basingstoke: Macmillan, 35–55.
O'Grady, T. (2006) 'Memory, Photography, Ireland', *Irish Studies Review*, 14 (2), 255–62.
Page, R. (ed.) (1999) *The City Life Book of Manchester Short Stories*. Harmondsworth: Penguin.
Page, R. (ed.) (2002) *Comma*. Manchester: Comma Books.
Pearce, L. (1998) *Fatal Attractions: Rescripting Romance in Literature and Film*. London: Pluto Press.
Pearce, L. (ed.) (2000) *Devolving Identities: Feminist Readings in Home and Belonging*. Aldershot: Ashgate.
Pearce, L. (2004) *Devolving Identities: Feminist Readings in Home and Belonging*. London: Edward Arnold.
Pearce, L. (2007) 'Women Writers and the Elusive Urban Sublime: The View from Manchester, England', *Contemporary Women's Writing*, 1 (1), 80–97.
Pollard, C. (2002) 'Kirsten vs the City' in Page, R. (ed.) (2002) *Comma*. Manchester: Comma Books, 129–43.
Procter, J. (2003) *Dwelling Places: Postwar Black British Writing*.

Manchester and New York: Manchester University Press.

Rau, R. (2005) *The Many Voices of English: An Anthology of Postcolonial Short Stories*. Braunschwig: Diesterweg.

Riley, M. (2004) 'The Ashes of Betrayal' in Hughes, A. (ed.), *Drawing Breath*. Manchester: Scribhneoiri, 5–8.

Rouse, R. (1991) 'Mexican Migration and the Social Space of Postmodernism', *Diaspora*, 1 (1), 8–23.

Schoene, B. (2009) *The Cosmopolitan Novel*. Edinburgh: Edinburgh University Press.

Shahraz, Q. (1988) 'A Pair of Jeans' in *Holding Out* [no named editor]. Manchester: Commonword/Crocus, 123–30.

Shahraz, Q. (2007 [2001]) *The Holy Woman*. London: Black Amber.

Sissay, L. (1998) *The Fire People, A Collection of Contemporary Black British Poets* (Edinburgh: Payback Press).

Smith, C. (1994) 'Legoland on Mescalin' in Bolton, C. et al., *No Limits: Urban Short Stories*. Commonword/Crocus, 35–44.

Smith, H. (2002) 'That's Adolescence' in Bolton, C. and Hartnett, P. P. (eds), *City Secrets*. Manchester: Commonword/Crocus, 249–57.

Stanley, J. (2006) *'Die, You Bastard' in* Chowdhry, M. and Sharratt, M. (eds), *Bitch Lit*. Manchester: Commonword/Crocus, 187–99.

Stockdale, R. (2002) 'After the Queen's Head' in Bolton, C. and Hartnett P.P. (eds), *City Secrets*. Manchester: Commonword/Crocus, 259–68.

SuAndi (1988) 'Maidenhood, Motherhood, Womanhood' in *Holding Out* [no named editor]. Manchester: Commonword/Crocus, 91–106.

Walker, K. (1989) 'Black Sisters' in *Talkers through Dream Doors*. Manchester: Commonword/Crocus.

Ward, J. (1978) 'Who Are the English?' *Voices,* 19 (1), 38–9.

Willner, M. (2002) 'DeValera's Wild Geese' in Hinchcliffe, S. and Hughes, A. (eds), *A Stone of the Heart*. Manchester: Scribhneoiri, 48–51.

Internet sources

www.cultureword.org.uk
www.dkrenton.co.uk/anal/anl.htm
www.iwhc.com/oldsite/education/htm
www.mancvoices.co.uk.
www.neworderonline.com
www.savetheshortstory.org/our-manifesto
www.suitcasebooks.info
www.transculturalwriting/movingmanchester.com
http://uaf.org.uk/

5

'Rebels without applause':[1] Manchester's poetry in performance (1960s to the present)

Corinne Fowler

For out of those far Northlands did one Teller, still mighty in his speed of Telling and blade-sharp in his Wit and Humour, come dressed all in skin-tight Black ... and the Poet-Scribes responded thus: 'no ... Women, Ethnic Minorities or Damned Mancunians'. (Joolz Denby in Munden and Wade, 1999: 17)

Poetry in performance is not the preferred terrain of postcolonial literary criticism. Despite the burgeoning literature on popular literary forms,[2] there remains widespread critical and pedagogical resistance to what Duncan Brown identifies as the 'oral challenge' presented by poetry in performance to literary studies (in Hoyles and Hoyles, 2002). Some of the best scholarly work to date has concentrated on more accessible cultural products such as novels and films.

This chapter discusses 'poetry in performance' in its broadest sense. The category encapsulates poetry's oral performance for an audience, whether that audience is seated near a stage, a radio or a computer screen. Resisting the artificial separation between 'page and stage' poetry, however, the chapter also understands performance as a page-based phenomenon. This aspect of performance is expressed in Patience Agbabi's poem 'The Word': 'give me a page and I'll perform on it' (Agbabi in Sissay, 1998: 34) or Lemn Sissay's sense of 'actual work with words' (in Grabner, 2007: 70). Both Agbabi and Sissay reject the label 'performance poet' as limiting, partly because it implies some sort of spectacle. This aspect of poetic performance therefore pertains to word-craft as much as to poetry's visual, typographical or grapholectic features. Ranging more widely still, the chapter focuses on poetry's 'infinite delivery' in the form of landmark poems (Osborne, 2011: 199) on Manchester's buildings, pavements and walkways. It is this expanded definition of performance that most accurately reflects Manchester's poetry scene. For this reason, a great deal of the discussion below deals not with particular performances but with poetry by poets who regularly perform their work. Correspondingly, I examine what Manchester's poetry in performance tells us about the dominant critical pretexts for literary approbation in Britain, as discussed in Chapter 2. As I will argue, these limitations are also exposed by black poets' struggle not so much for applause as for literary approbation.

This chapter evokes the figure of 'the neighbour' as a compelling metaphor to describe black poets' relationship with contemporary English poetry. Crucially and perhaps uniquely, the focus on the neighbour allows the chapter to concentrate both on the cultural politics of belonging and on the extent to which black Mancunian poets and their white counterparts may be considered as 'compatriots in craft'.[3] The chapter contends that diversity should, as Richard Appignanesi suggests, be considered as 'a condition *within* cultures' (Appignanesi, 2010: 5). To this end, I closely attend to the literary affinities between black poets and their white counterparts, focusing on black Mancunian poets' engagement with, and reshapings of, significant developments in English poetry.

Since the 1980s there has been a new surge of popular interest in British poetry. This popularity is not unprecedented. It is reminiscent of mass poetry readings associated with the British Poetry Revival[4] (1960–75), and Manchester's poetry in performance is strongly associated with the devolved cosmopolitanism[5] of poets associated with the revival, such as Roger McGough and Brian Patten from neighbouring Liverpool. To my knowledge, this is the first time that the British Poetry Revival has been discussed in connection with the work of British black and British Asian poets but my research has revealed a number of parallels and intersections that make a compelling case for dealing with both poetic developments together. British poetry in performance is more commonly discussed in the contexts of Jamaican dub poetry, the black arts movement[6], and rap, hip hop and the poetry slam from the United States. The case of Manchester reveals the 'home-grown' quality of work by the city's second- and third-generation black poets, whose poetry is shaped by the distinctive poetic topographies associated with the Poetry revival. Manchester's black poets, I will argue, are most accurately understood as indigenous British poets.

The status of poetry in performance

In his study *Voicing the Text*, Duncan Brown points out that all poetic forms have a debt to oral rhythms and vocalizations' (in Hoyles and Hoyles, 2002: 41). Introductions to books about poetry in performance invariably allude to the orality of ancient and classical poetic traditions by highlighting revered poets such as Theocritus, Virgil and Chaucer. 'In the beginning', writes John Coutts, 'all poetry was performed [and] "silent reading" was a rarity in the ancient world' (Coutts in Hoyles and Hoyles, 2002: 20).

Such comparisons are made with great regularity and they are largely born out of a collective desire by academics and practitioners alike to contest the subordinate status of poetry in performance.[7] As can be seen in Andrew Motion's 'Poetry in Public' lecture, given for the Arts Council in 2000, the dominant politics of literary taste conceives of poetry as a private, rather than a communal affair:

> Poetry is vitally ... an art that depends on solitary reflection – solitary in the way that it is meditated and created, and also solitary in the way that it is mediated and received. (Motion, 2000: 1)

Motion's conception of poetry clearly militates against the poetics and aesthetics of poetry in or as performance. He is not alone in his view. Since the early twentieth century, page poetry has become the main pathway to literary prestige (Munden and Wade, 1999; Hampson and Barry, 1993). Meanwhile, as Chapter 2 examines, Britain's leading publishing houses routinely discriminate against poetry associated with the performance scene.

A handful of literary scholars, notably Eric Doumerc and McFarlane (2011), Arturo Casas (Grabner and Casas, 2011) and Cornelia Grabner (2007),[8] have now begun to publish studies of poetry in performance. This emerging scholarship tends to provide a forensic analysis of poetry's oral and aesthetic dimensions, paying close critical attention to poetic craft and technique.[9] Writing in the same vein, Dana Gioia advocates critical readings that attend to the 'structure' of poetry in performance and he scolds critics for 'sh[ying] away from analysing the new popular forms. Performance poetry has been studied almost exclusively as a sociological phenomenon rather than in terms of its ... aesthetics' (Gioia, 2003: 26). While this approach helps to dispel the critical prejudice against poetry in performance by foregrounding technical sophistication, it can unintentionally work against poetry's popular appeal. Critically, too, by treating poetry in performance as a category in its own right, they risk endorsing the perceived distinction between page and stage by overlooking its relationship to British poetic traditions.

Many of Manchester's poets share a widespread concern that oral performance is a route to literary ghettoization. Yet, as this chapter explores, exclusionary practices cannot be justified on the grounds that poetry by the city's black poets has developed separately from the British poetic tradition. The unadorned accolade of 'poet' remains elusive. As Kwame Dawes (2005) observes, black poets throughout Britain have adopted a range of strategies to reconceptualize their poetry, and Dawes's description applies equally to Manchester's poets as to those elsewhere:

> The position of the Black poet in Britain has become inextricably linked to the notions of 'performance poetry' and the reductionist way in which the co-opted use of the term has created in many Black poets a desire to either run away from the label, or embrace it with defiance and as a kind of statement of race and aesthetics. Many Black British poets, even those who began as 'performance poets' have begun to seek ways to avoid the label. Some have taken to calling themselves 'spoken word artists' borrowing from the American scene, while others have simply insisted on being called 'poets' not 'performance poets'. (Dawes, 2005: 282)

The dilemmas posed by the persistent relegation of work by British black poets to a sub-category of poetry has given rise to a number of creative responses, such as Bernardine Evaristo's *Emperor's Babe* in which a Pictish poet called Hrrathaghervood recites his work to an audience of Romans:

> Hrrathaghervood sprang barefoot
> on to the rostum, face dyed blue with woad,
> snarling wolf tattooed on his forehead,
> ginger dreadlocks down his back.
>
> *They're only three groups of fowk I hate,*
> *de Romans who're trying tae thief Scotland,*
> *de Celts who've sold oot tae de Romans,*
> *and de Christians who dinnae wint nae bigger*
> *tae enjoy thaimsels ...*

> ... He finished to a standing ovation,
> and comments on how beautifully
> he shook his plait-things,
> the exotic charm of his Pictish patois,
> the symbolism of the knuckle-duster
> and how brilliantly he *did* Anger
>
> (Evaristo, 2002: 196)

Projecting today's practices of literary exclusion on to yesterday's historyscapes, this excerpt problematizes current modes of perceiving poetry in performance. As the less-than-subtle reference to 'dreadlocks' makes clear, Hrrathaghervood resembles British black poets in being called upon to perform his Pictishness. His appearance is fetishized and commodified: the audience admires the bare feet, the tattoo and the blue woad. As Manchester's Lemn Sissay has observed, the dominant mode of reception suggests that style supersedes substance: Hrrathaghervood may be hero-worshipped, but he will never be listened to. The audience of Romans gives his condemnation of slavery and imperialism a standing ovation. Hrrathaghervood's political subversion is contained by his art. Neither does his poetry receive any serious critical attention; he is praised for his ability to produce a cultural performance that corresponds to dominant notions of Pictishness. Evaristo's concern with the status of poetry in performance echoes that of poets such as Benjamin Zephaniah whose 'Angry Black Poet' reads:

> Next on stage
> We have the angry Black poet,
> So angry
> He won't allow himself to fall in luv,
> So militant
> You will want to see him again
>
> (Zephaniah in Doumerc, 2005: 202)[10]

Zephaniah's poem is similarly concerned about the ongoing public appetite for 'authentic' performances of blackness (Caro, 2011) which continues to neutralize both the politics and aesthetics of such work. One line hints at the way in which the thematic mainstays of English poetry, such as love, have remained out of bounds for black poets ('He won't allow himself to fall in luv'). Slam poetry, too (as discussed in Chapter 2), has been dogged by the call for authentic cultural performances (Somers-Willett, 2005: 52).

Manchester's writing organization Cultureword has consciously resisted the relentless focus on identity and ethnicity by commissioning themed poetry anthologies such as *The Suitcase Book of Love Poems* (2008), *Hair* (2006), *Peace Poems* (2003) and *Kiss* (1994), as discussed in some detail by Lynne Pearce in Chapter 4. The recently published anthology, *Red* (2010), edited by Kwame Dawes, makes a related point about the need to move beyond the expected remit of angry black poet: 'Black British poetry', he writes, 'has now arrived at a place where the pressure to justify itself through works that somehow seek to explain, by theme and focus, what Black Britishness is as an ethnicity can now be resisted' (Dawes, 2010: 17). Dawes here expresses a view – widely supported by British black and Asian writers – that the time has arrived to move beyond old thematic staples such as 'identity' (usually in crisis), migration or crime.

SuAndi is an influential Manchester-based poet as well as a founding member of the black feminist poetry collective Blackscribe and the former director of the Manchester-based Black Arts Alliance.[11] The epigraph to her 1992 poetry collection *Nearly Forty* is written by the English comedian Henry Normal, whose words try to combat the inferior status of poetry in performance:

> SuAndi is not just a performance poet
> she's a poet who performs.
> Her accessible images beg to be
> cherished on the written page ... HENRY NORMAL
>
> (SuAndi, 1992: 3)

Normal's epigraph poem hints at the *shared* struggle of white and black wordsmiths against the pernicious distinction between page and stage. The collective nature of this battle is indicated, not merely by the diminutive 'just' of line 1 ('not just a performance poet') but, more subtly, by the reference to SuAndi's 'accessible images'. By celebrating the accessibility of SuAndi's work, he links it to the democratizing philosophy espoused by Normal's Live Poets Society, which was established in Manchester with the motto: 'poetry so good you can actually understand it'. Normal's quarrel is not merely with an unspecified audience in front of the microphone, but to the much-maligned 'poetry establishment'. This quarrel is summarized by Sissay in his Afterword to *Morning Breaks in the Elevator* (1999):

'Rebels without applause'   213

If Lemn Sissay's audience is moved by his work – and he loves reading live – this does not equate with his readings being 'performance'. He believes the description ... is often used as a disingenuous accolade, particularly in Britain. To truly see the misapplication of the term simply look at its supposed opposite ... 'Page Poetry'. (Sissay, 1999: 70)

Normal's epigraph to SuAndi's collection is easily overlooked yet it provides a glimpse of intricate webs of influence and counter-influence that tell some untold stories about the evolution of contemporary British poetry.

Devolved poetry in performance: Manchester's Rebel Voices

> Peaceniks, heretics, rebels, refugees
> (Peter Kalu, 'Manchester' 2007: l. 4)

This section introduces the key players and developments in Manchester's poetry scene. As discussed in earlier chapters, Manchester has become an important regional forum for debates about the devolved expression of Britishness, and nowhere is the debate more vocal than in those clubs, bars and theatres that host its spoken word events. The city's poetry scene has, indeed, attracted large audiences to a range of venues across the city since the 1980s. Popular venues have included the Green Room and, more recently, the Contact Theatre. Manchester's poetry in performance is often informal and neighbourly in tone and it frequently engages with local history and politics. This chapter considers the wider significance of such expression, exploring what the devolved aesthetics and poetics of the city's poetry reveal about the cultural politics of belonging and exclusion in multiracial Britain. As observed in the Introduction with reference to James Procter's 2006 essay 'The Postcolonial Everyday', popular discourses have long preferred to construct northern England historically and as 'closeted from, and innocent of ... cultural difference' (Procter, 2006: 73). This is in signal contrast to popular representations of 'multiracial' London. As this chapter will now go on to show, the reality could hardly be more different, especially with regards to the region's poetry performance scene where the black and white communities have historically influenced one another in the most dynamic of ways.

An important feature of Manchester's poetry has been the figure of the poet-as-historian. In 2007, and following in the footsteps of grassroots organizations such as the Black Arts Alliance,[12] eight of

Manchester's museums and art galleries collaborated to explore the legacy of slavery to England's North West region. The 'Revealing Histories' project invited the public to explore the collections of its participating museums and galleries. Among other things, the project aimed to promote public awareness of Manchester's significant black population from the late 1700s.

Manchester's poets have commonly represented their city as a diaspora space. For example, Manchester's museum archives have been explored extensively by the city's poets, including by the Leeds-born Shamshad Khan, whose poetry collection *Megalomaniac* (2007) contains a commissioned poem called 'Pot', which is 'dedicated to a Nigerian pot currently in the Manchester Museum without charge or access to legal representation' (2007: 114). The poem's speaker imagines the pot's journey from Nigeria, creating a parallel with her own journeys to Pakistan in ways that both highlight the speaker's postcolonial consciousness and promote a sense of Manchester as a postcolonial city.

In pages that follow, I will detail black poets' conscious engagement with Manchester's radical and postcolonial histories. As many of today's Mancunian poets attest, the city is associated with some of Britain's most significant political developments. As the 'Revealing Histories' project stressed, Manchester was an important centre for the abolitionists' campaign. The city's activists frequently welcomed former slaves and activists such as William Wells Brown, Henry Box Brown, Frederick Douglass and James Watkins.[13] Manchester was also home to Emmeline Pankhurst and the Suffragettes as well as being the site of the infamous Peterloo Massacre of 1819, which took place in Peter's Fields near the site of the modern St Peter's Square. Gathering under banners reading 'Reform', 'Universal Suffrage' and 'Equal Representation', 60,000 pro-democracy and anti-poverty protesters gathered in the Square but many were injured by hundreds of armed Hussars and infantrymen.[14] Percy Shelley wrote about the massacre and the poem, 'The Masque of Anarchy', was banned for thirty years following its publication in 1819. Perhaps inspired by the event's literary pedigree, an independent publishing house called Peterloo Poets, originally sited in Manchester, took its name from the massacre.[15] The Peterloo Massacre is widely credited with goading the public to press for universal voting rights (Mansfield, 2011)[16] and many of Manchester's black poets have followed Percy Shelley's example by making references to it in their poetry.

Manchester is also a significant site of the notorious General Strike of 1926 when, according to an eye-witness, Manchester's 'mill chimneys ceased to smoke and [its] wheels ceased to turn ... Over Gorton, Openshaw, Clayton, Newton Heath and Collyhurst the air grew clearer' (Stella Davies in Irving, 2009). Crucially, too, the city was also a meeting place for anti-colonial nationalists. A leading figure was Ras Makonnen, whose restaurant The Cosmopolitan was situated on Manchester's busy Oxford Road. As John McLeod relates, the restaurant allowed 'ad hoc and adversarial links' to be forged between pan-African radicals, Indian Nationalists and Jewish groups resisting anti-semitism (McLeod, 2002: 53).[17] Makonnen set up a publishing company and a bookshop in Manchester together with a monthly periodical entitled *Pan-Africa*. Profits from The Cosmopolitan were used to fund the Fifth Pan-African Congress in 1945. McLeod argues these meetings between members of the Manchester-based pan-African intelligentsia paved the way for the 1945 Congress, which was attended by Kenyatta, Wallace-Johnson, Padmore and W. E. B. DuBois (McLeod, 2002: 61), and the Congress in Manchester advanced the case for decolonization and African nationalism. Over the past few decades, Manchester's black writers have engaged with all of these contexts.

Manchester's poets are highly conversant with the city's radical and anti-colonial histories. Poets often express the desire to document Manchester's present for posterity. Sissay's poetry collection *Rebel without Applause* (2000) is dedicated 'to James Baldwin, who in his last recorded interview said black writers should 'bear witness to the times' (Sissay, 2000a: 1). Peter Kalu, too, has echoed the words of Baldwin, publicly stating his commitment as a poet to 'bea[r] witness to the times' by 'document[ing]' events in the city and elsewhere. As discussed in Chapter 1, Kalu remembers the 1980s as a period of intensified anti-racist struggle in the region and beyond; he has stated in an interview that a whole generation of poets have been committed to documenting this struggle.[18] These struggles were not merely confined to regional concerns. The Black People's Writing Group, for example, was established in Manchester during the 1980s to accommodate a burgeoning interest in the Black Panthers,[19] anti-apartheid struggles and local anti-racist campaigns.[20]

As discussed at the end of Chapter 2, the concept of poet-as-historian is widely embraced by black poets and is clearly inspired partly by the 'versified headlines' of African griots and Jamaican dub poets (Kelly Smith and Kraynak in Somers-Willett, 2009: 370); Benjamin

Zephaniah famously called himself an 'alternative newscaster' (Doumerc, 2005: 199). Sissay and Kalu are influential figures on Manchester's poetry scene. Both held the post of Cultureword worker at Commonword, with Sissay eventually embarking on poetry tours while Kalu was to become Commonword's Artistic Director. Both Sissay and Kalu have striven to instil this ethic into the city's poetry. Zephaniah's introduction to one of Manchester's landmark poetry anthologies indicates that the very location of the city's poets means that their voices are less likely to be heard:

> These words come from a generation who have no voice in [...] society. They are their own historians; the historians of the future shall have to relate to them if they are to obtain an insight into Black British life in the 1980s.
>
> (Benjamin Zephaniah, 1987: x)[21]

A great deal of Manchester's poetry in performance gives the role of poet-as-historian a distinctive local flavour. Perceiving the need for a city-based forum for black female poets, a group of women founded in 1987 a poetry collective named Blackscribe, which was together for three years (see also Chapter 2).[22] Members of Blackscribe gave writing workshops and toured in Leicester, Liverpool, Leeds, London and Sheffield. Breaking away from Blackscribe was another group called Nailah, a collective that focused on the need to foster new writing talent among young black Moss-Siders. Suffering from a lack of arts funding, Nailah lasted only two years, but during its short lifetime its members managed to tour Liverpool and York with Zephaniah and Sissay.

The title of this chapter alludes to absent applause, yet this cannot be said of the mushaira. Debjani Chatterjee, Britain's most faithful chronicler of British mushairas, observes that such events take place in many of the nation's inner cities (Chatterjee, 1999: 54). Manchester's annual mushaira attracts staggeringly large audiences of many thousands of people. 'Mushaira' is Arabic for 'gathering of poets'. In the British context, however, it has mainly served as a forum for Urdu-speaking poets from North India and Pakistan. Although Chatterjee is not herself an Urdu speaker, she has energetically promoted the *ghazal* form throughout the English North and beyond. The *ghazal* is a popular short lyric poem that is generally set to music. As Chatterjee explains:

> *Ghazals* are recited in mushairas ... where there is an instant and vocal response from the audience. This has meant that poets deliver their work

in bite-sized couplets ... Great *ghazal* composers like Nasir Kazmi have enjoyed the adulation reserved in the West for pop stars ... their work being sung by the greatest singers of the Indian sub-continent. (Chatterjee, 2003: 13)

Nasir Kazmi was one of the most celebrated 'modern champions' of the *ghazal* form[23] (Chatterjee, 2003: 12). His son, Basir Sultan Kazmi, came to live in Manchester in 1990. Also a celebrated Pakistani writer of *ghazals*, Basir Kazmi formed a regional 'mini-mushaira' together with Chatterjee, which developed into a multilingual group of poets. Basir Kazmi and Chatterjee jointly translated his *ghazals* and most of his father's.[24] This joint effort resulted in Chatterjee's edited collection of *ghazals* by father and son called *Generations of Ghazals. Ghazals by Nasir Kazmi and Basir Sultan Kazmi* (Redbeck Press, 2003). By means of 'mini-mushaira' performances and workshops, Kazmi has promoted the *ghazal* form throughout Manchester and beyond, spawning a new generation of *ghazal* writers whose work has yet to be published.[25]

For Urdu-speaking composers of *ghazals*, poetry has always been about performance. Since the advent of radio and cinema, *ghazals* have reached large audiences not merely through mushairas but by means of popular music and film, using the tools of the entertainment industry (Gioia, 2003: 28). While this chapter concentrates on Anglophone poetry in performance, it is important to recognize that Britain's Anglophone performance scene co-exists with a larger Urdu one.

One of Manchester's most active poetry collectives has been Speakeasy. The collective began in 1999 as an 'open mic' jam session at the Green Room theatre, which recently closed after losing its Arts Council funding.[26] Founded and hosted by Segun Lee French and the DJ Chris Jam, the collective expressed its goal in local terms:

> Speakeasy is where Manchester people express their soul. It's a funky mix of ... poets, rappers and vocalists flippin [*sic*] their lyrics to the sounds of live soul jazz and hip hop [...It is] a collective spirit of Black music and words.[27]

The Green Room theatre provided a forum for audience members to perform their poetry with live musicians. The monthly 'open mic' session gradually gave way to a more distinctive 'ensemble' of poets and musicians who frequently received guest poets such as Lemn Sissay and who performed regularly at the Green Room and a range of other venues, drawing audiences from Moss Side, Rusholme and Hulme. Peter Kalu believes that Speakeasy was a prominent example of the way in which the city's performance scene evolved to provide a popular and alternative form of reportage to that offered by Rupert Murdoch's press.[28]

Despite its recently diminished internet presence, Speakeasy continues to nurture new talent and has been active in promoting 'Young Identity', which was formed in Moss Side in 2006 under the direction of poets Shirley May and Ali Gadema. A collective of over twenty members, Young Identity has embraced the poetry slam and competed in a number of local, national and international poetry slams, sometimes under the supervision of Speakeasy's Segun Lee French and, before he died of cancer, the many-time slam champion Dike Omeje.[29] The members of the Speakeasy collective are profiled on a dedicated webpage, which contains individual author profiles, photographs and sound recordings. Young Identity has very much inherited the ethos of Speakeasy, as has another of Manchester's emerging performers, Chanje Kunda, who describes herself as a 'poet, playwright and performance artist' and profiles her poems on a website called Afrique. Kunda's poems are often spoken over a soundtrack. Like Nailah and Young Identity, Afrique combines its touring activities with community work. This is communicated in the following statement about Afrique Performs:

> Afrique Performs [... works with] marginalized groups and young people. We aim to improve confidence and communication skills, as well as [to] help to break down barriers to participation in the Arts, Music and Cultural Industries. (www.afrique-performs.co.uk/)

This section has provided an overview of the poetry scene in Manchester. As Chapter 2 has already detailed, poets in Manchester, as elsewhere, have, in the light of recent funding cuts, increasingly relied on podcasts of performances, webpages and social media to reach their audiences. As this section implies, young poets who perform their work have had some success with this strategy but nevertheless still depend on funded organizations such as Commonword to support and promote their work.

Indigenous Britons

The urban street has historically been an arena for anti-racist protest and expressions of black political struggle (Procter, 2003: 88) In racialized discourse, too, the urban street has historically been defined as the prime locus of black criminality (Procter, 2003: 80). The British historian David Starkey drew on the latter association in his remarks about the British riots during the summer of 2011 on BBC *Newsnight*. Arguing that 'the whites have become black' Starkey referenced Powell's infamous 1968 'rivers of blood' speech as follows:

> I've just been re-reading Enoch Powell. His prophecy was absolutely right in one sense. The Tiber didn't foam with blood, but flames lambent wrapped around Tottenham and wrapped round Clapham. (BBC *Newsnight*, 13 August 2011).

Starkey's assertions here rely on established cultural association of the street with black criminality. He extends his comments to accommodate a further concept of the 'street' as a site of degraded black cultural expression, a move that allows him to attribute the riots' cause to 'a particular sort of violent, destructive, nihilistic, gangster culture' (Starkey, ibid.) that he linked to rap music and hip hop.

By contrast, suburbia has gradually become the locus of what Procter describes as a form of literary expression that is 'self-consciously detached from the sophisticated cosmopolitanism of the city' (Procter, 2003: 4). This expression reflects the 'increasingly differentiated, *devolved* cultural geography of black Britain over the last fifty years' (Procter, 2003: 3). The case of Manchester suggests that the work of black poets has significantly broadened the cultural topography of black Britishness by comprehensively exploring new terrains of tenure.

A more concrete assertion of cultural belonging and entitlement can be found in the landmark poetry of Sissay and SuAndi, which consciously subverts the 'street' as an emblem of black criminality. Both poets have quite literally left their mark on Manchester's walls,[30] paving stones and walkways. Painting and inscribing poetry on to various sites across Manchester provides a whole new dimension to the concept of performance. A good example of this is Sissay's poem 'Rain' (from *Listener*, 2008), which is painted on to a white wall above a takeaway along Manchester's Oxford Road (Figures 5.1, 5.2). With its playful configuration of words, 'Rain' is as much visual as it is verbal. The passer-by is forced to take a more than usually active role by mentally reassembling the words to make sense of them. As 'Rain' demonstrates, the poetic performance here has nothing to do with stagecraft and everything to do with the strategic arrangement of words. This works against what Kwame Dawes has identified as:

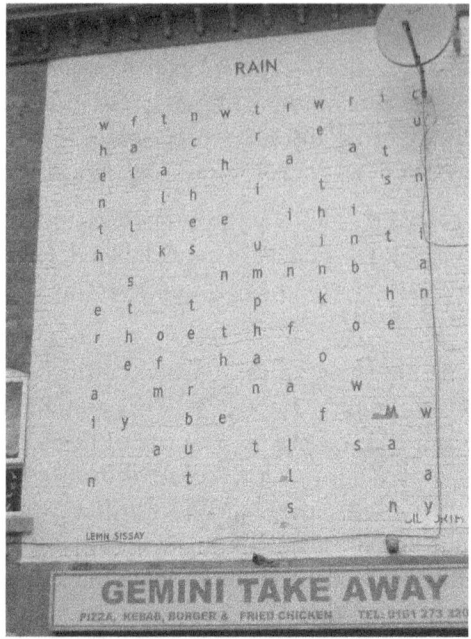

5.1 Lemn Sissay's 'Rain' poem on Manchester's Oxford Road, 2011. © Corinne Fowler

5.2 Lemn Sissay's 'Rain' poem on Manchester's Oxford Road, 2011. © Corinne Fowler

> [T]he totalising dichotomies often created between 'book poetry' and 'performance poetry' ... If we accept that a page is as much a performance space as is the stage, we may begin to find ways to speak about poetry without some of these prejudices. (Dawes, 2005: 284).

Sissay's 'Rain' poem poses a clear challenge to such dichotomies. The poem performs its cultural work by evoking the Mancunian 'rain' trope as a sign of local belonging by referring to the Mancunian Way, a dual carriageway that cuts through the city's heart. The metaphor serves its familiar function of foregrounding a shared experience of post-industrial malaise. This appeal is activated not merely by the rain metaphor itself but by the wordplay of the last line: 'it is the Ma n / cun ian way'. It is this line more than any other that forces the reader of the poem to acknowledge Sissay, the black poet, as neighbour. The street here appeals to a local audience that shares the poet's intimate knowledge of the city. The street is reclaimed as a site where neighbourliness co-exists with the parochial and the mundane. The poem performs in the sense that it repeatedly displays that intimate local knowledge, delivering its message again and again as people make their daily trips along the Oxford Road (Osborne, 2011: 199).[31]

Another of Sissay's poems, 'Flags' (*Listener*, 2008: 40) is set on to the pavement of Tib Street in Central Manchester (see Figure 5.3). The poem's lines provide a manifesto for landmark poetry itself:

> These pavement cracks
> Are the places where
> Poets pack their
> Warrior words
>
> (Sissay, 2008: 40)

As public property, poetry is presented here as fundamental to daily existence. Its rightful place is in the street and in free, civic spaces. The words of the poem, too, are imbued with a special agency: they are 'warrior words'. Most particularly, as Osborne argues, landmark poems have a 'cleansing agency' in a city scourged by slavery and racism (Osborne, 2011: 199). In this way, Osborne writes, it operates as a 'repository for the future' by functioning 'as a public record and public art' (Osborne, 2011: 199).

Manchester's landmark poetry testifies to Manchester's postcolonial and working-class histories. SuAndi has similarly striven to secure the longevity and public presence of her own work and that of her fellow

5.3 The opening lines of Lemn Sissay's 'Flags' poem, situated on Tib Street in Central Manchester, 2011. © Corinne Fowler.

5.4 The first plaque on the Manchester Ship Canal Walkway, 2011. © Corinne Fowler.

poets. Some of her poems are inscribed on to metal discs and set in to the Manchester Ship Canal Centenary Walkway. The inscribed discs run along the length of the walkways (see Figure 5.5). In the final disc of the series (Figure 5.6), Manchester figures as a central locus of transnational commercial exchange. As with Sissay's work, these lines promote a sense of Manchester's transnational geographical and

5.5 One of SuAndi's discs *in situ* on the Manchester Ship Canal Walkway, 2011. © Corinne Fowler.

> Here
> the world formed an axis
> down cobbled streets
> of shipped immigration
> all nations
> in a global dockyard.

5.6 The final plaque of SuAndi's Manchester Ship Canal Walkway poem near the Lowry Theatre, Salford, 2011. © Corinne Fowler.

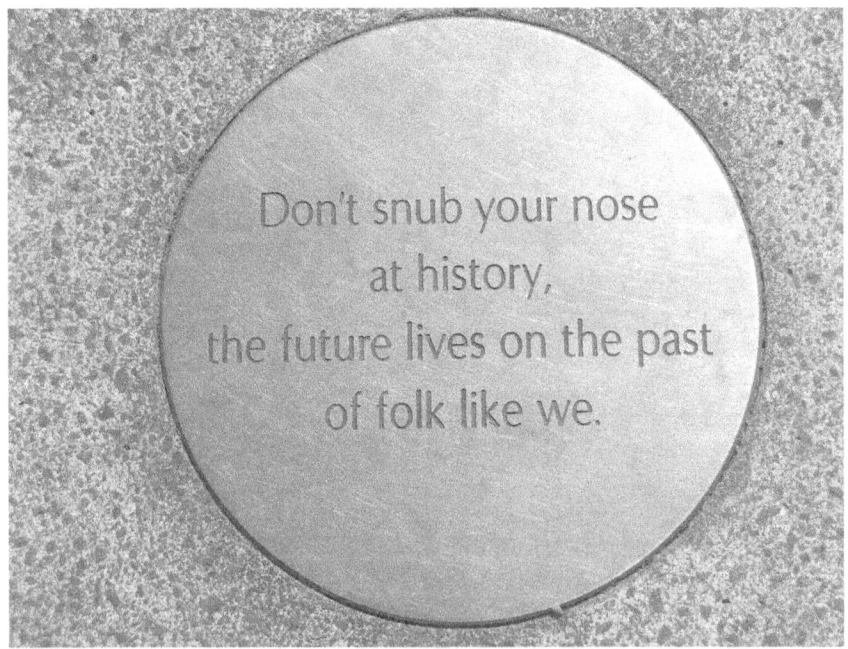

> Don't snub your nose
> at history,
> the future lives on the past
> of folk like we.

5.7 Another of SuAndi's discs along the Manchester Ship Canal Walkway, 2011. © Corinne Fowler

historical identity, contextualizing the city's immigration in terms of the city's global trade. Manchester figures here as a postcolonial city born of international commercial networks that converged on its 'global dockyard'. The discs similarly commemorate the docks' working-class histories, as can be seen on the disc pictured in Figure 5.7. These lines serve as a direct critical counterpoint to the docks' recent architectural facelift since, all around the nearby Lowry building, luxury apartments have sprung up to serve the BBC's new headquarters in Media City (see Figures 5.8 and 5.9).

Sissay's Tib Street poem similarly operates as a counterpoint to local development, continually performing itself anew as the street evolves around it and becomes increasingly gentrified. In Figure 5.10, Sissay's poem is a counterpoint to the new offices and retail units as the city's facelift proceeds apace.

For decades, Manchester's City Council has emphasized that the city's architectual redevelopment is designed to benefit its own citizens (Mellor, 2002: 216). As Rosemary Mellor argues, however, not only has priority historically been given to road access by dual carriageways such as the London Road and the Mancunian Way, which 'scythe

5.8 Luxury flats near the Lowry Theatre, Salford Quays, 2011. © Corinne Fowler.

5.9 BBC Media City, Salford Quays, 2011. © Corinne Fowler.

5.10 New construction work on Tib Street (2011) with the opening lines of Sissay's landmark poem, 'Flags', laid into the pavement in the foreground. © Corinne Fowler.

'Rebels without applause'

through old neighbourhoods, destroying their local centres' (Mellor, 2002: 230), but the 'gloss and gleam' of the city's new architecture have tended to exclude the poor from Manchester's 'revitalised core', which is designed to cater for those who visit its many restaurants and bars (Mellor, 2002: 230) (see also discussion in Chapter 1). In the face of such development, however, there are indications that the days of poetry's 'infinite delivery' (Osborne, 2011: 199) are numbered. As with the rotting Blackscribe anthologies described in Chapter 2, there lurks here another cautionary tale. Sissay's Tib Street poem is already in a sad state of repair (these photos were taken in 2011), with cracked tiles and missing words that the City Council has simply tarmacked over (see Figures 5.11 and 5.12). One of SuAndi's landmark poems, too, which was unveiled by the poet Benjamin Zephaniah in the 1980s, was recently demolished alongside a school building in Moss Side. Poets' hard-won endeavours to make their voices heard are thus easily forgotten. Further, as noted in Chapter 2, as Sissay's career has developed, he is increasingly associated with London. In his role as Associate Artist at the Southbank Centre, Sissay has been able to create

5.11 Damaged, repaired and worn tiles of Sissay's 'Flags' poem, 2011.
© Corinne Fowler.

5.12 Damaged, repaired and worn tiles of Sissay's 'Flags' poem, 2011.
© Corinne Fowler.

landmark poems in the Royal Festival Hall, Toynbee Hall, the City of London's financial district and (as discussed in Chapter 2) most recently the Olympic Park. These more lucrative landmark commissions, associated with his Southbank role in London, are sadly more likely to remain *in situ* than those in Manchester.[32] Given the literary dominance of London, it is hard to miss the irony that it is most likely the London-based landmark poetry of a black Mancunian poet that is set to endure in the public memory.

The cultural politics of belonging

In his study *Postcolonial London: Rewriting the Metropolis* (2004), John McLeod observes that many black writers in Britain have begun to deploy aquatic metaphors to express the complex cultural and historical dimensions of personal identity. He writes:

> [Following] the publication of Paul Gilroy's important study *The Black Atlantic* (1993), it has become increasingly popular [for poets and

novelists] to conceive of diasporic cultures in terms of aquatic metaphors. The fluidity and flux of the sea across which cultures, peoples and politics move have been appropriated as dynamic tropes of the restlessness, provisionality, adaptability and itinerant character of diasporic (and especially black) cultures. (McLeod, 2004: 163)

One of the British black poets whom McLeod identifies as using aquatic imagery is Bernardine Evaristo, whose 'novel in verse', *The Emperor's Babe* (2002), reimagines London as a waterway to the world. Aquatic metaphors are also important to some of Manchester's poets. A prominent example is Sissay, whose poetry has long contested dominant modes of Britishness by means of such imagery. This can be seen in his poem 'Island Mentality' (2000), for example, in which Britain figures as a claustrophobic nation obsessed with its own imaginary parameters. The speaker of 'Island Mentality' condemns Britain's insular self-fashioning by drawing playfully on the childhood rhyme 'The Gingerbread Man', where a gingerbread man gets eaten by the fox, who tricks him into riding on his back to get across the river:

> This ink blot on my world map is hemmed in by the sea
> Hemmed in by the sea, hemmed in by the sea
> I can walk on water and you can't catch me
>
> (Sissay, 2000a: 43)

This playful aquatic image allows the speaker to express an expansive postcolonial consciousness. Imbued with visionary, Christ-like powers, his ability to walk on water presents him as unconfined by national boundaries. More than this, his enhanced geo-political awareness actually renders him as a more fitting commentator on the nation's affairs than those who claim greater indigeneity on the grounds of their whiteness. In both respects, the poem's aquatic dimension insists upon Britain's situated geography as discussed in the Introduction to this book.

Taken together, then, Sissay's poems present a clear challenge to the practice of setting black Britons apart from the nation's shared cultural life. As discussed in the introduction to this chapter, the figure of the neighbour is highly pertinent both to the cultural politics of belonging and for understanding the extent to which black Mancunian poets might be considered as 'compatriots in craft'.[33] In his 2008 poetry collection Sissay writes:

[W]hen I hear of Oasis or Weller, and the great Beatles influence, when I hear of young up-and-coming artists harking back to The Beatles in some kind of retro-chic way, I remember not what they produced in this enlightened summer [of 1967, the year of Sissay's birth] but the misinformation of the time and how black people ... were either demonised or hero-worshipped *but god forbid they would be accepted as neighbours.* (Sissay, 2008: 102, emphasis added)

Sissay's insistence on the term 'neighbour' is critically relevant to a growing sense of indigenous black Britishness since neighbourliness suggests both communal belonging on the grounds of physical proximity and shared local sensibilities. Yet, as the experience of many black poets indicates, acceptance as a neighbour remains an impenetrable final frontier.

Mancunian rain is also central to Sissay's visual assertions of black neighbourly identity (see Figure 5.13). This photograph represents a subtly transgressive foray from 'the street' into the neighbourly setting of 'the park', which is by definition the most local and parochial of England's green spaces. Sissay wears a white suit and both his feet are planted on the grass. He holds an umbrella aloft and stares directly into the camera. Rain clouds gather behind him, but the sky above Sissay's head and shoulders is brightly illuminated. The incongruous white linen suit seems unwarranted by both the rainy weather and the locale. Yet the suit perhaps alludes to Alexander Mackendrick's 1951 film *The Man in the White Suit*, set in the north of England, in which the protagonist invents a strong fibre that never wears out. An allusion to this film, of course, would place Sissay and his poetry in the context of the textile mills of the North, which both accounted for the region's wealth and exploited working-class and immigrant workers in the process. As a redemptive, anti-sleaze figure, Sissay's pose offers us the black poet as a fitting wearer of the white suit whose insights illuminate the scenes described by his poetry, an impression that is enhanced by the brightening sky behind him. In this picture, then, a postcolonial sense of locale is insinuated into the decidedly parochial setting of the local park. Meanwhile, the clear, plastic panes of Sissay's umbrella arch above him like a canopy in a gesture mirroring that of the surrounding trees, suggesting that the metaphor of roots – which Salman Rushdie has decried as overly static – retains its usefulness as a pertinent metaphor of tenure. At once static and itinerant, these visual elements belie the apparent stasis of the 'roots' image by simultaneously communicating both the external and the internal geographies of belonging.

5.13 Lemn Sissay. Photo © Toby Madden.

SuAndi similarly emphasizes the significance of northern black neighbourliness:

> I think it's my cultural heritage as both Nigerian and Liverpudlian Irish and [I engage with] both their oral traditions. I want to make it gossipy, over the garden fence ... I think my style reflects a working class education ... You can be a working class poet, if you have a 'eh by gum' accent for people to hook on to. But if you're black, working class, you're non-exotic because you don't speak patois, and don't produce Dub Poetry ... the literary world doesn't seem to have any use for you. (SuAndi in Munden and Wade, 1999: 42)

It is a powerful irony that SuAndi's work could be discounted on the grounds of her regional, working-class identity. SuAndi suggests here that blackness and northerness are commonly perceived as mutually exclusive identifications. This perception is borne out by the experience of fellow writer Joe Pemberton, whose identities as black, northern and working-class were consistently perceived as anomalous, contradictory and mutually exclusive by national reviewers of his novel (see Fowler, 2008). Sissay describes what he sees as audiences' 'unconscious resistance' to the neighbourliness of black poets with regional accents (Harris, Brandes 2007: 24).

Procter's concept of the 'postcolonial everyday' seems particularly pertinent to the work of SuAndi, whose poems are stridently local, chatty and domestic. The conversational tone of SuAndi's poem 'Nearly Forty' gives a flavour of the collection:

> I was in the shop the other day,
> You should have seen this girl's outfit –
> It was disgusting – she had everything on display
> (SuAndi, 1992: 5)

Such poetry is both spoken (performed) and voiced (as a poetic register) in regional accents by cultural insiders to British provincial life. SuAndi's account of her inspiration in and of itself serves as a reminder that Britishness is always already transcultural: '[my mother's] Irish genes were so embedded in oral history that my storytelling is an art inherited. However, no-one was interested in women like her, ordinary working class women' (in Grabner and Casas, 2011: 220). This commentary accompanies an excerpt from one of her poems, which uses word order to subvert the charge of parochialism that so frequently attends devolved poetic expression:

> I am an ordinary woman
> Nothing special
> Ordinary.
> Nothing.
> Nothing.
> Ordinary.
> There is nothing to show
> Nothing to tell
> Ordinary.
> Nothing.
> Ordinary.
>   (SuAndi in Grabner and Casas, 2011: 220)

By her own account, while SuAndi initially wrote poems about Africa, she quickly found that England, and the North West region, was her natural poetic terrain (SuAndi in Grabner and Casas, 2011: 221). SuAndi's account of her early career, performing with Lemn Sissay and Henry Normal, recognizes that Mancunian poetry by black poets is not amenable to commodification:

> As each of the group went on [to establish] successful careers, I ... slowly began to understand that what made a performance poet special was the ability to speak in a voice that they, the poet, believes in. (SuAndi in Grabner and Casas, 2011: 220)

This is not so much an insistence on biographical authenticity (SuAndi's work explores multiple voices and subject positions) as an ethical commitment to writing poetry against the commercial grain.

As discussed in Chapter 1, the most consistent poetic expression of Mancunian black poets' local sensibilities is the rain metaphor. For earlier, migrant writing in Britain, rain has typically communicated something of the gloom and dread of arriving in Britain. More recently, however, it has come to signify belonging. John Agard's poem 'True Grit' is a good example of this:

> Here comes a black Englishman with a brolly
> To forget either would indeed be folly
>   (Agard, 2006: 10)

Yet for Mancunians rain has a distinctive cultural resonance. Sissay's poem 'Moods of Rain' (1988) uses rain to assert the speaker's status as cultural insider. This is notwithstanding the poem's exploration, discussed in Chapter 1, of the racist exclusions that would deny this shared sensibility. Nonetheless, by drawing on a collective Mancunian experience of rain and gloom he does assert his right to identify himself as a neighbour: 'I've got those winter dark blues / Wet, cold, and skint' (Sissay, 1988: 17). Some of Manchester's first generation migrants have also adopted the rain metaphor. Basir Kazmi has frequently performed his own 'rain' poem, which he calls his 'Manchester couplet':

> So that others may take pleasure in your talk, Basir
> Don't talk of your tears, talk rather about the rain
> (Kazmi in Chatterjee, 2003: 68)[34]

Although much of Kazmi's poetry is set in his Pakistani homeland, he argues that his experience of life and work in Manchester has impacted in subtle ways on his work.[35] The Manchester couplet registers rain's Mancunian province but conveys it in the form of a *ghazal*, with all of that medium's propensity for philosophical musing (Chatterjee, 2003: 16). There can be no doubt that the force of this poem relies on the cultural stereotype that the English like talking about the weather. When performed in Manchester, however, the couplet acquires a distinctive local inflection. On the two occasions I have seen Kazmi perform these lines in English, they have been greeted with laughter and shouts of pleasure by Mancunian audiences.

The Manchester couplet both embraces *and* critiques the rain trope as an index of local belonging. The trope's power to assert belonging pressurizes the poem's speaker to conceal the troubles he is experiencing in his experience of dwelling in Manchester. Kazmi might smile at the couplet's enthusiastic reception, yet the couplet presents the rain trope as a form of local tyranny. Such lines bear out Chatterjee's observation that, while the *ghazals* of Basir Kazmi's father are famed 'for their air of pathos and nostalgia ... those of Basir Sultan Kazmi often express a feeling of frustration and thwarted ambition' (Chatterjee, 2003: 16).

I began this section with a meditation on how black poets in Manchester, along with their counterparts elsewhere in Britain, have explored rural and regional locales that go beyond the traditional loci of black Britishness. Yet explorations of belonging by British black poets have increasingly enabled them to make poetic forays into the supposedly white preserves of rural England. Water flows through the urbanscapes of Sissay's Manchester but, equally, his metaphors of tenure take the shape of fields, sand, sea and rock. Valerie Bloom's introduction to Lemn Sissay's first poetry collection tentatively describes a number of his poems as 'almost pastoral' (Bloom, 'Introduction' to Sissay, 1988: xi), yet the body of Sissay's work increasingly justifies a more definitive statement. In one of a group of pastoral poems, Sissay's 'Barley Field' (2008: 82) pictures its speaker 'looking for inspiration' in a 'sea of barley' (ll. 9 and ll. 13). The poem's central focus is an oak tree, which 'stands, centre page' (l. 4). As a symbol of ancient England, Sissay's oak tree metaphor indirectly asserts the right to participate in British pastoral traditions of poetry. Ironically, too, the poem's speaker almost leaves the field without spotting his initials carved into the trunk, a detail that gives rise to an italicized realization: '*I had been here before*' (Sissay, 2008: 82), depicting the prior, habitual presence of a black man in an English rural landscape. The speaker's 'inspiration' derives not merely from his engagement with English poetry's pastoral traditions but from his sense of belonging to rural scenes and settings.

The pastoral dimension to Sissay's work has yet to register in reviews of his poems, which are overwhelmingly represented as urban, or, as an *Independent* review states, 'songs of the street'.[36] Nevertheless, poems such as 'A Black Man on the Isle of Wight' (2000b: 44) and 'A Reading in Stansted' (1999: 56) similarly address the lingering sense that British rural landscapes are subtly policed. 'A Black Man in the Isle of Wight' reads simply:

> Faces cold as the stone
> stuck to the sea's belly
> with seaweed for hair
> sculpted into expressions of fear
>
> (Sissay, 2000b: 56)

In 'A Reading in Stansted', meanwhile, the speaker's apparently incongruous presence in 'a real country pub' (Sissay, 1999: 56) sparks a similar sense of public alarm when he is asked to present his work to people sitting in the bar. Yet the poem emphasizes the speaker's devolved sensibility: he has 'travelled two hundred and fifty miles' south from his usual Manchester location. Once in the pub, he performs his poetry to the startled audience, who mistakes him for a 'gangster', a mistake that hints at the persistent association of black man and black poet with 'the street' (Sissay, 1999: 56). Both these pastoral poems reveal, and breach, the hidden territorial limits of multiracial Britain. The Lewes-based Agard has similarly drawn attention to these limits in his poetry collection *We Brits* (2006), which pictures 'a monocled Black Brit in jodhpurs',[37] depicts black bodies on beaches in 'Seaside Etiquette' and describes poets such as John Lyons ('Caribbean Eye over Yorkshire') as well as black and white poets taking country walks together in the snow.[38]

An important parallel with Sissay's pastoral poetry is the work of the British black artist Evewright. Evewright has photographed sand sculptures on a number of English beaches. In photographs of his sand sculptures entitled 'Coloured People', photographed on Silecroft beach in Cumbria, a multiracial line of people dressed in blue and green anoraks walks in single file along looping furrows that have been ploughed in the sand. By dressing the subjects in coloured anoraks, Evewright uses a literal description to interrogate the apparent anomaly of black people's presence in a rural setting. The term 'coloured' harkens back to a particularly fraught moment in British race relations as well as gesturing to transnational contexts, such as the apartheid struggle, while the alignment of the photographic subjects in single file evokes the context of slavery. Using these visual mechanisms, Evewright's image evokes past contexts of oppression to test the concealed limits of belonging in today's multiracial Britain.

The subtle nature of these limits surface regularly in relation to what happens when poetry is performed. This is exemplified in Cornelia Grabner's account of Linton Kwesi Johnson performing his poetry at the University of Stirling. Grabner writes: 'throughout [the reading] ... the contrast between Johnson's heavily rhymed dub poetry on the one hand and ... the surrounding rural campus created a productively disconcerting atmosphere' (Grabner and Casas, 2011: 11). It is hard to mistake the source of such disconcertion. The statement, and its likely comprehension, makes it abidingly clear that, even for established black poets such as Kwesi Johnson or Lemn Sissay, rural landscapes are perceived to be incongruous. In this setting at least, Kwesi Johnson cannot be a neighbour.

Black poets' intensified engagement with rural England coincides with recent work by local historians, revealing black people's long association with rural England, which dates back to at least 1650. Archival research by SCAWDI[40] shows that Britain's black population was widely dispersed throughout the countryside due to the rural locations of stately homes and mansion houses (Callaghan and Willis-

Brown, 2011: 3). As is now more widely known, plantation owners brought slaves back to England to work as servants. Not only was it fashionable to have black servants but their free labour made economic sense (Callaghan and Willis-Brown, 2011: 3). SCAWDI has found archival records of black slaves, gardeners and pageboys in the 'old' Midlands counties of Warwickshire, Shropshire, Worcestershire and Staffordshire. Of particular significance are some cave drawings by black slaves, who carved images of their faces into chalk caves below Guy's Cliffe House. Owned by the Greatheed family, which had plantations in St Kitts, this 1750s home in Warwickshire was the workplace of black slaves from the Caribbean. SCAWDI has battled to promote this find as one of 'national significance' (Callaghan and Willis, 2011: 2).[41]

The visual aspect of Sissay's work has acquired an ever more marked pastoral and nautical flavour. In January 2012, a new poem was projected on to the Turner Contemporary building in the seaside town of Margate. His newly designed website features several photographs of him swimming just off the British coast. It is clearly productive to understand such gestures as a performer's response to the intellectual archaeology of black Britain as outlined above.[42] In a collective attempt to counter the primacy of the 1948 'Windrush' moment as *the* moment of arrival of black people in Britain, researchers and historians have systematically uncovered evidence of a black presence in Britain dating back to Roman times. Archaeologists from the Universities of Liverpool and Reading have discovered the remains of black centurions at the village of Burgh-on-Sands and the 'ivory bangle lady', a black member of York's fourth-century elite. Long before these more recent discoveries, the historian Peter Fryer wrote his influential study *Staying Power: The History of Black People in Britain since 1504* (1984), which inspired Evaristo's depiction of black Romans in Londinium. These efforts complement the work of local historians, such as Dominique Tessier in Manchester, who have developed black history trails throughout Britain for Black History Month since the 1990s.[43]

On 23 July 2012, the National Trust invited Lemn Sissay to read his poetry to commemorate the lifelong friendship between Haile Selassie and Roger Grey, the tenth Earl of Stamford, who welcomed Selassie many times to his stately home called Dunham Massey, near Altrincham outside Manchester. An Ethiopian flag was flown above the hall while Sissay read his poetry to an elderly white audience and a handful of black Mancunians. A few days later, Danny Boyle's Olympic opening ceremony featured black people in classic English pastoral scenes, perhaps prompting MP Aiden Burley's now infamous tweet: 'leftie multi-cultural crap', followed by the explanation: 'I was talking about *the way it was handled in the show*, not multiculturalism itself' (BBC News, 28 July, italics mine). Despite the vast number of hidden black histories of rural Britain, then, this aspect of the nation's heritage continues to be relatively unexplored. For black Britons, the countryside remains symbolically out of bounds (see Procter, 2003; Robinson, Kay and Procter, 2012).

Indigenous British poets: the Manchester performance scene, 1960 to the present

> I loved the Mersey Beat poets and I read them a lot ... I remember it was my older sister's copy of *The Mersey Sound* that I first read.
>
> (Peter Kalu)[44]

Manchester's performance scene has always been diverse and – as well as the slams, mushiaras and landmark commissions outlined above – must be seen to include more conventional events such as the readings associated with the prestigious publishing house Carcanet, as well as those arranged by the University of Manchester's Centre for New Writing and Manchester Metropolitan University. The city's poetry in performance may thus be seen to speak to a range of local, national and transnational traditions and reflects multiple poetic developments.

An enduring influence on all Mancunian performance poetry is the ever-popular John Cooper Clark. A figurehead for youth culture in the 1970s, Cooper Clark is often referred to as the 'Punk Poet' or the 'Bard of Salford'.[45] He became known for his political satire and rapid-fire delivery, which the poet Joolz Denby alludes to in the epigraph to this chapter. Dressed in the 'skintight black' of his iconic drainpipe trousers, Cooper Clark has performed alongside bands such as the Sex Pistols, Elvis Costello and New Order. Many of his poems, such as 'Beasley Street' and 'Belladonna', are renowned for their bleak depictions of urban decay. Manchester's punk poetry phenomenon is teasingly captured in line 6 of Peter Kalu's poem 'Manchester' ('swindlers, poisoners, punks, poets' (2007)). A slightly younger contemporary of Cooper Clark is Henry Normal, who co-founded Manchester's Live Poets Society.[46] The Live Poets Society evokes the democratizing spirit of the Mersey Beat poets. Poets such as Tamsho and SuAndi frequently attended gigs by Cooper Clark, Normal and Brian Patten, while Sissay performed with Cooper Clark and Normal in his early career.

The Mersey Beat, or 'Liverpool', poets Adrian Henri, Roger McGough and Brian Patten, are widely considered as the founding fathers of British poetry in performance. Their 1967 poetry anthology *Mersey Sound* became one of the best-selling poetry collections of all time (Beasley in Munden and Wade, 1999: 31). As this chapter explains, influential Mancunian poets such as Peter Kalu,[47] SuAndi, Tina Tamsho and Lemn Sissay are heirs to the Mersey poets' democratizing spirit, local accent and formal experimentation. As Sissay proclaims at the end of his 2008 poetry collection: '[The 1970s] was a wonderful time for poetry ... The first book of poetry I received in adolescence was *The Mersey Sound*, published in 1967. I judge all proclamations of poetry's popularity against this year' (Sissay, 2008:101). Similarly, the black poet Levi Tafari, who was born in Liverpool, says that the performances of the Mersey poets were one of the reasons that made Liverpool 'the place to be in the Sixties' (in Hoyles and Hoyles, 2002: 147).

This historical contextualization is important since it reveals that Manchester's performance scene was established some twenty years before the poetry slam format (with which it more typically associated) arrived from the United States in the 1990s. While many of its poets have very evidently been influenced by the slam ethos, together with the performance styles of first-generation black poets such as John Agard and Linton Kwesi Johnson, in Britain or the jazz-infused style of Amiri Baraka in the United States, I would argue that it is equally important to situate Manchester's post-1980s poetry in performance in the context of both the local and national poetic expression of the British poetry revival (1960–75).

Before pursuing this hypothesis, I need first to reflect further upon the dominant scholarly approaches to the performed work by British black poets. Researchers invariably situate such work in one of two contexts. As noted at the beginning of this chapter, some scholars concentrate on the poetics, politics and aesthetics of dub poetry, focusing in particular on the work of African-Caribbean poets as John Agard, Jean Binta Breeze and Linton Kwesi Johnson. As these critics rightly suggest, dub poetry has been an important vehicle for denouncing exploitation and institutional racism in Britain and beyond (Williams, 2011: 109). Particular historical contexts that are indexed here include the 1980s riots, the New Cross massacre and the Black

People's Day of Action[48] (D'Aguiar, 1993: 59). These scholars have observed that, in Christian Habekost's words, dub poetry 'bridg[es] the "black" oral tradition and the white literary tradition' (Habekost in Williams, 2011: 109). Moving the discussion on to consider work included in Sissay's 1998 showcase of 'accented'[49] second-generation poets, *The Fire People*, Blake Harris Brandes similarly argues that contemporary work by British black poets occupies 'a liminal space between dub poetry and hip-hop' (Harris Brandes, 2007: 21). Such statements are not inaccurate. Yet it is hard not to notice that the dominant scholarly metaphors used to describe the poetics and positioning of work by British black poets remain that of 'the bridge' or 'interstices'. Such metaphors seem inadequate. It is a mistake to isolate the work of British black poets from the putatively more literary work of their white British counterparts. Among poetry practitioners, too, the common 'page or stage' binary promotes a form of collective amnesia about the oral dimensions of British poetry itself, particularly those associated with the British poetry revival, in which poets privileged both formal experimentation and public performance.

The second, less established, context for the analysis of British black poetry in performance is that of the countercultural poetry slam which, as noted above, arrived from the United States in the late 1980s. Books about poetry slams invariably retell the following story. In 1986 a poet and former construction worker called Marc Smith sought new venues for his poetry and lighted upon the blue-collar bars and cabarets of Chicago's white, working-class neighbourhoods. As legend has it, Smith ran out of material during an ensemble show at a venue called the Green Mill and stumbled upon a new format: the poetry slam. He held a mock competition in the show's final set and encouraged the audience to boo and applaud the poetry that they heard (Somers-Willett, 2009: 4). It is a mark of the slam's popularity and commercial viability that Marc Smith was able to author *A Complete Idiot's Guide to Slam*, which came out in 2004. Coinciding as it has with the development of information and communication technologies, the popularization of Anglophone poetry in performance (alongside that of rap and underground hip hop music) has indeed fundamentally altered poetry's province and modes of transmission. As Chapter 2 has already noted, Dana Gioia, Chair of the National Endowment for the Arts in the United States, argues that poetry in performance reaches its audiences less by means of print culture than by the tools of the entertainment industry, by means of

YouTube videos and podcasts (Gioia, 2003: 28).⁵⁰ In this 'manifesto', Gioia excitedly declares that the typical poetry venue for performance of poetry is no longer the university but the bookshop, the concert hall, the bar, nightclub or theatre.

In this enthusiasm to make manifest the ways in which post-millennial poetry is being transformed by new venues and new sciences of transmission it is, however, easy to forget that Britain's counterculture has been here before. Poets associated with the British poetry revival, such as Michael Horovitz or Adrian Henri, preferred the same sorts of venues, and shared many of the same values, as those now associated with contemporary slam poetry. Recognizing this is also important in that it helps us avoid viewing the devolved poetic expression of British black poets through an Anglo-American lens (Williams, 2011: 7)

It is, moreover, but a short political step from here to a crucial revaluation of slam's overwhelming significance for black poets. In her book *The Cultural Politics of Slam* (2009), Somers-Willett points out that, while slam has white, working-class origins, it quickly became a significant forum for 'poets of colour'. This is partly because the slam managed to absorb poets such as Amiri Baraka, whose work had long since explored the relationship between poetry, cultural heritage and jazz. Utopian accounts of the slam might easily proceed to associate the predominance of black poets with a wider tendency to embrace poets from traditionally marginalized groups (Somers-Willett, 2009: 11). Nonetheless, the case of Manchester tells a more complex story of restricted opportunity and literary ghettoization. While the slam format might be said to have partially revitalized Manchester's poetry scene, providing a productive focus for poetry collectives such as Brothatalk, Speakeasy and Young Identity, it has alienated established poets, such as SuAndi, who resisted the trend for a variety of reasons. SuAndi objects to the slam scene partly on the grounds that slam compères do not have to pay the performers. Echoing the concern of Jean Binta Breeze that 'slam is the fast food of poetry' (Breeze, Agbabi, Tipene, Harrison, and Bertram, 1999: 10) and troubled by the slam's three-minute performance rule, she asks: 'but can [these poets] hold an audience for an hour?'⁵¹ Large audiences are the province of poetry slams, which are highly amenable to a climate of Arts Council funding in which bids are assessed in terms of their ability to reach new audiences. In Manchester, the slam format does appeal to large audiences and it has absorbed young poets who draw from a range of traditions such as Jamaican dub, African storytelling, hip hop music and the figure of the griot. Nevertheless, reading the city's poetry in an Anglo-American context misses an important parallel story about poetry in performance.

To date, there has been very little scholarly work that examines the relationship of Britain's black poets to more established literary traditions. Fred D'Aguiar's 1993 essay on Britain's multiracial literary pedigree is an exception. In this piece, entitled 'Have You Been Here Long? Black Poetry in Britain', D'Aguiar traces black poets' influence on British literary traditions as far back as Phillis Wheatley's *Poems on Various Subjects, Religious and Moral*, which was published in 1773 (D'Aguiar, 1993: 53). Taking the long view, D'Aguiar asserts that 'black poetry ... invigorated poetry in Britain' (D'Aguiar, 1993: 53).

D'Aguiar's is a lone voice, however. The unexamined question of British black poets' relationship with more canonical British artistic, cultural and literary traditions is illustrated by Sissay's account of a rift between himself and the sculptor of one of his landmark poems, this time in London. Sissay rejected the initial design by the sculptor Michael Vissachi for his 'Gilt of Cain' poem because Vissachi planned to set Sissay's poem on top of a plinth where nobody would be able to read it. Instead, Sissay insisted that the lines of his poem be carved into the sugar cane itself, which represented 'the people, the Slaves' who were commemorated by his poem (Sissay in Osborne, 2011: 201). Sissay argues that Vissachi initially resisted his suggestion because he considered that the new design would somehow deface the sculpture. As Osborne relates, Vissachi's sense of defacement renders a black poet's poetry about the slave trade as a kind of 'graffiti' on the pure surfaces of his sculpture (Osborne, 2011: 202). The incident provides a pertinent metaphor for understanding the subordinate relationship of work by black poets to British poetry. Persistently figuring black poets as 'performance poets' or 'spoken word artists' risks relegating them to a kind of graffiti at the margins of British poetry.[52] This is apparent in the subtle policing of the apparently innocent and neutral title of 'poet'. As D'Aguiar observes, work by second- and third-generation British black poets is rarely analyzed or reviewed in relation to its engagement with local poetic traditions (D'Aguiar 1993: 70). However, the case of Manchester reveals that the city's black poets are active participants in key debates and developments in British poetry.

When D'Aguiar notes that Linton Kwesi Johnson's *Dread, Beat and Blood* was 'a departure from anything that had ever been published in Britain ... in terms of the kind of English used', he takes the unusual step of aligning Kwesi Johnson's poetry collection with the tradition of the Mersey Beat, or 'Liverpool' poets:

> [T]he poems had startling resemblances in their social concerns to the best of the Liverpool poets of the decade before, making them anti-establishment in their appeal and popular – qualities unfamiliar to most poets operating in Britain at the time. (D'Aguiar, 1993: 54)

Almost in passing, D'Aguiar recalls that Kwesi Johnson gave a joint concert with Salford's 'Punk' poet, John Cooper Clark (D'Aguiar 1993: 54), which he attributes to the poets' shared roots in contemporary youth culture and the political protest associated with anti-Nazi league and gay rights activism (D'Aguiar, 1993: 57). This detail potentially substantiates his earlier, more generalized observation that 'black poetry reinvigorated poetry in Britain' (D'Aguiar 1993: 53). His claim also parallels claims made in other contexts that the British poetry revival, and its associated poets, had a similarly re-energizing effect on the British literary scene. Significantly, too, D'Aguiar mentions that Kwesi Johnson's *Dread, Beat and Blood* (1975) coincided with the end of the Revival, though he draws no further conclusions about the significance of the parallels.[53] Worth noting particularly, however, is his closing remark in the conclusion to his essay:

> With the regional loyalties which poets like Jackie Kay or Levi Tafari carry ... surely critical attempts to isolate their work and group them together will look more and more absurd ... The reality is that poets of a particular age, class and locality, often have more in common, in terms of their craft and themes ... than poets of the same race who belong to a different generation and class and live at opposite ends of the country. (D'Aguiar, 1993: 70)

D'Aguiar's insight here relates strikingly to the importance of looking more closely at Britain's devolved literary cultures in order to understand the extent to which British black and white poets may, indeed, be considered as both 'compatriots in craft' (D'Aguiar 1993: 70) and 'poetic neighbours'.

It seems important, therefore, not to underplay the regional status of Manchester's poetry in performance nor, given the Mersey poets' centrality to the British Poetry Revival, to ignore its emblematic, countercultural Britishness. In the following discussion I detail the technical and philosophical legacies of Liverpool's 'Mersey Beat' to Manchester's parallel history of poetry in performance.

The Mersey Beat poets, and their followers, were inspired by famous performances such as Allen Ginsberg's first ever rendition of his poem 'Howl' in Gallery Six in 1955 (Raskin, 2011: 24). As Stephen Wade relates in his discussion of British poetry in performance:

> [A]lthough the Beats and Rexroth, Ginsberg and even Dylan played a part, surely our own British brand [of poetry in performance] owes most to the Mersey poets. It was the poems in that slim red and black Penguin paperback of *The Mersey Sound* that reflected direct displays of autobiographical pastiche and confession that the three poets [Adrian Henri, Roger McGough and Brian Patten] dealt in. What they did was show how eclectic influences from a more bohemian culture, a European type of student *dolce far niente* could be turned to a gentle love poetry and a sharp social satire all in one set of poems. Most of all, they had fun – in language, in their personae and in their media constructions [they] … established a discourse that was situated well clear of the Americans and yet also distant from … middle-class academic readings … [Their] impetus was always … [the] Liverpool / cosmopolitan delivery … creat[ing] moods … [and] emotional landscapes with voices at the centre. (Munden and Wade, 1999: 10)

The poetic expression of this devolved cosmopolitanism is further elaborated upon by Roger McGough, who describes writing about Liverpool as 'a breakthrough – to make your homeland into a real place … We read in smoky pubs [and] the evening would include music' (Munden and Wade, 1999: 37).

What I wish to propose is that many of the characteristics of the Mersey Beat poets are clearly discernible in poetry by black Mancunians. This is not to argue that the city's black poets exclusively derive their commitment to poetic renderings of everyday speech by figures such as the Mersey Beat poets. Rather, I am suggesting that the poetics of influential poets such as the Leicester-based Jean Binta Breeze or the Lewes-based Grace Nicols, who argue that poetry exists 'in any person speaking',[54] has a clear affinity with the democratizing spirit of the Mersey poets and the British poetry revival. The link is not straightforward, but it is easily missed.

One of the formal legacies passed down to the Mersey poets by figures such as Allen Ginsberg is the poetic technique of telescoping, or compressing, images (Dwividi, 2002: 65). Ginsberg himself inherited this technique from T. S. Eliot, whom he greatly admired. The poetics of telescopic images was outlined in an essay by Eliot:

> When a poet's mind is perfectly equipped for its work, it is constantly amalgamating experience: the ordinary man's experience is chaotic, irregular, fragmentary ... in the mind of the poet these experiences are always forming new wholes. ('The Metaphysical Poets', in Lind, 2011)

As the title of the essay implies, Eliot's work was itself inspired by that of the metaphysical poet John Donne, who was a key innovator of the technique. As Eliot observes, Donne frequently telescoped objects with the aim of connecting apparently unrelated planes of experience (Dwividi, 2002: 65). In 1919, Eliot coined a new critical term, the 'objective correlative', to describes the means by which concrete objects and visual images may be seen to embody an emotion that communicates itself vividly to the reader (Dwividi, 2002: 63). External objects thus correlate with the emotion that they themselves evoke.

Telescopic images which utilize Eliot's objective correlative' abound in many of the poems from the 1967 *Mersey Sound* collection. The technique is used to striking effect in Adrian Henri's 'Liverpool Poems', in which apparently disparate experiences are juxtaposed to build up a distinctive yet multilayered picture of Liverpudlian life:

>   1
>
>   GO TO WORK ON A BRAQUE!
>
>   2
>
>   Youths disguised as stockbrokers
>   Sitting on the grass eating the Sacred Mushroom
>
>   3
>
>   Liverpool I love your hornyhanded tons of soil
>
>   4
>
>   PRAYER FROM A PAINTER TO ALL CAPITALISTS:
>   Open your wallets and repeat after me
>   'HELP YOURSELF'
>
>   (Henri et al., 2007 [1967]: 65)

The telescopic technique is similarly deployed in Henri's poem 'The Entry of Christ into Liverpool', in which three apparently conflicting slogans are juxtaposed:

> Keep Britain White
> End the War in Vietnam
> God Bless Our Pope
> (Henri et al., 2007 [1967]: 69)

The placards' conflicting messages are clearly designed both to embody and to transmit the emotions associated with diverse political and religious experiences. The telescopic technique here allows Henri to evoke a particular city at a particular moment as a complex, multivocal whole: Liverpool.

The telescopic technique is, of course, nothing new. The comic songs of Victoria Wood – mentioned in the Introduction – are a case in point since they offer a cultural summary of 'the North', again in 'list' form. Wood sings of 'brass bands ... butties in your hands ... headscarves and mushy peas ... fog, smog, sitting on the bog, gaslight and games in the street'.[55] The North as depicted here has a strong association with cabaret, comedy and variety performance (Dearden, 2007: 14)

Telescopic images proliferate in poetry by Manchester writers. I discuss two especially vivid examples here: SuAndi's 'Contempt' (1992: 48) and Peter Kalu's 'Manchester' (Robinson, Kay and Procter, 2012). Written, like Victoria Wood's comic song, in 'list' form, 'Manchester' humorously juxtaposes disparate aspects of the city's culture and history. Kalu nevertheless imbues the telescopic technique with an additional postcolonial twist:

> Fire stokers, bridge builders, ball jugglers
> weavers, tunnellers, atom chasers
> guitar thrashers, cyber geeks, sausage sizzlers
> peaceniks, heretics, rebels, refugees
> carnivalists, miserablists,
> swindlers, poisoners, punks, poets
> centurions, slave barons
> divas, destroyers,
> rocket scientists, revolutionaries
> all live/d here.
> ('Manchester' in Kay, Procter and Robinson, 2012)

The telescopic technique is used in 'Manchester' to compress disparate identities and perspectives into a single poem and, by extension, into a single city. By capturing what Eliot described in his essay as the 'chaotic' and 'fragmentary' nature of everyday life, the poem 'amalgamates' an array of uneven social and political experiences into the multivocal and multi-temporal entity of 'Manchester'. The poem's final line effects a material act of temporal and experiential unification by compressing the diverse elements of the city's past into a single act of dwelling: 'all live/d here' (line 10). As he describes in his reflective commentary on the poem, Kalu aims to capture Manchester's 'political and creative energ[ies]' (Kalu, 2007; 'Moving Manchester' Writers' Gallery). What the telescoping technique also enables him to do is to present Manchester as a postcolonial city that is 'still wrestling with its imperial past' (Kalu, 2007):

> The poem ... attempts to capture Manchester's cultural and creative diversity, while also setting down its engagement with the slave trade, and other more shameful aspects of its history. The poem would probably work better on the Internet, where for each word there could be an html link to another file, which would unpack the history of that particular element of the poem. To give one example: Miserablists is a reference to the music of Morrissey and The Smiths – I grew up close to the cemetery where Morrissey apparently liked to wander – but it is also a reference to the UK's post Empire melancholia that fuels some of its contemporary racism. (Kalu, 2007)

As an instance of the 'postcolonial everyday' (Procter, 2006), Kalu's telescopic technique creates connections between seemingly unrelated Mancunian phenomena such as a specific band, The Smiths, and broad ideological orientations, such as colonial nostalgia, that adversely affect the everyday experience of those living in the city. His term 'miserablists' is placed in line 5, alongside only one other word: 'carnivalists', which may also be seen to conceptualize Manchester as a diaspora space with a strong history of immigration. However, the juxtaposition of 'carnivalists' and 'miserablists' modifies celebratory expressions of multiracial Manchester with a reminder of the city's persistent racism.

'Contempt', by SuAndi, which appears in her collection *Nearly Forty* (1992), is a poetic indictment of race relations in the late twentieth century. The poem depends throughout on the telescopic technique in order to provide a snapshot of the Thatcher era and to make humorous connections between seemingly unrelated elements. The poem again deploys the 'list' form to evoke and pour scorn on phenomena associated with Thatcher's government. The poem juxtaposes terms such as 'equal opportunities policies' and 'tokenism', thereby managing to capture the dominant concepts and terminologies of the period while also making a succinct critique of the divisive and ineffectual nature of governmental policy on social inequality based on ethnicity. The following lines illustrate how SuAndi uses the telescopic technique to satirical effect:

> The National Front
> Dick Heads
> ...
> Norman Tebbit.
> The English cricket team
> Football hooliganism
>
> (SuAndi, 1992: 48)

The name Norman Tebbit immediately evokes the former cabinet minister's infamous 'cricket test'.[57] The phrase 'cricket test' was coined by Tebbit as a means of questioning the patriotism of immigrants and their children on the grounds that many of them did not support the English cricket team. SuAndi's poem subverts Tebbit's notion of the cricket test by its listing strategies. The placement 'Football hooliganism' below the line 'The English cricket team' erodes Tebbit's assertion of disloyalty by foregrounding the relationship between patriotism and violence.

Kalu has argued that the work of the Mersey poets is highly relevant to Manchester's poetry in performance. So, too, is the British poetry revival. Eric Mottram argues that the revival's 'first representative collection' was *The New British Poetry*, published by Paladin in 1988 (in Hampson and Barry, 1993: 16). Work in this collection, Mottram argues, showed a range of formal influences ranging from open field, projective verse, sound text, concrete poetry, surrealist and dada developments and pop lyrics (in Hampson and Barry 1993: 16). Before and after this collection, he observes, work by poets associated with the revival was published largely by small presses and poetry magazines largely because the revival went 'largely unrecognised by the big controlling presses, the universities ... and the reviewing fraternity' (in Hampson and Barry, 1993: 15).

At the end of October 2006, several newspaper obituaries discussed the life and works of the recently deceased Scottish poet Ian Hamilton

Finlay. Hamilton Finlay's work was published in Michael Horovitz's landmark selection of British Revival Poetry called *Children of Albion: Poetry of the Underground in Britain* (Penguin, 1969). His poetry emphasizes formal experimentation and he specialized in concrete poetry, whereby the visual shape and form of the poem is intrinsic to the text's meaning. As Prudence Carlson (2006) observes, Hamilton Finlay's early concrete poetry could be characterized as modernist in the sense that it showed a formalist concern with the shape, colour and scale of his poems. Equally, however, Hamilton Finlay was interested in the power of language to shape perceptions and even inspire action (Carlson, 2006). This dual emphasis on the form and agency of language found its ultimate expression in Hamilton Finlay's famous Scottish garden in the Pentlands, which was called Little Sparta. Carlson has noted that Little Sparta has been described by Carlson as 'the epicentre of Hamilton Finlay's cultural production' because it both charts the grand historical events of the Western world and explores the relevance of art and poetry in that world (Carlson, 2006).

Lemn Sissay has also written a quantity of concrete poetry and he identifies Hamilton Finlay as a major inspiration. One of his poems called 'Advice for the Living', for example, is written in the shape of a coffin (Sissay, *The Listener*, 2008: 42).[58] 'Advice for the Living' mobilizes the power of poetry to promote reflection on the seemingly innocuous nature of language. Using a continuous play on the word 'dead', the poem lists conversational idioms – 'deadline', 'dead heats', 'dead right' – and promotes meditation upon the numbing effects of over-familiarity with language, which blinds us to the presence of death. As with the poetry of Hamilton Finlay, the poem's visual shape and wordplays combine to enforce its symbolism.

As my earlier discussion of the 'Gilt of Cain' sculpture indicates, Sissay's work has been inspired by Hamilton Finlay's formalist inscriptions of poetry on to sculptures. Equally, he inherits from Hamilton Finlay a concern to imbue poetry with a material physical presence that brings the language of poetry to public attention. Recognizing the ethical commitment implied by Sissay's interest in inscription, Osborne relates that, '[a]s part of his aesthetic *oeuvre*, Sissay has ... had [his work]... set in the counterweight of London's Royal Festival Hall, projected onto building facades, engraved upon walls, and inlaid into pavements' (in Grabner and Casas, 2011: 197).

Sissay's 'Gilt of Cain' landmark poem erodes the boundaries between slavery and modern day commerce, city and coastline. Its sculptural dimension echoes Hamilton Finlay's concern with poetry's potential agency to transform social consciousness. Sissay's resistance to the sculptor's initial design had everything to do with the principle of making the poem as visible as possible.

Mottram has characterized poets of the British revival as 'continuous[ly] awar[e] of the poet's function within finance capitalism, political corruption and concepts of law' (Mottram in Hampson and Barry, 1993: 24). Sissay's 'Gilt of Cain' clearly shares the kind of reflexive politics expressed by poems such as Adrian Henri's famous poem entitled 'The New Fast Automatic Daffodils' which explores the penetration of the capitalist ideology into the realm of everyday language and consciousness by re-rendering Wordsworth's 1807 poem 'Daffodils' in capitalist terms:

> beside the lake beneath the trees
> in three bright modern colours
> red, blue and pigskin
> (Henri et al., 2007 [1967]: 95).

Osborne argues that Sissay's oral performance of the 'Gilt of Cain' at the sculpture's unveiling ceremony 'activated multiple performances of his poem' (Osborne, 2011: 197). Not only was the poem both visual and grapholectic, but Sissay's Mancunian pronunciation of 'Wilberforce' ('Will Be Force') enacted a 'nuanced reversal' of the commissioned praise for Wilberforce since Sissay was not primarily concerned with commemorating the work of white abolitionists. Osborne therefore argues that Sissay's Mancunian accent 'undercu[t] the printed name Wilberforce' thereby giving the poem a more subversive ending that communicated a more ambiguous response to the commission than the printed or grapholectic versions of the poem had allowed (Osborne, 2011: 205).

Sissay identifies Hamilton Finlay's work as an important context for the poetry he wrote for the '2012 Winning Words' commission,[59] whereby inscriptions of his poems are stationed permanently throughout the Olympic Park in London. He writes in his blog: 'two of the three poems I wrote for the Olympic Park are directly influenced by the work of Ian Hamilton Finlay' (Sissay, 2011a). As explained in Chapter 2, one of these poems, 'Spark Catchers', is etched into a wooden structure that houses an electricity transformer to the north of the Olympic Park. The commission's brief was that the poem should relate directly to the area in which the Park was built. Sissay provides the following account of the thinking behind this poem:

> In my mind these East End women working with matches, with fire, were forging some connection with the Olympic flame. They had fire ... I am proud that my poem 'Spark Catchers' upholds these women on the 100th anniversary of International Women's Day. I am proud that this poem amongst two others I wrote will be placed on a structure that will stand long after the Olympic Games has passed. (Sissay, 'The Emperor's Watchmaker' blog, 2011a)

'Spark Catchers' thus provides an insight into the complex poetics and literary inspiration behind Sissay's work. Above all, his poetry shares the commitment of poets of the British revival to document the times, to transform public consciousness and to democratize poetry by bringing it into civic spaces.

It is more than a passing coincidence that Linton Kwesi Johnson shared a stage with John Cooper Clark since the major legacy of the Mersey poets and the British revival is an ethical one. Close examination of Manchester's performance poetry suggests that the city's black poets have simply picked up where the revival poets left off.[60] Mottram notes that 1960s Britain saw a dramatic growth in audience numbers when crowds flocked to see the performances of the Liverpool poets or to attend one of 'over a thousand' public poetry performances modelled on a successful event in 1964 called *Wholly Communion* that was organized by Michael Horovitz and Pete Brown (Mottram in Hampson and Barry, 1993: 29). Quoting Adrian Mitchell's essay 'Poetry Explodes' in a 1970 edition of *The Listener*, he argues that Horovitz and Brown did 'one hundred times more than the Arts Council to encourage poetry in this country ... these concerts ha[ve] brought into the open a huge new audience for poetry, as well as many new poets' (Mitchell in Hampson and Barry, 1993: 27). Significantly, however, Mottram believes that the closest Britain got to a powerful poets' union was the London Poetry Secretariat, in which Adrian Henri, among others, played a significant part. As part of his involvement with the London Poetry Secretariat, Henri and others his fellow poets produced the following declaration:

> Poetry is no longer the preserve of a cultural élite – it has become an art which is widely enjoyed ... the poet has gained a new audience through reading his work in public. (Hampson and Barry, 1993: 19)

Contemporary British black poets are demonstrably the heirs to this democratizing spirit: a politics summed up by SuAndi's declaration that that poetry is fundamentally a communal rather than a private affair, 'a contract of public contact' (in Osborne, 2011: 212). Shared by many British poets today, this ethic is in keeping with the 1960s belief in poetry's role as 'Fourth Estate' in the public sphere.[61] Citing John F. Kennedy's maxim that 'politicians are the men who create power', while artists are the 'men who question power', Zofia Burr argues that the poet's role in the last decade has been to question the sphere of politics from a position of integrity (in Williams, 2011: 63). Nerys Williams points out that Carol Ann Duffy's first act as poet laureate was to write a public poem about the expenses scandal in Westminster (Williams, 2011: 58). Subsequently, in 2011, she wrote a poem about the trial in January 2012 of two men accused of Stephen Lawrence's racist murderer.

In the autobiographical essay – quoted earlier in this chapter – Sissay presents himself as an heir to the Mersey poets phenomenon:

> [The Seventies were] a wonderful time for poetry ... The first book of poetry I received in adolescence was *The Mersey Sound*, published in 1967. I judge all proclamations of poetry's popularity against this year. (Sissay, 2008: 101)

However, Sissay's discussion of British cultural life also suggests that being denied the status of neighbour is bound up with the racism that denies the centrality of British life to his own poetic sensibilities (Sissay, 2008: 103).

These sensibilities are apparent in the extent to which Manchester's black poets inherit their forebears' emphasis on the local, the countercultural and the vernacular. It was the Mersey poets, among others, whose poetry implied that the most powerful expressions of place can be found in the most parochial of settings. This is famously communicated in Adrian Henri's poem entitled 'Liverpool Poems', which is set:

> outside chipshops
> in sidestreets
> on landings
> (Henri et al., 2007 [1967]: 41)

Set to music like many of the poems of the Mersey poets, John Cooper Clark's performances frequently dwell on the grit and grime of Manchester's streets. His poem 'Beasley Street' depicts its 'boarding houses and bedsits / Full of accidents and fleas' (Cooper Clark: 2002 Sony recording). Provincial settings also abound in the work of Manchester's black poets, such as Holden Caulfield, whose long poem 'Men's Morning' takes place in a council-run recreation centre where men of all races come to exchange their weekly gossip (Caulfield, 2000). Not only does Sissay's poetic material explore post-industrial working-class settings but it reflects the wider devolution of British poetry with its emphasis on everyday speech and mundane human action. His poem 'Olympic Invocation' depicts 'poetry sprayed in aerosol under the arches' (2008: 46) and provides the following account of football commentary, which 'Cuts through the defence, dessicates the attack / And scores a goal – "Poetry, poetry", Jimmy Hill Growls' (2008: 46). This espouses the notion, so central to the Mersey poets, that poetry is integral to everyday life. As a meta-commentary on poetry in performance, however, the poem is primarily concerned with poetry's oral and visual manifestations. The television weatherman is described as 'a closet poet' who '[p]erforms his piece' (page 46, l. 14). The poem asserts, too, that poetry's proper place is in the popular public domain: 'It's poetry on buses and poems on tubes' (l. 20). The reference to buses is particularly meaningful to a local audience since it refers to an advert he participated in for First Buses for which he received some criticism.[62] The reference to tubes, meanwhile, concerns the celebrated 'Poems on the Underground' campaign to which Sissay contributed and which aimed to popularize poetry by showcasing it on the London Underground and in a range of urban spaces, thereby bringing it to new audiences. As a meta-commentary on the evolution of British poetry, however, 'Olympic Invocation' recontextualizes the poetry slam in ways that gesture toward British everyday cultural life. Rather than offering a view of British poetry in performance as a US import, the local cultural references in 'Olympic Invocation' emphasize continuity both with northern oral traditions and with the efforts of poets associated with the British poetry revival to move poetry from the private to the public realm (Mottram, in Hampson and Barry 1993: 43).

This emphasis is by no means limited to a handful of individuals. As a recent Arts Council report on poetry in performance observes, promoters of live poetry events are committed to 'making the cultural activity open, friendly and non-elitist [and in] ... defining ... region[al] identity through the voices of its people' (Dearden, 2007:13). It seems no surprise, then, that John Agard recently dedicated his poem 'On a Yazoo Stem' to Michael Horovitz, editor of the publishing house closely associated with the British poetry revival called New Departures. Horovitz was also organizer of 'Live New Departures', a series of over a thousand large public gatherings where poetry was set to music (Mottram in Hampson and Barry, 1993: 27). He also organized several Poetry Olympics and edited several volumes of poetry associated with these events. In Agard's poem, Horovitz's efforts as an editor are reflected in the comparison of Horovitz to a squirrel, 'gathering nutty poems / from Albion's unsung corners' (Agard, 2006: ll. 4, 5). Similarly, the poem celebrates his work in organizing several Poetry Olympics and editing volumes of poetry associated with the live events: 'Torch-bearer schemer / of poetry olympics' (Agard, 2006: ll. 17, 18).

Sissay's own 'Olympic Invocation' makes its own contribution to this debate with its opening lines:

> Not a poetry picnic for the bards to enthral
> But Poetry Olympics at The Festival Hall
> (Sissay, 2008: 46, ll. 1–2)

The 'Olympics' of line 2 serves the dual purpose of referring to the slam's Olympic-style scoring and to the large audiences attracted to slam events. In this way the slam is obliquely linked with poetry's wider democratization. Conversely, and perhaps disingenuously, the poem conjures up the 'picnic' to represent the small-scale gatherings of poets associated with what Mottram calls 'the official British poetry'. As a parochial 'family' affair associated with the 'literary establishment', this picnic figures as both quaint and trivial. Indeed, by asserting that performing in a poetry slam is 'no picnic', Sissay's poem cheekily challenges the lowly status of poetry in performance by redirecting the criticism at poets who read their work to small, select gatherings. John Betjeman, a clear representative of the canonical poet, appears later in the poem as old and decrepit, sitting in a wheelchair and bemoaning a life with 'not enough sex' (line 17). Such references imply that canonical British poetry is anachronistic. This derision of outmoded forms of poetic expression echo Brian Patten's 1967 'Prosepoem Towards a Definition of Itself', which reads:

> Poetry asks the head-office for its files on the Nightingale
> for all information regarding its colour,
> its shape, the kind of song it indulged in.
> The message comes back:
> 'Subject obsolete. File closed'
> (Henri et al., 2007 [1967]: 45, ll. 14–18)

Sissay's 'Olympic Invocation' thus provides an implicit commentary on some long-standing debates about British poetry. While this commentary reflects recent poetic developments, it clearly also draws some inspiration from earlier critiques of the 1960s and the likes of Brian Patten, who was intensely conscious of the degraded status of devolved poetry in performance. In 'Prosepoem Towards a Defence of Itself', Patten depicts scholars as snipers on 'the roofs of articulate houses' (Henri et al., 2007 [1967]: 48, l. 19).

The Mersey poets are also an important influence on the poetry of SuAndi, whose poem about rape was inspired by Patten's 'Portrait of a Young Girl Raped in a Suburban Party' (Henri et al., 2007 [1967]). The very title of Patten's poem indicates a shift in literary focus from the male artist (indicated by the reference to James Joyce's novel *Portrait of the Artist as a Young Man*) (1916) to the experience of male violence. Together with her other poems about female suffering and male abandonment, SuAndi's poem about rape mirrors this shift. SuAndi's work is similarly influenced by other northern traditions. She has performed her dramatic poem called *The Story of M* to local and international audiences. The piece eventually appeared in print in 2002. Two years before the poem's publication, SuAndi wrote an account of the poem's development:

> When I was in Blackscribe, I wanted to develop a longer piece of poetry with characters ... I watched Alan Bennett in *Talking Heads* [first broadcast by the BBC in 1988]. There was an actress in it who looked like my mother and it was a year after she had died. The piece is about a women who is dying of cancer and I watched it and sobbed my heart out over it ... *The Story of M* [is]... my own *Talking Heads*. (SuAndi in Munden and Wade, 1999: 44)

The 'M' of the poem stands for SuAndi's mother Margaret, an Anglo-Irish Catholic brought up in Liverpool who moves to the city after the Second World War. However, the story is fundamentally an intergenerational one:

> 'M' for Margaret,
> 'M' for Mother,
> And now 'M' for Me
>
> (*The Story of M*, 2009: 18)

As Robert Crawshaw has observed, *The Story of M* is composed in the style of personal reminiscence, an impression reinforced by the photographs of SuAndi and her mother in the margins of its printed version (Crawshaw, 2009: 5). SuAndi's poem develops the preoccupation of *Talking Heads* with the theme of social isolation: 'M's sense of alienation is heightened by the racism of people and institutions who define "M" as an outsider such as the Salvation Army, the Catholic Church, the Police and racist neighbours' (Crawshaw, 2009). This positioning militates against the poem itself, the Mancunian and Liverpudlian idioms of which and intertextual relation with Bennett's work mark SuAndi's status as a cultural and literary insider.

As D'Aguiar predicted in his 1993 essay, 'Have You Been Here Long? Black Poetry in Britain' (D'Aguiar, 1993), the regional identities of British black poets make a nonsense of attempts 'to isolate their work and group them together' into the 'Black British' category (D'Aguiar, 1993: 70). The close literary affinities described in this chapter reveal the inadequacies of the metaphors of bridges and/or interstices to describe such poets' relation to English poetic traditions. Manchester's poets have shown a clear affinity with what Peter Barry describes as 'submerged poetic traditions' that have since become assimilated into mainstream British poetry. Barry writes: 'As so often, the ... repudiated "Other" is actually now a part of the self with which we were not yet ready to come to terms' (Barry, 2006: 180). Barry's context here is clearly poetry rather than the exclusion of black poets from the British literary canon. Yet his erudite book frequently deploys terms such as 'empire' and 'diaspora' as metaphors for these internal poetic struggles. Combined with Barry's reference to the 'repudiated "Other"', these terms are suggestive of another, overlooked dimension to the issue of British poetry. We might therefore be led to ask whether the repudiated British black poet might not have been integral to the nation's poetic self all along. Yet it also seems important to ask how British black poets figure in accounts of the British poetry revival itself. Barry's account tends to talk about British Black poets as practising *outside* the revival. The phrase 'by contrast' is frequently used to suggest that their poetry runs only in parallel to the revival. While revival poets, he writes, like to juxtapose slang and street talk with 'highly technical, abstract or learned language', British black poets, 'by contrast ... prefer 'interlingualism, in which Black British or Caribbean speech forms are used as well as standard English' (Barry, 2006: 142–3). This points, once again, to the fraught cultural politics of belonging whereby blackness, dialect and regional identity are forever seen as mutually exclusive. 'God forbid', as Sissay writes, that black Britons 'be seen as neighbours' (Sissay, 2008: 102).

Conclusion

When David Starkey made his now infamous contention that 'the whites have become black' (see discussion above), he repeatedly resorted to the concept of 'black culture' to sustain his argument, which he defined as 'a particular sort of nihilistic gangster culture'. His comments, made during a discussion with authors Dreda Say Mitchell and Owen Jones,[63] provoked over seven hundred complaints to BBC *Newsnight*. Jones and Mitchell firmly rejected Starkey's conception of 'black culture'. Nonetheless, they had only two main objections to it: first, that it criminalized black people in Britain and, second, that it did not reflect the diversity of British blackness. Mitchell insisted that 'black culture' be pluralized to 'black cultures'. However, by conceding the validity of any such categorizations, Starkey's critics unintentionally allowed him to equate blackness with foreignness, first as an import from Jamaica and then, as a concession by Starkey to Mitchell, from US rap. Many commentators dismissed Starkey's comments as pathologically racist. Yet work by black poets is typically defined as 'black poetry' from 'outside' the British cultural traditions with influences that are always-already predominantly transnational. Towards the end of the *Newsnight* discussion, Mitchell argued that British people need to 'start using words like *we*'. Her plea echoes the exhortations of D'Aguiar, Sissay, SuAndi and others: that, just one day, British black poets might be perceived as neighbours, even as 'compatriots in craft' (D'Aguiar, 1993).

In 'The Postcolonial Everyday', Procter argues that 'the habitual, the mundane and the taken-for-granted are all performing, or capable of performing, important cultural tasks after Empire' (Procter in Fowler, 2008: 87). Manchester is a significant regional hub of multiracial Britain. The regional inflections of work by the city's black poets testifies to a major, settled black presence, indicating poets' 'unquestionable belonging' to a range of urban and rural British settings and British poetic domains. While it is important to acknowledge the significance of dub, slam and rap, the case of Manchester suggests that what is typically classified as 'performance poetry' is also umbilically connected to older English poetic traditions.

In the introduction to his recent edited volume entitled *Beyond Cultural Diversity* (2010), Richard Appignanesi calls for an end to the 'myth' of cultural diversity in the arts. He argues that diversity should be understood 'as a condition *within* cultures and not simply of the obvious differences *between* them' (Appignanesi, 2010: 5). Yet, as Appignanesi argues, 'the official, sanctioned arts policy of cultural diversity' itself has written black artists out of mainstream art history[64] (Appignanesi, 2010: 10). This should be taken as justification not for diverting much-needed funding away from British black artists and writers but rather to move away from the kind of funding priorities satirized by Shamshad Khan's poem 'I've Been Waiting For Funding So Long', in which the speaker tries without success to meet 'the funding criteria' of 'vision and imagination, quality of execution' but finds the funders are interested in funding her only if she wears a 'razzle dazzle tunic with a pinstripe shalvaar / and union jack headscarf' (Khan, 2007).

Taking his inspiration from Enoch Powell, Starkey implied that 'black culture' has disrupted the established order of British society. Yet, in present-day British society where race, class and regional identity are so often posed as mutually exclusive categories, it remains the case that British black poets 'ask too much' to be black, northern and working-class, especially when their work is confined neither to 'black' issues nor to foreign literary traditions. Until this changes, Starkey's archaic conception of British cultural life will remain in the ascendant.

Notes

1. The title refers to Lemn Sissay's collection *Rebel without Applause* (2000a).
2. These forms include theatre plays, crime fiction, travel writing and middlebrow writing.
3. This phrase is taken from Fred D'Aguiar's essay, 'Have You Been Here Long? Black Poetry in Britain' (1993).
4. 'The British poetry revival' is a term coined by Eric Mottram, once editor of the *Poetry Review* and a central protagonist in Peter Barry's erudite study *The Poetry Wars* (2006).
5. This phrase is used by Munden and Wade in *Reading the Applause* (1999: 34).
6. The Black Arts Movement was the artistic branch of the Black Power movement led by Amiri Baraka.
7. As mentioned in the introduction to this chapter, I speak here of poetry in oral performance and will proceed later in the chapter to complicate the duality of page and stage.
8. Dana Gioia (2003: 26) argues that critics in the academy have shied away from analysing the new popular forms, and rap has been studied almost exclusively as a sociological phenomenon rather than in terms of its content and aesthetics.

'Rebels without applause' 259

9 The 'Crafts of World Literature' conference at Oxford University, September 2012, advocated 'fixing at the centre of our critical practice a close attention to techniques and craft of writing' (http://call-for-papers.sas.upenn.edu/node/44163) (accessed 8 February 2012).
10 In his essay 'Benjamin Zephaniah, the Black British Griot', Eric Doumerc draws attention to a poem by the US poet Mutabaruka whose poem 'Revolutionary Poet' contains the following lines: '"revolutionary poets" / 'ave become entertainers / babblin out angry words / about / ghetto yout' / bein shot down / guns an bombs / yes / revolutionary words bein / digested with bubble gums / popcorn an / ice cream in tall inter conti nental / buildins' (Doumerc, 2005: 203).
11 SuAndi has continued to direct the Black Arts Alliance after 2009, when the organization had its Arts Council funding withdrawn. See: www.blackartists.org.uk.
12 'Acts of Achievement' was run in conjunction with Black History Month but lost its Arts Council funding in 2009. In 2009, the Acts of Achievement website read: 'The Black Arts Alliance (BAA) regrets that due to loss of revenue funding from the Arts Council it is not possible to host Acts of Achievement 2009 ... [The] BAA is active in securing new funding for its work and this includes organising future Black History Months. Wish us luck.'
13 See: www.revealinghistories.org.uk (accessed 20 September 2011). The 'Revealing Histories' project notes that twenty per cent of Manchester's entire population signed the 1787 petition in support of abolition.
14 As the organizers of Manchester's Black History trail also note, Peterloo saw the conviction and deportation of a black labour leader and prominent Chartist activist called William Cuffay. Cuffay is commemorated on Manchester's Black History Trail, which can be found at: www.actsofachievement.org.uk/blackhistorytrail/ (accessed 20 September 2011).
15 Peterloo Poets is no longer based in Manchester and has moved to York.
16 Manchester's 'Peterloo Massacre Campaign for A Fitting Memorial to the Martyrs of Democracy' recently succeeded in replacing a euphemistic blue memorial plaque with a red one with updated figures of the dead and wounded: 15 people were killed and 600 were injured.
17 By the 1940s Makonnen's club had become the West Indian Social Club.
18 Kalu was speaking at the Diversity Exchange Network, held at Manchester Central Library on 14 March 2006.
19 Tina Tamsho Thomas in interview with Corinne Fowler for the 'Moving Manchester' project, 29 September 2011.
20 Tamsho Thomas in interview with Corinne Fowler for the 'Moving Manchester' project, 29 September 2011.
21 This publication was the outcome of the 1987 Peterloo Black and Asian Writing Competition.
22 Okoro, SuAndi and Tamsho Thomas in interview with Corinne Fowler for the 'Moving Manchester' project on 16 September 2011, 17 September 2011 and 29 September 2011 respectively.

23 The *ghazal* form originated in fourteenth-century India and is influenced by the Qur'an and Persian literatures (Chatterjee, 2003: 10)
24 Basir Kazmi provided Chatterjee with a literal translation of the *ghazals*, which she reworked into poetic form.
25 Basir Kazmi's son also writes *ghazals*, as does his granddaughter.
26 The Green Room has now closed but in February 2012 a group of poets managed to launch 'Word of Warning', a series of low-cost performance events in venues across Manchester.
27 This statement was posted on the now defunct website of the Green Room at www.greenroomarts.org/speakeasy/ (accessed 9 January 2006).
28 Talk by Peter Kalu at a day for black writers organized by the Diversity Exchange Network in Manchester Central Library, 14 March 2006.
29 The 'Moving Manchester' project's exhibition of writing, called 'Writing Manchester' bore Dike's image and was dedicated to his life and work. The exhibition was held in Manchester Central Library in the summer of 2009. See Moving Manchester website for archived details of this event: www.transculturalwriting.com/movingmanchester.
30 Sissay's poem 'Hardy's Well' is painted on to the wall of a pub of the same name.
31 Another of Sissay's poems, which also appeals to shared local knowledge, is about the number 32 bus, and can be found above a walkway in Shudehill bus exchange.
32 This does not imply that Lemn Sissay's commitment to landmark poetry in Manchester has waned. On 28 February 2012 he unveiled a new landmark poem called 'Let There Be Peace', which is painted on to a wall belonging to the University of Manchester.
33 This phrase is taken from Fred D'Aguiar's essay, 'Have You Been Here Long? Black Poetry in Britain' (1993).
34 As Debjani Chatterjee explains (2003), the 'signature line' is a convention whereby the *ghazal*'s last couplet introduces the name of the poet.
35 Basir Kazmi, group discussion at 'Writing South Asian Manchester', an event held at the Indus 5 restaurant, Stockport Road, Longsight, Manchester on 21 March 2007.
36 The *Independent* review is featured on Lemn Sissay's website www.lemnsissay.com (accessed 1 December 2011).
37 John Agard, 'Ethnic Eccentric' (2006).
38 Agard, 'Caribbean Eye over Yorkshire' and 'Three in the Snow' (2006).
39 In a provocative reversal of 'the street' as a domain of degraded black culture, the epigraph to Sissay's poetry collection *The Listener* (2008) reads: 'If, as Marx said, religion is the opiate of the people, then nationalism is the crack cocaine' (Sissay, 2008: i).
40 SCAWDI began as the Sparkbrook Caribbean and African Women's Development Initiative in Birmingham, 1997.
41 The caves are owned by the Masons and opening is currently restricted only to specified days.

42 The Archaeology of Black Britain: Approaches, Methods and Possible Solutions', www.blackpresence.co.uk (accessed 1 December 2011).
43 There is plentiful work on black Edwardians, notably Jeffery Green's book *Black Edwardians. Black People in Britain 1901–14* (1998).
44 Email from Peter Kalu to Corinne Fowler, 25 January 2012.
45 The recent revival of the British punk phenomenon has introduced a new generation to Cooper Clark's work.
46 The Live Poets Society is indirectly alluded to in Lemn Sissay's praise poem to the northern vernacular called 'Advice for the Living' (Sissay, 2008: 42).
47 As this book went to press (2012), Peter Kalu was Artistic Director of Commonword.
48 On 2 March 1981, many thousands of black people marched in protest against the New Cross massacre, a suspected racist fire bomb attack in which killed thirteen black people and injured twenty-seven.
49 Three years before Sissay won his commission as the first Olympic poet for 2012, a sculpture of his 'Gilt of Cain' poem (2008) was unveiled in the City of London's autonomous financial sector. A powerful critique of the enduring relation between slavery and the banking industry, 'Gilt of Cain' juxtaposes commercial terms extracted from Bloomsbury's glossary with graphic images of slaves' suffering during the Middle Passage. In this poem, the roaring sea erodes the boundaries of city and coastline in ways that emphasize the city's 'external geography'. Sissay performed the poem at the unveiling ceremony, which was witnessed by the scholar Deirdre Osborne. Describing a crowd of pinstriped suits and white faces, Osborne provides a compelling account of the assertive and subtly subversive nature of Sissay's public rendering of the poem which subverts the terms of the poetry commission, which was to celebrate primarily the abolitionist work of Wilberforce rather than to lament the suffering of the slaves. Osborne argues that Sissay's accent rendered 'Wilberforce' as 'Will Be Force', which enacted a 'nuanced reversal' of the poem's commissioned praise for him and giving the poem an entirely different 'aural ending' (Osborne, 2011: 204).
50 This leads Gioia (2003) to a more radical and controversial claim. Drawing on a statistic that the average US citizen daily spends just twenty-four minutes reading compared with four hours of television and three hours of radio, he argues that the revival of popular poetry in performance indicates that the United States, at least, is entering a new phase of oral culture, or 'secondary orality' (Gioia, 2003: 27–8). Specialists in literacy and orality have yet to determine how justified is Gioia's claim that developments in electronic media have 'readjusted the contemporary sensibility in favour of sound and orality' over print culture (Gioia, 2003: 25).
51 Author's interview with SuAndi on 14 September 2011. This is one of the 'Moving Manchester' project's series of interviews with writers and arts workers based in the city (see Chapter 6 for further reflection on these texts).

52 This assumption of separateness, led, in the late 1980s, to funding for 'ethnic arts' by organizations such as the Arts Council (Araeen in Appignanesi, 2010 Aran, 2011: 51).
53 D'Aguiar also briefly discusses David Dabydeen's engagement with the poetry of his British counterparts in 'Coolie Odyssey' in terms of its disparaging intertextual references to Seamus Heaney's *North* and the working-class poetry of Tony Harrison. The implication of these details are almost lost in D'Aguiar's contention that 'state[s] categorically [that] what black writers are doing in Britain is so unlike what their white compatriots in craft are practising that it merits a category entirely of its own' (D'Aguiar, 1993: 70).
54 Jean Binta Breeze has said, '[T]here's something called poetry and it exists in language ... in any person speaking: a fisherman on a beach ... so poetry for me exists outside of form ... people do it all the time in their daily lives ... So I have no difficulties [choosing] between page or stage. Poetry is ... using language well, and it crops up everywhere that people use language' (Breeze, Agbabi, Tipene, Harrison and Bertram, 1999: 29).
55 I am grateful to David Law (2004) for drawing attention to Wood's cultural summary of the North.
56 Kalu wrote the poem and adopted the list form to tackle the challenge of the restricted number of lines allowable for a Manchester-wide poetry competition.
57 Tebbit served as Secretary of State for Employment (1981–83), Secretary of State for Trade and Industry (1983–85) and Chair of the British Conservative Party (1985–87).
58 *The Listener* is a now defunct magazine that provided a significant forum for debates between advocates and opponents of the British poetry revival.
59 As detailed in Chapter 2, the 2012 Winning Words programme was funded by the Forward Arts Foundation and Arts Council England. As also discussed in Chapter 2, the Winning Words scheme also commissioned work by Carol Ann Duffy, John Burnside, Caroline Bird and Jo Shapcott.
60 Writing at a time when Britain's performance scene was less popular than it is now, Mottram makes the following observation: 'Large-scale poetry readings have never reached the extent and power of those in the American campus and city scene from the later 1950s into the 1960s and 1970s' (in Hampson and Barry, 1993: 19).
61 This key feature of Manchester's poetry scene since the 1980s perhaps coincides with the wider social endorsement of poetry's public role indicated by the importance of poetry at US presidential inaugurations. Zofia Burr observes that 'the occasion of the inaugural poem resurrects an ideology about the role of poetry in the public sphere that is as influential now as it was in the early 1960s'. In particular, she argues, the poet's role has become increasingly 'analogous' to the role of the press in being a Fourth Estate (Williams, 2011: 63 and 53).
62 The criticism was directed against the possibility that Sissay's involvement

in the campaign signalled complicity between poetry and the commercial sector.
63 Owen Jones is author of *Chavs: The Demonisation of the Working Class* (2011) and Dreda Say Mitchell is a British crime novelist. The discussion was chaired by presenter Emily Maitlis, who was herself criticized for not being more openly critical of Starkey's racist line of argument.
64 In the same volume, Rashed Araeen notes that the centrality of black artists to modernism has been overlooked in his essay 'Cultural Diversity, Creativity and Modernism' (Appigananesi, 2010).

References

Agard, J. (2006) *We Brits*. Newcastle-upon-Tyne: Bloodaxe.
Amaye, M., de Mello, M. and Hussain, Z. (2008) *The Suitcase Book of Love Poems*. Manchester: Suitcase.
Appignanesi, R. (ed.) (2010) *Beyond Cultural Diversity. The Case for Creativity. A Third Text Report*. London: Third Text.
Barry, P. (2006) *The Poetry Wars: British Poetry of the 1970s and the Battle of Earls Court*. Cambridge: Salt Publishing.
Bloom, V., Lewis, F., Munshi, R. and Walker, F. (eds) (1987) *Black and Priceless: The Power of Black Ink*. Manchester: Commonword /Crocus.
Breeze, 'Binta' J., Agbabi, P., Tipene, G., Harrison, R. and Bertram, V. (1999) 'A Round-table Discussion on Poetry in Performance', *Feminist Review*, 62, 24–54.
Callaghan, D. and Willis-Brown, B. (eds) (2011) *A Day in the Life. A Black Heritage Trail of the West Midlands*. Birmingham: Scawi, Friends Institute.
Carlson, P. (2006) 'Ian Hamilton Finlay', www.mycontemporary.com/en/artistes/ian-hamilton-finlay-0, 19 October, (accessed 3 January 2012).
Caro, S. (2011) Arts Council, Creative Case Symposium, 12 September.
Caulfield, H. (2000) *Men's Morning*. Manchester: Cheers Ta.
Chatterjee, D. (1999) 'South Asian Poetry in Performance: an Evolving Scene' in Munden P. and Wade S. (eds), *Reading the Applause: Reflections on Performance Poetry by Various Artists*. York: Talking Shop.
Chatterjee, D. (2003) *Generations of Ghazals. Ghazals by Nasir Kazmi and Basir Sultan Kazmi*. Bradford: Redbeck Press.
Cooper Clark, J. (2002) *Word of Mouth: The Very Best of John Cooper Clark*. London: Sony.
Crawshaw, R. (2009) 'Translating the In-Between. SuAndi's *The Story of M* or Reflections on Sociological Approaches to Literary Analysis'. Unpublished paper, Gesellschaft übersetzen' conference, University of Konstanz, 29–31, October.

D'Aguiar, F. (1993) 'Have You Been Here Long? Black Poetry in Britain' in Hampson, R. and Barry, P. (eds), *New British Poetries. The Scope of the Possible* (Manchester: Manchester University Press, 1993)

Dawes, K. (2005) 'Black British Poetry: Some Considerations' in Sesay, K. (ed.), *Write Black, Write British: From Post Colonial to Black British Literature*. London: Hansib, 2005.

Dawes, K. (ed.) (2010) *Red. Contemporary Black British Poetry*, Leeds: Peepal Tree.

Dearden, S. (2007) *Live Literature Review*. Nottingham: Arts Council North East.

Doumerc, E. (2005) 'Benjamin Zephaniah, the Black British [G]riot' in Sesay, K. (ed.), *Write Black, Write British: From Post Colonial to Black British Literature*. London: Hansib.

Doumerc, E. and McFarlane, R. (eds) (2011) *Celebrate Wha? Ten Black Britsh Poets from the Midlands*. Middlesbrough: Smokestack Books.

Dwividi, A. N. (2002) *T. S. Eliot: A Critical Study*. New Delhi: Atlantic Publishers.

Eidemarim, A. (2008) 'The Pleasure Seeker', *The Guardian*, 1 March, 39–40.

Evaristo, B. (2002) *The Emperor's Babe*. London: Penguin.

Fowler, C. (2008) 'A Tale of Two Novels: Developing a Devolved Approach to Black British Writing', *Journal of Commonwealth Literature*, 43 (3), 75–94.

Fryer, P. (1984) *Staying Power. The History of Black People in Britain since 1504*. London: Pluto, 1984.

Garry, M. (2006) *Mancunian Meander*. Manchester: Cheers Ta.

Gilroy, P. (1993) *The Black Atlantic. Modernity and Double Consciousness*. London: Verso, 1993.

Gioia, D. (2003) 'Disappearing Ink: Poetry at the End of Print Culture', *The Hudson Review*, 56 (1), 21–49.

Gómez Peña, G. (2000) *The New Global Culture: Somewhere Between Corporate Multiculturalism and the Mainstream Bizarre*. Los Angeles: California State University Northridge.

Grabner, C. (2007) '"Here to Stay": The Performance of Accents in the Work of Linton Kwesi Johnson and Lemn Sissay', *Thamyris*, (Spring), 51–70.

Grabner, C. and Casas, A. (2011) *Performing Poetry: Body, Place and Rhythm in the Poetry Performance*. Amsterdam: Rodopi.

Green, J. (1998) *Black Edwardians. Black People in Britain 1901–14*. London: Routledge.

Hampson, R. and Barry, P. (eds) (1993) *New British Poetries. The Scope of the Possible*. Manchester: Manchester University Press.

Harris Brandes, B. (2007) *Anthologies Without Apologies: An Analysis of*

Contemporary Black British Poetry Anthologies. Canterbury: University of Kent.
Henri, A., McGough, R. and Patten, B. (2007 [1967]) *The Mersey Sound.* London: Penguin Classics.
Horovitz, M. (ed.) (1969) *Children of Albion: Poetry of the Underground in Britain.* London: Penguin.
Hoyles, A. and Hoyles, M. (2002) *Moving Voices. Black Performance Poetry.* London: Hansib Publications.
Irving, S. (2009) 'The General Strike in Manchester, May 1926', 'Manchester's Radical History: Exploring Greater Manchester's Grassroots History' at: radicalmanchester.wordpress.com/2009/10/07/the-general-strike-in-manchester-may-1926/, accessed 4 December 2011.
Jones, O. (2011) *Chavs: The Demonisation of the Working Class.* London: Verso.
Kalu, P. (2003) *Peace Poems.* Manchester: Crocus.
Kalu, P. (2007) 'Manchester'. 'Moving Manchester' Writers' Gallery. See: www.lancs.ac.uk/fass/projects/writersgallery/content/Pete_Kalu.html (accessed 1 November 2010).
Khan, S. (2007) *Megalomaniac.* Cambridge: Salt Publishing.
Kunda, Chanje, www.afrique-performs.co.uk/ (accessed 5 May 2010)
Kwesi Johnson, L. (1975) *Dread, Beat and Blood.* London: Bogle L'Ouverture.
Law, D. '"Guddling for Words": Representations of the North and Northerness in Post-1950 South Pennine Literature'. Lancaster University. Unpublished PhD thesis.
Lind, J. (2011) 'Telescoping of Images in "The Wasteland"'. See: www.eagerimagination.blogspot.com, 23 November 2011, accessed 9 January 2012.
Mansfield, M. (2011) 'The Peterloo Massacre. Campaign for a Fitting Memorial to the Martyrs of Democracy'. See: www.peterloomassacre.org/campaign.html (accessed 4 January 2011).
McLeod, J. (2002) 'A Night at the Cosmopolitan. Axes of Transnational Encounter in the 1930s and 40s', *Interventions*, 4 (1), 53–67.
McLeod, J. (2004) *Postcolonial London. Rewriting the Metropolis.* London and New York: Routledge.
Mellor, R. (2002) 'Hypocritical City: Cycles of Urban Exclusion' in Peck, J. and Ward, K. (eds), *City of Revolution: Restructuring Manchester.* Manchester and New York: Manchester University Press.
Mex Glazner, G. (2000) *Poetry Slam: The Competitive Art of Performance Poetry.* San Francisco: Manic D Press.
Motion, A. (2000) 'Poetry in Public', Sixth Arts Council of England Annual Lecture at RSA, London, 1 January 2000. London: Arts Council England.

Munden, P. and Wade, S. (eds) (1999) *Reading the Applause: Reflections on Performance Poetry by Various Artists*. York: Talking Shop.

Nath Dwidevo, A. (2002) *T. S. Eliot: A Critical Study*. New Delhi: Atlantic Publishers.

Osborne, D. (2011) '"Set in Stone": Lemn Sissay's and Suandi's Landmark Poetics' in Grabner, C. and Casas, A. (eds), *Performing Poetry: Body, Place and Rhythm in the Poetry Performance*. Amsterdam: Rodopi.

Procter, J. (2003) *Dwelling Places: Postwar Black British Writing*. Manchester: Manchester University Press.

Procter, J. (2006) 'The Postcolonial Everyday', *New Formations: A Journal of Culture / Theory / Politics*, 58, 62–80.

Quinn, B. (2011) 'David Starkey Claims "the whites have become blacks"', *The Guardian*, 13 August, 23–32.

Raskin, J. (2011) 'Allen Ginsberg' in Grabner, C. and Casas, A. (eds), *Performing Poetry: Body, Place and Rhythm in the Poetry Performance*. London and Amsterdam: Rodopi.

Robinson, G., Kay, J. and Procter, J. (eds) (2012) *Out of Bounds: British Black and Asian Poets*. Newcastle-upon-Tyne: Bloodaxe.

Sesay, K. (ed.) (2011) *Black British Perspectives. A Series of Conversations on Black Art Forms*. London: Saks Publications.

Sissay, L. (1988) *Tender Fingers in a Clenched Fist* (London: Bogle L'Ouverture.

Sissay, L. (ed) (1998) *The Fire People: A Collection of Contemporary Black BRitish Poetry*. Edinburgh Payback Press.

Sissay, L. (1999) *Morning Breaks in the Elevator*. Edinburgh: Payback Press, 1999.

Sissay, L. (2000a) *Rebel without Applause*. Newcastle-upon-Tyne: Bloodaxe.

Sissay, L. (2000b) *The Emperor's Watchmaker*. London: Bloomsbury.

Sissay, L. (2008) *Listener*. Edinburgh: Canongate.

Sissay, L. (2011a) 'The First Olympic Poet', *The Emperor's Watchmaker Blog*. See: http:/blog.lemnsissay.com/blog_archives, 10 December 2011.

Sissay, L. (2011b) 'Winning Words'. See: http:/blog.lemnsissay.com/archives/2011/3/8/4768322.html, 8 March 2011, accessed 13 May 2011.

Somers-Willett, S. B. A. (2005) 'Slam Poetry and the Cultural Politics of Performing Identity', *The Journal of the Mid-Western Modern Language Association* (Summer), 51–73.

Somers-Willett, S. B. A. (2009) *The Cultural Politics of Slam Poetry: Race, Identity and the Performance of Popular Verse in America*. Ann Arbor, MI: University of Michigan Press.

Speakeasy (2010). See: www.speakeasymcr.org/, accessed 5 May 2010.

SuAndi (1992) *Nearly Forty*. Liverpool: Spike Books.

SuAndi (ed.) (1994) *Kiss: Asian, African, Caribbean and Chinese Love Poems*. Manchester: Commonword/Crocus.
SuAndi (2000) 'Why Would Anyone Want to Write a Poem about a Grecian Urn?', *Diverse*. Liverpool: Diverse.
SuAndi (2009) *The Story of M*. Lancaster: Lancaster e-prints.
Williams, N. (2011) *Contemporary Poetry*. Edinburgh: Edinburgh University Press.

Internet sources

http://call-for-papers.sas.upenn.edu/node/44163
www.actsofachievement.org.uk/blackhistorytrail/
www.blackpresence.co.uk
www.lemnsissay.com
www.greenroomarts.org/speakeasy/
www.revealinghistories.org.uk
www.winningwordspoetry.com/
www.youngidentity.org

6

Giving voice: the writers' perspective

Robert Crawshaw

Interviews, context and discursive recursivity

As is common in most projects which draw on ethnographic and sociological fieldwork, a central component of the 'Moving Manchester' project was the series of interviews and subsequent discussions with the writers and cultural agents who had agreed to be involved with the research. As will be clear from the other chapters in this book, the project was an interactive agent in the process it was seeking to examine. The research was 'action-led' in both a theoretical and practical sense in that it rapidly became a medium of communication in its own right, one which generated reflection by the participants on the activity of writing or performing, promoted published outputs and reinforced pre-existing networks. A workshop including a focus group would generate commentary on other textual material in the project: the text of the original proposal, written communication with the informants, draft summaries of initial findings and the outcomes of the interviews.

Twenty-eight writers and performance poets were interviewed. Eight of these could also be described as 'cultural agents' (CAs) in virtue of their role as promoters or facilitators of the artists' creative output. The participants were 'interviewed' individually and were well known to the 'interviewer'. The relationship between the interlocutors was as much institutional in a sociologically discursive sense as it was personal. The context 'positioned' them. Whilst positioning themselves in relation to the interlocutor as individuals, they were knowingly fulfilling the role in which the project had cast them: as Mancunian writers, many of them of diasporic origin, or as cultural agents in the development and promotion of the literary scene in Manchester. The validity of the questions themselves was not challenged, though some of the presuppositions inherent in the language used by the interviewer were qualified. The participants subscribed to the conditions of the interaction and participated fully. Questions nevertheless remained concerning the interpretation of the answers and the extent to which their content and the formal patterns which emerged from them could legitimately be used as a framework for making broader social generalizations.

In addition to the interviews whose analysis forms the basis of this chapter, there was also a focus group, held subsequently. Eight writers and three CAs took part in the workshop and focus group discussions. These consisted of recorded break-out groups of between two and four participants leading to a plenary discussion of the reactions of the sub-groups to the questions raised. The questions had been formulated by the research team and had arizen directly out of the findings of the interviews. The event was more 'performative' than the interviews in that the participants were not simply in a one-to-one situation but were differentiating themselves from the other members of the group in a semi-public context.

According to the standard principles underlying discourse analysis (Van Dijk, 1977; Teubert, 2010), the language of informants in a semi-formalized interview situation or in a focus group cannot be seen as entirely transparent. The meaning of what they say is not exclusively defined by what they say. Their underlying relationships towards each other and the subject matter of their description (their writing, their personal circumstances, their backgrounds, their negotiations with publishers and so on) are not merely referred to; they are embedded in the form of the language they use and in the external context in which the discussion takes place. The stated aim of the project was to explore how the creative writers had come to write in the first place, and, with reference to their motivation, to what extent their diasporic heritage (where appropriate) had been instrumental in causing them to write. Further, the project sought to capture the manner in which the form of their writing and the act of writing itself had been a necessary means of defining their identities in relation to the Manchester community. It sought to examine how the writers interacted with the agencies that enabled their writing to reach a wider public: the state-funded local groups which promoted creative writing and performance and the national and international publishers who represented the path to public recognition and financial security.

Underlying these questions was a further fundamental one: taken collectively, did the writers' output reveal characteristics of a specific class or genre of writing which defined migratory displacement in a uniquely insightful way? For obvious methodological reasons, these questions could not be imposed on the interviewees. According to the best principles of 'grounded research' (Glaser and Strauss, 1967) and context-based ethnography (Knorr-Cetina and Cicourel, 1981), they had emerged from the stated preoccupations or patterns of behaviour of the informants themselves – as writers or agents. So it was that, before the questions for the conversations were drawn up, the participants were invited to reflect on the project and on their own activities and to adapt or construct the proposed questions accordingly. Even then, as already suggested, the structure of the exchanges generally followed its own dynamic. There was a framework within and against which, in a Bakhtinian sense (Voloshinov, [1926] 1988) the interlocutors were simultaneously operating. They were both accepting the institutional constraints of the conversation imposed by the project in which they were voluntarily participating and in some cases reacting against them.

The reasons for writing

The first section of the interviews constituted a discussion of why the writers had started writing in the first place. With regards to the writers belonging to one of the city's diasporas, the hypothesis underlying the exercize was that this was due, at least in part, to a sense of displacement which, having affected their parents, grandparents, great-grandparents or other close members of their families directly, had been inherited by them. Further, that their writings had affected and were affecting their experience of belonging, or not, to the city. This assumption on our part as researchers could be seen – and was seen by many of the writers themselves – as a product of the postcolonial or 'multicultural' context in which the 'Moving Manchester' project had been set up. The project had after all been funded by a government agency bent on promoting multicultural 'integration'. What was being negotiated was as much the discursive framing of the project itself as the factual truth of what was being said. In any case, where was the dividing line between the two? In the tradition of Goffman's definition of 'frame analysis' (Goffman, 1974), the truth value of the statements could be interpreted only in relation to the discursive context in which they had been made. How justified was it to draw general conclusions from what was, after all, a highly situated interchange? Before one could answer these questions, it was necessary closely to analyse its dynamic.

So why had the writers started writing? To what extent was it the product of their background? For the vast majority, it was something that came from them, stemming for the most part from a natural love of reading and storytelling. At the same time, the association between reading and a specific person, usually a parent, was the leading determinant of the type of story with which the young child and thereafter the aspirant writer identified. Personal experience derived from a place of family origin was often the impulse which triggered the desire to write as was that of projecting an identity which the prospective writer felt to be different from that expressed in existing texts:

RB I hadn't really read the canon until I was in my twenties and before that the Mahabharata and the Ramayana were the first stories that I encountered, initially because they're the first stories I was told and they were told to me by my father. I really think it must have been these stories being told to me; like psychologists say, you can't give love unless you've received love and I think the same thing is with telling stories.

ZH Well looking back I'd say, the impetus probably does come from my mother. She's always had an abiding passion for reading; I think my earliest memories of my mother are actually of her reading, so I think I've always had that. In terms of writing, I went to Pakistan with my mother when I was nine years old. I actually kept a diary and I've still got that diary and I refer back to it. I think that was the kind of point where I did actually physically start to write and create things.

ASIJ Actually something happened when I was on holiday and I wanted to write that story, some incidents happened when I was on holiday in the Caribbean and I was inspired to want to write a story about that.

BSK I was born in Lahore, Pakistan. My father [Nasir Kasmi] was a famous poet. He died at the age of forty-six, in 1972, when I was an undergraduate student at the Government College Lahore. My mother was the head teacher of a local school and retired as an Assistant Director of Education, Punjab. I always thought of translating, wished to translate [my father]. Now, at the moment, he is recognized as one of the leading Urdu poets. The form of poetry is *ghazal*, which my father revived. He is regarded as the person who revived this form and I too started writing *ghazals*.

CK When I turned sixteen I ran away from home because I didn't like not being able to go out and do what I wanted. I stayed in about three different homeless hostels and I ended up in a bedsit; I loved that bedsit. As a housewarming present somebody gave me the collected works of Maya Angelou's poetry and then when I read it I thought 'Wow, it's amazing!' I was just really inspired and thought 'Oh wow! I'd love to be like that' and 'If she can do it I can do it.'

AMcV Well there are sort of two events really I suppose. The first, very briefly and privately for about a year in my late teens, and the writing was intensely political, I was doing politics at school and this was a period of the race riots in Moss Side. I had a boyfriend at the time who came from Northern Ireland – so I had this intense need to write and to explore what I was feeling.

AM I've been writing all my life I think, as a kid I've always been writing so I wouldn't know what started me. I think it's a family thing, from my mum's side. We have writers and artists and quite a few have done quite well back in Pakistan.

SM I'm a second-generation child from the West Indies. My parents came from Jamaica in the sixties and I was born here. I write poetry and short stories and at the moment I'm trying to attempt a novel about my parents' life and my experiences of living in Moss Side.

VM In my late twenties, why I don't really know, but suddenly I started to feel very creative. I found fault with many films, both Hollywood and Indian films, and kept thinking I could have written the story better. This thought then also extended to books. Travel, my many trips to India and experiencing the huge contrasts between my life in England and over there seemed also to encourage me to write.

JP Why did I start writing? I think there was an urge to do something at the very start and it turned out to be I managed to do something creative and then that urge to do something creative turned into doing some creative writing and eventually that urge turned my creative writing to writing creative novels; it was a gradual process.

JR The main reason [I started writing] was that my father was a writer, his name was Namba Roy and he was a writer, sculptor and painter but he was working in the fifties when it was very hard for black writers and artists to get recognized. He died when I was seven and my mother certainly believed that if he'd been recognized more in his lifetime that wouldn't have happened. At his funeral, I think it was just in the way adults quite carelessly say these things: 'One of the children's got to carry on' and I took that very, very seriously and from that time all through my life I've been thinking 'That's what I've got to do'.

QS I think from the very beginning... what I felt I wanted to do with my writing was to attract not just the British readers and people settled here but also other readers, like in Pakistan for example. Both my novels were set in Pakistan and take part in other parts, even Malaysia etc., so coming from another country originally, for me, readership was wide in that context... The main premise behind my writing is the feeling inside me that it's what I want to do. But then what I write is dictated by what I feel strongly about... Having studied literature all my life I have read lots and lots. And my favourite really is *Pride and Prejudice* ... and *Middlemarch*. But the recent one is Vikram Seth's *A Suitable Boy*.

KS I've mainly been seen as a crime writer but I write anything. I think when I started taking writing seriously was when I had children and I ended up as a single parent in Moss Side with two children and I think as a way of dealing with the stressful situation of being a single parent and also living in Moss Side at a time when there was a lot of shooting.

SA I kind of wrote sloppy love poetry to boys that didn't want to go out with me when I was at school but my first major piece of writing was a book about my mum after she died because I don't have any grandparents, so it was kind of therapy. One night I watched Alan Bennett's *Talking Heads*, the very first one done by Patricia Routledge who is the living image of my mother. I didn't catch the beginning of it, I turned the TV on, she's there on the screen talking to camera, she's obviously dying, she's obviously got cancer, I watched the whole thing, stood up and wept, you know wept forever and later thought 'There's a black version of this'.

SK I was just inspired by bits of things I found, poetry and things in my sisters' books and at school and a fantastic English teacher who, I think it was her personality as well as her love of literature I think that just inspired me. I thought I'd better do something about it and starting going to Commonword, that writers' group, and I think that was really the starting point of developing towards a sort of career in poetry.

PK Back in the days when Maya Angelou was being published, I think it was *I know Why the Caged Bird Sings*. It was the first book I'd read that was a story of a black life, and that was the first time I thought that, maybe it was my own ignorance, but I thought, oh right, so this is also literature. So, that was the spark actually when I thought one could have something interesting to say that is worthy of putting down on print. So, that's how I started out.

As situated voices contextually defined by the research model, is it surprising that they confirm the hypothesis of the project? Do they not simply correspond to the stereotypical expectations of a predominantly white hegemonic majority: that diasporic writers write specifically in order to retrieve a heritage derived from their parental origins and that it is this which has instilled in them a sense of difference? The answer to the second question must be 'yes', but this does not necessarily undermine the representative validity of the writers' statements. In ten out of twenty interview extracts which deal directly with motivation, the parental model is invoked as one to be imitated or preserved, either because of the cultural identity inherent in the form and the subject matter of the stories or out of the awareness of an emotional bond with origins which demand to be better understood – or both ('I think it's a family thing' (AM)'; 'The main reason [I started writing] was that my father was a writer' (JR); 'It must have been these stories being told to me; like psychologists say, you can't give love unless you've received love" and I think the same thing is with telling stories' (RB). Stories are seen as 'constitutive' of identity (RB), and, in most cases, the stories emanate from a different cultural tradition. However, there are at least three other impulses referred by the writers: reading, the conditions of life in Manchester and personal relationships. And in each case, the predominant theme is one of difference.

In the case of reading, what is striking at first is the combination of fortuitousness and predetermination in the nature of the reading matter encountered by the prospective writer of diasporic origin. In all but one case, the writers interviewed see themselves as predisposed to reading ('I saw myself as a sponge', 'I just read anything' (KS)). Of course what comes to hand derives first and foremost from the cultural environment to which the young person happens to be exposed: pop music (JP), feature film, television (ZH), popular fiction (MG), comics (KS). At the same time, several of the writers interviewed encounter examples of the English, European or American literary canons through their education in Britain and are influenced by their potency as a source of stories (VM, QS). In this respect the nature of the influences to which the young writer of diasporic background is exposed is no different from that of a member of any culturally identifiable group. Yet, as described by the writers interviewed, the reaction to the encounter with the subject matter is to draw differential comparison with material derived from the culture of origin, a differentiation which initiates a process of cultural translation. *Middlemarch* is compared with *A Suitable Boy* and finds an immediate echo in an extended trans-generational tale of cultural and emotional emancipation experienced by a woman brought up in a traditional Pakistani village (QS). The response to a chance viewing on television of one of Alan Bennett's *Talking Heads* programmes, is that 'There is a black version of this', leading to the reflection that 'I did have a connection with African-American literature which I read now but I also have a connection with British-based literature, but from a Black perspective' (SA).

In one case, the association between crime fiction and the distinctiveness of black identity is made almost inadvertently ('as I got older, in my thirties, I was drawn more to Deep South American crime novels [...] things with black characters in it or things that involved maybe prejudice and crime' (KS)). The context is changed but elements of the original form are retained. A distinction can be made between these processes involving the intertextual transfiguration of reading material and actual translation described by at least two of the writers of poetry whose current form of writing has been transposed from cultural originals from India or China or has been directly affected by them (BSK; MYW). In this case, there is an involuntary identification with the original form associated with the writer's personal cultural background. The form is deliberately preserved through translation in a new life context determined largely by educational priorities (BSK). Not surprisingly therefore, the interviews bear witness to a creative impulse which the writers represent as culturally distinctive. That this distinctiveness is specific to someone of diasporic origin is explicitly mentioned in several of the statements and is strongly implied in others.

If reading and exposure to popular culture are identified as major sources of inspiration by the interviewees, the compulsion to translate conditions of life in Manchester into narrative form is another. In a general sense, this is of course true of all narrative writing. The question remains as to the extent to which the circumstances giving rise to the impulse are linked to the diasporic condition. Three of the interviewees in particular refer to the Mancunian experience as a direct stimulus, all with reference to Moss Side. One deals with her own life as a single mother in a neighbourhood afflicted by violence ('there was a lot of shooting' (KS)), another to the lives of her immigrant parents who run a household of tenants from a variety of social and cultural backgrounds as well as reflecting on her own life and that of her siblings (CK). Yet another (JP) uses the device of deliberately melding past memories of childhood experiences with stories told to him by others. These are simultaneously located in Moss Side and the surrounding area at different historical moments and in the atemporal context of the Caribbean island from which his parents and grandparents emigrated after the Second World War. Their combination creates an inner mental space in which time and place are compressed into a fragmented omnitemporal moment embodied by the form of the text. The text world becomes an autonomous reality, epitomizing perhaps the condition of the creative artist whose sense of belonging is rooted in a displaced past as much as in the present (Crawshaw and Fowler, 2008). Taken as a whole, the implications of the writers' statements are that Manchester is not seen as an independent, self-standing place with its own inherent properties but, like a linguistic sign, as one which derives its meaning from its alterity, that is from its relation to somewhere or something else. Thus, for the Irish-born writer (AO'R), Manchester is the adopted home to which he wishes to return precisely because it is different from the Middle East country where he spent five years. He wants to go back so that he can understand it better: the place itself and his own relationship with it. The impulse is, as he puts it, 'partly homesickness and a great desire to find out more'.

It is hardly coincidental that even extra-familial relationships are described by the writers as bound up with cultural concerns. In one of the three (all female) cases where partnership is referred to, the (male) 'friend' concerned is from Northern Ireland and an association is made between the troubles in Ireland and the disturbances in Moss Side where the writer (AMcV) was then at school. In the case of SA, a poet of mixed-race heritage, writing and reading habits had been conditioned by her relationships: with boys at school and later with a partner who had tried to interest her in black American literature. The data suggest that the emotion of the relationship is conditioned by a sense of cultural difference and that it is this which triggers or directs the subject's reading and his or her desire to write.

Finally, at least three of the writers (SA, MG, SK, PK) mention their membership or initiation of writers' groups as instrumental in causing them to present their writings to a wider public. You 'become' a writer in virtue of being a member of the group which in turn generates the network which gives the prospective author a readership, an identity as a writer and opportunities to participate in public readings:

> **AM** I had to keep saying Yes I am a writer, and in fact Pete [PK] came up to interview me and said: 'So what do you say when people say to you what do you do?', and I said 'Well, I'm trying to be a writer but it's really hard.'

Seeing their own writing in relation to that of others plays a catalytic role which is explicitly referred to by two of the three writers concerned, leading in one case to a shift from performance poetry to fiction writing (PK). This interactive factor which has played such a crucial part in establishing the community of writers with whom the project had the most contact is a topic to which I return under the heading 'articulation': the reinforcement and stimulus which derives from the sense that a 'message' or at least a personal vision is being shared with a wider community whilst simultaneously affecting the outlook of the writer or performer. That this space should be identified with Manchester as a place is a function not of the city per se but of the social and institutional networks which have been established over time: a historical-cultural phenomenon which other chapters of this book have analysed in detail.

The message ... what message?

One of the next presuppositions, which had informed the 'Moving Manchester' project initial proposal, was that the creative outputs of the writers fulfilled a social function which went beyond personal expression. To what extent did the writers see themselves as having a message which they felt should be communicated to others for didactic or even polemical reasons? Did they see themselves as having 'impact'? As Stuart Hall (1996: 3) would have put it, did they see themselves as 'hailed into place' in the sense that their writing was the product of a historical heritage and hence of a given social context which the act of writing enabled the author and a potential readership to understand better? As the following extracts illustrate, there was indeed an immediate link between 'black' identity – where the term 'black' implied an identification with cultural and ethnic difference from what the writers themselves perceived to be 'the mainstream', and the need to communicate a message about the forms of racism they or their families had encountered:

MA I want to explore big things, I want to explore and teach about different aspects of black British life, not the mainstream, not the things that are being talked about, not putting us in a pigeonhole, not saying that OK we can only be dealing with gang culture because we're from Manchester and that kind of thing. I want to write about the Africans that were in Britain because it's not been written about.

RB It's all very individual I find; it's very personal, I think the whole thing's very personal. There has to be a frustration rising with these kinds of pseudo-narratives: *Brick Lane*, *White Teeth*, *Bend It like Beckham*, all this sort of thing. I think there is just a need for realism but also without detracting from literary substance.

ASIJ I'm hoping like *The Goat Thief* that it would become a semi-important piece of literature, not because it's fantastically well written in any way but simply because I would like it to be something that my daughter, who isn't born in the West Indies, Jamaica, and who doesn't live there ... I'm hoping like for her and for her generation that it will be something that they could read and it would give them a good sense of Jamaica.

BSK Almost everybody who has settled here has relatives and friends there. They have a link. Then there are themes, for example, loneliness, a search for identity etc.. So one of my audiences are the people who are here, and then people back home, who want to know how we feel here because they have heard different stories.

AMcV What interests me with the writing is the relevance of elsewhere and else-when in the here-and-now.

AM Mine's always about people caught in between places and people and cultures, so all my heroes and heroines are in those places and they can't decide where they belong or whether they can easily adapt.

SM My role I feel is somebody who will document the past and also document some of the future. I think for me documenting the evidences of true life rather than fiction.

AO'R It's simply to share a knowledge, to share my knowledge and experience because I know that people find it interesting. I also have a terrible sort of desire to document and to photograph things if they're changing.

Giving voice 279

JP I saw an article about troubles in Moss Side, Manchester and there was an overwhelming feeling in me saying 'Hey I don't remember Moss Side, where I was born, being like that', and therefore the urge to redress the balance in my own way came and was expressed in my writing.

JR It's certainly to do with wanting to be part of a body of work that re-inscribes black people into British experience. It still seems important to try sometimes and to think about which voices are silent in our society and to try and voice some of those experiences.

QS I think from the very beginning ... what I felt I wanted to do with my writing was to attract not just the British, but also other readers, like in Pakistan ... For the Western readers, I wanted to really take them on a journey, I wanted them to go to that part of the world.

KS The purpose of my writing I think is to number one entertain and number two educate and number three inform ... I've done a lot of workshops in prisons and schools and colleges. They learnt a lot about certain issues that were facing people in Moss Side or facing single parents.

SA I didn't start out wanting to tell anything. I kind of wanted to play around with it, see if I was any good. It's because, as a black woman, this time I live in is so heavily burdened by the past that in a sense you reflect on the past but the impact is 'bumph' right now in this moment. I don't write for readers, I write for an audience.

PK I think over the years that as people began to understand what development work was and what can be achieved through a process of engagement with new writers and working out what they need to become more successful: getting that voice, the voice of those who may not really have access to these resources, you might call them marginalized, you might call them excluded, whatever, these different communities getting their voices on and bringing it to the fore.

It is apparent from the writers' comments that the desire to project a message is by no means common to all. Eight out of the eighteen writers explicitly state that they wish to raise the awareness of their readers either of the 'true' conditions of life in ethnically diverse parts of Manchester or of the religious and cultural heritage of the place of family origin. However, the impulse to 'educate and inform' (KS) is very strong, whether it be the public at large, especially young people in schools, or the writers' own children. 'Education and information' in this context implies revealing what the writers believe to be the truth underlying popular stereotypes promulgated by the media or projected by certain mainstream fictional publications (RB). Here the 'truth' is represented as an expression of personal experience ('I've got to show there's another side to this; it wasn't like that for me' (JP)), as if aspects of the writer's past, that of his or her culture of origin or the social conditions of being brought up in Manchester, in short the writer's complex 'sense of self', had somehow been traduced by texts in the public domain and that there was a need to put the record straight or to provide a corrective to 'official history'.

Associated with the need to differentiate between personal experience and public record was an urge to promote 'realism'. The term is mentioned at least twice in the interviews (RB; SM). It implies an inner obligation to reveal the complexity of living in between – 'people caught in between places and people and cultures' (AM) – and to 'explain' the social circumstances which give rise to those feelings. This sentiment or sense of collective responsibility is grounded in the visceral belief that creative narrative structure has, or should have, a counter-discursive function which raises awareness. By 'giving voice', it enhances, or restores balance to public perception by counteracting the influence of the media. At least one case (QS) bears witness to an almost evangelistic mission to increase Western understanding of the condition of women in Muslim society, another to a determination to act as a spokesperson for groups whose circumstances remain unheard: 'to think about which voices are silent in our society and to try and voice some of those experiences' (JR) or alternatively 'getting their voices on' (PK).

At the same time, many of the writers refrain from ascribing any overtly social objective to their work, though in almost all cases they acknowledge the benefits both of being able to share their personal experiences with others and of translating the condition of cultural displacement into aesthetic form. They prioritize the act of creation itself, the putting into words whose authenticity derives from its correspondence with the sense of being of the creator: 'Writing gives me enormous pleasure. I haven't thought too much about the relationship of my writing to others' (VM). Statements such as these are a potent reminder of the dangers of associating the situation of 'displacement' with a migrant state of being which is especially conducive to creative writing. All writing, but creative writing in particular, is at one and the same time both an act of displacement in its own right and a means of giving 'presence' – materiality – to a generalized ontological condition which according to postmodern orthodoxy is inherently unstable and fragmented. If instability and fragmentation of identities are general phenomena of postmodern, mobile societies, they are not exclusively peculiar to people of diasporic origin. Indeed, it would be profoundly patronizing to suggest that such a condition were felt to a greater extent by second- or third-generation immigrant writers than by any other social category of the population though, as the present study illustrates, the analysis of the works themselves may reveal common traits related to inter-generational mobility.

For many of the writers, the act of communication, sharing feelings with others, the sense of an audience, was paramount:

> **AM** What's always been important to me is that the ordinary people who just work in ordinary jobs will listen to my work whether it's poems or plays and connect with it. It's important to me that it goes out to a lot of people. I think it's just connecting with them really, on a human level.

Not surprisingly, this was particularly true of poetry written specifically to be read or 'performed' in public where the sense of provisionality – the immediacy of an experience generated by the context of communication: the collective event – predominated over the notion of imparting a given pre-mediated message: 'I hope that a performance, somebody thinks it speaks to them, you know. But because I don't think – I should write about this – then I can't say again it's an intentional thing, I just hope the link's there' (SA). For at least one of the writers, the three functions – expressive, communicative and poetic – were intrinsic to each other. There was a message, but it was not one designed simply to change the reader's social outlook. Rather its intention was that of sharing, creating a communal identity which responded to a social need and which was frequently associated with physical and cultural displacement: 'Almost everybody who has settled here has relatives and friends there. They have a link. Then there are themes, for example, loneliness, a search for identity etc. So one of my audiences are the people who are here, and then people back home, who want to know how we feel here because they have heard different stories' (BSK).

A final category of writer understood perfectly the complex inter-relationship between dominant discourses and the plurality of reference points against which the qualities of this or any other form of creative writing could be evaluated. One (ZH) recognizes that the 'status quo' is not a uniform concept when translated into social norms. As he puts it,

'There's always a status quo it appears and people may say that what we are interested in is the cutting edge, is the latest thing [...] It doesn't matter to me, to me they are different styles, different nuances. It's like different dialects of the same language and each has its own place.' The comment can be read as a restatement of the Bakhtinian principle that each generic context imposes its own formal features in relation to which the creative writer defines an identity through dialogic, even playful, contestation (Bakhtin, 1981). Such open-ended tolerance of diversity precludes dogma and returns the commentator to the principle that this writer and performance poet, like others, such as SK, prioritizes first and foremost the authenticity of the form of expression and its interrelationship with others over the imperative to 'state a position' which represents the interests of a particular social group.

Impact and reception

As has just been seen, a significant proportion of the writers interviewed wanted to reach out to an audience in order to raise awareness or to correct public misconceptions concerning the conditions of life of specific ethnic groups in Manchester. Yet few, beyond one or two of the most successful authors, had a clear sense of the reading public's reception of their work. They might be conscious of its relative success in terms of book sales, commissions from the BBC or the demand to give talks, perform in public or participate in educational or social programmes. But despite their stated objectives, they had little insight into the extent or manner of the change in outlook which their work might be instrumental in promoting. Or so they claimed. One of the relative shortcomings of 'Moving Manchester' was the difficulty in capturing the nature of the public's response to events such as the *Black Writers Conference*, the reception to the performances of poets, the constitution of audiences in clubs on the Manchester circuit at which performances took place, the reactions of visitors to the writers' exhibition set up in the Manchester Central Library (2009), the modifications in perception and awareness amongst students or schoolchildren which might have resulted from workshops with the writers concerned. There were of course exceptions, particularly within the secondary education sector in Manchester and abroad, where texts by at least two of the authors (JP and QS) featured on school syllabuses in Manchester and abroad as works to be studied. In another instance, Manchester Metropolitan Council had published extracts of an author's work on its website as an example of the way in which the city had changed and also as an illustration of the 'authentic' experience of being brought up as the children of immigrant parents in Moss Side (Crawshaw and Fowler, 2008).[1]

However, while it was a central aim of the project to pinpoint the process of social articulation at the 'points of suture' (Hall, 1996: 5), the examples given by the writers were, with few exceptions, symptomatic rather than conclusive:

> MG It's really difficult to say what impact I wanted to have because I don't necessarily want to take a kind of polemical approach.
>
> ZH My experience of publishing has been that I think that my approach is very much the case of 'Look, I am not a great novelist' ... The whole world has changed. The world of publishing is about the cult of celebrity nowadays.

Yet ZH's novel has known considerable success and has provoked enthusiastic responses from members of the public at training sessions. As he acknowledges, 'it was that sort of novel. It's meant to be very, very accessible'. Statements by JM, regional reader development co-ordinator in Manchester Central Library, reveal that ZH actively discussed the subject matter of his book *The Curry Mile* with a wide range of local groups in Manchester. It was this, she claimed, which had contributed to the book's profile in the city and had led to its being constantly in demand by library users (JM Focus Group 3). In this and other cases, it is partly through public self-promotion and subsequent integration into institutionalized educational environments that the creative text takes on its catalytic social function. Apart from raw data such as library borrowing and sales statistics, it seems that it is only in this context that the character and extent of social impact can be realistically gauged. Impact and success as a writer are seen by the writers as closely related, but success in publishing terms does not necessarily mean the resulting impact conforms to the aspirations of the writer or that it can be satisfactorily measured. A play by MC, a highly successful, well-known playwright and scriptwriter, was integrated into the machinery of municipal anti-racist policy in Glasgow. Her play 'went to every 14/15 year old in Glasgow' and was accompanied by television advertising and posters, so as she says: 'I feel like it was part of a cog in a wheel of working towards some change on all sorts of different fronts.' As with so many of the writers, for MC, the success of the play was directly linked to the follow-up educational visits to schools, even though as she explains: 'the young people I've been working with just want to work with video'. Once again, the written text is more a medium or a trigger to further action than an end in itself. If the scriptwriter obtains a commission 'it goes out to a lot of people' (AM) but only if the text is embedded through an institutionalized follow-up activity does the author become aware of its effect on the listening or viewing audience and whether or not any changes in attitude are lasting or collective. This is not to say that the public are indifferent to the writers' works on more controversial issues such as gang warfare in Moss Side where one writer (KS) describes being heckled and then cheered at the book launch of her first novel: 'Everybody started clapping; then I knew that I'd got over the first hurdle and that just spurred me on and after that I got a bit of negative press but the majority of the press at the time was more positive about what I was saying and how I had said it' (KS).

For at least two of the most prominent writers, the principal readership of their works is not located in Britain at all, let alone Manchester. A significant and paradoxical feature of the writing by certain first- and second-generation diasporic authors from Manchester is that their work is better known in other countries than it is in England. In such instances, the traffic is two-way. In the case of Basir S. Kazmi (BSK), as has been seen, a poetic form inherited from Pakistan has been translated into English and has become more widely known in educated circles, opening up a new audience for a culturally specialized genre. In another, Qaisra Shahraz's (QS) *The Holy Woman*, a book raising an issue which has been at the heart of much political debate in Western Europe – the status of women in Islamic societies, their clothing and relationships, the balance between mind and body – has proved to have had its most major impact in countries other than Britain such as Germany, Turkey, the Indian subcontinent and Indonesia and has been translated into many languages.

Yet writing as a member of a diasporic community about a country in which the writer no longer lives has its pitfalls. A reverse effect of writing in English against the British cultural mainstream about a country of origin is that it provokes opposition from commentators native to that country. The author finds himself or herself the object of the same accusations of falsification that she or he directed towards the best-selling authors describing the conditions of life of immigrants in Britain:

RB It's not for me to say what is a correct reading or a misreading, particularly if your writing is idiosyncratic, you have to accept such responses. A couple of Indian critics read it [the writer's first novel] as belonging to this emerging canon of Indian writing in English which is realistic and reflects contemporary society ... and those critics read it in that way and read me as an imposter.

Whether or not the topic and location of the writing is physically displaced relative to the place of upbringing and residence of the writer, the space it occupies remains a 'space in-between'.

What emerges from the interviews is that while impact on society at large is hard to assess, even for the writers themselves, the culture of writing and performing in Manchester itself constitutes a powerful communal bond between the creative actors:

MG There's a real sense of some kind of artistic community or communities here ... a lot of different kinds of art. People work together, people support each other and encourage each other and that's really amazing.

Only a minority of the writers interviewed by the 'Moving Manchester' project had achieved national and international recognition, though the project itself, through its conferences, publications and website, provided a platform for the impact of their work to be more widespread and far-reaching in its effects. As for local impact, a common pattern was that a written proposal led to a commission to run workshops involving a writing project exploring a local population's relationship with a given space such that the writing would become part of a community built on shared experience. A prizewinning poem would even literally be inscribed in stone, so, as the writer said, 'I'll have a little mark in Manchester' (CK). Once established, writers like this one relied on commissions, bursaries and residencies to support their activity, the most commonly mentioned broadcast outlet being the BBC, where the relationship with individual producers appeared to hold the key and where the audience for a particular programme was known in advance. Surprisingly, little mention was made of local media, a lacuna which deserves to be further explored. In parallel, the impact on the cultural life of Manchester implied by the very existence of a community of writers and performance artists was a social phenomenon in its own right. That and the multiple links between the municipal institutions which supported the network through cultural facilitation were the dynamics which made the level of activity possible, to the extent that, for the writers themselves, it had become a way of life.

Facilitating production

As will have become clear from the early chapters of this book, and as the project team knew from the outset, the culture of writing and performance in Manchester had had a long history. The role played by 'minority', 'independent' or 'community' publishers and their relationship with municipal authorities and national sources of funding were crucial to the processes of articulation already referred to. It was clear that the *raison d'être* of community publishing was precisely its distinction from the 'mainstream' and equally that, from a financial point of view, it was not self-sustaining. Not surprisingly, the emphasis of the interviews was on success in terms of publication, dissemination and the experience of communication, the social benefits of which were taken as axiomatic. As far as the writers themselves were concerned, their main objectives, as has been seen, were to write well, make a difference and get published. Whilst some undoubtedly harboured ambitions for their works to be widely circulated, few had any illusions that writing alone would offer them material security. This was even true of the most widely internationally reputed writer in the group, who had not even been paid royalties for the translations of her work. Another, who had been nationally honoured for her contribution to intercultural understanding, was not in paid employment, the funding for her group set up to promote black culture in Manchester having been cut. Several had had work commissioned by the BBC and were well known, but to be broadcast on radio or television was scarcely sufficient to secure a living. At least one taught in universities on full or part-time contracts. A number of others survived on bursaries and residencies. Most were directly or indirectly involved in educational support and so were dependent on public-sector finance. By definition, these were writers who were outside the economic and publishing mainstream but who saw themselves as the living pulse of a certain strand of Mancunian culture. Their survival and the cultural values they stood for depended on dwindling public sector support. A separate study of the structure of cultural financing in Manchester is still required so that a proper evaluation of its impact can be adequately appreciated. In the meantime, one thing was clear: few if any of the writers would have been able to project their writing in the way that they had without the assistance and advice of the small writing and publishing groups with which they had been associated.

Apart from the sense of being a member of a like-minded group which promoted their abilities and ambitions as writers, the element most frequently stressed by the writers was the editorial assistance they had received:

> **KS** I think it [the editorial advice] was very good. I did resent it, at first, because it was my first novel and I suppose in a way I knew what I was doing and I sort of had a talent but I didn't have the craft of writing and my editor was very good and he sort of like showed me basically how to make the novel flow, which I'm really grateful for.

Admittedly it was not always clear whether, as in the above case, the writer was referring to the editor of the publisher who eventually published the work or whether she or he was describing the encouragement received from a community publisher before seeking an imprint with a wider circulation. Both were mentioned as core elements in the process of achieving success as a writer. It appeared to depend on the stage of development of the writer as to whom they turned to for advice. The 'community publishers' had a social role which went beyond simply promoting market-led output. They relied on public financial support to sustain a developmental mission which combined supporting writers' craftsmanship with providing opportunities to use writing or performance as a means of raising awareness and promoting community. A small number of others, although regionally based, were financially independent and placed greater emphasis on publishing itself. The Arts Council Literature Officer (AH) regretted that more aspirant writers in the region did not take greater advantage of the community writing groups or publishers before dealing directly with a prospective mainstream commissioning editor. As the Arts Council co-ordinator pointed out, the role of the groups was crucial as a conduit for funding and a more efficient structure for meeting the Council's objectives: namely to foster the wider development and dissemination of writing for social as well as purely aesthetic or cultural ends:

> **AH** Some of the publishers just collect submissions and they scan some of the small literary magazines looking for talent. There's no middle agent if you like in that relationship. What's happened is a lot of writers just go directly to publishers and of course a lot of those manuscripts are unsolicited and perhaps not looked at in every case... I think it would be more efficient and more effective for other agencies to act as a kind of conduit if you like for grants. We can fund directly with a direct relationship but it's not going to be as cost efficient. I think the main issue for

writers is distribution of their work and I think that the individual writers themselves don't understand always. Obviously their energies and attentions, particularly for emergent writers, is to focus on the actual writing of the book. Very often they don't have recourse to an editor.

This view was echoed by the former literature development officer for the region (BW), who described earlier tensions facing the Arts Council writing development team between offering individual bursaries and supporting small publishers in order to sustain an infrastructure. Unlike her successor in the job, she saw the latter option as problematic, seemingly because of the difficulty in selecting the most appropriate publishers to fund and because of their hybrid, semi-independent status:

> **BW** I think that Arts Councils generally have a slightly ambivalent view of publishers. As literary publishers they're within that kind of subsidized art form area, and on the other hand they're a kind of creative industry. I think they tend to fall between the stools and I've never felt that the small publishing sector anywhere I've come across it has been adequately resourced by Arts Councils. What they [the Arts Councils] tend to do is fund the cost of production but not the infrastructure, not the costs of editors and commissioning editors or people who are actually running the businesses, even though they're small business. It's a battle everywhere really for literature officers. One that falls back on the writers inevitably because the publishers themselves then struggle for the resources to market and distribute work, they struggle to pay royalties. I mean it depends at what level they're operating.

Not surprisingly, the actors themselves, the writers who were also CAs (cultural agents) and publishers, saw things somewhat differently. Their preoccupation was to do the job as well as possible with whatever funding they could get from whatever source, including foreign embassies, charities and cultural foundations: to act as spokespersons and leaders for the writers of a certain type of literature perceived as 'local' and therefore by definition 'non-mainstream'. As Pete Kalu (PK), the long-standing editor, director or co-ordinator of the community publisher Commonword with which the project was most closely associated put it:

> **PK** We started growing that [a distribution network for recordings of poetry performances and live readings known as 'The Listening Post'] and we've now got quite a strong set of processes and programmes that

contribute to the advancement of black literature in, certainly, Manchester. So, that's been my major involvement up to about a year or two ago in the Manchester writing scene; so the groups are probably the most important contribution. Much of the initiatives that we've taken I feel have subsequently been copied, not just around Manchester but sometimes around the UK.

The nature of the funding sources had changed over time according to shifts in political culture:

> **PK** [F]rom that sort of job creation schemey type feel, I can't itemise it, I wasn't absolutely around, but from that feel we moved to revenue clients of the Arts Council, I can't remember exactly when. And we've also had backing from the Manchester City Council and then through the Association of Greater Manchester Authorities. But now we're attracting funding in different ways from different funders who have different goals.

Individual CAs had different priorities, the priority of each lying somewhere on a differentiated spectrum from promoting publication at one end to social improvement at the other, but in either function they emerged as catalysts, the hubs of a distinctively local process, without whose agency it was difficult to see how the infrastructure and sense of cultural community derived from creative writing could survive. It was they more than anybody who defined their role as distinct from the mainstream and who missed no opportunity to rail against the market-led ethos of the London publishing scene. It was this which lent Manchester its distinctiveness: Manchester was not London:

> **PK** the publishing industry works out of London and it's a very upper middle class, white institution, that power at the top of the publishing world that are quite homogenous I think. And so the writers that we come across share nothing with them particularly. So, it becomes a question of what appeals to that group.

> **RP** Any publisher not based in London has an in-built sort of inherent need or purpose, which is to offer non-London-based perspectives. Publishing is a very expensive business, it's always been a privileged pastime of the educated classes and it's also been centred in London. Inevitably publishing's worked like every other large industry or commercial industry in Britain in that, if it works, if it's seen to work through a London audience, and the surrounding commuter belt audience, then it

will automatically work and apply to everyone else. When the first big inroads are made into novels and writing about Asian or Caribbean, African communities comes out, the first bright young things of that generation of writers, their novels are about areas of London and the interest is rolled out … One of the things we do with Comma and with our short stories is we do books of short stories set in each northern city, one of four northern cities. We started with Leeds and we're next in Liverpool and then we're doing Manchester and Newcastle. We're actually commissioning writers to set stories against specific milieus and events and backdrops over the last fifty years of those cities, just giving alternative perspectives and individual rooted perspectives from specific places outside of London that are not homogenized. It's what short fiction allows you to do, it allows you to increase the number of voices and be slightly more democratic in a very undemocratic art form.

The same interviewee extends this definition of what he refers to as 'independent' publishers', one which focuses on particular genres (such as the short story) and places (such as northern cities), to one which reflects their developmental interface with prospective writers:

> **RP** I think writing is often a sort of collective kind of a self-help, grassroots exercise and the most important thing that writers need is feedback so a lot of the time, in poetry for instance, it's fairly easy to get. You set up at a workshop, you then ditch that workshop because nobody there has a clue and you set up a better workshop or you find people who are better at it and you join your own workshop. The actual editorial process doesn't need as many resources as you think, what they do need though is they need access to quality contemporary literature. So, ten years ago Manchester had a very active Waterstones and it had really, really good readers, international standard authors coming pretty much every night. That's gone and the access points to hearing good contemporary literature has kind of reduced, which has increased the importance of festivals. I think also generally writers suffer from the growing power of the agent. Agents have replaced readers in publishing houses. The only place you're going to get a developing editor and an editor who will take you on knowing that you're a bit rubbish to start with but you show promise and to work through you and point you in the right direction are the editors that you get with the independent presses. There's an increasing gulf between the celebrity next new thing author and the rest of the writers who are trying to improve their craft, and there's not much improvement. They're either the done deal or in the package or they're on the heap.

From the evidence of the interviews, there was little sense that this difference in outlook and function between 'mainstream' and 'local' publishing was likely to change. If anything, the cutbacks in national funding would make it more difficult for the operations initiated by Ra Page (RP), Pete Kalu (PK) and others like them to achieve their objectives. Even now, there were hints of a potential disconnect between the act of writing as a mutually supportive, communal activity and the forms of social embedding to which it might give rise: 'publication', 'broadcasting', 'live performance' and 'education' were complementary discursive functions which in terms of their impact on society ran in parallel with each other rather than being fully joined up. Assessing the relationship between them deserved to be more closely scrutinized. The need to find a balance between the oral and written traditions, itself a powerful cultural signifier, made the relationship between publication and community building more complex still. As the writers saw it, the social impacts of 'performance poetry' and extended written prose text were different in kind:

> **PK** I think in the early days we bypassed the entire, you know, publication [process] to make [ourselves] known to a wider audience. I always loved that definition of a publication because it gets us away from paper, and we can bypass the whole print business by basically going into community centres, going into youth clubs, going into libraries, going to carnivals, things like that, and we would really perform there and build our own audience, an audience that ... Again, you go back, back, back in black writing terms.

Assisting the writer and benefiting the community did not necessarily involve the same type of activities, even assuming it was possible to agree on what such social benefit might consist of, itself a highly charged cultural and political issue. It was true, however, that you could not have the one without the other. The greater the number of writers who articulated the issues crucial to their identities, the greater would be the opportunities for their voices to be heard in day-to-day social activity and for their concerns to be registered in educational environments such as schools and universities. This had been one of the main aspirations of the 'Moving Manchester' project and for Peter Kalu, as for many of the writers, they were two sides of the same coin.

PK I would say that that was probably one of the biggest and most important contributions we made to Manchester: in bringing that live literature, spoken word, to the fore, and again through repetition and example, making it understood, acknowledged as a genre, as a form, that we performed with some power. If you're not brought up into a family or a culture or a society where writing is seen as anything worthy or as worthwhile doing, then it's quite hard to persevere and believe in yourself when you've got no support network. So, I think we provide that as well, but that's another hard thing to do. And I'm sure that it overlaps and grows into other societies, communities.

Thus while the interviews with the CAs underlined the powerful sense of difference from the mainstream, certainly of the cultural specificity associated with being an ethnically identifiable Manchester writer or performer, they also revealed the schisms and tensions involved in reaching out to a local audience. The fact that not all the writers saw their readership in local terms and were not themselves all permanently located in Manchester, together with the shortage of funds and the changes in communication practices, meant that it was constantly necessary to reassess the types of initiative and creative forms most likely to benefit the cultural and educational environment of the city. Apart from the quality and volume of the writing itself, the success of local publishing initiatives bore witness to the social role that writing and performance was playing. What was less clear from the evidence of the interviews was how widely read the writings were and what their impact had been on the perception and behaviour of their audiences. And in the background was the fact that the nature of communication was changing rapidly even as the project progressed. Apart from print on demand, writing through paper publication was being overtaken by downloadable e-stories, collective composition online, storytelling through networks and so on. The oral and the written traditions had already emerged as creating different types of relationship with their audiences or readerships and themselves represented different types of association with a cultural past. Now a new generation was taking over which was altering the very nature of articulation, space and place.

'Manchester ... why Manchester?', 'them' and 'us'

At the outset of this chapter, I referred to the positional dynamic which was embedded in the language of the participants in the project. I saw this as replicating the very differences which the project was seeking to explore. At one level, 'Moving Manchester' was an enabling initiative which exemplified, and was itself part of, a network of relationships existing between creative writing, literature development organizations such as Commonword, political concerns for contemporary urban society and ethnic relations and government-sponsored institutions such as the Arts Council, municipal authorities, schools and universities. The project opened up a space of dialogue between the different actors and offered a facility which promoted the wider dissemination of the work of a relatively diverse group of Manchester writer/performers. In so doing it was supporting the work of the independent publishers with whom the team was collaborating and, as this chapter has sought to do, to give a voice to the various parties involved in what, from the outset, the project had sought to represent as a transformative cultural process. At another level, the discourse employed by the project team, the types of questions to which it was seeking answers, the project's very objectives could be seen as emanating from a position of privilege, even intellectual posturing, from which the writers felt excluded and sought to distance themselves. It was as if 'the academy' were engaging in an act of cultural appropriation which involved generating a set of categories to which the writers felt they did not belong and with which they took issue. As has been seen, this distancing between interlocutors had not been apparent in the one-to-one interviews because of the face-to-face character of the exchange and the relationship of trust which existed between them. If there was a challenge, it was not provoked by the terminology used by the interviewer or even the nature of the questions asked, since these had emerged as much from the writers' own engagement with the objectives of the project as from the project team.

It was the function of the writers' workshops and focus groups on the other hand to interpellate the researcher/informant relationship, to establish a forum in which the writers or CA participants were free to comment in the form of reflexive research data on the research process and on the nature of the questions posed. As already stated in the introduction to this chapter, the format lent an internal autonomy to their exchanges which was independent from their direct dialogue with the members of the research team. By definition their commentary qualified some of the statements made in the interviews and, most notably, offered further insight into the validity of the project's own terminology. The participants commented not only on the nature of the issues identified as the outcomes of the interviews which this chapter has, if anything, further reinforced (see Appendix), but also on the language in which they were expressed and the institutional or social assumptions which underlay them. This did not gainsay the value of the research, but further emphasized the dynamic, dialogic, recursive and thus ultimately partial nature of qualitative investigation to which this chapter deliberately and self-consciously bears witness.

The reference to Manchester as a place was not simply to a physical environment which could be encompassed by a series of writings and whose climate was different from that of Nigeria or the Caribbean. It was a perceived space, the understanding of which was expressed through what the participants said about it. As far as the interviews and focus groups were concerned, the Manchester of writers or publishers and CAs found substance as much through their comments as through their works. 'Displacement' was a generalized phenomenon which could apply to any physical location. To what extent it could legitimately be applied exceptionally to a former colonial metropolis and especially to a predetermined group of citizens was an acutely sensitive and debatable question which the focus groups addressed head on:

A How do you feel about displacement? You're British born aren't you like me?
B Yeah, yeah, but ...
A You're ...? What's your background?
B Caribbean, my parents were from the West Indies.
A I'm of mixed heritage, I'm Nigerian. I'm as British as a bacon butty, but I'm black. I don't feel a sense of displacement.
C Because I'm British born as well and I feel, I do actually because I've moved around so much as a child, it's been close to thirty times in my life I've moved around England and around Canada, and in Canada I lived as an immigrant the whole time, but because I'm white skinned, I never got asked, 'What are you doing here?' Not once. And here the same thing, although I've moved around, you know, I've got this privilege and that's what I move around with. But for me it pops up, my displacement pops up really visibly to me. I suppose it's to do with class because my family are, they're labourers and cleaners and I got to go to university and so I got to kind of rub shoulders with people who went on holiday in a cabin and who had access to this world. And I kind of fit in with them sometimes, and I guess I feel ... And something I've been aware of with this project is I feel kind of this friction, the university, it's a space I had a bit of access to for some reasons, but also it's not my world in other ways.
A It's actually the alienation rather than displacement on that level.

C Yeah, right. Do you ...?
A I belong to a country that denies me. People are not saying to you 'Where do you come from?' People are always saying, 'Where do you come from?' And sometimes we say it between each other as people of colour.
C But that's different.
A No, but, and then the other is (laughs) kind of taken aback by what do you mean? And then Corinne [the researcher responsible for the interviews] will say, 'Manchester, why?' Even if not, do you understand me? So, alienation I think is a different thing, to just, I can't feel displaced if this is where I set down with my first footsteps. But it can alienate me.
C Yeah, and that's a totally different thing.
A Do you agree, disagree?
B Well, I mean, displacement yeah, it's just an ongoing thing, I can't think of the word, displacement at all, because it's like saying a fish in water.
A Well, displacement assumes that we don't belong here.
B Yeah, but it's like a condition which has always existed, so it's like well, but it's always been like that, I didn't know there was a situation. It's like so what? I mean, you don't say, 'So what' but it's like a situation which has already existed, or you take it for the norm, and it's only whether you ask the question and you think, oh, displacement, I didn't know it was that.
(Others agree.)

At one and the same time, this extract illustrates the different ways in which the notion of 'displacement' was understood while questioning the meaning which, as the writers saw it, the project team had attached to it. For one, writer A, 'displacement' was the outcome of attitudes and behaviours of marginalization – even 'rejection – on the part of the society into which she had been born. For writer B, displacement was an ontological state of being which emanated from the individual, an inherent sense of difference which could be the product of a number of factors, one of which, as writer C points out, was class. It was about people, culture and identity rather than about place. Furthermore, the term could be applied to the different perspectives of the two main parties defined by the research project: the writers or CA informants, and 'the university'. Not only did the informants feel 'displaced' in relation to the institution which was conducting the research; by implication, the use being made of the information and insights gained was itself, inevitably and quite literally, in a Foucauldian sense (Foucault,

1969) a form of discursive 'displacement'. If the argument were taken to extremes, it could be said, paradoxically, that the research was reinforcing the very phenomenon it was seeking to investigate. Or was it? 'Giving voice' meant listening and quoting, not extrapolating and placing language in a new frame; in reality, the project was doing both.

While re-echoing several aspects of the interview responses, in the focus group discussions, the distinction between 'them' and 'us' becomes explicit. It is clearly an involuntary form of articulation, unmotivated by aggression, but one which identifies a 'position' with social implications which helps to understand where many of the writers stood in relation to the issues being investigated by the project:

A The problem is, you know, you'd think I was a visual artist but academia identifies and understands shapes and forms and then desperately tries to. . . .
B And publishing. . . .
A Well, desperately tries, in order to understand where we're coming from, needs to fit us into these forms. And it can't allow us to move these shapes over here and to exist over here. And that's why I found this process problematic. It's trying to say well, 'We want to know what you're doing and then we want to know what you're doing and then bring it over here so we can file it over here.' I don't want to be filed.
B I can add to that, it's even worse for publishing, it's even worse for the market.
A No, but I'm talking about academics, we survive and again, oh God, I was doing a performance somewhere and somebody asked 'Would you like your books to live after you?' (laughter). And I didn't know. But to exist, do we have to fit the boxes, because, if we don't fit them, will we get discarded? That's my problem with it. Do you understand me?
C Yeah, I do. And this is one part of, like you say, publishing.
B Oh yeah!
C And the certain words and it changes all the time too, there's a word that's used today, shifts and tomorrow it's a different thing, just like learning other people's languages as well. Like how do I frame what I'm doing?
B And you might disagree with this, but I'm only going by my experiences but I'll say it anyway, in my experiences the academics have been the less of the evils, in my experience, okay.
C In terms of . . .?
B Yeah, in terms of boxes.

A As opposed to what, sorry?
B Publishing! (*laughs*)

As for the links between the writings and the perception of Manchester as a place, at least three anecdotal references from the focus groups acted as reminders of the relationship between symbolic representation, place references and everyday life. The inclusion of a short story by Qaisra Shahraz in the syllabus of the German *Abitur* had, she claimed, excited the curiosity of her young German readership, inducing them, as she said, to visit Manchester to observe 'multiculturalism' at first hand. The realism behind the setting of Zahid Hussain's *The Curry Mile* (2006) had been a source of negotiation with the marketing department of the City Council. Having at first refused, the Council finally agreed to mount banners advertising the novel on the Wilmslow Road (the location of the concentration of Indian restaurants known as 'the Curry Mile') but ironically did so only following the novel's publication. For Joe Pemberton, the author of *Forever and Ever Amen* (2000), Manchester remained an amalgam, conditioned by its contrast to the Caribbean background of his family as much as by that between Moss Side and Ashton-under-Lyne: 'When I pick up this pen, the fact is that the amount of energy that is produced is the fact that there's a difference' (JP, Focus Group 1).

The truths which emerge from qualitative data such as these are relative, but they tell stories. Interviews and focus groups and the subsequent commentaries to which they give rise are stories about stories which are conditioned by their setting and the factors influencing their production. As Luhmann puts it, 'There's no such thing as the last word!' (Luhmann 1997: 141). What emerges is an infinite ricochet of partial truths. The evidence of the fieldwork describes a vibrant creative writing scene in Manchester whose distinctiveness thrives on a sense of difference: from the 'mainstream', from social privilege, from the academy, a distinctive group culture where the interplay between the oral and written traditions is a frequently recurring theme. But in terms of the relationship between the writers, their writings and Manchester as a space, the picture was self-limiting. Major nationally recognized authors such as Howard Jacobson whose novels offer close insight into the life of Manchester's Jewish community in the 1950s and 60s were not interviewed, and doubt remains as to the precise nature of the impact on life in Manchester resulting from the writers' outputs.

What the fieldwork data of the 'Moving Manchester' project do reveal, however, is the character of the interaction between writers, publishers and institutional agencies. This analysis in itself allows the nature of social impact as a concept to be better understood. It also forces the analyst to consider the exact nature of the relationship between creativity and social benefit. It affords an insight into the operation of cultural actions which enable the voices of certain social groups to be more widely heard. One clear distinction which emerges from the data is that between purpose or message and outcome: the fact that meaning is inherent neither in the intention or vision of the writer, nor in the hermetic form of texts, nor in the socio-economic structures which have 'produced' them. Nor is reception relevant in itself unless it is accompanied by changes in attitude and behaviour on the part of those members of society to whom the message has been communicated and unless the evidence of change can be traced to the discursive structures in which it is embedded.

Only an oblique insight into the nature of such changes was offered by the interviews and focus groups. There was an underlying assumption on the part of the participants that the articulation in language of a certain condition of 'being in society' should in principle be socially beneficial. But the nature of 'benefit' was an open-ended and endlessly renegotiable concept. It could not simply echo the discourse of government or its avatars. In that sense, the funding priorities of the Research Council, the aims of the 'Moving Manchester' project and the aspirations of the creative participants were themselves in a differentiated, dialectic relationship with each other, especially in the way in which such terms as 'relevance' and 'impact' were understood. As researchers, we did not have a predetermined view of what 'impact' or the nature of 'social change' entailed. Neither did the writers or participants in any consensual or conclusive sense. Many felt that their writing was contributing to an educational mission while the 'cultural agents' clearly had an agenda which went beyond simply promoting publication. The structure of the networks on which the process of writing, reading, publication and dissemination depended pointed towards a form of social action which we and they felt was culturally important and which of its very nature we believed was potentially beneficial to a social environment which was best understood in terms of a given urban location: the City of Manchester. What was apparent was that for such networks to operate effectively, public finance was paramount. The 'Moving Manchester' project offered no evidence to suggest that privately sponsored 'social enterprise' initiatives would fill the gap left by reductions in Arts Council or municipal support. Rather, the interface between writers, publishers, public performance venues, libraries, official agencies and educational institutions was conditional on the existence of a publicly funded, grassroots local cultural policy which promoted creative writing and its dissemination, not simply for its own sake but as a part of a wider political project whose ultimate goal was social well-being.

Appendix: Focus group questions
'Moving Manchester' workshop, 21 March 2009: questions for discussion

While the wording of the questions below is obviously 'ours' as members of the 'Moving Manchester' team, they derive directly from the interviews with 'you': 27 creative writers and 'agents' responsible for promoting creative writing in the Manchester area. They are designed as stimuli for open-ended discussion: as a means of verifying the extent to which the provisional hypotheses emanating from the interview data are 'justified' in the sense that they correspond – or otherwise – to your own perceptions of your activities as writers.

1. Your responses in interview and the subject matter of your writings reflect motivations either arising out of your membership of a group perceived as an ethnic minority or derived from the past experience of your families – or both. To what extent do you feel this to be true?
2. We would like to think that your writing helps the experience and the consequences of 'displacement' to be better understood – by yourselves and by a wider public. To what extent do you feel us to be justified in thinking this? How do you perceive the relationship between your writing and the phenomenon of migration?
3. Many – if not all – of you refer to the past: either to the influence of your parents or grandparents in causing you to start writing in the first place, or as the cultural legacy of a place of familial origin whose way of life you feel an urge to recapture ... for personal reasons or in order to bring it to public awareness. To what extent is it accurate to see this as one of the mainsprings of your motivations as writers?

4. There seems to be a strong desire on the part of many of you to convey a message: to inform or correct popular misconceptions, to draw attention to political repression, to give voice to feelings shared by a wider social group. To what extent do you in fact see yourselves as representing the voice of a collectivity and a voice of contestation? And if you do, which collectivity – or collectivities – do you see yourselves to be representing? … and if a voice of contestation, which cause do you see yourselves as defending?
5. One of the most striking features of your writings is its diversity of form. But there seems to be a common quest for originality on the part of virtually all of you, as if seeking to draw attention to the special status of the experiences you wish to represent. Is this true? And if it is, what do you see as the defining property of your work?
6. Your responses to the role of place and space in your writings and that of Manchester in particular are very varied. Yet the evidence of the interviews is that Manchester remains a central point of reference, even if several of your writings are located wholly or partly in another place. Could you explain more fully the relationship between the image of Manchester which emerges from your writings and what you consider to be the 'real' Manchester?
7. One of the hypotheses behind the project is that the image of Manchester has actually been, and is being, modified as a consequence of your representations of the city or of other places which might be seen as 'complementary' to it. To what extent do you feel this to be true? And if you do, how can this best be demonstrated?
8. Your interview responses suggest that you consider yourselves to be operating outside the publishing mainstream. Further to this and associated with it, there is a strong sense that you understand your writings to be fulfilling a communal function. How accurate is this impression? How widespread is the 'community building', interactive effect of your creative writing and performance in Manchester and what do you see as the factors hindering and/or promoting its successful development?
9. If the association between community and writing is a reasonable one, how is it possible to gauge its impact and to what

extent do you feel that your own writing has been instrumental in promoting social change?
10. There may well be other important questions relating to your writing and its social impact which we have not raised in the interviews or in discussion so far. If so what are they?

Robert Crawshaw
'Moving Manchester' Project
20 March 2009

Note

1 See also: www.manchester.gov.uk/info/448/archives_and_local_studies/788/picture_book_moss_side/22).

References

Bakhtin, M. (ed.) (1981) *The Dialogic Imagination: Four Essays*. M. Holquist. Trans. C. Emerson, and M. Holquist, Austin, TX: University of Texas Press.
Crawshaw, R. and Fowler, C. (2008) 'Articulation, Imagined Space and Virtual Mobility in Literary Narratives of Migration', *Mobilities*, 3 (3), 455–69.
Derrida, J. (1967) *De la Grammatologie*. Paris: Les Editions de Minuit.
Foucault, M. (1969) *L'Archéologie du savoir*. Paris: Gallimard.
Glaser, B. and Strauss, A. (1967) *The Discovery of Grounded Theory*. Chicago: Aldine.
Goffman, E. (1974) *Frame Analysis: An Essay on the Organisation of Experience*. New York: Harper and Row.
Hall, S. (1996) 'Who Needs Identity?' in Hall, S. and du Gay, P. (eds), *Questions of Cultural Identity*. London: Sage, 1–17.
Hussain, Z. (2006) *The Curry Mile*. Manchester: Suitcase.
Knorr-Cetina, K. and Cicourel, A. (1981) *Advances in Social Theory and Methodology. Toward an Integration of Micro- and Macro-sociologies*. London: Routledge and Kegan Paul.
Luhmann, N. (1997) *Die Gesellschaft der Gesellschaft*. Frankfurt and Main Suhrkamp.
Pemberton, J. (2000) *Forever and Ever Amen*. London: Hodder Headline.
Shahraz, Q. (2001) *The Holy Woman*. London: Arcadia.
Teubert, Wolfgang (2010) *Meaning, Discourse and Society*. Cambridge: Cambridge University Press.
Van Dijk, T. (1977) *Text and Context: Explorations in the Semantics and Pragmatics of Discourse*. London and New York: Longman.
Voloshinov, V. (1988 [1926]) 'Discourse in Life and Discourse in Poetry:

Questions of sociological Poetics' in Shukman, A. (ed.), *Bakhtin School Papers*. Colchester: Essex University Print Centre, 5–30.

Internet sources

www.manchester.gov.uk/info/448/archives_and_local_studies/788/picture_book_moss_side/22).

Key to interview/focus group participants included in the text

AH – Avril Heffernan
AM – Anjum Malik
AMcV – Allison McVety
AO'R – Aidan O'Rourke
ASIJ – Audrey Saint Ivy Johnson
BSK – Basir Sultan Kazmi
BW – Bronwen Williams
CK – Chanje Kunda
JR – Jacqueline Roy
JM – Jane Mathieson
JP – Joe Pemberton
KS – Karline Smith
LT – Libby Tempest
MA – Muli Amaye
MC – Maya Chowdhry
MG – Michelle Green
MYW – Mei Yuk Wong
PK – Pete Kalu
QS – Qaisra Shahraz
RB – Rajeev Balusubramanyam
RP – Ra Page
SA – SuAndi
SD – Steve Dearden
SK – Shamshad Khan
SM – Shirley May
VM – Vijay Medtia
WL – Wyllie Longmore
ZH – Zahid Hussain

Afterword

Corinne Fowler and Lynne Pearce

In 2008, the 'Moving Manchester' project received an enquiry from a local radio producer in connection with a programme about Eastern European migration to Manchester. Advising the producer to contextualize new arrivals to the city with Manchester's history of Jewish migration, we recommended Bill Williams's comprehensive study *The Making of Manchester Jewry 1740–1875* (1977), as a useful source of information. As its title suggests, Williams's study provides detailed historical account of Jewish immigration to Manchester. It tells the complex story of how, during the eighteenth and nineteenth centuries, the city's established Jewish merchants, shopkeepers and share-brokers often distanced themselves from newly arrived hawkers and pedlars[1] in their fraught quest to gain a strong social standing in the city. The radio producer did not take up our suggestion; she explained that reference to this older history of settlement might detract from the programme's focus on the newness of Eastern European migration to Manchester in the twenty-first century. The incident serves as a reminder of another tenacious formulation: the concept of the 'indigenous white Mancunian'. As we have noted on several occasions in the preceding pages, this formulation promotes collective amnesia since, of those who might conceivably fall into the 'indigenous' category, a large proportion is descended from Irish, Scottish, Welsh and European migrants. What our research for the 'Moving Manchester' project has shown us is that it is crucially important to take the historical long view on 'multiracial' Manchester so as to properly accommodate a sense of migrants and refugees as formative of, and integral to, Manchester rather than as late additions to it.

Experience tells us that it is extremely difficult to counter the persistent emphasis on newness in popular debates about immigration, a focus that hints at a restricted cultural politics of 'belonging'. Yet, and as demonstrated in Chapter 1, Manchester's very architecture testifies to the fact that the city has been so much more than a place of temporary refuge for peoples of wide-ranging ethnicity and culture. The city's rival synagogues tell a centuries' old story of expansion and social diversification. Similarly Rusholme, a nineteenth-century suburb of Manchester, was transformed by immigrant Asian restauranteurs into nearly a mile of neon-lit restaurants (the internationally renowned 'Curry Mile'), thereby utilizing old Victorian housing to counter the economic malaise of post-industrial Manchester. However, nothing counters the nation's obsession with the supposed newness of immigration as much as Manchester's graveyards. The city's Southern Cemetery in Chorlton-cum-Hardy contains within its bounds a long-standing Jewish graveyard, with a Muslim section adjacent to that, testifying to the fact that Manchester has been 'home', in the archaic sense (see Chapter 1), to a multiethnic demographic for centuries.

Manchester's graveyards have inspired several of the city's writers to consider the significance of place to the interment of skulls, ribs and femurs in local soil. Lemn Sissay's poem 'For My Headstone' (1992) is about the inscription on his prospective gravestone to the Ethiopian mother who gave him up for adoption, while Zahid Hussain's novel *The Curry Mile* (2006) depicts the death and burial of Ajmal Butt, an immigrant restaurateur who made Manchester his home. Another exploration of national and local tenure associated with Procter's (2006) postcolonial everyday can be found in a short story called 'The Escape' (2009), by Qaisra Shahraz. In the story, seventy-three year-old Samir flies from Manchester airport to his birthplace of Lahore after thirty years of living in Cheadle. During his visit to Pakistan, he sits by his parents' graves:

> The tranquillity around him had him thinking about his own burial place. Of course it would be Manchester's Southern Cemetery. He could not imagine his children traipsing back to Pakistan to visit his grave in a land that was foreign to them ... He turned back to look at the graves ... Was this going to be a final farewell? Standing over his mother's grave, soft sobs shook his large body. It was a strange world. To be buried continents away from one's parents. (Shahraz, 2009: 121)

'The Escape' offers a poignant counterpoint to the racially motivated vandalism of twenty Muslim graves in Manchester's Southern Cemetery in 2009 (*Manchester Evening News*, 2 October 2009). While Samir's children consider Pakistan as 'a land that was foreign to them', his death impresses upon him the strange finality of his migration to Manchester. In the story, however, he comes to terms with his inevitable interment in the Southern Cemetery, an acceptance that is perhaps prefigured in his walk through Longsight in the story's opening paragraphs: 'he savour[ed] the walk down streets he had cycled and scooted along for over three decades' (2009: 115). As he does so, he notes the city's evolving demographic and architecture: 'He noted that the Roman Catholic church and its primary school on Montgomery Road had disappeared, joining the quaint little National Westminster Bank branch that had been in the middle of Beresford Road with a communal vegetable plot at the back. That had been pulled down twenty-odd years ago' (2009:115). It is this sense of long-standing intimacy with the city's streets that marks Samir's transition from immigrant to 'neighbour' – a term that has been invoked frequently in the course of this book to signify the everyday reality of how Manchester's citizens inhabit Manchester's 'diaspora space' (Brah, 1996), notwithstanding still-unresolved issues with the city's residential housing. Indeed, it is the graves of protagonists such as Samir and Ajmal Butt that may be seen to confirm the profoundly devolved and hybrid *community* that both Manchester and Britain have become.

Following on from the conclusion advanced in Chapter 5, an important area for any future study of postcolonial literary production in Britain must be the extent to which regional writers, such as Joe Pemberton, Lemn Sissay and SuAndi, might be said to be 'compatriots in craft' with white counterparts such as Brian Patten, Adrian Henri and Ian Hamilton Finlay. We hope that this book has shown that, in literary terms too, the concept of the neighbour can promote a productive shift from notions of difference, otherness and foreignness towards a vocabulary of affinity, collaboration and exchange. Close attention to local, translocal and national literary connections can tell us new kinds of stories about contemporary literary cultures. When Linton Kwesi Johnson holds a joint concert with John Cooper Clark, Henry Normal writes a preface to SuAndi's poetry collection, or John Agard dedicates a poem to Michael Horowitz, it seems important to understand what these collaborations can tell us about the development of contemporary British writing and performance. Manchester's devolved literary cultures point to the wisdom of emphasizing difference as, in Appignanesi's words, 'a condition *within* cultures and not simply as the obvious differences between them' (2010: 5). Crucially, the degree of literary exchange, influence and counter-influence in the work of

Manchester's writers makes a nonsense of outworn cultural and literary metaphors such as 'bridges' and 'interstices' that have positioned Britain's diasporic literatures as marginal and/or secondary to a white, 'indigenous' mainstream. As far as the post-Second World War literary history of Manchester is concerned, the city's white and black literary cultures have progressed hand in hand: an achievement given material acknowledgement by the 'Moving Manchester' project's 'Writing Manchester' exhibition held at the Central Library in the autumn of 2009 (see Figure 7.1).

As is the case with all research projects and books that take the contemporary and/or the recent past as their focus, we must accept that any conclusions we advance in *Postcolonial Manchester* will have been overtaken by new developments even as this book goes to press. Since the 'Moving Manchester' project was conceived (2004) almost a decade ago, a great many national and international events have impacted upon everyday life in Manchester and Britain, in addition to which both academic life and the world of publishing (academic, transnational, independent and community) are undergoing radical restructuring on account of changes in the global economy and the impact of technology on the dissemination of the written word (see Pearce, 2010). Taken together, these changes make any coherent prediction for the future of Britain's devolved literary culture virtually impossible, though we are hopeful that our intervention in ongoing debates concerning 'English literature' and 'Englishness' in a postcolonial context will have a bearing upon the history and profile of the subject as it continues to be conceptualized and taught.

As we observed in the editorial to one of the journal special issues (Pearce, 2011) that came out of the 2009 'Glocal Imaginaries' conference, the way in which late twentieth-century predictions concerning the impact of globalization both are and are not being lived-out is of particular interest and concern to all those working in the fields of postcolonialism and migration studies. In brief, one of the most serious consequences of the mass globalization of people, capital and technology (as originally outlined by Robinson, 1992; Urry, 1999; Bauman, 1998: Beck, 2000) in the past two decades is that it has resulted in a reification of the nation-state and its immigration policy:

> In other words, while the processes of globalisation have clearly been instrumental in creating the financial crisis that Europe is presently [2011–12] grappling with and does, indeed, expose the extent to which the world economy now operates outside the control of the nation-state,

7.1 View of the 'Writing Manchester' exhibition (Catalogue Hall, Manchester Central Library), 2009. Photo © Lynne Pearce.

> the nation-state still exists very palpably for all its citizens ... as an agent of control, welfare, and social justice. This may, indeed, cause us to conclude that [Zygmunt] Bauman's vision of a world in which *globalisation would make itself felt very differently for some groups than others* [emphasis in the original] came closest to what is taking shape: true, the transnationals *have* seized significant political and economic power from the nation-state, but this has not meant the *end* of the nation-state; rather, the change is being experienced as a re-trenching of whatever power the nation-state still has (and this, of course, is considerable) over its citizens in their 'local', everyday lives. (Pearce, 2011)

With regards to Manchester's future as Europe's flagship 'migrant' city, such policies are already having a negative impact on the daily lives of the city's diasporic communities in terms of increased personal and institutional racism and obstructions to international travel (including, of course, visits to and from their countries of origin). Combined with the dramatic increase in Islamophobia in Britain during the past decade, partly as a consequence of 9/11 and – within the life of the 'Moving Manchester' project – 7/7, this entrenchment of the nation-state and its border security must register in the conclusion to this volume as the latest, unwelcome twist in Manchester's two-hundred-year-long struggle to gain acceptance for its 'multiracial' or 'multicultural' demographic. In terms of the city's literary response to these developments, meanwhile, there is a sense of 'business as usual': as we have noted on many occasions in the preceding chapters, racism has long been *the* pre-eminent concern of Manchester's writing community, and recent work by long-established Mancunian writers like Shamhad Khan (see the poem 'Megalomaniac' 2007: 79–82) and Tariq Mehmood[2] (2011) which engages directly with the post-millennial upsurge in hostility towards Muslims is probably best understood as part of an *ongoing* intellectual resistance to racist violence and oppression, both on the streets of Manchester and across the world. Moreover, such an understanding is arguably the best way of remaining positive about literature's role at a time which cannot but feel like a backward step *vis-à-vis* Britain's attempt to free itself from its inhospitable, colonial past.

The final area of change that is important to mention by way of conclusion is funding: that is, both the funding available for writers, publishers and the arts in general and that which has supported academic projects like 'Moving Manchester'. As we have noted elsewhere (O'Neill and Pearce, 2011), it is doubtful that the government-funding made available (through the Arts and Humanities Research Council (AHRC) and Economic and Social Science Research Council (ESRC)) for projects like 'Moving Manchester', 'Devolving Diasporas' and 'Making Connections'[3] will be as available in the medium to long term as the recession bites deep into public funding, and the principal source of arts funding in England (Arts Council England (ACE)) has already withdrawn its support from a large number of organizations and agencies including, regrettably, the Black Arts Alliance. So far, Manchester's Commonword, the catalyst for so much of the writing considered in this volume, is keeping its head above water and had its funding renewed for a further five years in 2010.[4] This, we trust, will continue to be the case given the demonstrable achievement of this unique organization – its groups, imprints and individual success stories – for well over thirty years. Writing, one could argue, is now so much part of the cultural fabric of contemporary Manchester that it would be senseless for funders, city planners, public services and universities not to build it into whatever plans are being put in place to carry us through and beyond these difficult times. Certainly, close inspection of any number of the novels and poems we have cited here proffer warnings, suggestions and solutions that local and national government would do well to heed. Manchester is a city that – as Dave Haslam (2000) observed over a decade ago – has had its history (social, cultural, architectural) 'rubbed out' too many times; we therefore appeal to all those who have a hand in the matter to listen to the writers and not let the same mistake be made again.

Notes

1 As Williams explains in his study, wealthier Jews who had been established for some time in the city, worked hard to establish their reputation in the city and the co-presence of poorer, less established Jews continually threatened their fragile standing as immigrants to the city (Williams, 1977: 57).
2 Tariq Mehmood, who completed a PhD in Creating Writing as part of the 'Moving Manchester' project, has been a writer and activist within the North West region for over thirty years. His first novel, *Hand on the Sun* (1983), was published by Penguin Press, and his second, *While There Is Light* (2003) by Comma Press. Both texts, as well as the novel *The Last Act of the Terrorist*, written as part of his PhD portfolio, detail the material and psychological expression of racism within British society and culture. For full details of Mehmood's life and work see the 'Moving Manchester' Writers' Gallery (www.transculturalwriting.com/movingmanchester (accessed 12 August 2012)).

3 The two other large, AHRC-funded research projects mentioned here (which developed links with 'Moving Manchester') are: 'Devolving Diasporas: Migration and Reception in Central Scotland, 1980 – the present' (see www.devolvingdiasporas.com (accessed 30 April 2012)) whose principal investigator was Dr James Procter (University of Newcastle-upon-Tyne) and 'Making the Connections: Arts, Migration and Diaspora' (see www.makingtheconnections.com (accessed 30 April 2012)) whose principal investigator was Professor Maggie O'Neill (University of Durham). Both projects were sponsored under the auspices of the AHRC's 'Diasporas and Migration' initiative.

4 In the Autumn of 2010 Arts Council England had £100 million stripped from its funding budget, which resulted in two hundred organizations losing their funding. See www.bbc.co.uk/news/entertainment-arts-12892473 (accessed 27 March 2012) for the full story.

References

Appignanesi, R. (ed.) (2010) *Beyond Cultural Diversity. The Case for Creativity. A Third Text Report*. London: Third Text, 2010.

Bauman, Z. (1998) *Globalization*. Cambridge: Polity.

Beck, U. (2000) *What Is Globalization*. Trans. Patrick Camiller. Cambridge: Polity Press.

Brah, A. (1996) *Geogaphies of Diaspora*. London: Routledge.

Haslam, D. (2000) *Manchester, England: The Story of the Pop Cult City*. London: Fourth Estate.

Hussain, Z. (2006) *The Curry Mile*. Manchester: Suitcase.

Khan, S. (2007) *Megalomaniac*. Cambridge: Salt Press.

Mehmood, T. (1983) *Hand on the Sun*. Harmondsworth: Penguin.

Mehmood, T. (2003) *While There Is Light*. Manchester: Comma Press.

Mehmood, T. (2011) *The Last Act of the Terrorist*. Lancaster University. Unpublished PhD thesis.

O'Neill, M. and Pearce, L. (2011) 'The Arts of Migration' in special issue of *Crossings: Journal of Migration and Culture*, 2 (1), 1–11.

Pearce, L. (2010) 'Writing and Region in the Twenty-First Century: Epistemological Reflections on Regionally-located Art and Literature in the Wake of the Digital Revolution', *European Journal of Cultural Studies*, 13 (1): 27–42.

Pearce, L. (2011) Editorial to 'diasporas', *M/C Journal*, 14 (2). Online journal available at: http://journal.media-culture.org.au/index.php/mcjournal (accessed 30 April 2012).

Procter, J. (2006) 'The Postcolonial Everyday', *New Formations: A Journal of Culture/Theory/Politics*, 58, 62–80.

Robinson, R. (1992) *Globalization: Global Theory and Social Culture*. London: Sage.

Shahraz, Q. (2010) 'The Escape' in Amaye, M., De Mello, M. and Fowler, C. (eds), *Migration Stories*. Manchester: Crocus Books.
Sissay, L. (1992) 'For My Headstone' in *Rebel without Applause*. Newcastle-upon-Tyne: Bloodaxe, 27.
Urry, J. (1999) *Sociology Beyond Societies*. London: Routledge.
Williams, W. (1977 [1976]) *The Making of Manchester Jewry 1740–1875*. Manchester: Manchester University Press.

Internet sources

http://journal.media-culture.org.au/index.php/mcjournal
www.devolvingdiasporas.com
www.makingtheconnections.com
www.transculturalwriting.com/movingmanchester

Index

Note: with the exception of collectively authored anthologies and periodicals, literary works can be found under authors' names; 'n.' after a page reference indicates the number of a note on that page.

academia 16, 17n.8, 71, 197, 201n.33, 209, 258n.8, 293, 296–7, 306, 308–9
ACE (Arts Council England) 11, 12, 41, 73n.12, 83, 89, 177, 209, 217, 241, 251, 253, 259n.11, 259n.12, 262n.52, 262n.59, 287, 288, 289, 293, 299, 309, 310n.4
  Free Verse (Decibel report) 83, 90, 96, 102
  Read: Write (report) 94, 96, 102
Adebayo, Diran 80, 94–5
Africa 8, 96–7, 160, 165, 215, 233, 241
Afrique Like Me *see* Chanje Kunda
Agard, John 97, 239, 305
  'Caribbean Eye over Yorkshire' 236
  'Memo to Professor Enoch Powell' 17n.4
  'On a Yazoo Stem' 253–4
  'Seaside Etiquette' 236
  'Three in the Snow' 236
  'True Grit' 233
  We Brits 236

Agbabi, Patience 81
  'The Word' 207
Aghedo, Nayaba
  'Invasion' 165–6
  Talkers through Dream Doors see anthologies
AHRC (Arts and Humanities Research Council) 309, 310n.3
Alexandra Park *see* Moss Side
Ali, Monica 95–6
  Brick Lane 10
  In the Kitchen 96
alienation 2, 10, 11, 40, 56, 167, 192, 194, 197–8, 256, 294–5
Amaye, Muli xiv, 202n.35, 278, 302
Ancoats 4
Angelou, Maya 272, 273
Ansar, Louise
  Talkers through Dream Doors see anthologies
anthologies 154–206
  Bitch Lit 180, 182, 184
  Black and Priceless 159–60
  City Life Book of Manchester Short Stories 43, 155, 172–3, 176

Index

City Secrets 178–80, 184
Comma 155, 176–7, 179, 183, 184
Fire People, The 82–3, 87
Hair: A Journey into the Afro & Asian Experience 181–4
Healing Strategies for Women at War: Seven Black Women Poets 169–72
Herzone: Fantasy Short Stories by Women 200n.19
Holding Out 161–4, 167
Life, Death ... The Whole Damn Thing 200n.15
No Limits: Urban Short Stories 167–8
Talkers through Dream Doors: Poetry and Short Stories by Black Women 161–4
see also FWWCP; Manchester Irish Writers' Group
Appignanesi, Richard 208, 257–8, 305
architecture 13–14, 30–6, 39, 304–5
  colonial 23–4, 30–6, 111
    Castlefield Quay 34
    Corn Exchange 112
    Royal Exchange 31–3, 112
    Whalley Range 112
  gentrified
    Canal Street 34, 147
    Castlefield Estates 34–6, 112, 113, 147
    Merchant's Warehouse 34–5
  see also ghettoization; housing
Arndale Centre 113
Ashton-under-Lyne 29, 48, 54, 65, 297
asylum seekers 11, 143–5
automobility 58, 60–5, 74n.23, 115

BAA (Black Arts Alliance) 42, 98, 212, 259n.11, 259n.12, 309
Baker, Shirley 27, 28, 30, 72n.2
Bakhtin, Mikhail 270, 282
  chronotope 148n.6, 201n.27
Balasubramanyam, Rajeev 148n.3
Banks, Ray 126, 146, 150n.24
Barry, Peter 256
BBC (British Broadcasting Corporation) 72n.3, 225, 226, 282, 285, 286
Beasley, Paul 6
Bee, Malcolm 20
Belle Vue 52, 111
Bennett, Alan 37–8
  Talking Heads 255–6, 273, 275
Besant, Annie
  'White Slavery in London' 87
Bhatt, Sujata 82
black
  British writing 2, 5–6, 10–11, 16, 17n.3, 70–1, 79, 80–1, 82–4, 86, 90–1, 92, 96, 100–3, 172, 197, 200n.14, 208, 210–11, 212, 219, 228–9, 234, 237, 239–41, 242, 256,
  identity 12, 48, 275, 277–8
Blincoe, Nicholas 126, 172
  Manchester Slingback 120, 130–1, 141
Bloom, Valerie 235
  Black and Priceless see anthologies
BNP (British National Party) 22
Body, Seán 187, 200n.23
  'Blight' 187–8
  Seasons 4, 189–90
  see also Manchester Irish Writers' Group
Bolton 38, 96, 185

Index

Bolton, Cathy 178–9
  City Secrets see anthologies
  Life, Death ... The Whole Damn Thing see anthologies
  No Limits: Urban Short Stories see anthologies
Boyle, Danny
  Olympic opening ceremony 237–8
  Slumdog Millionaire 69
Bracewell, Michael 173
  'Blackley, Crumpsall, Harpurhey' 55–6, 173–6
  'Nocturne' 177
Brady, Ian *see* Moors murders
Brah, Avtar
  diaspora space 1, 8, 11, 12–13, 48, 68, 166, 168, 305
Breen, Catherine
  'Coming Home' 194
Breeze, Jean 'Binta' 82, 239, 241, 244, 262n.54
Britishness 9, 169, 212, 213, 219, 229–30, 232, 234, 243, 258
  Citizenship Test 10, 17n.6
Bromley, Roger 67, 198n.3
Broughton, Jane
  Herzone: Fantasy Short Stories by Women, see anthologies
Brown, Duncan 207, 209
Brown, Norma
  Herzone: Fantasy Short Stories by Women, see anthologies
Burgess, Anthony 37, 72n.6
Burke, Vanley 97, 105n.36
Burn, Sean
  'Edgecity' 179
Burr, Zofia 252, 262n.61

Canal Street *see* architecture and Gay Village
Carlson, Prudence 249

Cartwright, Jim 38
Casas, Arturo 209
Castlefield *see* architecture
Caulfield, Holden
  'Men's Morning' 253
Chatterjee, Debjani 216–17, 234, 260n.34
Cheetham Hill 48, 49, 73n.16, 111, 126, 200n.23
Chorlton 111, 304
Chowdhry, Maya 169, 180, 182
  'Acting Real' 180, 182
  Bitch Lit see anthologies
  Healing Strategies for Women at War: Seven Black Women Poets see anthologies
  The Seamstress and the Global Garment 84
Clews, Wayne
  'Going to the Dogs' 177
Collins, Merle 6
colonial legacy 22, 23, 31, 34, 42–4, 47, 49, 56, 60
Commonword 9, 15, 85, 103, 154–6, 158–9, 177–8, 179–80, 182–3, 199n.9, 199n.10, 200n.21, 216, 288–9, 309
Cooper Clark, John 16, 238–9, 243, 251, 261n.45, 305
  'Beasley Street' 252–3
cosmopolitanism 11, 23, 90, 111, 155, 179, 180, 200n.20, 208, 219, 244
Coutts, John 209
Cox, Ailsa 158, 197, 198n.2, 198–9n.5
  'Be a Good Girl' 162–3
Craven, Judy
  Talkers through Dream Doors see anthologies

Crawshaw, Robert 55, 74n.19, 74n.21, 255–6, 276, 283
crime 14, 48–50, 110–53, 275
  causes 115–45
    bad seed, the 135–8
    greed 127, 140–2
    indifference 142–5
    psychopath, the 132–5
    racial inequality 122–6
    social inequality 116–22
  fraud 117, 138
  and gangs 14, 48–50, 58, 63–4, 88, 123–5, 126, 146, 273, 284
  institutional 113, 127–31
  and masculinity 138–40
  paedophilia 131, 134
  see also police
Curry Mile, the 3, 297, 304
  see also Zahid Hussain

D'Aguiar, Fred 242–3, 256, 257, 262n.53
Dawes, Kwame 82–4, 87, 101, 210, 212, 219–21
Delaney, Shelagh 38, 172, 173
  'Abduction' 177
  Taste of Honey, A 38
De Mello, Martin xiv
  if our love stays above the waist 84–5
Denby, Joolz 207
devolution of literary culture 1, 6, 9, 253
diasporas
  African 4, 6, 12, 23–4, 27, 44, 47, 48, 49–50, 62, 70, 73n.13, 260n.40, 278, 290, 294
  African-Caribbean 4, 6, 12, 13, 22, 23–4, 27, 44, 47, 48, 49, 52, 58, 62, 72n.3, 73n.13, 73n.16, 163, 169, 237, 239, 256, 260n.40, 276, 290, 294, 297
  Asian 2, 4, 6, 9, 10, 12, 13, 22, 23–4, 47, 58, 67–8, 73n.13, 73n.16, 169, 290
  Chinese 4, 12, 158, 169
  Irish 4, 13, 22, 38, 70, 154, 155, 184–96, 232, 255, 303
  Jewish 4, 22, 215, 297–8, 303–4
  Scottish 4, 22, 303
Didsbury 3, 26, 119, 147n.1
Doumerc, Eric 209, 259n.10
Duff, Mike
  The Hat Check Boy 110
Duffy, Carol Ann 86, 91, 252

EDL (English Defence League) 22
Eliot, T. S. 188
  objective correlative 59, 245
  telescopic images 244–8
Engels, Friedrich 4, 25–6, 39, 55, 189
Englishness 10, 306
Evaristo, Bernardine 83
  The Emperor's Babe 210–1, 229, 237
Evewright
  'Coloured People' 236
Ewers, Karryn 159

Farnworth 38
Farrand, Julie
  'The Dragon on the Wall' 167–8
femininity
  and hair 163, 183–4
  performance of 162–4
feminism
  black 97, 161–2, 212

consciousness raising 161, 180, 182
critique of patriarchy 138–40, 182
and lesbianism 182
and socialism 142, 158
flânerie 39, 114–15, 118–19, 148n.3
Fowler, Corinne 8, 10, 55, 66, 74n.19, 74n.21, 74n.25, 80–1, 95, 96, 202n.34, 220, 222, 223, 224, 225, 226, 227, 228, 232, 276, 283
Frangopulo, Nicholas Joseph 29–30
French, Segun Lee 84, 217–18
FWWCP (Federation of Workers Writers and Community Publishers) 155–6, 158–9, 177
Voices 155–8, 198n.5, 199n.6, 199n.7

Gatehouse 45, 155
Gay Village, the 112, 120
Gayle, Mike 96
genres (fiction)
 autobiography 36–7, 38, 39–40, 72n.6, 97, 167, 244, 252
 cyberpunk 59, 121–2, 168, 174
 dystopia 57–9
 magic realism 51, 52–3, 55
 noir 13, 56–7, 59, 110, 115, 121, 124, 147
 science fiction 60, 96, 110, 121, 168, 174
 see also crime
genres (poetry)
 concrete 248, 249
 dub 208, 215, 232, 236, 239–40, 241, 25
 ghazal 216–17, 234, 260n.23, 260n.24, 260n.25, 260n.34, 271
 landmark 7, 15, 86, 87–8, 89, 207–8, 216, 219–28, 242, 249–50, 260n.32
 pastoral 234–8
Gioia, Dana 81, 84, 88–9, 91, 92, 101, 209, 240–1, 258n.8, 261n.50
globalization 306–8
glocalization 160
Goffman, Erving
 frame analysis 270–1
Grabner, Cornelia 209, 236
Gray, Breda 185, 195, 201n.31
Green, Michelle 274, 276, 283, 285, 302
 'Forklift Trucks' 182
Guise Williams, Marie 166
Healing Strategies for Women at War: Seven Black Women Poets see anthologies
Gunning, Dave 84

Habekost, Christian 240
Hall, Stuart 277
Hamilton Finlay, Ian 248–50, 305
Hannan, Noel 168
Hare, Robert D. 149n.15
Harris Brandes, Blake 240
Hartnett, P. P. 179
 'CCTV Eyes' 179
 City Secrets see anthologies
Haslam, Dave 22–3, 43–6, 50, 51, 72n.2, 72n.5, 73n.14, 100, 122, 123, 124, 172, 309
Headley, Victor 127, 148n.8
Heffernan, Avril 287, 302

Henri, Adrian 16, 239, 241, 244, 251, 305
  'Entry of Christ into Liverpool, The' 246
  'Liverpool Poems' 245
  'New Fast Automatic Daffodils, The' 250
  see also Mersey Beat poets
Hewison, Robert 41–2, 43
Highmore, Ben 54–5, 115, 116–17, 148n.3
Himes, Chester 124, 127, 146, 148n.8
Hinchcliffe, Stella see Manchester Irish Writers' Group
Hindley, Myra see Moors murders
Hirsch, Marianne 201n.28
Holroyd, Eileen 185–6
home
  belonging 10, 11, 66–7, 71, 86, 90, 91, 160, 197, 208, 213, 219–21, 228–38, 256, 257, 271, 276, 303–4
  destination homes 2, 26, 68–9, 174
  displacement 72n.2, 160, 270, 280–1, 294–6, 299
  exile 154, 186–7
  homeland 2, 13, 48, 186, 192, 195, 234, 244
  homelessness 2, 104n.16, 147, 272
  homesickness 10, 276
  homophobia 130–1, 146, 149n.13
Horovitz, Michael 241, 249, 251, 253–4
Horsley, Lee 124, 127, 141, 145, 150n.22
housing 24–30, 34–6, 51, 55, 66
  city planners 25, 29, 66, 116, 147, 309
  gentrification 34–6, 66, 88, 104n.16, 112, 113, 116, 147, 225
  ghettoization 25, 36, 48–9, 60, 113, 117, 124–5, 147, 189
  Ministry of 30
  redevelopment 24, 26, 27, 29, 34–6, 39, 72n.2, 113, 116–17, 147, 225–7
  residualization 147, 148n.5
  slum clearance 26–7, 39, 51, 63, 111, 116, 147
Huab, Sua
  'You' 164–5
Huggan, Graham 91, 105n.24, 106n.52
Hughes, Alrene 200n.23, 200n.24
  'A Missed Heartbeat' 191–2, 193–4
  'Incidental Snow' 191, 193
  see also Manchester Irish Writers' Group
Hulme 26, 27, 28, 36, 39, 51, 63, 65, 72n.2, 110, 111, 112, 116, 124, 147n.1, 168, 217
Hussain, Zahid 92, 96, 101, 271, 274, 281–2, 283, 302
  The Curry Mile 67–8, 110, 283, 297

industrial heritage 20–3, 31, 36, 47, 57, 60, 111, 221, 304
  Corn Laws 31
  cotton trade 13, 20, 22, 23–4, 31, 34, 72n.4
  see also architecture; Engels; housing; slave trade; Thatcher, Margaret
IRA (Irish Republican Army) bomb (1996) 31, 33, 113, 120

Islam 177
  Islamophobia 304, 308
  and women 163, 280, 284

Jam, Chris 217
Jones, Owen 257, 263n.63
Joy Division 27, 44, 200n.17

Kalu, Peter 86, 92, 101, 121, 122, 125, 126, 131, 136, 138, 149n.12, 159, 168, 199n.9, 215, 216, 217–18, 238, 239, 248, 273, 276–7, 279, 280, 288–9, 291–2, 302
  'Adventures of Maud Mellington, The' 160
  Hair: A Journey into the Afro & Asian Experience see anthologies
  Lick Shot 57–9, 61–2, 127–30, 136–8
  Little Jack Horner 130
  'Manchester' 213, 238, 246–7, 262n.56
  'Old Radicals' 5–6
  Professor X 129
  Yard Dogs 23, 57, 67, 125, 129, 131, 140–2
Kazmi, Basir Sultan 217, 234, 260n.24, 260n.25, 271, 275, 278, 281, 284, 302
  'Manchester couplet' 234
Kazmi, Nasir 217, 234
Khan, Shamshad 166, 183, 273, 276, 282, 302
  Healing Strategies for Women at War: Seven Black Women Poets see anthologies
  'I've Been Waiting For Funding So Long' 258
  'Manchester Snow' 68–70, 71, 74n.25
  Megalomaniac 82
  'Pot' 214
  'Silver Threads' 170–2
KKK (Ku Klux Klan) 136–7, 150n.19
Kunda, Chanje 92, 218, 272, 276, 285, 302
Kwesi Johnson, Linton 97, 98, 166, 200n.4, 236, 239, 251, 305
  Dread, Beat and Blood 87, 242–3

Law, David 3, 16n.1, 36–8, 81, 103n.3, 262n.55
Leonard, Tom 6
Levenshulme 117, 118, 134
Lin, Tang
  Healing Strategies for Women at War: Seven Black Women Poets see anthologies
  'naked frame' 169–72
literary canon 3, 138, 186, 196–7, 202n.34, 242, 254, 256, 271, 274, 285
literary ghettoization 2, 210, 241
live literature *see* poetry in performance
Live Poets Society 212, 238, 261n.46
Liverpool poets *see* Mersey Beat poets
Lloyd Thomas, W. 157
local government 30, 40–3, 66, 282–3
  CMDC (Central Manchester Development Corporation, also MDC) 34, 66, 72n.5, 112

GMC (Greater Manchester Council) 42, 73n.11, 73n.12, 147
London 2, 3, 6, 7, 9, 13, 15, 22, 23, 48, 71, 80, 87, 89–90, 96, 148n.4, 159, 213, 227–9, 242, 251, 253, 289–90
　GLC (Greater London Council) 40–2, 43
Lowe, Adam 96–7, 100
Lugosi, Rosie
　'My Dear' 182
Luhmann, Niklas 297
Lukács, Georg 123, 148–9n.9
Lyons, John 16, 47, 166, 183, 199n.12, 236
　'Englan no Muddercountry' 159–60

McDermid, Val 65, 112, 117, 126, 134, 140, 142, 145, 146, 147, 173
　Kick Back 117–18, 138–9, 140
　Mermaids Singing, The 112, 132–3
McFarlane, Roy 209
McGonagle Johnson
　'Cleaning the Slate' 193
　'Famine Imagined' 188
McGough, Roger 16, 208, 239, 244
　see also Mersey Beat poets
McKenzie, Val
　'One Voice, Many Voices' 157–8
McKenzie, Victoria
　Just Lately I Realise 97
McLeod, John 6, 17n.3, 17n.5, 23, 215, 228–9
McVety, Allison 272, 276, 278, 302

Madden, Toby 231
Makonnen, Ras 215, 259n.17
Malcolm X 129, 149n.11
Malik, Anjum 272, 274, 277, 278, 280, 281, 284, 302
Manchester Irish Writers' Group 155, 184–96, 200n.23
　exile 186
　Great Famine 186–9, 195
　Irish Troubles 191–2, 195
　journey home 184, 190–4
　mythic past 186–90
　national mourning 186
　post-memory 187–8
　Scribhneoiri 184, 186, 195, 200n.24
Mantel, Hilary 8, 80, 95
Marangoly George, Rosemary 201n.26
marginalization 9, 11, 61, 94, 101, 197–8, 218, 241, 279, 295
Massey, Doreen 8
　external geography 6–8, 261n.49
　world city 47, 66
Mathieson, Jane 283, 302
May, Shirley 218, 272, 278, 280, 302
　Hair: A Journey into the Afro & Asian Experience see anthologies
Medtia, Vijay 272, 274, 280, 302
Mehmood, Tariq 308, 309n.2
　'The Peacock's Dance' 177
Mellor, Rosemary 225–7
Mersey Beat poets 16, 238–9, 242–6, 248, 250–5
　see also Henri, Adrian; McGough, Roger; Patten, Brian

Messinger, Gary 22–3
Mex Glazner, Gary 89
Michael, Livi 8
  'Robinson Street' 173
  Their Angel Reach 59–60
migration 13, 22–3, 26–7, 47, 71n.1, 155, 189–90, 193, 196, 212, 225, 247, 299, 303–5
  circuits of 184–6, 195, 200n.25
  economic 34–6
  forced 25, 27–30, 36, 54
  internal 22, 44, 303
  middle class 38–9, 51, 167–8
  student 22, 37, 39–40, 69–70
Miller, Kei 82, 92, 106n.49
Mitchell, Dreda Say 257
Montoute, Carlene
  'Simmy' 162–3, 183–4
Moors murders 131, 134, 149n.14
Morrissey 38, 39, 150n.17, 247
  'Over the Moors' 134
Mort, Graham 74n.25, 202n.35
Moss Side 3, 14, 26, 27, 29, 36, 39, 44–5, 47, 48–55, 58, 62–4, 65, 72n.2, 73n.16, 73n.17, 74n.18, 74n.19, 74n.20, 80, 97, 98, 99, 100, 105n.43, 110, 112, 113, 116, 121–5, 126, 135, 140, 147n.1, 150n.18, 216, 217–8, 227, 273, 275–6, 279, 283, 284, 297
  Arts Group 46
  riots 130, 272
Motion, Andrew 209
Mottram, Eric 248, 250, 251, 254, 258n.4, 262n.60
Moving Manchester e-catalogue 11, 13, 70, 103n.6, 146, 150n.24, 176, 186, 198n.1, 199n.6, 199n.11
multiculturalism 2, 4, 9–11, 17n.7, 42, 68, 70, 177, 238, 270
  and New Labour agenda 10, 66
  and 'feel-good' texts 10, 65–6, 70–1, 90
mushaira 216–17
music 2, 24, 27, 31, 36, 41, 43–6, 50, 53, 55, 73n.14, 73n.15, 92, 94, 100, 167, 172, 174, 197, 217, 218, 219, 240, 241, 252, 254, 274
  Haçienda nightclub 43, 112, 113, 172
  see also ghazal; Joy Division; Morrissey; New Order; punk
Muslim identity *see* Islam

Nagra, Daljit 83, 84
narrative devices
  absurdism 124
  denouement 60, 63, 99, 116, 131, 192, 250, 261n.49
  focalization 51–4, 60–5
  social realism 120–5, 149n.9
  surrealism 38, 51, 53, 168, 176, 248
Naughton, Bill 37, 173
  Alfie 38, 72n.7
  On the Pig's Back 38
  Saintly Billy 38, 185
Nazism 136–7, 201n.28
  Anti-Nazi League 156, 199n.8, 243
Neaser, Sally
  'Being a Woman' 162, 163
neighbourliness 1, 3, 5–6, 90,

208, 213, 221, 229–36, 243, 252, 256, 257, 305
New Order 43, 174, 200n.17, 238
NF (National Front) 5, 57, 59, 129, 130, 136, 137, 160, 248
Nicols, Grace 97, 105n.38, 244
Noon, Jeff 121, 168, 172, 173
  'Cobralingus Remix' 174–6
  Pollen 121–2, 148n.7
  Vurt 59, 61, 148n.7
Normal, Henry 212–13, 233, 238, 239, 305
  see also Live Poets Society
northernness 3, 4, 8–9, 16, 20, 22, 36–8, 39–40, 80–1, 86, 90, 95–6, 112, 134, 176, 197, 213–14, 230, 232–3, 246, 253, 255, 258, 261n.46, 290
nostalgia 2, 3, 11, 37, 48, 90, 234, 247

O'Brien, George 186
O'Grady, Timothy 190
Okoro, Elaine 97–8, 100, 105n.38
Olympics 58–9, 88, 91, 104n.16, 104n.17, 237–8
  Cultural Olympiad (2012) 89, 102
  Poetry Olympics 88–9, 104n.18, 254
  Winning Words commission 15, 79, 85, 86–8, 89, 90–1, 102, 250–1
  see also Lemn Sissay
Omeje, Dike 106n.50, 218, 260n.29
Omoboye, Pauline
  'Innocent Until Proven Guilty' 98–9

'24th December 1956' 99
O'Neill, Maggie 308–9, 310n.3
O'Rourke, Aidan 35, 276, 278, 302
Osborne, Deirdre 221, 242, 249, 250, 261n.49
  Hidden Gems: Contemporary Black British Plays 104n.14

Page, Ra 9, 15, 43, 104n.23, 155, 172–3, 176, 184, 197, 289, 290–1, 302
  City Life Book of Manchester Short Stories, The see anthologies
  Comma see anthologies
page vs. stage see poetry in performance
Parkes, Nii 91, 94, 97, 106n.54
Patten, Brian 208, 239, 244, 305
  'Portrait of a Young Girl Raped in a Suburban Party' 255
  'Prosepoem Towards a Definition of Itself' 254–5
  see also Mersey Beat poets
Pearce, Lynne 2, 13, 24, 25, 25, 38, 39, 55–6, 61, 62, 64, 68, 110, 113, 119, 120, 124, 129, 135, 148n.2, 167, 173, 174, 179, 201n.27, 306–8
Pemberton, Joe 29, 48, 55, 74n.20, 92, 96, 100–1, 232, 272, 274, 276, 279, 280, 282, 297, 302
  Forever and Ever Amen 10, 29, 50–5, 63–4, 65, 74n.19, 74n.21, 79, 80–1, 85, 94–5, 103n.2

performance poetry *see* poetry in performance
Phillips, Mike 96, 114
Piccadilly Gardens 3
poetry collectives
  Blackscribe 97–8, 99–100, 198n.4, 212, 216, 227, 255
  Brothatalk 241
  Nailah 97–8, 99–100, 105n.38, 216, 218, 227
  Speakeasy 217–18, 241
  Young Identity 92, 93, 218, 241
poetry in performance 2–3, 5, 11–12, 14, 15–16, 46, 47, 60, 71, 81–2, 86–7, 88–9, 91–2, 98, 99, 100, 101–2, 154, 166, 196, 199n.12, 207–67, 268, 277, 282, 288–9, 291–2
  see also poetry slam
poetry revival 16, 208, 239, 240, 241, 243, 244, 248, 253–4, 256, 258n.4, 262n.58
poetry slam 88–9, 90–2, 102, 104n.18, 106n.50, 208, 211, 218, 238, 239, 240–2, 253–4, 257
police 98–9, 128–31
  Detective Inspectors 127–8, 142
  GMP (Greater Manchester Police) 130–1, 146, 147
  Private Investigators 114–15, 118–19, 127, 140, 142
Pollard, Clare
  'Kirsten vs the City' 177
postcolonialism 2–3, 4–5, 6–8, 11, 13–14, 17n.5, 20–78, 96–7, 127, 154, 156, 160, 165–6, 167–9, 172, 177, 197–8, 207, 213, 214, 221–5, 228–30, 232, 246–7, 257, 305–6

see also colonialism; multiculturalism
Powell, Enoch 17n.4, 156, 219, 258
Poynting, Jeremy 94, 95
Princess Parkway 49, 113
Procter, James 2–3, 5–6, 48, 66, 90, 200n.14, 213, 219, 232, 238, 247, 257, 304, 310n.3
publishing 8–10, 13–14, 15, 79–109, 196–7, 269, 283, 296–7, 306
  community 9, 42, 45, 71, 82–5, 90, 94, 96, 100, 101, 103, 154–6, 214, 215, 248, 286–91
  electronic 92, 94, 96–7, 100, 101–2
  mainstream 10, 79–86, 92, 94–6, 100, 101–2, 209, 289
  print-on-demand 102
  self 97–100
  see also Commonword; Gatehouse
punk 16, 40, 44, 46
  post- 27, 46, 73n.15, 200n.17, 238, 243, 246, 261n.45

racism 11, 53, 54, 56, 57, 59, 61, 97, 114, 123, 125, 129–30, 138, 142, 146, 156, 159–60, 161, 164–5, 174, 198, 221, 234, 252, 256, 257, 261n.48, 263n.63, 278, 304, 308, 309n.2
  institutional 67, 98–9, 125, 126, 127–30, 239–40, 247, 256, 308
rain 8, 55–60, 171, 174, 193, 219–21, 230–1, 233–4

Index

Riley, Marion
   'The Ashes of Betrayal' 195
Rouse, Roger 200n.25
Roy, Jacqueline 96, 169, 272,
   274, 279, 280, 302

Said, Edward 185, 201n.26
Saint Ivy Johnson, Audrey 271,
   278, 302
Salford 3, 16, 27, 28, 30, 38,
   106n.50, 126, 224, 238, 243
   Quays 112, 225, 226
Sandhu, Sukhdev 23
SCAWDI (Sparkbrook Caribbean
   and African Women's
   Development Initiative)
   236–7, 260n.40
Sebald, W. G.
   The Emigrants 25–6, 38–9, 61,
   72n.9
Sesay, Kadija 81
sexuality
   gay 41, 101, 113, 120, 130,
      149n.13, 155, 158, 177,
      178–9, 243
   heterosexual 158, 179
   lesbian 41, 119, 139, 155,
      178–9, 182
   LGBT 178
   queer 131, 178, 179
   transsexual 133
   transvestite 139
Shahraz, Qaisra 104n.23, 160,
   161, 167, 195, 201n.32,
   273, 273, 275, 279, 280,
   282, 284, 297, 302
   'A Pair of Jeans' 162, 163
   'The Escape' 304–5
   The Holy Woman 199n.13
   Talkers through Dream Doors
      see anthologies

Sharratt, Chris 173
Sharratt, Mary 180, 182
   Bitch Lit see anthologies
Siddique, John 166
   Poems from a Northern Soul 84
Sissay, Lemn 15, 46–7, 79, 85–6,
   87, 90, 91, 92, 96, 98, 101,
   102, 103, 103n.9, 103n.14,
   155, 159, 166, 207, 211,
   212–13, 215, 216, 217,
   223, 232, 233, 234–6, 237,
   239, 252, 253, 256, 257,
   260n.31, 260n.39
   'Advice for the Living' 249,
      261n.46
   'Barley Field' 235
   'Black Man on the Isle of
      Wight, A' 235–6
   'Flags' 221, 222, 225, 226, 227,
      228
   'For My Headstone' 304, 305
   'Gilt of Cain, The' 7, 242,
      249–50, 261n.49
   'Hardy's Well' 260n.30
   'Island Mentality' 7, 229–31
   'Let There Be Peace' 260n.32
   'Mill Town and Africa' 7–8
   'Moods of Rain' 56–7, 60,
      233–4
   'Olympic Invocation' 85, 253,
      254–5
   'Rage' 7
   'Rain' 219–21
   'Reading in Stansted, A' 235–6
   'Spark Catchers' 87–8, 250–1
slam *see* poetry slam
slave trade 7, 22, 23, 31, 72n.4,
   211, 214, 221, 236–7, 242,
   246–7, 249–50, 261n.49
Smith, Catriona
   'Legoland on Mescalin' 51, 168

Smith, Helen
  'That's Adolescence' 180
Smith, Karline 126–7, 146,
    148n.8, 150n.23, 173, 273,
    274, 275–6, 279, 284, 287,
    302
  Full Crew 125, 150n.18
  Moss Side Massive 48–50,
    54–5, 62–5, 74n.18,
    74n.21, 121, 122–5,
    135–6, 140
Smith, Marc 240
Smith, Zadie
  White Teeth 80, 95–6, 103n.2
social media 9, 79, 86, 87, 88, 90,
    92, 94, 96, 102, 218
Somers-Willett, Susan 88–9, 91,
    92, 104n.18, 241
spoken word *see* poetry in
    performance
Staincliffe, Cath 117, 118, 126,
    134, 142–3, 146, 150n.23,
    173
  Bitter Blue 119, 132–3, 135,
    143
  Dead Wrong 111–12, 126,
    139–40
  Looking for Trouble 114–15,
    131, 134, 141
  Missing 119, 134, 139, 143–5
Stanley, Jo
  'Die, You Bastard' 182
Starkey, David 219, 257, 258
Storey, David
  Flight into Camden 37
SuAndi 15–16, 47, 92, 97, 101,
    104n.23, 161, 166, 169,
    183, 212–13, 219, 221–5,
    227, 232–3, 238–9, 241,
    252, 257, 259n.11, 273,
    275, 276, 279, 281, 302,
    305

'Contempt' 246, 247–8
'Maidenhood, Motherhood,
    Womanhood' 162, 163–4
'Nearly Forty' 232
Story of M, The 255–6
see also BAA
suburbia 5–6, 22, 26, 34, 58, 130,
    134, 219, 304
Sutcliffe, Peter *see* Yorkshire
    Ripper

Tafari, Levi 239, 243
Tamsho Thomas, Tina 238–9
Tebbit, Norman 248, 262n.57
telescoping (poetic device) *see*
    T. S. Eliot
Thatcher, Margaret 40–3, 44, 45,
    47, 73n.10, 117, 123, 141,
    159, 161, 247–8

Wade, Stephen 244, 258n.5
Walker, Fiona
  Black and Priceless see
    anthologies
Walker, Kanta 183
  'Black Sisters' 161–2
  Talkers through Dream Doors
    see anthologies
Ward, Jim
  'Who are the English?' 156
Whalley Range 48, 73n.16, 110,
    111, 112
Wilberforce, William 250,
    261n.49
Williams, Bill 34, 303, 309n.1
Williams, Bronwen 288, 302
Williams, Di
  *Herzone: Fantasy Short Stories
    by Women see* anthologies
Williams, Nerys 252
Willner, Mary
  'DeValera's Wild Geese' 195–6

Wilson, Anthony 177
Wilson, Elizabeth 148n.3, 148n.5
Withington 111, 112, 142
Wong, Mei Yuk 275, 302
Woodruff, William 37, 72n.6
Wood, Victoria 3, 246
Woolf, Virginia 119, 148n.6
Wythenshaw 110, 143–4

xenophobia *see* racism

Yorkshire Ripper 134, 150n.16

Zephaniah, Benjamin 82, 159, 215–16, 227
   'Angry Black Poet, The' 5, 211

EU authorised representative for GPSR:
Easy Access System Europe, Mustamäe tee 50,
10621 Tallinn, Estonia
gpsr.requests@easproject.com

www.ingramcontent.com/pod-product-compliance
Lightning Source LLC
Chambersburg PA
CBHW070232240426
43673CB00044B/1768